SITTING BULL RUN

PAT J DALY

SITTING BULL RUN

Published by Willis Court Press.

Copyright © 2024 by Pat J Daly
www.patjdaly.com

All rights reserved. This Book may not be reproduced in whole or in part, in any form (beyond copying permitted by Sections 107 and 108 of the United States Copyright Law, and except limited excerpts by reviewer for the public press), without written permission from Pat J Daly.

This is a work of fiction. Names, characters, businesses, places, events and incidents are either the products of the author's imagination or used in a fictitious manner. Any resemblance to actual persons, living or dead, or actual events is purely coincidental.

*Cover by Chasson Higdon of Indiana University Southeast

The map of Bellport was drawn by Patrick Daly, III

Author services by Pedernales Publishing, LLC.
www.pedernalespublishing.com

Library of Congress Control Number: Pending

ISBN 978-0-9960453-9-1 Paperback Edition
ISBN 978-0-9960453-8-4 Digital Edition

Printed in the United States of America

v15

This book is dedicated to my former teammates at Holy Trinity High School and Bradley University

To the Reader

For those not familiar with the sport of cross country, which has a language all its own, the author supplies two resources in the back of the book: an overview of major cross-country topics as they relate to this novel, and a glossary of running terms. To the uninitiated, the author recommends a look at these sections before taking on the novel itself. But first, a brief visual of the sport...

God made me an Indian who runs not from death.

> — Chief Sitting Bull

The best pace is a suicide pace, and today looks like a good day to die.

> — Steve Prefontaine

The mind is its own place, and in itself
Can make a heaven of Hell, a Hell of heaven.

> — John Milton

Youth can perhaps be described as the illusion of your own durability.

> — Martin Amis

The devil can cite Scripture for his purpose.
An evil soul producing holy witness
Is like a villain with a smiling cheek,
A goodly apple rotten at the heart.

> — William Shakespeare

Losing is like knowing that in the movie scene where a thousand die but the hero lives, you're one of the obliterated.

> — David Guterson

But now secure the painted Vessel glides,
The Sun-beams trembling on the floating Tydes,
While melting Musick steals upon the Sky,
And soften'd Sounds along the Waters die.

> — Alexander Pope

Cross country at its heart is still kids running through woods to exhaustion on a Saturday morning. To me, the sport embodies honor and dignity, and at meets I am often moved to tears by how kids will put out, collapsing into adult arms or falling splat on the ground at the finish...You can't buy that courage.

— Marc Bloom

When I'm running, I don't have to talk to anybody and don't have to listen to anybody. This is a part of my day I can't do without.

— Haruki Muraki

For the aging cross-country runner, fall is the season of eternal return – a chance to wallow in the past and, perhaps, regain the illusion of once more....For certain macabre souls, to race at Vanny [the Van Cortlandt Park cross-country course] is to engage in a little jock necromancy, to feel a supernatural connection with anyone who may once have felt the sting of the back hills, or the sense of being hunted as you emerge from the woods and start pushing for home.

— Martin Fritz Huber

Prologue

It was 1974, and the summer on Long Island was drawing to a close. The three boys were just days away from entering their senior year at St. Theresa High School in the bayside town of Bellport. As members of a powerhouse cross-country team, they had spent the last few months busting ass for Coach Jack Hogan. On most days in June, following the taxing outdoor track season that had ended in late May, they typically ran easy miles along the shore or on country roads. With formal practice starting July 1st, their coach demanded a much higher volume. All told, the boys, along with their varsity teammates, averaged seventy-five miles per week during July and August, which included one run of at least fourteen miles. Now with the cooler air of September just days away, and having stockpiled deep aerobic reserves over the summer, the three boys were hungry to get at it, for the crisp autumn racing season to begin. They knew that their St. Theresa's team, come early November, was among the favorites picked to win the state title.

But on a late August evening, just hours after the annual parish picnic ended, the same three boys with horror on their faces knew only that they had just splashed across the town creek, this after having left behind the old custodian, Mr. Malagati, in the parish woods. Now on the creek's residential side, they dodged more trees and stopped just short of the open field. They paced in circles. They stammered terms of disbelief.

William Flanagan, the first to take flight out of the woods, shouted over his shoulder that his two friends burn everything. Peter Walker, nodding his head, next took off. Dennis Hurley, however, called out to his friends, telling them to stop, that they needed to talk about what had just happened.

But his two friends barely heard him. They were hell bent on getting home.

Dennis took a moment to peer back across the creek and then deeper into the cemetery woods. There he spotted the distant figure of Mr. Malagati as they had left him, except that the old man was now on a knee, head down, as if in prayer. Dennis took off, and once on the field, he saw that William and Peter had already crossed Crocus Lane. The two were heading down Dahlia.

The Hurley family lived right there on 32 Crocus, directly across from the field and the woods beyond. Dennis took dead aim at it. He found the house dark throughout, just as he had left it a few hours earlier. He lightly trod the stairs up to his bedroom so as to not awaken his parents. His alarm clock read 1:18. He stripped down, his clothes thrown atop his trainers on the floor. His foot nudged the pile under his bed.

Through the front screen window, he stared across the field to the wall of summer trees that blocked all of the parish cemetery except for scattered headstones that, flickering like birthday candles from the moon's light, broke through on its crest.

Good God, he muttered as he stepped back to his bed and collapsed on it. If we had just left well enough alone after the picnic. Had we just stayed home!

He tossed a good while, the night's ghastly images crashing one into the other.

Come, sleep, come, he pled with the night.

Oddly enough, it was only after the town's foghorn bellowed that he felt the approach of sleep. This led, for a few brief moments, to his thinking that everything that happened tonight, like magic, would disappear once he awoke the next morning. That, in fact, just as he and William and Peter had been planning for many months, the three of them would nail every Saturday race in the run-up to state at Van Cortlandt Park, where brilliant sunshine would undoubtedly pour over a race trail littered with burnt red and brown leaves. There at beloved Vanny, the team would hoist a championship trophy, outsized grins plastered on every face.

But when Dennis finally fell asleep that night, he did so unaware of just how unforgiving the new world would be when morning came. Nor could he possibly know at the time that the seeds of it all were planted on a winter morning years earlier when he stumbled into the inner sanctum of the more important parish players. Dennis was in sixth grade at the time, just on the cusp of his teenage years.

Part 1

1

Like other bayside towns on the south shore of eastern Long Island, Bellport's first houses sprang up at the turn of the twentieth century. Over time, the town, with its sandy beaches just beyond the inlet bridge, became a summer playground for the more affluent from New York City who built a few dozen homes in the acreage across from the town's meandering creek. From there, a residential area of some thirty square blocks emerged over the coming decades.

Perhaps the most coveted of all blocks was Crocus Lane, which faced an enormous field and the large stretch of woods beyond. Property owners there liked to brag about the unique advantage that Crocus offered. Country living, they might say, complemented by a white sand beach just a few hundred yards away. A generation passed, and the original homeowners, not much liking that Bellport was attracting cash-strapped WWII veterans on the GI bill, packed their bags and moved farther east, the Hamptons becoming the next playground for the rich and famous.

Dan and Catherine Hurley, both reared in the Hillside section of Queens, knew that they were damn lucky when Dan's Uncle Billy, a retired New York City cop who had amassed a fortune shaking down perps, sold his three-story summer getaway on 32

Crocus to them for a song. Their little Christine had just turned two, and Dennis was still an infant. Nearly a decade would pass before Tommy, their third and last child, would arrive. The couple loved their new house. But not unlike other city transplants, Dan and Catherine struggled to get by, taxes and utility bills not the least among their problems.

So, when on a January morning in 1968, their twelve-year old son awoke, he was characteristically oblivious to his parents' ongoing financial struggles. His only concern was staying out of the way of his high-maintenance sister, whose rummaging about the house in nervous preparation for the school day often escalated into a seismic boom. Anything might cause it. Lost homework. A wrinkled blouse. Their mother would enter the fray, dish towel in hand, and try to calm down his sister. As for their father, he'd stand by, trying to give the impression he was ready to step in and take control. Dan Hurley did so because he never wanted to get caught by his wife with a look that conveyed his real desire, that he'd much rather be in his seat by the kitchen window sipping hot morning tea and reading the *Bellport Citizen* while she attended to the vagaries of the children.

On the morning in question, Dennis' groggy eyes first went to a framed painting on the opposite wall—the outstretched arm of The Babe pointing to the fence at Chicago's Comiskey Field, the bleacher crowd waiting for the ball to fall into the ocean of splashing hands. On another wall, a poster of Pele doing his upside-down bicycle kick that sailed past the goalie's outstretched arms. Dennis liked to imagine himself one day scoring such a goal playing for the parish soccer team. But as he lay there trying to wake up to the radiator's drawn-out hiss, he suddenly realized the house was too quiet. It sounded as if nobody was home.

He jumped out of bed and went to the front window where he was surprised to find that a heavy snow had fallen during the night and blanketed the field and the wall of trees beyond it. He anxiously scanned the road until he noticed, with some relief, his father on the far side of the field walking Coco, the family basset hound, burrowing through the snow. Then his eyes went big after he looked down at the driveway and discovered that the blue station wagon was gone. No sooner had he noticed that than the wagon was seen coming down Crocus and rolling back into the drive, his mother behind the wheel. Her sister, Pearl, was in the passenger seat, his little brother, Tommy, on her lap. Christine was in the middle seat. The wagon coming to a full stop, William and Peter, his two friends, spilled out of the back. Dennis couldn't believe his eyes. He couldn't quite piece together how this had come to be, how they all had been thrown together while he slept. Where had they been?

One of Peter's snowballs splattered against William, who reacted with his own missile, but not before yelling out, "I'll fucking kill you."

"William Flanagan!" Catherine Hurley shouted with a scowl as a return snowball smashed Peter. "Watch your mouth. Or else a phone call will go out to your parents." She grabbed Tommy from Pearl, who cackled some, and climbed the front porch steps.

Dennis met his mother in the kitchen. She walked right by him, Tommy squirming to free himself. She put him in his highchair and poured some Cheerios on the tray to keep him preoccupied.

Aunt Pearl next appeared. "So, you're up, old sleepy head."

Then Christine, who couldn't wait to begin an elaborate account of the morning, started in. "Oh, Dennis, while you were sleeping, we all ventured out to Father Mulski's wake. Or viewing, as Mommy calls it. In fact-"

"Christine!" Catherine Hurley yelled. "Don't be teasing on a hard morning like this. We have breakfast to think about. And chores."

"Dennis," Aunt Pearl rushed to console with her wild tongue, though speaking as if of an old annoyance. "Don't you worry yourself about Mulski face. You didn't miss a thing. After years of cranky sermons, the old goat got what he deserved. Besides, sometime tomorrow he'll be in the ground. Poof! Like he was never here."

"Pearl!" protested Catherine, clearly trying to suppress a grin.

Heading for her attic bedroom, Aunt Pearl sputtered, "Dulski, Mulski, Bulski!"

The news hit Dennis like a whack across the head. He had forgotten that the night before his mother announced they would all rise early to attend the public viewing.

"It's a real shame, Dennis," Christine was not done. "Every kid in the school except you saw Father Mulski in his final hours."

"Christine, please!" her mother again urged. "See if you can't attend to Tommy while I make breakfast. In fact, take him to his toys in the den."

Lifting Tommy out of the highchair, Christine kissed his face with loud slurping sounds as she carried him away.

"Mom," Dennis said, "why didn't you wake me up? And what's with William and Peter?"

She first filled the kettle with running water, then glanced at his bare feet. "If it will help matters, Dennis. But it's nothing, really. Early this morning, your father took part in a special Knights of Columbus predawn service for Father Mulski. When he returned, I called to get everyone up so we could pay our respects. But you didn't respond. I called again. Nothing. So I thought it best to let you catch up on your sleep. You had already served early Mass twice this week. As for Peter and William, I simply offered them a ride home. Now, if you don't mind, do drop the sad face! Let us get on with the morning!"

As Dennis stomped back upstairs, Coco pawed his way in and collapsed under the table. Dan Hurley followed, and swatting wet snow off his pants, he looked around to see if his sister-in-law had retired upstairs.

"Not to worry, Dan, Pearl went up top."

"As if, Cat, I was on the lookout for her." He poured hot water into his mug and dunked the tea bag in, followed by two heaping tablespoons of sugar and an ample dose of milk.

"Listen to you," said his wife, who had sworn to her husband after Pearl divorced Carl that her move out from Queens was temporary. Just a few months, she told him. As the few months passed, and oily suitors came a-calling, Pearl in preparation for each date smeared a mask of cream on her face that flaked and crumbled by the early afternoon. When Dan once asked Pearl why she dumped the barrel-chested Larry Mann, she replied, "If not for the weak chin, Dan Hurley, Larry would have been the perfect package." She finally accepted the marriage proposal of John Remkinski, a retired electrician, her senior by some fifteen years. For Dan, the sixteen months to get his sister-in-law out of the house was not a minor point.

Nor was it for Dennis on the morning of Mulski's viewing. When he returned downstairs for breakfast, he was in no mood for his aunt's bluster. But there Aunt Pearl was, sitting alongside the mulish Christine, both lying in wait. Dennis had only the Cheerios box to shield him from those two.

"You know, Dennis," Christine took the lead. "I bet there were hundreds of us kids there, maybe a thousand, all paying our respects to the Most Reverend Mulski."

"And for what?" his aunt muttered, biting off a piece of buttered toast.

"Why, Aunt Pearl," Christine blurted, "to experience one of the most dramatic events in the whole history of St. Theresa's."

Dennis' spoon fell to the bowl. He stormed back up to his bedroom where he swore he'd stay the rest of the day.

LATER THAT AFTERNOON, after Dan Hurley called up to his son to shovel out front, Dennis armored up in winter wear; and with the sun low in the sky, the shoveling became a lonely, arduous affair. Worse, the morning's visitation thing still stuck in his craw.

It wasn't like he didn't know Mulski better than most. He served as his altar boy for many liturgies. One morning, Dennis watched him discover a stray guitar on the altar and proceed to smash it repeatedly on the sacristy's concrete steps, the splintered handle and its dangling wires tossed out onto the pavement.

As Dennis continued to shovel snow, he wished there had been some other excuse than his having overslept for not taking part in the morning visitation. Not helping matters was the black mutt that kept coming back to sniff each new stretch of shoveled sidewalk. Even as the morning blunder lingered in his mind, however, Dennis started to feel wild musings taking shape. He looked down at his winter boots. At least they'd offer him the needed traction. He stole a look at the kitchen window, and with the coast clear, he speared the shovel into a mound of snow. He took off running as best he could across Crocus Lane, the earlier slush having hardened to ridges. The field was no better, each footstep crunching the top layer.

Passing through the woods, Dennis slowed to a walk as he crossed over the creek water on the usual rocks. The snow on the opposite bank caused him to slip backwards a few times. Finally up and over, he stepped onto what was known as the town path, a wooded byway that sat on parish property and that ran north to south from the parish to Old Montauk Highway. To the path's west was the creek itself, to the east, the parish cemetery a few hundred feet through more woods. Bellport's youth often straddled the creek rocks and used the path as a short cut to and from the parish.

Once up on the path, Dennis passed the Sitting Bull plaque, which was welded to an iron pole and cemented in, the chief's face obscured by snow. At the time Dennis didn't know the origins of the plaque. He knew only that it was there. The boots again finding traction, he resumed running, slipping at times but quickly finding his feet again. Soon, the cold air burned his lungs. His shoulders tightened. But he didn't care. No matter the season, he liked to run whenever he found himself on some open stretch. Running at times seemed easier, and more natural, than walking. Of course, in just a few short years, he had forgotten all about the terrible hardship he had endured between the ages of four and nine when he wore a corrective brace that ran along his entire left leg, this from a degenerative hip condition. After dinner each night, Dennis would take off the brace and read in bed. He'd often take breaks from reading, and on his good leg hop over to the window and watch neighborhood kids playing on the field. He dreamed of the day he would join them.

Once the hip had healed and the brace came off for good, those five years from hell were history, and as he raced along that cold January day, he thought only about the exhilaration running gave him. It didn't matter where he was. Voices in his head simply told him to take off, and once in stride, he visualized the luster about his legs, buoyant and fast, and of the driving force of his arms. He could go on forever. That's how he felt that day running along the path, hidden by snow but outlined by large trees on either side whose limbs made slight cracking sounds, like distant pops on the Fourth of July. It wasn't until the path ended that he came to a hard stop, the parish grounds now in full view. As he caught his breath, he had no choice but to stare down the church wherein Mulski lie.

He made his way over and tugged on the massive entrance doors. Locked. He walked around to a large evergreen on the church's rear side, behind which hid a window whose frame Peter Walker one night the previous summer had jimmied open. His friend did so for no other reason than the adventure, and after climbing in, he challenged Dennis and William to do the same by hurling digs about them being cowards. The three soon found themselves mulling about the empty church.

But that was then, and today with dusk emerging, Dennis stood staring at the window, his only access to the dead Mulski. The same voices that told him to run now told him to wheel around and go home, to leave well enough alone. Yet, Christine's taunting returned. She'd never stop teasing the hell out of him for sleeping through the viewing. He rattled the window frame open and dropped inside.

As he moved along the back wall, he looked up at the long narrow reach of the empty nave saturated with dim air that hung like ocean mist. At the middle aisle, he turned and saw Mulski way up there in an elaborate brass-trimmed coffin, illuminated by tall glowing candles. Hands in loose fists, Dennis resumed walking, and once there, he eyed the black skullcap rarely worn except when posing for newspaper pictures. He tried not to study the tight sockets, the small nose, the crusty pink lips. A terrifying thought came. What was to prevent the old goat, sunken as he was in the coffin's plush interior, from snapping forward? Dennis had once witnessed Mulski stop a novena dead in its tracks to reprimand the chattering Mrs. McNally, a red-haired parishioner who liked a drop or two, and who under her breath slurred an obscenity at the pastor.

"Son, son!" came a raspy whisper.

Dennis turned. There to the right, a few skips away on the sacristy landing, stood the old parish custodian. Since 1938, Mr. Malagati, along with his wife, had resided in the small bungalow, the original rectory that stood adjacent to the convent, both structures tucked away in the corner of the grounds. Today, the custodian's large hand beckoning, Dennis made his way over to the small pencil of a man.

"How you get in?" Mr. Malagati asked. "Doors? They lock. How?" He said this stealing back-and-forth looks at the coffin. Even as Dennis was trying to follow the sorry English, he refocused on the old custodian: the wide brown eyes, the imposing forehead, the leathery face that had lost much of its roughness for a more delicate skin that comes with age.

"How?" Mr. Malagati demanded.

"A window."

Realizing the boy's transgression could not be overlooked, the old man returned a pained expression, as if someone had lassoed him around the stomach and yanked. "I sorry. I sorry. But you follow me."

Now a small ocean fish caught in the beak of a low-flying gull, Dennis was led by Mr. Malagati out into the cold air along a hedgerow and handed over to Mrs. Wooten, the matronly rectory secretary. After she made a hushed phone call, she sent the boy down the hallway to a bench across from the office of Mulski's successor. Monsignor James Francis Cassidy, a lean, supple cleric had been sent to St. Theresa's years earlier when Mulski was waiting on his open-heart operation. The diocese was sure, as was Cassidy, that the patient wouldn't survive the procedure. But the old goat had proven them all wrong. Returning to the parish, he wasted little time turning tedious pastoral duties over to his new assistant, who waited nearly a decade for his boss to take leave.

All of this was of little solace to Cassidy when he learned that among his first administrative tasks as pastor was dealing with an impish altar boy who had stolen into the church for a glimpse of Casimir Mulski in the long sleep. Still, the new pastor needed to play the part. He did so by making Dan and Catherine Hurley wait on the bench beside their son. All the while he sat in his office, his fingers lightly drumming the desktop, the wall clock given casual glances.

Finally, he stood and went to the full-length mirror. He adjusted his collar and tapped down a full head of wavy silver hair.

The three prisoners watched the office door open. Out came the arm. "Mr. and Mrs. Hurley, please."

The door closed on Dennis, but not before he felt the sting of Cassidy's pale blue eyes. He could hear little of what the Monsignor had to say during the brief meeting. Only muted tones heavy with meaning, followed by the bootlicking acknowledgments of his parents. A short, conciliatory response from his father brought the meeting to a close. His parents came out, shoulders sagging.

Dennis stood to follow them, the three in single file moving out past the purse-lipped Mrs. Wooten at her desk.

Nothing was said on the ride home, and before Dennis was sent to his room for the night without dinner, his father told him that the Monsignor had settled on a month of detentions. That was not exactly good news for Dennis. As the night wore on, moreover, he started to dread the prospect of the face-to-face contact he'd have the next morning with the new pastor. He was slated to serve early Mass, which Cassidy had presided over the last few months as Mulski's health deteriorated.

So, when his alarm went off at 5:45 a.m., Dennis felt nothing but fear as he got ready for his visit back to the crime scene. Heading downstairs, he met his mother, who in her bathrobe, spoke just above a whisper. "Dennis, don't let the Monsignor scare you up on the altar. But if it gets bad, just do what I always do. Say a prayer. As for Charlie Malagati, stay away from him. One never knows about him. Always looking cross, like he's about to erupt. Okay?"

"Okay."

"And, Dennis, there still might be a bit of action over at the parish. A Dalton's hearse was to take Father Mulski early this morning to the Cathedral for today's funeral service and then to Holy Rood for burial."

Catherine Hurley also told her son to avoid the path and take the safer downtown route. Dennis usually ignored such warnings, but not this time. The act of obedience felt vaguely reassuring as he walked briskly down Crocus, dodging ice spots in the predawn darkness. As he approached the empty downtown, he took off running. He liked his silhouetted reflections, fleeting though they were, in storefront windows. He picked up the pace when he turned off Main Street and onto the parish grounds, which Mr. Malagati had ploughed clean with a tractor. Dennis skidded to a stop to watch a hearse pass by on the way out of the parish. He turned for the church's sacristy door.

SITTING BULL RUN

Once inside and greeting a wall of radiated heat, he grabbed a cloth altar napkin and dried the sweat off his face and neck. He wasted no time peeking out onto the altar. Indeed, the coffin and all the tall candles were gone. But he was startled to see the new man, Father Ken Garland, a young priest not long out of the seminary who had joined the parish the previous year when Mulksi's health got bad. Working the tabernacle, Father Ken didn't look happy. Dennis had served Mass for him often enough to recognize his two faces. One, a gleeful oaf topped with curly black hair and a small square jaw set inside a blubbery countenance. The other, that of a tortured underling, which he resembled this morning on account of his having been shaken out of sleep by Cassidy. The pastor had been itching for a reason to broadside the new man ever since catching whiffs of his gaseous brand of sermonizing, of which Dan Hurley once said, "elevated the evangelical to a new level." When Father Ken wasn't saying Mass, he was teaching part-time for the high school's Religion Department where, by day's end, his collar was askew, his hair disheveled. On weekends, he was seen bounding around town in baggy khakis and a large pullover to hide the girth. Cassidy's nightmares featured his new man on the altar in tennis shorts, a guitar in hand, serenading the congregation.

Dennis, now in cassock and surplice, had just started lighting altar candles when he noticed the nuns in full dress out there in the front pews stealing looks at him. They must have heard about his breaking into the church. He finished up and scurried back into the sacristy to find Father Ken patting vestments down into place.

"Ready, Dennis Hurley?"

"Ready, Father."

"Good, then. Let the show begin."

With hands precisely joined, Dennis led Father Ken onto the altar where both genuflected before the Crucifix. Without any warning, and as if taking a cue from heaven, the young priest raised his arms upward and began singing, a cappella, a popular spiritual. At first the nuns looked startled, accustomed as they were to the austere manner in which Mulski or Cassidy conducted early Mass. But unable to resist the alluring melody, most joined in and filled the church with song. A stranger stumbling in off the street might have thought a trained choir was at work.

For Dennis, none of this helped him face the tight spot he was in. Sister Rosaleen, the very tall school principal with a long face and wide shoulders, seemed to be evaluating him. Her conclusion all but etched in stone, the Hurley boy was no longer the pure-of-heart acolyte responsible for lighting and extinguishing altar candles that symbolized Christ's ghostly presence. He was now one from a long line of parish thugs.

Averting his gaze to evade the principal's eyes, Dennis looked to the back of the church. In a rear pew was Mr. Malagati, whose habit it was to kneel in prayer for just a minute before leaving to unlock the school buildings. Dennis was relieved when he next looked and found the old custodian gone.

2

Some years later, in late October 1973, Dennis as a junior at St. Theresa's found himself part of the school's varsity cross-country team that had just won the sectional qualifying meet. They did so by defeating the powerhouse programs of William Floyd and St. Anthony's on the daunting Sunken Meadow Park course, located on the hilly north shore of Long Island. Running alongside William Flanagan and Peter Walker, the "core three" as Coach Jack dubbed them, Dennis and his two friends came across the line together (as they always did) in the top fifteen, each posting a PR for the three-mile course. Finishing before them was teammate Adam Feltman, who won the race, and George Legstaff, who passed some twenty runners in the last half mile for a third-place finish. And although non-scorers Mark Voit and James Fennessy fell apart over the last mile, St. Theresa's first-place finish of 62 points earned the team a trip to the state championship, to take place a week later at upstate Watkins Glen.

Before the St. Theresa team left Sunken Meadow that day, they posed for team photos for the local *Bellport Citizen* and the larger regional publication, the *Long Island Press*. Standing at one end and holding the team trophy was their brawny coach, Jack Hogan, whose pudgy face had widened considerably since his own running days. His elfin ears, a dark shade of pink, were pressed flat to his head as though he'd spent his whole life in a woolen cap. Like his team, he smiled broadly for the photos. Behind the smile, however, he was already brainstorming the workout schedule for the coming week. Forever taking measure of the world with a stopwatch, Coach Jack would relay that schedule to his varsity seven on the ride back to Bellport while they munched on their White Castle.

"Gonna get after it, boys, the next three days," he said looking into the rearview mirror of his old jalopy of a van. "Starting with a fast three-mile boardwalk run tomorrow. The last two miles, race pace, followed by bumrushes, a dozen of them." Bumrush was a tag the coach used instead of the more commonplace 'strides.'

"But tomorrow's Sunday," moaned James Fennessy. "We need a recovery day."

"Monday, Coach?" Adam Feltman asked.

"Five 880 repeats on the boardwalk. The last three, bare-knuckles fast. Tuesday, a breather of five junk miles."

"Uh oh," said William. "Afraid to ask what Wednesday brings."

"Our last mile time trial of the season on the Sitting Bull course."

"I dig it, Coach," from Peter. "We can beat the shit out of the Injun." Coach Jack used the Sitting Bull plaque as a starting or finishing point for interval workouts over the path.

"Bet your shiny white ass, Peter Walker! And from there, the tapering begins. Three very slow junk miles on Thursday. Got it, Adam?"

"Good luck, Coach," said William, "getting Adam to run junk miles."

"I'll fry his ass," Jack Hogan shouted back, "if I find out he runs anything faster than eight-minute pace. Got it, Adam? Good. And then on Friday, we'll stretch, jog a bit, and end up with bumrushes. Followed by the team meal at Sal's Pizzeria. Spaghetti and meatballs. Hell, I can already hear the garlic knots singing in the pan."

LATER THAT NIGHT Jack Hogan, pen in hand, sat alone at the far end of Chief's Bar and Grill, a popular watering hole in downtown Bellport. A notebook sandwiched between his empty beer mug and a bowl of pretzels, he was busy finishing up a to-do list in preparation for the run-up to the state meet.

"One for the road, Jack?" asked owner Billy Boyce from behind the bar.

"Why not? But then I've got to get home and get me some sleep."

The mug of beer delivered, Coach Jack put pen and notebook back in his briefcase. Wrapping his two hands around his mug, and looking out into space, he said to himself, Finally, dammit! We're there!

Back in 1963, in the basement of St. Francis Prep High School in Queens, Jack Hogan had led a regional group of Catholic high-school coaches in drafting a petition to the New York High School Athletic Association. The petition asked that private high schools be allowed to compete in the state cross-country meet, which, since its inception decades earlier, had been restricted to public schools. The petition was initially rejected by the powers that be, this despite the hundreds of signatures as well as copies of recent meet results that revealed New York Catholic teams outpacing their public-school counterparts. But persistent badgering by coaches continued. Jack Hogan was among the more vociferous, this given that his team for a number of years had won regional invitationals as well as the annual Long Island Catholic schools' championship meet. Still, it took a good decade before the state cross-country championship included private institutions.

But in order to qualify for the state, a team would still have to win the sectional meet. Today, St. Theresa's had done just that.

Coach Jack could barely contain himself as he took a hearty swig from his beer mug. His team would now travel to Watkins Glen, and if all went well, punish a few upstate public schools that had dominated recent state meets. Namely, Albany Hamilton and Syracuse Central.

"Hey, Jack," yelled Larry Mann from across the bar, "Good luck next Saturday, if I don't see you before then."

"Yeah, Jack," Roger Greer added, "thump those damn heathens."

Coach Jack waved back and said, "That's the plan." But behind a frozen smile, he thought that if only he could chain a five-hundred-pound anchor to both Roger and Larry and toss them over the inlet bridge into the bay. Neither has any fucking idea what it takes to get seven teenage boys, with Hostess Ding Dongs forever smearing their bright white teeth, to thump the heathens. Nor does either know what it takes to cajole and sweet-talk the same boys into seventy-mile weeks over the hot summer, followed by playing the free-of-charge shrink during the long fall season. All to goddam get his team to understand and embrace an all-consuming physical pain that constitutes cross-country running. Only then can each boy, hopefully with a burning fire in his belly, pop a magical race at state.

Coach Jack chugged the rest of the beer and left, shouting over his shoulder on the way out, "Until we meet again!"

When he got home, he called his assistant, Sister Jean Ruskin, and asked her if she would phone around and rally as many JV runners as she could to meet at the beach. "At the Field Six boardwalk tomorrow at three. And tell them to be ready to run a workout."

"But their season, Jack, ended last week with the dual meet against Holy Family. Plus, it's Sunday."

"Dammit, Sister, we go to state next week. Just tell them we'll splurge for pizza afterwards. Can you do that for Ole Jack?"

Upon arriving at Field Six, the varsity seven found a mob of underclassmen in their running gear. Each of the seven knew what their coach had up his sleeve. Several times during the season Coach Jack would invite the underclassmen to a beach workout, where he'd give them a two-minute lead ahead of the varsity on the out-and-back boardwalk run of three miles. Each time the coach demanded that his team use a racing strategy that he coined slow burn, which was little more than a conservative first mile, followed by a torch of a second mile and an all hands-on-deck final mile. Coach Jack would sometimes use the underclassmen for this workout because he knew it would motivate his varsity to begin mowing down one runner after another once they reached the mile mark at the first jetty. Legs hated it because he knew just how foolish he'd look if even one of the younger runners beat him. The other varsity members, however, thrived on the workout since it was a confidence booster passing a slew of runners once the surging began.

Of course, Coach Jack understood that nearly all coaches ask their runners on race day to use a disciplined pacing strategy through most of the three miles, holding off on the hard charge until the end. The St. Theresa's hard charge, however, always began at the mile mark, and by using slow burn repeatedly in certain workouts as well as race days, the strategy became ingrained in them. That was exactly the case with the Field Six run that Sunday afternoon, which pleased their coach to no end. So did Wednesday's mile time trial prove noteworthy. The five-man average of 4:27 was the fastest of any Jack Hogan squad to date.

"Okay, boys," he said afterwards, "I'd say we're ready. Let the tapering begin."

UPSTATE WEATHERMEN called for cloudy skies that early November day. Neither rain nor wind in the forecast, the temperature by race time would creep up into the low sixties. With racing conditions thus ideal, throngs of anxious fans scurried from parking lots and passed under the entrance banner.

*Welcome to Watkins Glen State Park
Home of the 1973 New York State
High School Cross-Country Championship*

Some fans bolted over to the starting line, there for a bird's eye view. Others swarmed to the park's crowning bluffs to cheer on their team's runners. Among these fans was the contingent of St. Theresa's parents who decided to go to a perch some six-hundred yards into the race. On their way, Harry Feltman, father of Adam, stopped to survey the makeshift tent city. There he saw all manner of runners in their team colors. Some were doing wind sprints; others on the ground stretching; still others standing upright, hands reaching for toes, slapping quads. Harry located St. Theresa's silver and maroon team tent.

"What in God's creation is going on over there?" Harry shouted to the other parents who had stopped and saw what he was gaping at. George Legstaff and James Fennessy were having a towel fight. Dennis Hurley and William Flanagan seemed to be lounging in the grass. Peter Walker, sitting atop a tree limb, was wildly kicking his legs out like a maniac. Captain Mark Voit lay on his back, as if sleeping. Only his Adam was engaged in intense stretching.

"Not to worry, Harry," said Dan Hurley. "The boys won on this course back in September. And I'm sure they've already done their drills. They're just relaxing some before the big race."

"But Coach Jack! Does he even approve of this?"

"Oh," Bill Flanagan said, "he's probably getting the team packet. And once he returns, all seven boys will snap to attention. Or he'll cut off their you-know-whats."

"Bill!" Kay Flanagan cried.

As the parents made their way, the P. A. system came to life. "Your attention, please. It is now nine-fifteen. The race will start in forty-five minutes."

Coach Jack Hogan, in fact, had been at the registration table retrieving the team packet. Arriving back at the tent, he told his team now stretching, "Inside, boys! It's time!" He said this just as Sister Jean steered the school bus full of her JV runners into a parking spot. She told them to hustle over to the team tent and form a corridor outside of it through which the varsity would pass and be cheered.

Inside the tent the nervous coach distributed bibs to his runners, whose jittery fingers attached them to their singlets with safety pins.

"C'mon, Fenny, strip down," William said to James Fennessy, who hadn't taken off his sweat bottoms.

When Fenny didn't move but flushed a crimson red, Adam Feltman exploded. "God, no, Fenny! Don't tell me you left your racing trunks at home!"

Coach Jack's mouth fell open and got stuck in the rigid shape of a half dollar, his runners left to take on that crazed-out-of-his-mind look that their coach could sometimes display. And he might have screamed bloody murder at Fenny but that the P. A. system came back to life: "It is now nine-thirty, the race to begin in thirty minutes. All teams should begin making their way to the starting line and respective team boxes."

Jack Hogan now looked downward at the grass floor. That prompted Dennis to say, "Coach, the race?"

The coach looked back at Dennis, and then at his runners, who stood knowing not what to say or do. Nor did Coach Jack for that matter, even though he had rehearsed a fiery pep talk countless times the previous week. He scoured his mind. Strangely enough, Fenny's fuck-up provided him with an opening.

"Well, if truth must be told, Ole Jack Hogan can't help but love Fenny the Fleabite. Why? For the same reason he loves all his Mary Janes. Not because they, too, have royally screwed up at one time or another. No, it's because they worked their tails off this summer. And because they followed that up with a mean ass-kicking of the enemy on regional courses during the season, not to mention destroying the prima donna schools last week at sectionals. And because, well, this race belongs to them and not the uppity teams from Albany and Syracuse, who, if I can be damn frank, can go straight to Hell."

The team muttered approval.

"Now remember the strategy that got us here in the first place. The first mile's all about biding your time and watching your goddam step over an early set of bumpy ups and downs. Then at the mile mark, it's time to poke the bear and start mowing down runner after runner over the next two miles, the whole time telling yourselves that slinging dirt back at your competitors is the road to victory. So, boys, wadda you say? The moment's at hand. The granddaddy of them all, the first ever state meet to include Catholic schools. Got it?"

"Got it!" his runners shouted back.

"Good!" he said, his hand jutting out. "Now, as I take my fat ass out to the course, you boys go win yourselves a big championship in the sky."

The team put their hands atop his and blasted, "Sitting Bull!"

Jack Hogan left the tent, his bouncing gut passing through the corridor of JV runners who cheered on the coach with fist pumps. The top JV runner, one of the Peterson twins, stepped out in front of Coach Jack and yelled, "Kick ass, Coach!"

"That's the plan, Carl."

Resuming his jog, the coach headed to a spot where he'd watch his team over the first few hundred yards.

Soon his varsity runners emerged from the tent and were greeted by the raucous high-fiving of their younger teammates, several of whom had smeared on silver and maroon face paint and were now waving enormous school flags. The charged expletives from their mouths made the scene all the more intense. Knowing better, Sister Jean stood away, pressing her rosary beads, a victory prayer in the offing.

Coach Jack's seven headed to Team Box 12. Once there, they

exploded with a few bumrushes, followed by fist-bumping and pats on the back.

Now crowded inside their team box, they waited on the starter, each runner in his own way keeping busy with a final pre-race ritual.

Captain Mark Voit did deep-knee bends.

Peter Walker, a fierce rotation of the shoulders.

William Flanagan shadowboxed, his fists moving slowly at first, then in smooth combinations, and finally in a blur of speed.

George Legstaff slapped his quads and hissed encouragement to each teammate.

The five-foot-four-inch Adam Feltman, with a mask of sheer intensity, stood hands akimbo, shifting weight from foot to foot as he peered down the opening stretch.

James Fennessy retightened the strings of his sweats.

Dennis Hurley looked down at his wiggling fingers, muscle memory from his piano-playing days when he had his leg brace on. He turned an eye to the Albany Hamilton team, the odds-on favorite to win, three boxes over. He might have stared longer had the bullhorn not ordered the field to toe the starting line. Most runners inhaled a pound of air.

The starter's pistol now pointing to the sky, the crowd's buzz dropping off, the teams stood frozen for several long, hellish seconds. Faces straight out, arms dangling, a knee bent forward.

"Runners, set…"

The crack of the pistol unleashed the sprawling mob in an all-out sprint that quickly devolved into a fight for position. Hard jostling. Wide swinging elbows and hand checking. Spikes meeting bony shins. All as the arrow formation gradually emerged, the tip of which today took aim at a large water fountain. Once reached, the field half-circled it and settled into race pace, faces reflecting the gut-wrenching grind that epitomizes cross-country running. Only the leader, the Bronson kid from Rochester North, looked as clean and fresh as a baby's ass.

After motoring to the first vantage point, Coach Jack saw that his team had gotten out in decent shape. Feltman near the front, the core three of Hurley, Walker, and Flanagan some rows back. Voit looked like crap not far behind them. Fenny and Legs, falling roughly in the middle of the massive field.

Coach Jack scurried through the woods and soon joined other coaches who surrounded an official whose job was to call out the first mile split. He arrived just in time to see Bronson pass by in 4:56, followed by a large group that included Adam Feltman, who came by in 5:04. Adam's slow-burn surge did little to encourage his coach, for a pack of three from Albany went right with his top guy. It only got worse after another dozen runners came by, the fourth and fifth men from Albany among them. This prompted the Syracuse coach to yell out to the Albany coach, "Got this race by the balls!"

"Only if," the Albany coach replied as he took off for the two-mile mark, "we can keep your boys at bay."

Coach Jack muttered harsh words. Barring a meltdown, the race indeed was Albany's to lose. But he was not willing to concede second place to Syracuse quite yet, despite that its own pack of five runners just then passed a good ten places ahead of his core three, who were positioned somewhere in the mid-forties. Like Adam, they, too, surged in slow burn, which was some consolation to their coach, even though a narrow race trail forced them to run unevenly, darting here and there, squeezing through runners. They did so as Coach Jack back at the mile marker waited on his next three runners.

Fenny was the first to appear, running his fastest first mile of the season, 5:33.

"Dammit, Fenny," Coach Jack yelled, "this is your day! Now go maul twenty runners by mile two!"

Fenny waved a fist and surged.

"It doesn't matter, Jack," the Elmira coach responded, "if your kid mauls fifty, he's out of uniform."

"Technically speaking," the Saratoga coach added, "your whole team's disqualified."

"Hell, yeah, Hogan," shouted the Syracuse coach as he took off for the two-mile mark. "Caput!"

Coach Jack lowered his head, and as he desperately tried to recall what exactly the state uniform rule was, Legstaff approached in that smug comfortable stride. His coach nearly jumping onto the trail, he rasped at his all-state half-miler, "What the fuck, Legs!"

Now he waited on Captain Mark Voit, whose season had turned to shit after the Jersey Shore Invite at Holmdel Park. There the boy sprained his ankle and never got back on track, even after it healed. When a long stream of runners passed, and still no Voit, Coach Jack muttered, "Hell with him," and ran up a wooded hill, stopping at its crest to gauge the race from a distance.

With Albany's three still on Adam's tail, Coach Jack saw that his top scorer had moved up into the teens and continued to pass runners. Syracuse's pack of five passed before the core three came into view. Coach Jack, however, thought his three were moving at a good clip, the Syracuse five within their grasp.

Soon Legs, having gapped Fenny, came by. Yet he still seemed to be floating along without a care in the world.

"Asshole!" cried Coach Jack, who could never get over George Legstaff's rejection of his slow-burn racing strategy. For Legs, who ran a 1:54 half mile during the track season as a sophomore, and who hated the slow creep of a three-mile race, his modus operandi during cross country was to coast the first two miles, and then pick up the pace some before torching the final half mile. And to the fucker's credit, Coach Jack had to admit, the kid typically ran a sub 2:10 last half mile. In several races, Legs moved up as many as fifty places from the two-mile mark, even finishing second to Adam in a few big meets. After hearing about this maniac kid from New York, *Runner's World* sent one of its people out to witness Legs in action. *This George Legstaff,* the subsequent article read, *runs most of the race with a profound air of sunny optimism before he morphs into a ferocious tiger on the prowl the last half mile.*

THE CORE THREE having just finished an up and down, Peter gasped, "Let's go grab a bunch more."

He took off, to which William shouted back, "Here we go, Denny Boy."

With that, the two of them caught up to Peter, and grinded up a long incline, passing a good dozen runners in the process. But just as the three gapped a large pack on the long backside, and set their sights on more runners, Peter caught William's spike and went down, Dennis forced to hurdle over him. William and Dennis slowed down to let Peter catch up.

"You okay?" Dennis asked Peter.

"Piece of cake!"

"Fuck!" William cried out. "Let's go."

They did just that, though forgetting that after another climb just around the bend was a steep descent on a rutted path. Each now found himself going down full stride, arms held out until the bottom came. There they negotiated a sharp right turn that led to a ravine of soft dirt and sand, a part of the course that was a nightmare on the legs and that for a few hundred yards ran along a stream, its trees with large roots clinging to its bank. Then, a small bridge that ushered in a long, slow climb to the other side. At its summit, the grimacing three were met by a torrent of fans who kept an eye on them even as they waited on their own runners.

At the two-mile mark, Coach Jack joined an enormous crowd of coaches and fans, the St. Theresa contingent among them. To the screaming delight of Harry and Ida Feltman, their Adam was now in the lead group of six runners, the Bronson kid at its tip. Coaches could tell things were really heating up for the six, each of whom seemed to be keenly aware of those around him. They seemed to be racing one another for the first time.

The Albany pack of three came by, soon followed by their fourth and fifth men still running together. Jack Hogan sneered at the Albany coach, whose team was crushing the field. His spirits were lifted, though, when his core three came by in 10:38, right behind Syracuse's pack of five, all of them positioned in the twenties. Legs had not yet kicked it into high gear. But he had moved way up, now in the thirties.

"What are you waiting for?" Coach Jack screamed at Legs when he came by.

"The man in the moon," gasped Legs. "That's who."

The sauciness brought a smile to his coach, one that grew wider when Fenny came by in 11:14, a PR two-mile split for the boy.

"Way to go, James Fennessy!"

"Doesn't matter, Coach," injected Sam Falconi, the Buffalo coach, "if your kid there wins the race. He's out of uniform."

"You think so!" said Coach Jack. He would have cold-cocked the guy except that his team, in the hunt for second place, propelled him through woods to a spot where he saw that Adam Feltman had gapped the lead group, and now in first place was approaching the water fountain on his way to the final half mile. So did Coach Jack nearly piss in his pants when he saw his core three closing in on the Syracuse pack of five. He crunched numbers on his clipboard.

Looking up with a startled expression, he muttered, Shit, if the core three can pass the Syracuse pack, second place is ours! That is, if damn Legstaff can work his magic.

As if Legs had read his coach's mind, he flew by more runners and was closing in on the core three. But, and this Coach Jack knew, a mountain of work remained if George Legstaff was to move into the top ten, the number probably needed for a second-place team finish. The coach kept his eyes on Legs, now flying past the core three, newspaper people snapping pictures of him. Legs soon went by Syracuse's five, who broke into smaller packs of two and three.

Coach Jack, taking off for the finish line, now saw Adam, still in the lead, circling the water fountain and heading for home. The coach barreled through fans right up to the rope, in time to see his top kid come down the final straightaway.

"C'mon, Adam Feltman," he screamed, "you got this, dammit! Just bring it home!!"

Jack Hogan knew the tumult and uproar drowned out his words. Still, he continued to shout encouragement. Soon, too soon, however, he noticed Adam's legs growing rubbery. The boy was jostling for balance, pain stretching wide on his face.

"Bumrush, Adam! Bumrush!"

It was only a matter of time, and Coach Jack now knew this, before Bronson and Albany's top two runners would reach and pass Adam.

Not far from the finish line, they did just that.

Fuck, Coach Jack snapped, Adam Feltman just got skunked.

Yet the St. Theresa's coach also knew that his top runner had just taken fourth at state, and that the team was still in the hunt for second place. All of which led Coach Jack to look up to heaven and ask his mother, Molly, to put in a good word for the rest of his team. The prayer seemed to work, starting with Legs who flew by runners and crossed the line in tenth place. Now it was up to Hurley, Flanagan, and Walker if his team was to grab second. They'd close the deal, Coach Jack figured, by picking off the second of Syracuse's small packs. Which the core three, turning on to the final straight, did in high style and with fierce expressions.

"Hell, yeah!" screamed Coach Jack, the core three now positioned in the high teens.

But no sooner did he throw a giddy fist to the sky than he noticed Syracuse's sixth man, coming out of nowhere, laying waste to the field. He watched in horror as the damn kid, with less than twenty yards left in the race, reeled in his own five Syracuse teammates, the core three, and several more runners, all before crossing the finish line.

With dead eyes, and ever so slowly shaking his head back and forth, Jack Hogan muttered, "We just lost second place."

He didn't wait for Fenny. He turned for the park's bathroom, and soon felt his head leaning against the cold cinder block as he took a long hot piss. His frayed mind, over and over, rechecked the math. Each time the scores remained the same. And when he eventually made his way over to the results board, a look at the places of the top three teams was tough to stomach.

1973 Watkins Glen State Championship
Albany Hamilton High School: 2, 3, 8, 14, 15 = 42 pts.
Syracuse Central High School: 7, 9, 11, 23, 24 = 74 pts.
St. Theresa High School: 4, 10, 20, 21, 22 = 77 pts.

"Three fucking measly points," Jack Hogan muttered under his breath.

3

Not long after the race, the Nanuet coach, his team a distant fourth with 151 points, rushed into the meet officials' tent with a rule book in hand. He demanded a St. Theresa's disqualification for a uniform violation. When Jack Hogan got wind of this, he charged the tent.

"What did you want the boy to do," he screamed at the Nanuet coach, "run in his jock strap?" The two coaches had to be restrained.

Coach Jack would not relent. "The goddam rulebook's fine print allows for extenuating circumstances."

"What possible extenuating circumstance," the Nanuet coach replied, "could there be? That one of my runners stole your boy's racing trunks? I don't think so."

A frantic Jack Hogan recalled that a few years back Fenny's younger brother died tragically. "Hey, Mister Know-It-All, the boy lost his baby brother to a drowning accident, that's what. And if that's not enough, you can go straight to Hell."

An influential meet official from Genessee County intervened on behalf of St. Theresa's. A decision finally reached, Fenny was disqualified. But the team score remained intact. Still, their coach continued to be racked by the thought that a few places here, a few places there, and second place would have been theirs. His runners thought the same thing once back inside the team tent, starting with William, who cried as he ripped off his singlet, "That peckerhead from Syracuse! Fuck, he came out of nowhere."

"The same," Adam echoed, "with the three who nailed me at the end."

"C'mon, you guys," said Dennis. "St. Theresa's just ran state for the first time. A podium finish. And William, you had a PR. Adam, fourth place overall. Ain't too shabby."

"And don't forget, Adam," Peter added, "you were the first junior to come across the line. You'll be the man to beat next year when we win state."

"And," Dennis added, "the meet's at Van Cortlandt, our stomping grounds."

"I say," declared Peter, "some gambling tonight at the bowling lanes. Dollar a game. You know, to celebrate our podium finish."

"I'm all in," said Legs. "The guy from the *Long Island Press* clocked me at 2:07 for the last 880. Should get my mug in the sports section."

"I'm in, too," said Fenny. "Gonna bleed you guys dry."

When the team started to take down the tent, their coach asked if anyone knew what happened to Voit during the race.

"He was right next to me a half mile into the race," said Fenny. "Then he pulled a Houdini."

"Traitor," said Legs. "Voit deserves a noose. We shouldn't have let him on the podium with us."

Coach Jack asked, "And where the hell is he now?"

"How about we fan out, Coach?" asked Dennis.

"Fucking Denny Boy, I can always count on you for sage advice."

But the search for the team captain came up empty. William told his coach that Voit was last seen with the Mepham High team.

"The little shit," fumed Coach Jack, who told his varsity to do a mile cool down, pack the tent, and meet him at the van. "I'm gonna see if I can't find him."

He grabbed the third-place trophy, and on the way to look for Voit, he heard, "Hey, Coach Jack."

He turned and saw Harry Feltman approaching. "You have a minute, Coach?"

"Sure, Harry. I always have time for you."

"Coach Jack, help me here. What business does Peter Walker, just minutes before the start of a state championship race, have climbing trees? Or some boys in a towel fight? Or Fennessy, that menace, showing up out of uniform?? All while my son is stretching by himself. I mean, how will any of this advance the cause of my Adam and the college scholarship you promised? You did promise a scholarship, which is why I agreed to transfer him from the public school."

Jack Hogan would need a moment to compose himself. He took stock of the overlapping gold chains around Harry Feltman's neck. The close eyes, the arching nose, the long black hair greased straight back that made him look like a plump Robert DeNiro. Then there was the straw hat that Jack Hogan wanted to rip off Harry's head and stomp to pieces on the ground.

"Huh, Coach Jack, I ask again. What business do they have?"

Over Harry's shoulder were Ida Feltman and the other families standing by. Trapped, the coach worked up a dull smile and waved to the other parents before returning to Adam's father.

"Thank you, Harry, for the concern. And trust me, the boys will pay dearly for their pre-race shenanigans. But do know that today was a massive victory for our program. In addition to a podium finish, six out of my seven runners will be returning next year. This includes your Adam. He not only broke the school record, he was a mere fourteen seconds off the Suffolk County record, which he will shatter next year. Goddam intoxicating, if you ask me."

"But my Adam had the lead! He let three runners pass him at the end. He looked pathetic out there. How does something like that happen in the first place?"

"It happens, Harry, because your son's a fucking string bean.

No upper-body strength. Hell, he can't do a single pull-up. That's why your Adam was fried by the kickers."

"So how do we fix that?"

Coach Jack took just a moment to search for an answer, which then came to him in a flash. "Easy, we beef him up next summer. Get him started on a weight-training program."

"Why not get him started right now? The indoor track season is less than a month away."

To that, Coach Jack puckered his lips. There was no way in hell that he'd admit to Harry Feltman that he always used the indoor and outdoor seasons as a launching pad for cross country the following fall. Since taking over the team back in the late fifties, he had done everything in his power to tone down the training of his distance runners during the track seasons. All so that they'd be healthy and primed for cross country, which Jack Hogan loved more than life itself.

"Listen, Harry! I thought Adam had told you about our plan for the indoor and outdoor seasons."

"No, he hadn't."

"Well, the strategy then is to focus on low mileage and high V02. That translates into leg speed. Which he sorely needs. From there we move onto core strength during the summer."

"And just how do we do that?"

"A summer weight-training program, that's how. One that gets him benching 150 pounds by September, all so that he'll be ready to crush the field at state, his scholarship signed no later than January 1st of next year. Got it?"

"I am not sure I do."

"All in due course, Harry. I'll explain in some detail over a shrimp chow mein dinner at Kwong Ming. As always, my treat. For now, let me find Voit and get on the road. Like you folks, we have a long drive back to the Island."

As Coach Jack made the rounds looking for his captain, several coaches congratulated him on his team's third-place finish. A staff writer from the *Long Island Press* stopped him for an interview. Only then, as he answered questions while looking up at a mass of slow-moving clouds across a blue sky, did it dawn on him that the third-place finish at state was nothing to sneeze at. Nor that six of his runners would return next year. Still, a consummate skeptic at heart, he reminded the reporter that the Syracuse team was returning four, Saratoga, the same, and Albany, three. Not to mention that Nanuet and Bishop Loughlin were both returning strong squads.

After the interview, he learned from the Mepham coach that "Voit probably left with one of my runner's families."

"Probably?"

"Best I can do, Jack."

"That little shit."

Coach Jack returned to the van, where he found that Dennis Hurley, as odd man out, would share the front with him, the monster trophy between them. Firing up the engine, Coach Jack shouted over to him, "Not a bad day's work, huh?"

"No, Coach, not bad at all. A podium finish."

"I like you, Dennis," he said revving the engine, the van then taking off. "But it's a ticklish situation when your team captain goes missing in action. Worse, that a goddam group of lousy coaches bitch over a uniform bottom."

Dennis knew that his coach was still agitated. But with the van out on the open highway, Coach Jack was soon singing along with Tony Bennett on his crooner station, his free hand drumming the dashboard, occasionally tapping the trophy to his side like it was a cymbal.

Not long into the trip Legs asked, "I imagine a third-place trophy translates into you greasing our palms with a ten spot for grub?"

"Got to love you, Georgie boy. Got to love all you boys. But shit no to a ten spot. I'm thinking an Honest Abe will do the trick." Dennis smiled at the exchange, knowing as he did that on van rides back to Bellport both the coach and his runners seemed to lose all inhibitions. Coach Jack especially loved it when George Legstaff riffed his bullshit.

After stopping at a Binghamton Hardee's, the interstate opened up to hazy mountains that bulged on either side. The runners yanked pillows out of their bags and fell asleep. All except Dennis. He could not get comfortable.

"Shit, Dennis, look," said Coach Jack, the traffic slowing to obey a construction worker waving a red flag, this amidst steam gushing from the large asphalt machines. And just as traffic started moving again, a rain began, bringing to life the sound of wheels on wet pavement and of churning hydraulics. Coach Jack knew enough to let the semis go by, their blowing past causing the van to sway. Dennis' body tightened each time. He closed his eyes and begged sleep to come. And when it did, he dreamt that he was out swimming in the ocean and was confronted by a giant seagull, the size of the Titanic, perched on the crest of a tidal wave. The hulking creature spoke to him in menacing gibberish. Dennis sprang up just as the van reached the toll booth at the George Washington Bridge, the sky having cleared to a sunny blue.

ANOTHER HOUR PASSED before the van looped around onto Old Montauk Highway, the trip's final leg, always a congested affair given the road narrowing to a two-laner bordered by sparse pines and strip malls that had mushroomed in recent years.

"Hey, Coach?" a groggy Fenny yelled. "Gotta piss."

Legs shouted up, "Make him hold it in."

"Yeah," Adam agreed. "Turn his balls blue for all I care. The idiot almost got us disqualified."

Coach Jack laughed. "I should, but I could use a good piss, too. And I'm getting low on gas."

After they filled up and took care of business, the van back on the road, Dennis noticed that they were racing a stopn-go commuter train. As a boy, Dennis with Peter and William sometimes rode their bikes up north to Sunrise Highway where the elbows of commuters hung out of windows as the train chugged into the station. So many drawn faces making the long commute, it reminded Dennis of farm animals being transported to the slaughterhouse.

The van arrived back in town in time for him to take stock of a family of herons flying over the courthouse smokestack. He followed them as the van slowed to a stop at a red light.

"Hey, Jack Hogan!"

Inside the van, heads turned to follow the voice. Over at the Shell station was the fist-pumping Ronnie Dabeers, a parish board member gassing up his Bonneville. "Way to go! Third place at state."

The light turning green, Coach Jack returned a thumbs up, to which Adam asked, "How does he already know?"

"Word, my little friend, travels fast out in the sticks. Real fast. Say, boys, I have a question."

"Shoot," said Peter.

"I'm thinking about giving my Mary Janes a few days off. Wadda you think?"

"The season's over anyway," Fenny said.

"Asshole, Fenny," said William. "I like your idea, Coach. A few days off sounds good."

"Huh, Denny Boy," Jack Hogan asked, "what do you think?"

"Sounds good. But what about you, Coach? A few days off yourself?"

"Hell, no. As soon as we're back at the parish, my measuring wheel gets a workout. I want to tweak the Sitting Bull course by looping it around the tennis court. Then and only then after I'm done, and after your moms tuck you boys into bed, I'll be off to Chief's. For a belt of sodi pop, of course."

"Hey, everyone, look," Legs called out as the van entered the parish grounds. "It's the Doughboy, the Amazon Woman, and

Merlin the Magician. And two unidentified urchins." No one in the van batted an eye, accustomed as they were to the Camelot fetish of George Legstaff, who had a tag for everyone. Legs today was referring to Father Ken, Sister Rosaleen, and Mr. Malagati. The urchins were two grade-school boys with somber looks, each with a baseball mitt. The priest and the principal were clearly having words over the cracked classroom window, at which an errant baseball apparently had made contact. Charlie Malagati stood by, a toolbox on the ground beside him.

"Well, boys, what do you know," said Coach Jack, the van coming to an abrupt halt. "My three favorite people in the whole wide world. Better yet, looks like we got a tussle on our hands."

"About what?" asked Fenny.

"About how to deal with those two kids for busting up the window. Amazon probably wants to flog them. The Doughboy, no doubt, wants to invite them to the rectory for a BLT, heavy on the bacon and mayo. And Charlie, well, he's just bloody annoyed that he has to look at their ugly mugs."

"Hey, Coach," said Fenny. "Look!"

"Damn!" said Coach Jack, "the plot thickens. Jimmy Boy, out on the school grounds."

Dennis and the others looked, and sure enough, there was the pastor, Monsignor Cassidy. He was briskly walking over to the fray, checking his watch as he moved along.

"You know, Coach," said Peter, "the only time you see Cassidy in public is when he scurries like a mouse to and from church. Or to and from the rectory garage for that fancy Cadillac of his."

"But why," Adam said, "are we stopping, Coach?"

"Because, my little friend, I can tell Cassidy's pissed. Really pissed. And since he was born with a blow torch up his ass, there's no way I'm gonna miss today's main event, the incineration of the Amazon Woman. Or the Doughboy. Or better yet, both."

"Bring it on, Jimmy Boy," said Legs. "King Arthur could use some bloodletting."

As Coach Jack predicted, Cassidy's sudden appearance brought to a halt the wrangling between Sister Rosaleen and Father Ken, both offering up bright deferential smiles to the pastor.

"Okay, my Merry Band," the coach said, "blink and you miss it all."

No sooner had Sister Rosaleen attempted to put forth her case to the pastor, Father Garland trying to interrupt, than the pastor raised an arm like a crossing guard, the two brought to heel. Sister Rosaleen was the first to walk away. Father Garland, next. Both with the sorry looks of children who had just been sent to their rooms for the day. From there, Cassidy waved off the two urchins, who left in a fast walk. He said something to Charlie Malagati, who promptly retrieved some cardboard and taped it over the window. The pastor turned back to the rectory, the old man left to lug his toolbox back to his basement office.

"Presto!" said Coach Jack, slamming the dashboard. "And to show you boys that Ole Jack ain't afraid of his shadow, watch what I'm gonna do now."

He slammed on the gas and detoured over to Cassidy. The pastor came to a stop just as Jack Hogan brandished the trophy out the window at him.

"Wadda you say, Monsignor, a podium finish in the first ever state championship to include Catholic schools!" Cassidy's ice blue eyes did all the talking. Head down, he strode back to the rectory.

"That took balls, Coach," William said as the van resumed in the direction of the locker room.

"Bet your ass it did. But Jimmy Boy and Coach Jack have an unspoken agreement."

"About what, Coach?" from Adam.

"That, my little friend, is classified."

4

As Cassidy climbed the rectory steps, he thought that on this day of days, when his dream was about to come true, he had just been forced to address that vulgar coach about a damnable sporting event, this moments after having to manage a wrangle by his staff over a window repair. Only yesterday Mrs. Wooten phoned from her desk to tell him that the archdiocese had called to announce that someone was coming out to Bellport today to meet with him.

That was yesterday, however, and today entering his office he told himself that he still had one foot in the briny patch of purgatory. Broken windows. Sports trophies. If only he had come a generation or two earlier, he could have bullied parishioners in Church Latin and excoriated damned souls who would invariably suffer light years in Hell. He didn't necessarily mind that his role at St. Theresa's afforded him regular opportunities to sharpen his wit with clever observations about doltish parishioners. Yet even after a particularly clever thought had come and gone, the muck remained. Regrettably, he didn't have a stable of young priests whom he could send off to hear confession while he enjoyed a solitary meal at a long, shiny table, set off with candles. Soon, though, he murmured as he plopped into his high-back swivel, such a stable would be had once today's visitor showed up with the official news of his nomination, one which he so richly deserved after all he'd done for the Church over the years.

The national work, for one thing. Not long after arriving in Bellport, he was appointed regional chair of the Catholic Education Committee. He was elevated to Monsignor in the process. Dioceses from all over the northeast sought his expertise. On an international level, he was invited to Rome as the guest of Cardinal Edoardo Laghi, the Vatican's Prefect of the Congregation, to help design a more conservative international curriculum. Then, after Mulski was laid to rest, Cassidy began an ambitious facelift of the St. Theresa property itself, beginning with the restoration of the church interior, a new vibrant color scheme about the nave transforming the drab appearance. From there he had Tobin Brothers Construction poke an enormous hole in his office, right behind his desk, and install a large bay window that allowed him to keep a close eye on nearly all the parish grounds. Workers from Gise Nursery leveled a large stretch of parish woods and created a sprawling, awe-inspiring lawn, populated with dogwoods and series of flowerbeds. A new twelve-foot statue of St. Theresa was placed at its head.

For solace, Cassidy often swiveled around to admire the sublime space, which in a well-attended ceremony he labeled, The Great Lawn. Charlie Malagati maintained it with exquisite care, so much so that the grounds took on the look of an Ivy League campus. The parish school board was thrilled. The aesthetic value aside, enrollment flourished.

FOLLOWING A KNOCK on the door, Mrs. Wooten entered with the parish checkbook to find her boss looking out over the grounds. "Excuse me, Monsignor, but the checks for the water and insurance bills need your signature." He paid little attention to his secretary. His eyes were fixed on Hogan who, with trophy in hand, was barking something to his runners right outside the locker room.

"Have you heard, Monsignor?"

"Heard what?"

"Them," she said pointing out the window. "The school's cross-country team. They apparently took third at state."

"No, I hadn't heard."

"Yes, what they call a podium finish. So I just got a call from Mrs. Feltman, inquiring about a pep rally."

After the pastor spun around in his swivel, the crossing-guard arm went up. "My dear Mrs. Wooten. Not today. Please."

"I think, Monsignor, you know my feelings about that crude man. The thought of Hogan with a microphone in front of the student body makes my skin crawl."

"Mrs. Wooten, you of all people know that pep rallies are the province of the principal, Sister Rosaleen."

Cassidy signed the checks.

"Are you sure, Monsignor, that you don't know what today's visit is all about?"

"Thank you, Mrs. Wooten."

As the pastor watched her leave, he knew she was right about a Jack Hogan pep rally, which the principal would be forced to approve given the squawking of Harry and Ida Feltman. Or the beady-eyed Carol Legstaff. And it's not like Hogan didn't make his own skin crawl. But the man has value. When he's not bringing in buckets of cash with his parish-sponsored events, especially the foot races, he's forever butting heads with staff, which Cassidy from his swivel sometimes took in with great relish. The pastor especially liked when Hogan got into it with the assistant pastor. Cassidy despised Father Ken, never more so than when he heard that the young priest demanded unfettered subjectivity of students in his religion classes, a teaching methodology that made the pastor recoil.

Cassidy heard voices. He spun back around and saw the cross-country team on their way to the town path, which was always a sticking point for him. He knew the path was used for waggery after dark, sometimes bringing with it bad publicity to the parish. At other times that same frolic extended into the parish cemetery whose boundary sat not more than a hundred feet from the path through more woods. And then there was the path's damnable Sitting Bull plaque, of which Hogan took full advantage by using it and its pagan lore to promote his cross-country program. Cassidy would have dynamited the plaque long ago. But before he came on board, the diocesan bishop, in the spirit of good will toward past Long Island tribes, signed an edict that publicly declared the plaque untouchable.

The pastor returned to the paperwork at his desk, trying to bide his time until the chancery visit. Unable to concentrate, he started pacing. He wondered if the bouquet of bright flowers that Charlie Malagati fetched from Gise's Nursery, and that now sat brilliantly in a reading table vase, were over the top. Perhaps a more somber-colored hue would have been more appropriate.

The limo finally arriving, Cassidy put on his clergy jacket and stepped over to the mirror for approval.

In due time, Mrs. Wooten tapped the door twice before entering, followed by the guest who dipped his head in staged ceremony and said, "Monsignor Cassidy."

The pastor took the guest's hand and kissed it. "Your Excellency, Archbishop Nellenberger."

Curtsying out of the room, Mrs. Wooten said, "Your Holy Imminence."

The door closing, the two men laughed and embraced. Cassidy went to the bourbon decanter, Nellenberger to the bay window.

"It's hard to believe, Jim," said the archbishop, "that after our seminary days together, my first assignment was here in Bellport. You've turned this place into the Elysian Fields. My goodness," he then said after noticing the old custodian on his knees troweling mortar, "Charlie's still at it, I see. Replugging the ancient walkway that he laid brick by brick when I was here. And I imagine he still lives in the bungalow?"

"He does, John."

Cassidy handed Nellenberger a drink.

"And his wife, Loretta?"

"She passed some years ago."

"Oh, I'm sorry to hear that. Charlie must have been devastated."

"He was. But you know him. Stoic through and through."

"And the son, Vincent, wasn't it? Always in trouble as a young boy if I remember."

"Yes, we thought Vietnam would straighten him out. But after the war, he came back to Bellport and got arrested for drugs. Got off with probation and fled to Florida, where I'm told he started a family."

"Still there?"

"No such luck. He returned last year without the wife and children. Speaking of the devil..." The two paused to take in the Harley roaring into the parish and parking under the carport of the bungalow, whose large yard butted up to the convent, separated only by a white picket fence.

Vinnie Malagati dismounted, *Good Soldier / Bad War* stitched on the blue denim vest he wore. He disappeared inside.

The archbishop saw the cross-country coach, whose one hand pushed the measuring wheel while the other pulled a wagon stacked with orange cones. He stopped to place a cone a few short yards from where the custodian was working.

"Say, Jim, who's that fellow?"

"Oh, that's our parish bumpkin, Hogan. Got his hands in everything. Bingo, dances, the parish picnic. Even coaches the cross-country team, for which he has this unfettered passion. They say he was a runner once himself, St. Peter's High in Staten Island."

Charlie stepped over to the cone and kicked it. The two clerics again fell quiet, both enjoying the spat between custodian and coach.

"You know, Jim, I've heard all about this dream team from the sticks of Long Island."

"Ahhh, the pride of Bellport. One wonders, John, how the town would react if it was the chess team, or the thespians, vying for a state title?"

Moving the cone back to its original position, Jack Hogan dared the custodian to kick it again. The old man obliged.

"Even so," Cassidy mused, "I guess one ought to be grateful that St. Theresa's is making such a splash."

"He's a good man, this Hogan?"

"Anything but. Yet with the coffers surging, who wants to send a money man packing? Even one who skims a little off the top. To which my parish ledger can attest."

"Yes, I, too, have kept men like that over the years."

"However, when the day comes for me to retire, spring cleaning will be in order."

Nellenberger handed his empty glass to his friend, who turned for refills.

"Speaking of retirement, Jim." Cassidy froze. "The Vatican contacted me yesterday morning with their pick for Lauder's successor as Bishop of Rockville Centre. I figured I'd come out myself to congratulate you."

Taking a deep breath, Cassidy poured the drinks and handed one glass back to his friend. "John, I don't quite know what to say."

"The diocese is all yours, and we both know you deserve it. You truly deserve it. And if you don't mind me saying," he nodded out at the squabble, "spring cleaning might need to come sooner than later. So that by the time you travel to Rome next November for the ordination, an impeccably clean parish is left behind. The Vatican likes that."

Just then Father Ken, returning on foot from the school,

rushed over to referee the battle between coach and custodian, which was still in progress.

"I somehow wish, Jim, that we could send the moving van right away to gather your things. But Vatican protocol, and this you know, requires that each candidate receive a pro forma review, which regrettably takes time. Sometimes a full year."

"To be honest, John, scrubbing the grounds clean could very well take that long anyway."

The two clerics clinked glasses.

"Say, how would you like to handle the formal announcement?"

"Perhaps next spring. When the Great Lawn is in full bloom."

"Next spring, it is."

After the limo had left to take the archbishop back to the city, Cassidy unlocked the top drawer, where side by side lay two books, the *Ledger* and the *Memorandum*. He retrieved the latter, which held the annual blacklists of those parishioners whom each year the Monsignor would send packing. Before adding new names, he typically skimmed through earlier lists for the satisfaction it brought. His thumb grazing the yellowed edges, he eventually found his way to the current list.

<u>*Spring Cleaning 1973*</u>
Water Commissioner
Sister Immaculata
Sister Florence
Usher – guy with a gimp

In the same spidery cursive, he penciled in a new entry, *Hogan*. Yet beside the coach's name, he also scribbled a question, *Now or later?*

After all, Cassidy muttered to himself, Hogan's a shrewdy who's been around long enough to know where skeletons are buried. I'll sleep on it.

He put the book back in the drawer and locked it.

SOME HOURS LATER, Dennis went up to his bedroom and stripped down to his briefs. He would have much preferred that he spent the evening at the bowling alley with his teammates. But after the team's success, his parents insisted that they all head out for a celebratory dinner at The Red Snapper in Southampton. He turned to the calendar over his bed and traced the weekly volume total he had penciled in each Friday, the volume decreasing from seventy-mile weekly averages in July and August to the sixties in September and to the fifties in October. During each of those weeks, however, was a long hard run that Coach Jack demanded. In the week leading up to the state meet, Dennis counted a total of just twenty-six miles.

As he often did before bed, Dennis turned off the lights and went to his window. Tonight, the wall of November trees, having lost most of their leaves, offered a direct view of the cemetery's crest. What if, he and his two friends earlier in the day had held off the lone Syracuse runner? What if? A second-place trophy, that's what if.

Turning for bed, he detoured over to the large wall poster of Steve Prefontaine in his Oregon singlet, running all by himself in an NCAA cross-country race. The moonlight filtering in, Dennis focused Pre's eyes, big and bold and dark, and forever peering about. It was as if Pre was always on the lookout for some alien spaceship that was about to swoop down and abduct him right there and then on the race trail. It was those eyes that Dennis often tried to penetrate. The best he could come up with was that they were the eyes of a hunter. Or a clansman like his great grandfather, Paddy Hurley, who, so Uncle Marty liked to say, took on the enemy in hand-to-hand combat off the craggy cliffs of County Mayo. Dennis made a silly game out of talking to the poster, often querying Pre in all matters running.

"So, Pre," Dennis asked tonight, "after today's podium finish, you think we got a chance at the title next year?"

Pre never replied to his questions, busy as he was crushing the field. Still, Dennis maintained the charade. He did so despite that Coach Jack let it be known on several occasions that he had no use for the "James Dean Cult," which is how he referred to the thousands of runners who, like Dennis, idolized Steve Prefontaine. "Raving mad" is how Coach Jack, once after practice, described the cult. "Dangerous, too."

"Why dangerous, Coach?" asked Peter, whose bedroom wall featured the Munich 5K poster of Pre. Peter loved the animal spirit in Pre.

"Because the cult inspires runners who have no damn business running from the front."

"What's wrong with running from the front?" asked Fenny.

"Cause, dummy, running from the front is the wheelhouse of a precious few."

"Like who?" Adam asked.

"Like crazy man Prefontaine who, during races, gets a kick out of his heart skipping beats, of his lungs going bone-dry. He's a rare breed who can't help but run from the front. Everyone else should learn to run from behind. Running ain't some exalted existence. It's a near death experience in fancy racing shoes."

5

By the time Dennis fell asleep that night, a tipsy Coach Jack was just arriving home after celebratory drinks at Chief's, the third-place trophy having stood on the bar where the regulars lifted and admired it. A few toasted the podium finish. The trophy in hand, Coach Jack unlocked his front door and passed inside, feeling the dark rooms more than seeing them. He headed to the den, his second office, filled with cross-country photos, newspaper clippings, a desk cluttered with running magazines and books. He turned on a small desk lamp and placed the trophy atop the fireplace mantel, above which was a large painting of the Indian warrior, Crazy Horse, flanked on either side by a crowd of smaller framed photos of legendary runners, each coming across in first place. The Flying Finn, Paavo Nurmi. Unbeaten Olympian, Aussie Herb Elliott. Bloke Roger Bannister. New Zealander Peter Snell. And the more recent upstarts: phenom Jim Ryan; fleet-footed Marty Liquori; the indomitable Frank Shorter; and Boston Billy Rodgers.

Studying their faces, Coach Jack suddenly felt himself choking on the glory that was the day. He even wondered if the race had actually taken place, if his team had really stood atop a podium, with just a thirty-six-second compression time between his first and fifth scorers! Or was it just a matter of the universe playing a horrible trick on him.

"What a goddam idiot I am!" he said laughing out loud. "I could slap myself silly."

His mind nonetheless ablaze with the day, a *Wild Turkey* nightcap came to mind. First, though, he'd start a fire to tamp down the cold draft that pushed about the house. He stacked several quarter pieces atop twisted newspaper in the fire box, crowned by pinecones from a ceramic jug. The paper lit with a match, it smoked, blackened, and erupted into flames. Soon Coach Jack, drink in hand, sat watching the flames.

"To top it off, all five of this year's scorers are returning next year."

But the coach also knew that each of those runners would have to pick up his game if a title was to become a reality next November at Van Cortlandt. For Adam, with his short torso and long legs and arms that always seemed to be swatting mosquitoes, that meant he'd need to come by the mile with the leaders in 4:55ish, and run anyone who dared to stay up with him into the ground. As for Legs and that stride to die for, and that toe-to-heel strike that never seems to hit the ground, he'd need a much faster first two miles than what he ran today to get a top-five next year. If only the smug asshole, for once in his life, would begin his slow burn at the mile mark.

"Surge, Legs, surge!" cried Coach Jack as he stabbed a log with the poker, sparks eddying about.

His core three. What would they need to do to help win state?

A hot pinecone exploded, prompting him to again laugh and think, Leave well enough alone. For what's there not to like about those three? Take the bowlegged William Flanagan, built like a brick shit house, born with a barrel chest and a scowl on his face, the broad calf muscles of a sprinter and the short bounding strides. Or crazy Peter Walker, a long jaunty body always leaning forward, always cocksure, always weaving the fuck about on the race trail, sometimes knocking runners off stride. Or Dennis Hurley and that quiet upper body, that effortless stride of his that seems too damn efficient for a runner. Yes, Denny Boy's the caretaker: his job is to keep wild Peter Walker from going out too fast. And if Peter goes out gangbuster, William and that angry mug of his can't resist following him, both dying like dogs.

Jack Hogan couldn't help but picture the core three at Vanny next year, slow burning a 5:10 second mile, and in the rhythm of teamwork moving up a good thirty places in the process. And over the last mile, in the fight of their lives, they'd throw all elegance to the wind. Contorted faces, dead arms, heads thrown back, unable to breathe except for gulps of air. That's how they'd find themselves that day crossing the finish line. A top fifteen for all three. A goddam spread under thirty seconds!

"Hell, yeah! Time for a refill."

While pouring his whiskey in the dark kitchen, he realized he forgot all about his sixth man, Fenny the Fleabite, the only sophomore on this year's team. He's nothing but a face spotted with menacing freckles. A body too loosely jointed. All wrists, elbows, ankles. And that goddam jerky stride of his seems like he's got rocks in his racing shoes. But Fenny's got a wild streak in him. I'll get him thinking 16:30, that's what I'll do. Yes, Fenny, a top-thirty at Vanny, in the race of his life.

As for a seventh man, Robert Mumbino, who Legs nicknamed Bobby Mumbles, had approached Coach Jack a few weeks ago. Mums told him he wanted to rejoin the team next season. The coach remembered that he had a great sophomore year. But then that next summer, the boy's big Italian cock got the Rafanello girl pregnant. His grandfather, who owned the Maaco body shop, thwarted expulsion with a sizeable financial contribution to the parish. The Amazon, however, declared that Mums sit out his junior year.

But, Coach Jack thought this while taking a swig, Bobby Mumbles wants back in. And the kid's got heart, he and that long, girlish stride of his. Yes, Fenny and Mums! The potato head and the wop running side by side next season. I like it. I like it a whole lot.

Coach Jack returned to the den, and again staring down flames, he lifted his glass for a toast. "To a goddam team for the ages."

Another log tossed in, he relaxed some, his mind going back years to that one night in the early sixties, on a bar stool at Chief's of all places. It was there that he concocted the plan that netted him his current dream team.

IF JACK HOGAN was honest about things, some credit for the dream team ought to go all the way back to his ex, Lorraine. After all, he had cursed up a storm in 1956 when she told him she'd divorce his ass if they didn't leave their Staten Island apartment and move to her hometown of Bellport. And who was he to complain! He had just lost a sales job in Bensonhurst. His wife's uncle promised him a similar position at an appliance store in Patchogue, a short drive from Bellport.

The move was a nightmare from the start. Less than seven months after they bought the house on Day Lily Drive, Jack Hogan found himself divorced, childless, and in foreclosure. He had no choice but to rent a yellow clapboard with brown shutters and a seeping septic tank on Azalea Lane, one of those properties everyone thought would lead to the deterioration of the entire neighborhood. The only saving grace was that Lorraine, not long after the move to Bellport, had signed him up to usher Mass at St. Theresa's. This, to get him out of the house.

Jack Hogan soon became part of a boisterous camaraderie of ushers who often met at Chief's for drinks. In a very short time, he came to realize that St. Theresa's offered ample opportunities to initiate any number of parish social events, such as Saturday night bingo, monthly dances with a cash bar, and a summer golf scramble, whose gate collected enough money to cover the parish utility bills for the year. It also allowed an opening to skim a bit off the top for himself.

Mulski and the parish council were bowled over by the new parishioner's energy and resourcefulness. Only Jack Hogan knew the true motive behind it all. He badly wanted the head coaching job of the parish cross-country team. Back in the day he had been a star cross-country runner at St. Peter's. After the army, even as a beer gut emerged, he'd sometimes jump into a road race and hold his own. But so long as Sister Rosaleen had anything to say in the matter, the job would remain with the rotund Sister Jean Ruskin, once a star sprinter and long jumper at Hofstra University. Yet after Jack Hogan in 1959 marched into Mulski's office armed with an enormous bag of cash from the first annual Firecracker 5K, the pastor reconsidered the head coaching position. "And, Father," Jack Hogan promised, "I can double the gate in this fall's Turkey Trot that I'm planning." Against the protest of the principal, Mulski appointed Jack Hogan the new head coach, in the process demoting Sister Jean, who in her new role as assistant coach would oversee the JV team, which included all freshmen.

Initially, it wasn't easy for the nun working under Jack Hogan. For starters, Coach Jack dictated all workouts for Sister Jean's JV squad. Moreover, JV would now convene practice at the county park, several blocks from the parish, which left the parish grounds to Coach Jack and his varsity team. As far as the race schedule was concerned, varsity runners no longer would run mid-week dual meets against Long Island's Catholic schools. They'd compete only in weekend invitationals. The dual meets thus fell to Sister Jean's JV runners who were elevated to varsity status on dual-meet days.

The new arrangement initially distracted Sister Jean to no end, banishing as it did the underclassmen to the county park for practice. It reeked of elitism. But in a few years, she warmed up to Coach Jack. For one thing, there were the unprecedented number of PRs and dual-meet victories for her runners, which forced her to admit the efficacy of Coach Jack's dogged insistence on high volume and increasing anaerobic intervals over the season, a kind of training that was foreign to her. For his part, Coach Jack came to enjoy the spunk in Sister Jean, and he came to depend on her. That's why the nun would find an occasional restaurant gift certificate in

SITTING BULL RUN

her mailbox, an enclosed note from Coach Jack always thanking her on behalf of the St. Theresa cross-country program.

To make the head job possible in the first place, Jack Hogan worked out a flexible schedule with his boss at the appliance store, which allowed him to be free to coach after school and on weekends. By 1963, he had built St. Theresa's into a powerhouse program. But while he was congratulated everywhere he went in town, he was fully aware he had just lost four seniors to graduation. Coach Jack would have to again start from scratch. And as he took up a barstool at Chief's to mull over his sorry options, the coach muttered to himself, "I don't have shit to replace them."

But even as he said that, his eyes clamped down on the bust of Sitting Bull on a shelf above the cash register, a single feather in the war bonnet. At the time he didn't fully understand why the locals were so enamored of Chief Sitting Bull. He knew only that the warrior's name and weathered image were used by local businesses, like the *Bull Brake and Muffler Shop*. Or *Sitting with Salvatore*, the popular pizzeria. Or *Chief's Bar and Grill*, his tavern of choice. He heard it all started when the mouthy library broad, Alice Crimmins, petitioned Bishop Lauder back in the early fifties to allow her to hire an outfit to weld a plaque of Sitting Bull to a steel pole and cement the pole into the parish path, this after Mulski rejected the idea. Having found the plaque in the library storage room, and not knowing where it came from, Alice Crimmins nonetheless told the bishop that the cemetery and surrounding woods were once the burial grounds of the Sachem Indians. Despite that Sitting Bull hailed from South Dakota, Bishop Lauder signed a diocesan decree that the plaque remain on the path in perpetuity. He mainly did so because he despised the cranky Bellport pastor, Casimir Mulski.

That night at Chief's Jack Hogan didn't give a rat's ass about the town's Sitting Bull fetish. His mind was too busy thinking about how he might replenish his team. Sure, Sister Jean's squads had beaten the snot out of the dual meet schedule. But she did so with a bunch of runners who lacked real star power.

"Goddam!" he said as he brought into focus next year's powerful rival teams and their impressive returnees. He was sure that a sorry conclusion had been reached, that his own team had been drained dry. All that was left was a bucket of horse shit.

But his eyes still resting on Sitting Bull, it was as if a light switch had been thrown, the idea coming to him.

Hell, why can't I take full advantage of the town path, as well as the plaque of Chief Sitting Bull on it, by throwing a series of summer races for elementary school kids. A big-time recruitment tool.

"Fuck, yeah," he yelled out to the regulars who knew not the reason for his outburst. He pictured how he'd get the Elks to help him widen the path in time for a weekly racing series that summer, to take place during the dead period in June when cross-country coaches are prohibited from having any formal coaching contact with their teams. The rationale behind the policy was that adolescent harriers needed some rest, given that most of them run three consecutive seasons—cross country in the fall, indoor track during the winter months, and outdoor track during the spring. Indeed, Coach Jack over the years had found ways to circumvent the policy, and that night, as he sat on a barstool at Chief's, he had a hunch he would do so again by taking advantage of the summer series concept that he had just stumbled upon. So, too, did the coach decide the series' course would be a mile long. As for a course route, right there on the bar surface he sketched three possible routes on the back of beer coasters. He ended up choosing the one that started near the school tennis courts, turned onto the path, looped around the Sitting Bull plaque at the halfway mark, and returned along the same path to the finish line at the flagpole.

"Say, Billy Boyce," Jack Hogan said to the bar's owner counting the till. "I have a question for you."

"Shoot, Jack."

"A series of weekly foot races over the summer on the parish path. To be called the Sitting Bull Run Series. Wadda you think?"

"For crying out loud, Jack, what took you so long?"

SITTING BULL RUN

"Asshole."

As Coach Jack smiled, his eyes refocused the bust of Sitting Bull. He now recalled that when he was still in grade school, his mother had bought him a thick illustrated history of the Native American, which he devoured over the course of a week. After that he went to the library and read books about famous Indian chiefs, and in the process came to admire the heroism and courage in them. While he was out running one day with his high school teammates, he passed a large framed painting of Crazy Horse propped up on a yard sale table. He went home, grabbed three dollars from his shoe box, and returned to buy the painting. Indeed, in his later years he would never admit to anyone, least of all his runners, that he held the American Indian in high regard, and that his admiration for them became a source of inspiration during his own high school cross-country years.

"Hey, Billy," he said as he stood and chugged the remainder of his beer, "time to go home and get some beauty sleep."

"Have at it, Jack. You need all the help you can get."

That next morning he called a buddy at the *Long Island Press* and placed an advertisement in the sports section. The wait was more than he could stand. A few days later, a cry escaped him when he saw the ad for the first time.

> *St. Theresa's of Bellport*
> *is pleased to announce*
> *The Sitting Bull Run Series*
> *When: Tuesday Nights in June @ 6:00 p.m.*
> *Where: Parish Grounds*
> *Entry Fee: 75 cents per Race*
> *Three Age-Group Divisions*
> *Prizes for All Participants*

Mulski's initial outrage subsided after the entries for week two ballooned to over fifty, to a hundred by week four. Sister Rosaleen informed the pastor that her office had received over two dozen new applications for the fall enrollment, the dramatic increase no doubt the result of the fancy flyers Jack Hogan was handing out at the race registration table. Each week the *Bellport Citizen* published the results. And each summer thereafter, as his varsity was making a name for itself by regularly winning Long Island's Catholic league championships, the Sitting Bull Run Series grew in prestige and size.

Coach Jack almost lost his mind when a Jewish kid named Adam Feltman, a public school eighth grader from Bellport, destroyed the field in the Bantam Division race. He posted a jaw dropping 4:54, beating the eighth-grade record by twelve seconds. The next night Jack Hogan took the boy's father out for a sweet and sour pork dinner at the Kwong Ming Restaurant. There he told Harry Feltman that a parent's signature on a simple diocesan *Intent to Convert* form was all that it would take to enroll his Adam in the parish high school.

"Dammit it, Harry," he added in confidence, "your Adam can bide his time and never become a damn Catholic."

"You think so?"

"Who needs the aggravation? Plus, the three hundred bucks per year tuition ain't nothing compared to the thousands you'll save with the college athletic scholarship that right here and now I guarantee will come Adam's way."

Jack Hogan drove home that night with a smile on his face, the Feltman boy his for the taking. He could see the kid winning major invitationals by his junior year. But no sooner had the thought crossed his mind than the brooding began anew. Once again, the nucleus of his team was graduating. Except for Feltman, there didn't appear to be a new crop to take their place. Some eighth graders showed promise in the Sitting Bull series, but none who ran eye-popping races. That all changed at the graduation ceremony of the parish elementary school. It was there that Coach Jack, while standing in a maroon blazer at the auditorium entrance and handing out promotional cross-country flyers, noticed four eighth graders in suits and ties about to slip by him.

"Gentlemen," said the coach, blocking their path, "what's the hurry?"

"Oh, nothing," said Legs. "Except that each of us is receiving the Purple Heart Medal for injuries incurred in the line of battle."

"How delightful," said Coach Jack, smothering his laughter. He knew that he had to maintain sober eye contact with this cocky kid with thick glasses and sandy wind-blown hair. "I know these other boys from the Sitting Bull Run Series," he said nodding at Dennis, William, and Peter. "That was a few years ago, and I haven't seen them since. But I don't think I've ever seen you at Sitting Bull. Your name?"

"George Legstaff. I go by Legs. And you wouldn't catch me dead running in Injun territory. I am a loyal servant to King Arthur! Besides, my three buddies and I play in the town's soccer league. We plan on playing for the parish team. King Arthur demands it."

"Well, Legs," said Coach Jack as he pulled out his money clasp. "I see that you've read your fair share of action comic books. But let's see just how loyal you are to this!" He waved a ten-dollar bill.

"Very," said Legs. "I would have voted for Alexander Hamilton back in the day."

"Clever boy," replied the coach, lips curving to a smile. "You know your currency, too. Well, here it is. This Alexander Hamilton goes to the boy who wins the private race I am about to host in the next few minutes. We'll call it..." he hesitated as he searched for what to call the race. But looking down at the boys' Sunday shoes, which would need to be taken off, he said, "Yes, we call it The First Annual Barefoot Race. Run on our parish Sitting Bull course, whose dirt surface is as soft as a baby's butt. And," a five-dollar bill yanked out, "I'll award an extra Abe Lincoln if the eighth-grade school record is broken."

"Exactly how long is the course?" Legs asked.

"Exactly one mile."

"A mile too long. And the record?"

"4:54. By a public-school kid named Feltman."

"Not Adam!" said Peter. "He lives right by us. We used to play at his house all the time."

"So wadda you boys say?"

"Coach," said Peter taking off his tie, "I'm always up for a challenge."

"Count me in, too," said William Flanagan. "How about you, Denny?"

"All systems a-go."

"Which leaves," said Coach Jack, "our knight in shining armor."

"This has pagan conspiracy written all over it. But King Arthur hates a coward."

"Off to the starting line, boys!" said Coach Jack. And once there, he added, "Just follow the markers that will guide you on the path and to the plaque of Sitting Bull, the halfway mark. Give the chief a tap for good measure before you head back to the finish line. Got it?" The boys nodded as the coach retrieved the stopwatch always stored in his pants pocket. "Good. Now take off your shoes and socks. Blazers and ties on that bush. And toe the starting line as I head on up the cemetery for a bird's eye."

With that, he dodged headstones to the top where he could see the entire race.

"Okay, my merry band," he shouted down, "all set?"

"Ready as ready can be, Coach," Peter shouted back. Their trousers were rolled-up, button-down white shirts hanging out, bare feet on the starting line.

"Runners, take your marks and...go!"

Jack Hogan punched the timer on his stopwatch.

While Dennis, Peter, and William charged forward, George Legstaff, a Three Stooges fan, started bouncing up and down, calling out Curly's "nyuk, nyuk, nyuk." Then, like a rocket he exploded, though slowing down after some fifty yards to a playfully slow pace.

"Cocky bastard," muttered the coach, who turned his attention to the three other boys, still running at a good clip. So much so that he was sure they had gone out too fast and any second would hit the wall. As the three entered the parish path, though, and Coach Jack studied them through trees, they maintained the brisk pace even after they tapped the plaque at the halfway mark and U-turned. Coach Jack's eyes went big at the fast 2:34 split on his stopwatch.

"Well, kiss my white Irish ass!" he shouted.

Legs coming by in 2:38, Coach Jack could not believe what happened next. The boy kicked it into gear, and in short order caught his three friends, flying right by them in breathtaking speed. After that, the coach wasn't even aware of the other three, fixed as he was on the maniac kid with the long, gorgeous stride.

"A fucking gazelle," he cried out, and over the final stretch, this George Legstaff put on an amazing burst of speed that made Coach Jack think of the quickness of light. But it wasn't until Legs came across the line that the coach's eyes popped out of his head, the 5:02 just eight seconds off the Feltman kid's age-group record. As the other three struggled over the final stretch, they nonetheless came across together in 5:13, which represented one of the fastest times ever run by eighth graders. Coach Jack felt himself falling back in space. He looked a second and third time at his watch. If you throw Feltman into the mix with these four mutts, the giddy coach thought, this would make for the greatest incoming freshmen class any coach could ever dream of.

He scaled low-lying headstones on his way back down.

"Well, boys," he said, catching his breath. "Obviously, you ran like a bunch of lightweights. But since I have you here, I might as well take pity on you. Give you all a little something for the effort."

"Coach," said Legs sticking out his hand, "I do believe I'm owed fifteen buckaroos!"

"Not so fast." Coach Jack handed a ten-dollar bill to Legs. "You won, yes. But you missed Feltman's record. That said, I'll be the first to admit that you ran like a rabbit on steroids. If you run for St. Theresa's, and if we can shut that trap of yours, you'll find more fame and glory than King Arthur ever dreamed of. Perhaps some fair Guinevere will be so dazzled by your speed that she'll take you behind the bleachers and play footsy in the tall grass."

"That'll work," said Legs.

"As for you three," said the coach handing them five dollars apiece, "you'll also have one hell of a running career at St. Theresa's. And with Adam Feltman on board, the five of you one day will hoist a state championship trophy. You can take that to the bank, boys. So, dammit, I'll see all four of you the third Monday in June for freshman orientation. There you'll enjoy a breakfast buffet of eggs, sausage, and the fluffiest of sweet rolls. A little something to properly motivate the next generation. So, wadda you say?"

Before the boys could answer, there came an unintelligible screech from across the parking lot. Standing at the auditorium entrance, arms akimbo, was Miss Margaret Mudhank, a lay social studies teacher who for years directed the eighth-grade graduation ceremony. She had the full attention of the four boys. "Get inside. And fast!"

With a wink, Coach Hogan whispered, "Don't you worry about Mudface! I got your backs. And mums the word about the green stuff."

As the four scrambled back into their clothes, Mudhank walked over and said, "Boys, I'll be right in." And after they had left, "So, Jack, this is how you get kids to come to St. Theresa's? Bribe them? I wonder what Sister Rosaleen, or better yet, what Monsignor Cassidy would think, if they were to find out that their star coach is paying kids under the table?"

"My dear Margie, the money I just gave those four was well earned. By the sweat of their fucking brows!"

"I think, Jack, I'll just wait until I'm at home tonight, and sipping on some brandy, to compose a little something on St. Theresa letterhead. I'll make copies and send them to the diocesan offices. Maybe, the *Bellport Citizen*, too."

SITTING BULL RUN

Coach Jack had to smile. "Well, hell, if you're going to do a letter, I'll whip one up, too. And to get the poetic juices flowing, I'll head over to Chief's right now for some bubbly. Only after a robust gulp gulp will I ask the proprietor and former lover of yours, Billy Boyce, if I might take the Polaroids he took of you over to Rite Aid and make copies. You know, the ones on his cabin cruiser in the Great South Bay. In a hot green bikini, quite diminutive in size, if my memory serves me."

The fuming mad Mudhank waited just a moment before storming back to the auditorium, ready to hollow out the first set of eye sockets she met.

Less than an hour later, she pulled on a backstage control-panel lever, the curtains opening to begin the ceremony. With confidence, and with more than a little flair, she strode across the stage to the podium. But no sooner had she begun to speak than her introduction was interrupted by shrill microphone feedback. The audience jerked.

Looking as if she had swallowed a bumble bee, Mudhank had no choice but to talk over the feedback. "Could Mr. Malagati…come backstage…and adjust the-" More feedback prompted her to signal to Jack Hogan who, having returned from Chief's, stood smirking by the doors. He knew she wanted him to retrieve the custodian from wherever he was. So acquiescing to her bidding, he disappeared behind the auditorium double doors and returned just moments later with Mr. Malagati in tow, who had been mopping up a spilled lobby drink. The two men headed for the control panel backstage, where Mudhank now stood.

"Miss Margaret Mudhank," Jack spoke softly in jest, "you owe me big time."

"And you, Jack," she whispered back, "can go fuck yourself."

To the old custodian, she then sputtered harsh words as he went to work on the panel. When more feedback crackled over the speakers, the desperate Mudhank reached for the panel herself. Charlie grabbed her wrist and held it away. Appalled, she broke loose as he again went to work. The feedback, finally subdued, gave way to bristling silence out in the auditorium. Mudhank waited for the old man to look up and acknowledge her injured look. He refused to give her the satisfaction.

"Wadda say, Margie," Coach Jack said, "you get out there on stage and knock 'em dead. Maybe a beer afterwards?"

"Over my dead body."

It was obvious to all who had experienced previous ceremonies presided over by Mudhank, always delivered with a round-mouthed flamboyance, that she was not herself tonight. Once the ceremony was over, she wasted no time going straight to the old custodian, already racking fold-up chairs on the auditorium stage and ripping into him. Charlie tried ignoring her. Yet throughout Mudhank's tongue lashing, he looked as if he was doing all he could to restrain himself from slamming her across the head with a chair. As she walked away, he sputtered harsh words at her in his native tongue. Dan, Catherine, and other parents waiting on their sons saw the whole thing.

When soon their graduate son reappeared to join them for the trip home, the Hurleys headed out into the lobby unaware that Jack Hogan was about to zoom in on them.

"Why, hello there," the coach said to Dan Hurley in a voice that oozed obsequiousness. "Coach Jack Hogan would like for you and your lovely bride to take this home." He handed Dan a flyer. "Information on St. Theresa's regionally ranked cross-country program." Here he stopped to shake hands with Dennis, and wink at him as if the two had never met. "And I take it this is your son?"

"Yes, Coach," said Dan. "His name is Dennis, Dennis Hurley."

"Nice to meet you, Dennis," said Coach Jack stealing another wink. "But if I recall, didn't you run in the Bantam Division of Sitting Bull Run a few summers ago?"

"He did," said Dan. "You must really love the sport, Coach."

"Lots of love in this big heart of mine."

"And Dennis," said Catherine in a testy voice as she started to walk away, "will have lots of love in his big heart while he's playing soccer for St. Theresa's. All four years."

Dan Hurley shook hands with the coach and caught up with his wife.

LATER THAT NIGHT, Catherine turned off the kitchen faucet and looked at her son who was eating cereal, a late-night ritual of his. Dan sat across from him reading the newspaper.

"Tonight's sound problem aside, Dennis, how do you think the ceremony went?"

"Okay, I guess."

The phone ringing, Catherine nodded at Dennis. "My hands are wet."

He picked up the receiver and said, "Hello?"

"Auntie Pearl, Dennis. Listen, do you know anything about Malagati attacking Mudhank backstage?"

"Here's my mom, Aunt Pearl."

Catherine relayed the details to her sister, the harsh terms of which startled Dennis. "Yes, Pearl, the whole night was a real embarrassment. First, that joke of a coach recruiting out in the lobby. As if he's the Pope or something. As for any backstage assault, I really can't confirm that, except to say the two of them got into it afterwards. And it seemed Charlie was seconds away from cracking Mudhank's head with a chair."

"You know," Aunt Pearl said, "I'm not the only one in town who thinks the old guy's got a violent streak in him. And probably a past. You ever ask yourself why all those years ago he fled Brooklyn and came out to Bellport?"

"No, I hadn't, Pearl, but it makes sense." With that, Dan rattled the newspaper as his wife continued. "It goes without saying that my husband calls it gossip mongering. He's forever on Charlie's side. Anyway, getting back to the sound problem, that's something that Charlie should have prevented."

Dennis headed up to his bedroom thinking that some crude power was at work here, that his mother got it all wrong. Sure, he thought, Coach Hogan is a strange bird. But from what Dennis could tell today, the coach is also a hoot and seems to know his stuff. Besides, Dennis had loved to run for as long as he could remember. Not to mention that he, along with his other three friends, were mediocre soccer players who wouldn't see a whole lot of playing time on the parish team. But a championship trophy in cross country! How could his mother scoff at that? And how could she blast Mr. Malagati for his inability to work magic on an ancient sound system held together by paper clips and electrical tape? And violent? He's just a guy who likes to keep to himself.

6

Following the graduation ceremony, Jack Hogan made several inquiries regarding the barefooted boys who mopped up the cemetery course. The news was promising, though one source told him that the mother of prospect Dennis Hurley was still declaring for the high school soccer team. The only option left was to invite the boy's father to Chief's for a bar burger. A few nights later, a tipsy Dan came home and informed Catherine that cross country was just the ticket for their son.

"Think about it, Cat. As Dennis transitions into high school, he becomes part of a powerhouse program. Shit, St. Theresa's won the league championship nine of the last eleven years. Plus, Coach Jack told me the New York Athletic Association is a year or two away from allowing Catholic schools to run in the state cross-country championship. Hell, Cat, he can smell a title in the not-too-distant future."

"A title, you say! But can that coach of yours smell the rot that comes out of his own foul mouth? He'll coarsen Dennis in no time. Corrupt him for good."

During family dinners that next week, Catherine tried as hard as she could to squelch Dennis' fixation on the cross-country team. She came up with every excuse in the book to choose soccer over running, ending each time with a lambasting of Jack Hogan. What she underestimated was the impact of the barefoot race on her son. With his father's help, Dennis eventually won the day. And when the June freshman orientation came, some twenty prospects—including Dennis, William, Peter, Legs, and Adam—were greeted by Coach Jack and Sister Jean with a hot buffet breakfast. The menu included blueberry cream cheese Danish, a favorite of the nun, who as JV coach moderated the affair.

Coach Jack was more than happy to have the good sister welcome the incoming class, gushing forth as she did about sacred bonding and lifelong friendship. He also knew that the prospects would need something to keep them busy until July 1st, when the dead period was over and practice officially began. So before the orientation broke up that day, Coach Jack announced, "I want to thank Sister Jean Ruskin for throwing one heck of a bash this morning. And as you will learn over your first year, she knows a hell of a lot about all things running. The proof's in the pudding. Look at her brilliantly undefeated dual meet record this past year." He dimmed the lights and flipped on an overhead projector whose transparency shot those results on the wall.

St. Theresa's 1970 JV Cross-Country Results

Date	*Opponent*	*Results*
9/7/1970	Bay Shore Invitational	2nd Place
9/14/1970	at St. John the Baptist	16-39 (W)
9/21/1970	Chaminade	27-30 (W)
10/1/1970	at St. Anthony's	15-50 (W)
10/8/1970	St. Mary's	21-38 (W)
10/15/1970	Jake Schoof Invitational	1st Place
10/22/1970	at Maria Regina	15-47 (W)
10/29/1970	Holy Family	24-33 (W)

"Not bad, huh! And for every away meet, all runners enjoy White Castle sliders and curly fries."

"I dig it, Coach Jack," Peter said.

"Now, since cross country is a sport that has a language all its own, Ole Coach Jack has some homework for you." With that, another transparency.

Glossary
St. Theresa Cross Country

Aerobic
Anaerobic
Bib
Chute
Cool-down
Fartlek
Hit The Wall
Hydrate
Intervals/Repeats
Invitational Meet
Junk Miles
Lactic Acid
Negative Split
Pace
PR
Recovery Pace
Sectionals
Slow Burn
Snot Rocket
Split
Starting Box
Strides
Surge
Switchback
Taper
Tempo Run
Threshold Pace
VO2Max
Warm-up

As Sister Jean handed out paper copies, Coach Jack said, "So, my Merry Band, your homework between now and the first day of summer practice is to define the terms and commit them to memory. A little something to cut your teeth on. Do whatever the heck you need to do to get the definition of each term, some formal, some not so formal, such as the infamous Snot Rocket."

"Say, Coach?"

"George Legstaff?"

"King Arthur's plate is full the rest of the summer. Public executions. Executive orders. Sweet Dalliance. You know how it is."

"I also know your dad, Hank. I bump into him at Chief's from time to time. Pretty sure it wouldn't tickle his fancy should you fail the quiz on the first day of practice. Now would it?"

Legs fell quiet.

"Good, and should any of you grow a wild hair up your ass," he paused to wink at Sister Jean, "you might want to mow a few lawns and buy yourself a pair of new trainers, the Nike Marathon, for example. All so you can get out on the roads, the shore, the parks, the wherever, for a whole bunch of easy miles."

"Sounds great," said Peter. "When's our first race?"

"Early September when Sister Jean takes you to the Bay Shore Invitational. There in our silver and maroon uniforms you'll toe the line in bad-ass racing spikes. And hidden underneath your race bottoms is a musty old jock strap whose only job in life is to keep your diddly at bay. Not to mention that on race day the stink of it cleans out the nasal passage." Dennis and most of the others laughed even as they stole a look at Sister Jean, now making the Sign of the Cross.

"And before you all leave, here's a little treat for you to also take home and tack onto your bedroom wall. The Ten Commandments, we call them." Sister Jean handed out copies.

SITTING BULL RUN

The Ten Commandments of St. Theresa's Cross Country

1. *Slow burn or bust!*
2. *There is magic in misery. Just ask any runner.*
3. *Bring uniform and racing spikes to every meet.*
4. *It's a hill. Get over it.*
5. *Stretch like crazy.*
6. *Be like a horse: be dumb and just run.*
7. *Kiss Sitting Bull on the cheek whenever possible.*
8. *Lots of push-ups and pull-ups.*
9. *Bumrush the first and last 100 yards of all races.*
10. *Running is a safe zone for farts. Let 'em rip!*

Adam Feltman asked, "Slow burn, Coach, what's that?"

"It's a race strategy that I'll explain in due course."

"Bumrush?" Peter Walker asked. "Got a cool sound to it."

"Hell, yeah. It's a term I coined for strides. Which is when you find a fairly flat surface and proceed to do strides of roughly 150 yards. You start off at about seventy-five percent pace, then gradually accelerate until you reach an all-out sprint. We do a good dozen bumrushes before and after most practices."

"And it helps how?" said Legs with some sarcasm.

"Gotta love George Legstaff. Gotta love all you boys. Bumrush helps in two ways. First, it develops the speed you'll need to nail the crap out of the start of a race, so that you can get in a good position without sucking in all kinds of wind. That same speed allows you at the end of the race to bore a hole in the back of runners on the final straight and reel them in, one goddam runner at a time. Got it, boys?"

Most muttered back, "Got it."

As THE ORIENTATION ENDED, and as Coach Jack laughed it up with several freshmen who remained behind, Sister Jean began the clean-up. She couldn't help but smile at Jack Hogan. He turned into a little kid when it came to underclassmen, forever chatting with them. Sometimes, he'd show up at the county park with pizza and soda that her JV squad, after a workout, enjoyed under the pavilion. Each year he invited their families to the Bear Mountain Invitational, where after cheering on the varsity, they all enjoyed a potluck in the park's picnic section. Coach Jack quarterbacked for both sides in a game of flag football. He encouraged a high stakes game of horseshoes for the dads, cash passed under the table. The climax of the potluck was Coach Jack mounting a picnic table, where in a heartfelt baritone voice he startled the crowd with a tender rendition of some Irish folk song his own mother sang to him as a young boy. Several moms found themselves fighting off tears.

As the last of the freshmen left the orientation, Coach Jack said, "Say, Sister Jean, you can take off. I'll finish up here."

"Oh, I don't mind sticking around, especially since I have a question for you."

"Shoot."

"I wonder why, at yet another freshman orientation, you once again avoided discussing that slow burn voodoo thing you do with the varsity team. After all, it's your bread and butter."

"For starters, Sister, the skill I teach comes not in a classroom but rather on the battlefield. And the enemy is not, as many think, a race trail with perils of its own. No, the enemy is the runner's mind. So my job-"

The nun interrupting, "I feel a nightmare coming on."

"So my job is that just as the Spartan warriors of ancient Greece learned that pain is a purifying process, which then allowed them to be great fighters, so, too, must my runners learn the same thing. But, and this gets to your question, who wants to tell a bunch of freshmen during their first interaction with the coaching staff that to become a great runner you have to learn to run with a gut-wrenching pain. And the optimal way to do that is through slow burn, especially since slow burn's pain predictably starts pretty much the same time in each race."

"And when is that?"

"Roughly halfway through the second mile, well after the surge has started. That's when the going gets rough. Real rough."

"A blood sport, Jack, is what cross country means to you."

"That's right, Sister, there's no getting around that cross country is a damn ugly business. And yet for a kid who gets after it, they eventually experience what St. Paul did on his way to Damascus. You know, when he got thrown off the horse. Yup, only then does the kid find the promised land. And that's when I usually take him to Sal's for a killer pasta dish and a high falutin game of chess."

"What if the boy doesn't know how to play chess?"

"I beat it into him."

Following the conversation that day at freshman orientation, Sister Jean took a closer look at the varsity races by positioning herself at the two-mile mark. And sure enough, she came to better appreciate the self-awareness in Coach Jack's varsity as they surged at the mile mark and began the gritty process of mowing down runners, all despite that it was sometimes hard for her to watch their bodies stricken with real physical pain. Of course, on most nights after a big race, Sister Jean in the confines of her convent bedroom would make the Sign of the Cross even as with a wry smile she recalled some of the salty language used that day by the head coach. It reminded her of what she heard as a girl on the streets of New York. She often told herself that life at St. Theresa's would be a very bland place without Coach Jack.

AT HIS DESK that same night, Dennis first tacked the Ten Commandments to the wall before turning to the glossary. The effort perplexed him. His dictionary failed to serve up working definitions for more than a few terms. Like his friends, however, he liked what he had heard today, especially the perks. The road trips, pasta nights at Sal's, the cookouts and the games. And then there's Coach Jack, whom William afterwards called, "A fucking rip."

Yes, Dennis thought, I like it all.

But by the time he went to bed that night, he was not aware that his life, once he was brought up to varsity his sophomore year, would become monopolized by the stern machinations of a Jack Hogan program. The team trained year-round. The practices, whether on the roads or over dunes and through sand, were grueling, unrelenting. Nor did the racing itself come easy, particularly over courses with stubbornly long inclines that burned calves, and unforgiving steep hills that made breathing impossible, and aching pain that shot through the shoulders. Catherine Hurley came to call Coach Jack a cruel despot, in response to which Dan Hurley produced a mocking yawn.

As for the incoming class, Adam was the only freshman to run varsity, third man most of the year. Midway during his sophomore year, Legs was brought up from JV. By sectionals that same year, Coach Jack demoted two seniors and a junior and brought up Dennis, William, and Peter. He especially loved those three. Slow burn suited their make-up. What they lacked in speed, they damn well made up for with grit and drive. All of this meant that five sophomores competed in the Long Island Catholic League Championship at Sunken Meadow Park, which resulted in a first-place finish. The expectations for St. Theresa's team were sky high, especially since the newly formatted state meet had been finalized for the following year at Watkins Glen, a championship trophy predicted all over town.

Perhaps that is why it took hours for Coach Jack to swallow the third-place finish at Watkins Glen. A few places here, a few there, he kept telling himself, and the goddam second-place trophy at state would have been theirs.

7

The morning after the Watkins Glen race, Dan and Catherine arrived home from the 9:15 Mass with Christine and little Tommy, a box of Dunkin Donuts in tow. Dennis was still in bed.

"Mommy," said Tommy, "can I eat my donut in the den? I want to draw."

"Yes, you can, Tommy. Christine, could you get him settled?"

"Sure, but after that I need to fill out my college applications."

As Christine left with Tommy, Dan grabbed the newspaper and started reading the account of the state meet.

"Did you notice, Dan," his wife said, "not a word at Mass from Monsignor Cassidy about the podium finish?"

"Let's enjoy the morning, Cat."

"Yes, not a peep from His Highness."

"Last time I looked, Cassidy's only job up on the altar is to teach us all a little humility."

"Blah, blah, blah, Dan. But now that I think about it, we should be grateful that the cross-country season's finally over. In fact, what do you say I go wake up Dennis, and we all head into Flushing Meadows to take my Aunt Dorothy to that Greek restaurant she so likes?"

"Aren't you forgetting that we just spent a bundle at the Red Snapper last night?"

"You're no fun."

"Fifty-two dollars in checking, Cat, that's to get us through until I get paid next Friday."

"No!"

"Yes."

A groggy Dennis appeared. He poured some juice and grabbed a seat.

"So, Dennis, your mother was just saying with cross country over, we can all go out today and rake leaves in the yard. All so that we're nice and hungry for a dinner of chicken pot pies. How much, Cat, is a chicken pot pie these days?"

"Your father, Dennis, is a regular riot."

Dennis grabbed a glazed donut. He was not at all interested in the money issues of his parents, who back in the day barely had enough to cover the first month's rent for their Queens studio apartment over a Jericho Turnpike coin shop. There, night after night, following a modest dinner atop a lumpy linoleum floor, Catherine opened the living room couch into a pull-out. Like some hotel wench, she whipped the bed sheets out and over the mattress. That's why Dan did a double flip when his Uncle Billy made him a generous offer to buy 32 Crocus.

Indeed, Catherine at the onset didn't know what to do with the drab old house. But that all changed when by chance she met Alice Crimmins, Bellport's library director and former religion teacher at St. Theresa's who took to herbal tea, baggy institutional clothing, and political outrage long before any of those became fashionable. As the young niece of Charlie Malagati, Alice moved from Brooklyn to her Uncle Charlie's when her mother died in 1947. Always lighting some new torch, she regularly pissed off Mulski. He finally fired her after learning that her students were using some alternative text instead of the *Baltimore Catechism*. The incident embarrassed her uncle who could barely stand to look at her after that.

Alice also rubbed Dan Hurley the wrong way. For one thing, Alice got Catherine hooked on antiquing, the main floor of their home soon filled with hutches, pottery, and tables adorned with dim lamps placed on lace doilies. Also under Alice's spell, Catherine dabbled in Protestant extracurriculars, attending lectures and reading ponderous books on spirituality that her friend recommended. After dinner one night, Catherine looked over her shoulder from the sink and informed Dan that she and Alice were going to attend a panel discussion at St. Paul's Lutheran Church in Yaphank. "Eventually, Cat," Dan replied, "the two of you will trade in novenas for tongues and other acrobatics." Dan didn't exactly mind, however, whenever Alice, as one of the more voluptuous women in town, showed up unannounced in his kitchen wearing one of her elastic outfits, this as a detour during one of her power walks. Dan would never tell his wife that her good friend had the rockin' body of a young cheerleader.

All of which is why the morning after the Watkins Glen race, Dan was not disappointed when through the window he saw Alice heading up the drive. Today she wore a shiny blue outfit with a gold lightning bolt running down her front. As was her habit, Alice tapped at the front door even as she opened it. "Hello, hello, wherever you are."

"Come in, Alice. Come in and pull up a chair," replied Catherine.

"Hi, everyone," Alice said entering the kitchen.

Dennis tried as best he could to avoid looking at what his father was also trying to avoid looking at, that which Coach Jack once described as boobs that stare back at you like eyeballs.

"Yes, Alice," said Dan. "Do sit."

"Tea?" asked Catherine.

"Pennyroyal Leaf, Catherine. Thanks."

Dan asked, "How about a Boston Creme, Alice?"

"All that processed sugar, Dan, never. And the town, young man," she paused to look at Dennis, "is all abuzz about the big race. Congrats!"

"Thanks, Mrs. Crimmins."

"And I imagine," she turned back to Catherine, "that Jack Hogan got good and drunk at Chief's last night."

"We try, Alice, not to mention him at the table. Causes indigestion."

Dan, rattling the newspaper, said to his son, "Dennis, remind these two where you and Coach Jack stood yesterday?"

"On the podium."

"Third place at state, if I'm not mistaken." Dan held up the back page of the *Long Island Press* that featured a photo of the team. "And knowing my bride, she will have this picture framed in no time at all. Right, Cat?" Turning to the article, "And listen to what Coach Jack had to say right after the race. *I am proud of my boys. Damn proud. And while I'm not about to jump the shark, with six of my top seven returning, we will be the team to beat at state next year.*"

"You hear that, Alice!" Catherine said. "His team just finished the season, and that man can't let them enjoy the moment. He's a brute, plain and simple."

"Your mother's right, Dennis," said Alice, "Jack Hogan's cut from the same cloth as Attila the Hun. Say, Catherine, did I ever tell you about the first time I bumped into him? Back in the days when I was running. Before my knees started acting up."

"Is it salty?" asked Dan.

"Dan!" cried his wife.

"In part," replied Alice. "But through no fault of my own."

"Proceed," said Dan. "But should we first send Dennis above? His virgin ears and all."

"Anyway, one day while I was out on a run and stopped at the traffic light on Main, I was jogging in place when a man with thick eyebrows and the remnants of acne approached to ask directions.

'Say, lady, I'm new in town,' he said, 'and just got off the train from the city. I'm looking to buy a house for me and my wife on Day Lily Drive. You know where this Day Lily is?'"

"And you told Jack Hogan what?" Dan asked.

"I pretended not to hear him. But it didn't stop him from leering at me and claiming he used to run for St. Peter's in the city. All I could think was turn light, turn, as I was stuck there running in place. I was ready to bolt the second the light changed. But then I caught him ogling me some more."

"I bet, Alice," Dan slapped the table, "you slugged him, and good."

"He actually had the arrogance to keep going with it! 'So lady,' he said, 'you know where this Day Lily Drive is or what?' Naturally, I didn't respond, to which he said, and these are his words, Dan Hurley, not mine: 'Say, lady, it's clear you got a set of tits on you. But do you speak the King's English?'"

"He didn't!" cried Catherine.

"Yes, he did! By the grace of God, the traffic light turned, and I was off, telling myself that with any luck the house on Day Lily had already been sold. That's the first time I met the infamous Jack Hogan."

"I would have contacted the police," Catherine said.

"Couldn't agree more," Dan said with a smirk, now picturing Jack Hogan taking in her pretty little ass before he headed across Main Street to Chief's to down a frosty mug as Billy Boyce told him exactly where Day Lily was located. "And yet, Alice," Dan added, "if it wasn't for your Indian mania back in the day, Jack Hogan might not have the team he has today. I mean, you were responsible for that plaque on the path. You know, the plaque with Sitting Bull that Coach Jack has used to create a running dynasty. Not sure if Dennis here knows that story."

"Oh, Dennis probably knows how I found the plaque in library storage and, thanks to the bishop's decree, had it cemented on the parish path where—"

A knock at the door.

"Come in," cried Dan, "whoever you are."

William and Peter entered in their running gear.

"Hey," said Dennis, "what's going on?"

"Tried calling you earlier," said Peter, "but your mom said you were sleeping. Thinking about some junk miles that end up at the Apollo for pancakes. Adam's gonna join us."

"C'mon," William added, "put a bunch of singles in your sock and let's go."

"But," Catherine said, "the cross-country season is over."

"Just a cool down, Mrs. H.," Peter replied, "after the big race yesterday."

"Boys," said Dan, "you're gonna miss the library director regale us with the story behind the Sitting Bull plaque."

While Peter glimpsed the accentuated curves, William said, "We'll take a rain check, Mr. Hurley. C'mon, Denny."

"Pray tell, boys," asked Dan, "how does Sunday Mass figure into your day?"

"Oh," said Peter, "we're gonna catch the five o'clock later."

As Dennis left to change upstairs, Alice Crimmins turned to his two friends. "As you boys wait, why not offer your opinion of Coach Jack, as he is called in these parts."

"People can say what they want," said Peter. "He can coach like nobody's business."

"And you?" she said, turning to William.

"Ditto."

"What I mean is, what is your opinion of his moral compass?"

The question pricking William, his eyes narrowed some. "Aren't you Mr. Malagati's niece?"

Alice returned an appalled look. The brazen boy's sarcasm was clearly a barb about her well-known estrangement from her uncle. So she decided to hit the boy where it hurt. "And aren't you Bill Flanagan's son?"

William knew immediately Crimmins was referencing his

father's combative nature. But rather than being quelled, he reveled in it. "I am, and what about it?"

Feeling the heightened tension, Dan intervened, "Hey, why don't you boys head up top and help Dennis double knot his shoelaces."

Alice Crimmins had fled by the time the three returned downstairs, Dennis now in his running gear. They went outside and found Adam stretching at the bottom of the drive.

"Okay, Adam," said Dennis, "you almost won state yesterday. You pick the route."

"You call fourth place almost won?"

"Hey, Adam," said William, "you beat the shit out of just about every runner. Lost by a few seconds. You'll get 'em next year."

When Adam couldn't decide on a route, Peter nodded to the far side of the field where Alice Crimmins power-walked. "In honor of Boobs-To-Die-For over there, I say we run poontang. Easy access to the Apollo Diner on the way back." It was Legs who bestowed the bawdy tag on the out-and-back route to Bellport High School that the team sometimes ran on junk mile days. They mainly did so to gawk at the public school girls going bra-less in frazzled jeans, with stringy hair and that stoned-out-of-their-mind look. Adam once described them as "high-assed broads training for careers in prostitution," all because of their jumping in and out of their boyfriends' slow-moving cars in the school parking lot.

Little was said as the four boys took off across the field. They made sure to slow down to allow Alice Crimmins to pass right in front of them. Once over the creek and on the path, they settled into a breezy pace. They soon turned onto the shoulder of Old Montauk, which they always liked for its shade.

"Say, Adam," William asked, "what were your splits yesterday?"

"5:08, my first mile. A 5:02 slow burn. Finished with a 5:03."

"Wow," said Peter. "I bet Coach Jack got a hard-on watching that."

"But look where it got me. Sucking wind at the end. Coach told Harry he's got a weight-training plan for me this summer."

It being a Sunday, the high school grounds were empty. After circling the school, Adam shouted as he picked up the pace, "See you boys at the Apollo."

"Let the fucker go," said William.

As the core three soon made their way back onto Old Montauk, they noticed a slew of Harleys coming in their direction. Vinnie Malagati on the lead bike swerved onto the shoulder, and, laughing hysterically, he took dead aim at them. They jumped into the bracken to avoid being hit. The bike passing by, Vinnie without missing a beat swerved back onto Old Montauk and continued on his way.

William bolted out onto the road and, flipping the bird, he cursed Vinnie, too far ahead to take notice. But not so for two rear riders who pulled up to the boys and dismounted.

"You gotta problem, Boy?" said a huge gorilla with a big gut, rangy long hair, and a beard.

"Cause if you do," said the other rider, "we can chain you to the back of our bikes and drag your asses along for a bumpy ride."

"Vinnie Malagati," William took a step forward, "is human garbage, if that's what you want to know."

With that, the gorilla pulled out a six-inch metal bar from his vest pocket. "You want to repeat what you just said?"

Dennis attempted to intervene, "We were just leaving."

"No, I'd feel better," said the gorilla lightly tapping his own head with the bar, "if this one here first says he's sorry. And fucking says it like he means it."

William spat on the ground.

"What he means," said Peter, "is he's sorry. I'm sorry. We're all sorry. Right, William?"

A plumbing truck in the west lane slowed to a stop. The driver was Bud Homa, the owner of the company where Mr. Flanagan worked. He yelled out the window, "Hey, William, everything okay?"

"Honky dory, Old Timer," the gorilla answered for him. "So why not get back to your roto-rootering?"

Bud Homa pulled over to the shoulder and reached into his truck's hub. He retrieved a hammer, and crossing over the two lanes, he went right up to the gorilla.

"There's only two ways, Son, this can go down. One, you can get back on your shiny little toys and enjoy the day. Or me and these boys can jump your fat asses and have the police clean up the bloody mess. And, my kid brother, Wayne Homa, the Chief of Police, can sign off on it all. So, what will it be?"

"Fuck off!" said the gorilla, turning for his bike.

With engines roaring, the two riders took off.

William explained what had transpired, to which Bud Homa replied, "Well, you boys stay away from Vinnie Malagati and his ilk. Nothing but trouble. And William, you cool it. Okay?"

William nodded.

After Bud Homa left, the boys resumed running along Old Montauk, a still angry William picking up the pace. Dennis knew that his friend would never forgive Vinnie Malagati for the bowling alley incident years ago, when the three were in grade school. Having just returned from Vietnam, Vinnie slapped William in front of a large group of classmates for refusing to give up the change in his pocket. To add insult to injury, Vinnie then threatened William with a second slap unless he got on his knees and kissed his boots. William, with keen embarrassment as classmates looked on, got down on his knees and kissed the boots.

William and Vinnie Malagati, Dennis thought to himself as they approached the Apollo, are on a damn collision course.

8

After the large crowd finished its meal at St. Theresa's fall sports banquet, the athletic director introduced one coach at a time. When it was Coach Jack's turn to discuss the season and hand out awards, he took his time itemizing each of the all-county and all-state honors his runners received. And when it came time for the big announcement of next year's team captain, he said, "My decision was a no-brainer. My heart and my head have been telling me for some time now that Dennis Hurley is an individual of high character. A born leader."

As the audience clapped, Catherine Hurley grabbed her husband's arm and whispered, "Please, God, no."

Dan was delighted with the news.

On the drive home, it only got worse for Catherine. Dennis announced that he and Coach Hogan were to meet at the Apollo that next morning for the traditional captain's breakfast. His mother gasped.

"Not to worry, Mom. Coach just wants to get a jump on things."

"What you mean to say is that he wants to get his tentacles all over you. And there's the horribly vulgar things he says to you boys. At one meet your father and I heard him say-"

"Leave me out of this, Cat."

"Yes, Dennis, we've been to enough races to see him in action. His veins popping out, belittling his runners when they are in horrible pain, when they can barely walk, much less run."

"Mom, that's his way of cheering us on."

"Cheering you on? Is that what you call that rot!"

"What your mother means to say, Dennis, is keep up the good work and knock 'em dead."

Later that night, Dennis lay in the darkness of his bedroom thinking about his mother's bitter reaction to him being chosen as captain. He told her not to worry. That all would be fine. But would it? After what Coach Jack put Mark Voit through this past season, he wasn't so sure.

"Good God," Dennis mumbled, turning restlessly in bed.

But as he pulled the pillow over his head and sighed heavily, he heard taps at his side window.

"Damn it, Peter," he said moments later pushing the slider open. When Mr. Walker was out of town as a regional salesman for Seagram's Liquors, which was often the case, Peter made an art form of scaling the attached garages of teammates. Tonight, Dennis found Peter in a sweatshirt and wool hat.

"Hey, Denny, get dressed. My cousin Eric's going out night-fishing on his boat. For blues."

"No can do. I meet Coach Jack at nine for breakfast."

"We'll be back way before the sun comes up."

"Ain't happening."

"You're no fun."

With that, Peter jumped down.

Dennis watched his friend take off on his bike and head down Crocus in the direction of Duckpond Drive, where Fenny lived.

"My captains," Coach Jack said once he and Dennis had settled into a booth, "usually get The Big Breakfast. Two meats, a stack of pancakes, a few eggs to boot. I get the same."

"Sounds good."

The order taken, Coach Jack laid out the captain's various responsibilities. Just when Dennis thought his coach was done, "But the biggest goddam thing you've got to do is this: after your teammates take a few weeks off next May following the end of outdoor track, you got to make sure they run most days during the dead period in June. Mixing up easy long and short runs. You know that, right?"

"I do, Coach."

"Damn, Dennis, the team can't let its guard down. Got to come into July with at least a small base, ready to take on the slog of high volume over the summer. And you probably also know that it's a bunch of bullshit that I can't train you guys during the dead period, right?"

"I do."

"What's worse, the top teams in the state stick the middle finger up at the rule. Everyone knows that cocksucker from Albany has his kids up to his family's cabin on Lake George, where they run up and down mountain paths when they're not chomping on burgers off the grill. Jack Hogan ain't got squat. Just the flat-as-a-damn-pool-table south shore of Long Island. Which is why we always got to mix it up in the dunes and beach sand as often as we can. So, anyway, you'll make sure the team gets after it for Ole Coach Jack?"

"I'll try."

"Try?"

"I can, Coach, and I will."

"Thatta boy. Now listen, Bobby Mumbles approached me a few weeks back and said he wanted to rejoin the team after sitting out this past year." He paused, seeing his captain return a surprised look. "Yeah, I get it. But I says to myself, sure, the whole school knows that Mums, with that black mop of hair and the face of a Roman god, got a monster cock that won't quit, knocking up that sophomore like he did. But he also ran 17:26 as a sophomore, in spite of the thwop of his gargantuan feet. Yeah, Dennis, Bobby Mumbles is back on board. So, can you pull him aside and have a man to man with him?"

"Sure. But what about?"

"For starters, the birds and the bees. Tell him he's got to put a lock on that zipper of his. Then you got to convince him that he's the perfect candidate to team up with Fenny next fall. Got it?"

"I like it, Coach."

"Which is why I included him in the entries for this year's Turkey Trot."

"Turkey Trot?"

"You know, the five-mile road race I started years ago but passed the baton on to the Elks. Always run the Saturday after Thanksgiving. While my team hasn't run it for years, I decided it would be good for this group. So, your first test as captain will be to get the lazy asses out of bed. I couldn't give a shit about how they run. My only concern is that they run. Got it?"

Dennis went silent.

"You do want to be captain?"

"Sure, Coach. But…"

"But what?"

"Adam and William and Peter are no problem. But Legs. And Fenny. And now, Mums. I mean, how exactly do I get them out of bed?"

"A good kick in the nuts is all it takes. Take your buddy William with you. He knows how to serve notice. And to help with motivation," he handed Dennis an envelope with thirty dollars in it. "For pizza afterwards. But, dammit, no one can know. No one."

That night, Dennis came downstairs for cereal and found his father with the paper and a cup of hot tea. "It says right here on page one, Dennis, that some sixteen hundred of our boys are still missing in action. That number to complement the fifty thousand already dead. And now the Paris Peace Accords are falling apart." His mother came up from the basement laundry room with a basket of clothes. "Did you hear that, Cat? Paris Accords look bleak."

"Enough, Dan. Enough of that war. And Dennis, I got a call from Carol Legstaff today. She passed on her congratulations to you about the captain business."

"Okay, Cat, do tell us why Carol really called."

"Now that I think about it, Dan, she did mention that the race times of Jack Hogan's past captains regress from the previous year, on account of severe psychological abuse. The Turley boy, for example, had to seek counseling when that man kicked him off the team right before sectionals, that after rubbing his nose in the dirt all season long. And let's not forget about what just happened to Mark Voit this year. The poor boy's nerves were so shot that he was unable to finish the race at state. His reward? Our coach-of-the-century left him behind in upstate New York."

"Let Dennis enjoy his cereal."

"Carol was just trying to convey that that man has made an art form of draining the life out of his captains. But since I can't talk Dennis here into quitting that team, I suggest he follows the angel of his better nature, which is to say that he ignores Coach Jack as best he can."

Dan rattled the paper. "Don't let Carol Legstaff or your mother, Dennis, fill your head up with nonsense."

"I get it, Dad. But..."

"But what?"

"I'm not sure that I will be any good at playing hard ball with my teammates, which is what Coach wants. They're my friends."

"Yes, they are, and I don't envy you there. Especially since that team of yours is something else, each kid marching to his own drumbeat. My advice is to put on your game face whenever Coach is around, but to enjoy the heck out of the season. Unless Fenny is destructive, or Peter breaks into a bank, turn a deaf ear to the background noise. Lead through example, kicking the shit out of each and every practice. And," he said waving the newspaper, "thank your lucky stars that you boys were born too late to be drafted."

Back upstairs and lying in bed, he heard his father's assessment of the team swirling around his head. He knew his father was right, and if anyone marches to his own drumbeat, it's Peter Walker, a taut wire of adventure. It's like he wakes up every day with a wild scheme springing to life. Dennis' earliest memory of his friend came during his brace days when through his bedroom window he saw Peter with a tennis racket chasing a raccoon into the woods. Then there's William, the polar opposite. He's a headstrong brooder with a wrestler's throbbing body who doesn't suffer fools, at all. But William would give his left leg to anyone who deserved it. He was the only parish kid who regularly approached Dennis for a chat, often offering him one of his Reese's peanut butter cups.

George Legstaff! For Legs, it's all about jumping up onto his soapbox and taking captive any audience with his acid wit. Living just six houses down on Crocus, Legs as a kid would show up on the Hurley doorstep with a briefcase overflowing with medieval comic books and plastic swords, immersing Dennis in the legends of King Arthur, which is what led to his dazzling inventory of lore.

Dennis also knew that Adam Feltman, as the only non-Catholic on the team, learned at a young age to keep the Jew-hating bullies off his back by running like the wind in any direction, day or night. Once back in grade school, a crowd of kids watched in awe as the neighborhood's biggest bully, John Miltenberg, failed to chase Adam down on the field. William loved the spunk in Adam and always came to his defense. Peter loved Adam for another reason, and it had to do with the dormer Harry and Ida Feltman built for their only son, including as it did a game room where *Playboy* centerfolds adorned the walls, the magazines themselves in a neat stack on a desk. Like his friends, Dennis studied the centerfolds, though he'd never forget the day when the gang was playing pool in the game room and Adam sent him downstairs to fetch a case of root beer. Once there, he heard faint voices at the end of a long hallway that had always been off limits to Adam's friends, but along which that day Dennis crept. Through a slit in a door, he saw a nude Harry and Ida in a hot tub. The show included a wall shelf that held statues of tall, curving African bodies waving spears. His brain a muddle, he grabbed the root beer and skulked back upstairs.

Dennis' inventory of the team moved on to Fenny the Fleabite, who by anyone's standard takes the damn cake. Born to wreak havoc, Fenny sets the bar for trash-talking opposition runners on the starting line. After post-race White Castles, a loud elastic belch never fails to escape him. Forever sniggering, Fenny drives Coach Jack batty. As for Mums, Dennis smirked at the idea of his former teammate, Robert Mumbino, rejoining the team. It was Legs who started calling him Bobby Mumbles after Mums got real drunk at a party and starting mumbling incoherently, eventually dropping to all fours and puking his brains out. Legs also dubbed Mums the Marvel of Carnal, this after classmates learned that Barbara McManus and Leslie Pinskey, two slack-mouthed cheerleaders with smokey eyes and wet lips, visited the Mumbino house while his parents were at their Friday night bowling league. That was before Mums got the Raffanelo girl pregnant.

Damn, Dennis muttered, Dad's right. That's one doozy of a team.

But creeping back into his head was the business about the Vietnam War that Dan Hurley had also mentioned. His father sometimes made the point that the cross-country team amounted to little more than a group of scrubbed prep boys born a few years too late to be drafted, and that they barely noticed the ebbing tide of the war, this despite that they were besieged by the newsreels and photographs. Their world was the sand and the dunes, the rough surf, the rural roads up north, the docks, the downtown storefronts. Dennis also knew that they regarded the war as one might impersonal scraps of newspaper. Except for popular antiwar songs on the radio, they gave little thought to the carnage, defoliants, and the angst.

Needless to say, that didn't stop members of the team from taking cheap shots at the returning neighborhood soldiers. "Rogue peasants" is what Legs once called Vinnie Malagati and his soldier friends. Just back from Vietnam, they started a lawn service where they seemed to be in competition to see who could move the slowest. Dennis occasionally from his window would catch one of them late at night walking along Crocus in his moon-bleached mane. He kept asking himself just who were these moping insomniacs, so unlike the spruce portraits of war casualties on the front page of the *Long Island Press* that he delivered some years ago as a paperboy.

9

Less than twenty-four hours after the captain's breakfast with Coach Jack, Peter called Dennis. "Hey, Denny, since you go by Captain Ahab now, I think it's high time you invite the team for a kick-ass game of you-know-what at you-know-where. It's been a while." Dennis knew that Peter meant a night game of poker on the humongous boulder, which sat some three feet high and five feet wide on the shoulder of the path, and just yards from the Sitting Bull plaque. As far back as eighth grade, Peter lured neighborhood kids there at night to play cards on the boulder's flat surface.

"Not sure that cards are a good idea, Peter. And I sure as hell ain't organizing it. I got enough on my plate. Like getting Fenny and Legs and Bobby Mumbles to show up to this Saturday's Turkey Trot."

"Turkey Trot? And Mums? Tell me, Denny!"

"Yeah, Mums is rejoining the team after a year layoff. And Coach Jack's already entered us in the downtown Turkey Trot. And to motivate his merry band, he's kicked in for pizza afterwards. Enough for three pies and a few dozen garlic knots."

"Sign me up! I'll kick ass. And you know what? We'll play

poker Saturday night after the race. So, Ahab, wadda you say? You'll call around and let the boys know?"

Dennis chuckled at his friend's persistence and replied before hanging up, "Like I said, Peter, that's all you if want to organize some poker."

Returning upstairs, Dennis gauged Peter's chances of mustering support. William and Adam were always a maybe when it came to a night game of poker at the boulder. Fenny and Mums, a probable. Legs, a yes, if for no other reason than it gave him yet another opportunity to remind the gang that they were the Knights of Camelot, that the large boulder was the Round Table, and that the creek was the River of Life, protected by the sanctity of the Church, only a stone's throw away.

On an unseasonably warm Saturday, the race crowd of a few hundred weekend warriors gathered in front of Bellport's First Federal Bank for the annual Turkey Trot. Indeed, Dennis finagled the varsity team, which now included newcomer Bobby Mumbles, into running. Of course, Legs, who sat on a curb eating a banana while his teammates stretched, was not happy. "This is pure crap. I should still be in bed."

"Say, Denny," Fenny asked "why ain't Coach Jack here?"

"Don't worry," Legs replied, "he's somewhere out there on the course, lurking about, ready to pounce."

"Hey, guys," Dennis said, "snap out of it. Indoor track is right around the corner."

"Which is why," William snarled, "Legs should get off his ass and start stretching."

"And boys," Peter said, "don't forget about the poker game. Tonight's balmy weather will be perfect for a trouncing!"

Legs popped up from the curb. "Arthur will be there to collect all outstanding tithes."

As to the task at hand, a Boston University junior, who was home for Thanksgiving and who took fifty-sixth in his year's NCAA cross-country championship, won the Turkey Trot by putting on a kick that left Adam in the dust. The core three ran an uninspired race. Fenny and Mums jogged the last mile. When it became apparent that Coach Jack was a no-show, Legs cut through back streets to the finish line. The team wasted no time making its way to Sal's for lunch, at which time Peter again reminded them, "Poker! Seven sharp!"

LATER THAT AFTERNOON in Room 12 of the Lantern Inn, a dated motel on Long Island's north shore, Jack Hogan got out of bed. Buck naked, he strolled over to the desk.

"Hey you, and that big hairy ass of yours," said Margie Mudhank, who apparently had reconciled the former antagonism with the coach since the eighth-grade graduation some years back. Today, she lie on the queen-sized bed holding a plastic cup of vodka on the rocks, the cup leaving a ring on the white sheet that covered her. "You promised, no phone calls."

"I lied." He lifted the receiver.

"You said that if I graced Room 12 for another weekend of boinkety-boink you'd not bring up anything remotely connected to that team of yours. I need a break is what you said."

"It's just one bloody phone call, Marge. I need to keep a finger on the pulse. Besides, you need to shower and powder your nose. In less than an hour, we got a big dinner reservation in the sky at Lenny's Lobster House."

"Fine!" she said, throwing the sheet aside and getting up. But before the bathroom door was slammed shut, she turned and shook her breasts from side to side.

Only after Coach Jack heard the shower's spray did he dial the Hurley number, which he would come to know by heart. He first asked Dennis if all seven showed up at the race.

"They did, Coach. All of them."

"Mission accomplished, then?"

"Adam ran great. The rest of us, not really."

SITTING BULL RUN

"Don't worry. The name of the game is simple. Just keep the team above water until winter track starts. After that, we'll run most days. Take off when need be. Got to stay healthy for the fall. Never tempt fate. Got it?"

"Got it."

"Anyway, gotta go. I'm in the midst of painting my kitchen an explosive shade of blue."

After Dennis hung up, his mother asked, "What pearls of wisdom today?"

"Just the usual. Though he did say something about painting his kitchen a shade of blue."

None were surprised when they found that Peter, a gleam in his eyes, had arrived early and placed on the boulder a pack of cards and a pint bottle of Seagram's whiskey pinched from his father's well-stocked liquor cabinet. Nor that he had strung a flashlight from a branch to illuminate the game of seven-card stud, where nickels and dimes were about to be won and lost.

As Peter dealt the first hand, Legs looked to Bobby Mumbles and said, "Well, Mums, Arthur's Court has a question for the Marvel of Carnal."

"Go fuck yourself, Legs."

"What Arthur wants to know is, are you still preoccupied in lewd anatomical wanderings? Or have you really settled down, and now only sadly dream of swelling boyhood exploits, of mouthing come-hithers, of conjoining with this or that whimpering one?"

"Hey, Legs," Bobby Mumbles shot back, "at least I wasn't seen blowing kisses at bathing beauty, Elsie the Cow." The others burst into laughter, high-fiving each other over the reference to Elise Fowler, a plump, square-faced classmate, Legs' junior prom date.

Spats like this between teammates might have discouraged the captain. But Dennis tonight ended up grinning back. The team's blood is thick, he reminded himself.

"Okay," said Peter, "back to poker."

"Heck, yeah," said Fenny, lining up his coins. "Time to win some money."

William got out of the blocks fast, winning the first two hands—the first with a bluff, the next with a full house, after which Adam cried, "Fucking William Flanagan!"

Moments after a jubilant Bobby Mumbles won the next hand, Fenny pointed to the cemetery woods. "There he goes again." Everyone turned and saw Mr. Malagati's dark figure passing by headstones, his German Shepherd, Rosa, nosing ahead of him.

"Still don't get it," Fenny added, "night after night."

"Fenny the Fleabite," Legs replied. "By now you should know that Merlin goes there in search of the ghost of Sitting Bull. On behalf of Christendom, he aims to snuff the life out of the chief in bloody combat."

"Wrong, Legs," said Dennis as everyone anted up a nickel. "He goes there to see his wife who's buried on the cemetery's north side."

"Maybe, Denny," said William. "But I bet these days he also goes there to get away from that piece of shit son of his."

"Hey, I heard Ida say," Adam replied, "that Vinnie Malagati joined a POW group that gives talks and all, and that he's turned his life around."

William snarled, "That's a joke if ever I heard one."

Dennis knew that William would never buy into the town's changing attitude toward Mr. Malagati's only child, a change that was the result of a feature story that Father Ken drummed up in the *Bellport Citizen* shortly after Vinnie's return from Florida. The article described Vinnie's dramatic escape as a prisoner of war.

"Sure," William had more to say, "he's posing as a model citizen. Going to the Legion Hall. Keeping his hair short. A load of crap is what that is!"

Several awkward seconds passed before Mr. Malagati and Rosa disappeared.

"Damn," said Peter. "Back to poker."

The poker game resuming, angry shouts emerged, but nothing that came to blows. During one hand, Legs made clear his intentions at next year's Golden West meet. "Go out in a middling 54 and come back in yeoman's 58, for a 1:52. Which will allow me to dictate the terms of my scholarship."

"Hey," said William, who was always butting heads with George Legstaff. "We all know why Legs is in love with his damn event. No goddam hills. No roots. No rocks. Just two short trips around a pussy of a flat oval track."

Fenny added, "Yeah, and no snot running down his face."

"You know, guys," the team captain intervened, "we shouldn't forget that even though Legs sandbags most practices, he never lets us down on race day. Just a few weeks ago at Watkins Glen, he nailed state with a top-ten finish and All-State honors. In fact, we all nailed state. With Adam leading the way, we almost upset Albany and Syracuse! They better look out next year!"

"Here, here," said Peter.

"And if I'm not mistaken," Legs added, "with less than eight hundred yards to go, I left William in the dirt."

"That you did, you fucker."

"And what about Fenny," Dennis said. "Also slinging dirt for a PR. And no doubt Mums will be in the hunt next year when we take state."

"Better be!" replied Bobby Mumbles.

"Hey," said Adam pointing across the path. "Is it possible we have another night stalker on our hands?"

They all looked, and sure enough they saw someone wandering aimlessly through the woods coming in their direction. Only when the figure reached the path did the moonlight reveal classmate Cindy McGallister, who stopped just across the path and leaned onto a tree for support as she glared at them.

"Oh, boy!" Legs howled. "The pangs of cursed passion!"

Bobby Mumbles was the first to move her way, the others following. And as it became a staring contest, none of the boys seemed too discouraged by the fact that Cindy was a far cry from the pose she struck when sauntering by in the school hallways, her eyes looking past most, plump lips colored a dark copper brown and always held open in high drama. Tonight, Cindy was anything but one of those special cheerleaders sprayed with a powerful protective film, plucky legs bouncing and snapping with energy. Instead, her hair was all tangled, the top half of her shirt unbuttoned.

"My, my," said Legs. "Fate doth play wicked games on the once golden damsel, who now staggers like a wretched milk maiden."

Bobby Mumbles moved closer.

With a dull smile, she said, "What are you all looking at?" Her words badly slurring, she grabbed the tree trunk tighter.

"No need to worry, Cindy," replied Bobby Mumbles, trying to keep an even tone while slowly working to within an arm's reach.

Lolling her head toward him, she shot back, "Twerp-face! I'll get Kevin after your ass. But," she looked out into the dark woods, "where is Kevin?"

"Ahhhhh," Legs mused out loud, "the jilted damsel of Killer Kilgallon and his bestial predisposition!" The others also understood. Cindy had just shared the outdoors with a stud on the parish baseball team.

"You with Killer tonight, Cindy?" Bobby Mumbles asked.

"Listen, asshole," she hissed. But noticing the ring of males closing around her, she grew fearful. She started running back through the woods and into the cemetery proper. Not far along, she fell and rolled onto her back. The boys raced towards her, where but for slight moans, she lay as if dead.

Bobby Mumbles crouched down, his eyes feasting on her as if readying himself for a grand meal. "Nice, Cindy," he said. His hand brushed aside a strand of hair from her face. He looked back up at his teammates, his clenched white teeth in full view.

Dennis was not the only one who would go to bed that night thinking of what might have ensued had not the rustle of Mr.

Malagati's Rosa broke in on them and went right to Cindy and sniffed her face. Then came the old custodian, undaunted by the numbers. Bobby Mumbles stepped back among his teammates.

"What you boys do? This parish cemetery! Don't you know-" He saw Cindy on the ground.

"Not to worry, Mr. Malagati," said Peter. "She's not dead. Just drunk as a skunk."

A nervous Dennis added, "She showed up out of nowhere."

"I know you boys. That team. Okay, you and you." He pointed at Peter and William. "Get her up!"

They reached down and struggled to raise her. Dennis lent a hand, the three now lifting her.

"You boys, follow me. Rest, go home. Go now!"

His voice vexed, severe, the others scattered like chaff through the trees. The old man and Rosa turned for the bungalow. The three boys followed with Cindy in tow.

Reaching it, they carried her through the back door and laid her on the couch.

"Last name?" Mr. Malagati asked.

"McGallister," Dennis said. "Cindy McGallister. A classmate."

No sooner had the custodian left for the kitchen to make the phone call than William muttered, "Wonderful. Forced to stand before her old man. His daughter passed out drunk on the couch."

The creaking of the stairs captured the boys' attention. They turned to see Vinnie Malagati appear in his briefs. The boys had seen him any number of times since his return to Bellport, the most recent being the Harley attack on Old Montauk. But they had not seen him so up close. Still the same short and stringy person, he now had a face tightened in a web of lines. Thick black hair, cropped army style, replaced the ponytail.

At first Vinnie's hard mouth displayed a condescending disinterest in the boys whose faces he vaguely recognized. His eyes fell on Cindy. "Wow! Who is she?"

A jittery Mr. Malagati returned. "Vincent! You go back up. Church business. No concern you."

The sound of more steps on the stairs preceded the appearance of Vinnie's girlfriend, sporting a long flannel shirt and not much else. All three boys recognized Liz Pearce as one of the clerks at Horizon East, a clothing store downtown, who was sometimes seen dressing a window manikin. "Hot as Hades," Peter had once labeled her as the team ran by.

Tonight, she had a wary look on her and was about to say something to Vinnie when he turned to his father, "Yeah, church business alright. What, were you drinking wine in the sacristy with this pretty little one?"

"Vincent!" said the old man, leveling an embarrassed look at the boys.

"Well, well, well, what do you know? Charlie Malagati, of all people. And the lectures you've been giving me lately!"

His father simmering in rage, Liz Pearce whispered something to her boyfriend. As the two disappeared back upstairs, there came a hard laugh from Vinnie.

When Mr. McGallister arrived, he went straight to his daughter and grabbed her wrist for a pulse. Her eyes opened, her lips forming a faint smile before a sluggish tongue stirred and she again dropped off. Visibly relieved at the signs of life, her father gestured for the old man to follow him into the kitchen where they talked in hushed terms. When they returned, Mr. McGallister addressed the boys who were standing stock-still near the front door as if afraid to move. "You three and the other boys who were in the cemetery are on the parish cross-country team, right?"

"We are," Dennis answered. "But we had nothing to do with this."

"Yes, I know. My daughter left against my wishes tonight with Kilgallon, a real beaut. Boys, could I ask you to have a talk with your teammates, and see if we all can't come to an understanding?"

"Of course, sir."

"I'd like the incident to be forgotten. That it never took place. What happened tonight, well, the parish administration would not be able to overlook. Not to mention that the cross-country team would be dragged into the thick of it. Reputations at stake."

Dennis nodding his head, said, "As captain, I'll make sure the whole team understands and that nothing is said."

With that, Mr. McGallister lifted his daughter up and carried her out the door.

Mr. Malagati turned to the boys, "You boys hear what he say? No one know! No good in woods. Now go!"

The three passed outside, Peter racing ahead to open the passenger door for Mr. McGallister, who positioned his daughter upright in the seat. The door closing on her, she teetered and tumbled over. As the car took off, Dennis turned back to find the bungalow's front door already closed shut.

"Well," Peter said as they reentered the path, "I'd say that Denny saved the day. The ironclad pact with McGallister, that is."

"What the fuck, Peter," William said. "Do you know what just happened?"

"Hey, we saved a drunk cheerleader from drowning in the creek. Not to mention that we ended up with a close-up of the chest berries on Vinnie's babe."

"A shitstorm will rain down on us if this gets out!"

"Not to worry, William. Captain Ahab will read the riot act to the others. Right, Denny?"

Dennis was too agitated to respond.

"Yes, sirree," Peter said, "the thing's already gone out to sea."

Dennis filled in the other teammates, waiting at the boulder, about the agreement with Mr. McGallister. William warned all that they were to keep their traps shut. Peter grabbing his poker stuff, the shaken team retreated back across the creek.

Dennis undressed in the dark and went to the window. For George Legstaff, whose house several doors down also faced the woods, the view was a martial one. Legs once said, "With Lancelot and other warriors on guard against the night, the forest glows with charm and powerful might." For Dennis, the slumbering woods always had the opposite effect, one that somehow soothed and often left him at peace right before bed. But that was before the disaster that was tonight. He couldn't say for sure what Bobby Mumbles would have done next had the old man not stumbled onto them. Maybe he would've brushed aside her shirt whose top buttons Killer Kilgallon had already undone. And had Mums followed through, what next? And how would the gang have reacted? Without any good answers, Dennis backstepped to his bed and sat on its edge. He listened for the night out there. He thought he heard an invisible wind, too great to check, sweeping across the field.

10

Early that next morning, while their sons were still in bed, seven varsity fathers, with deeply furrowed eyebrows, occupied a rear table at the Apollo Diner. Harry Feltman was in the midst of his explanation: "So when my Adam got home well after eleven, Ida smelled booze on his breath. I forced the truth out of him. It seems that while the team was playing a poker game on that boulder, and while a damn bottle was being passed around, this drunk cheerleader came stumbling through the woods and passed out. Her name, Cindy McGallister."

"Phil McGallister's girl?" asked Walt Fennessy.

"Adam said she's some sort of goddess at school. Anyway, the custodian, Malagati, showed up out of nowhere. He had William, Peter, and Dennis carry her back to his place."

"What the fuck, Harry?" Bill Flanagan said. "This is not good."

"And when the girl's father came to pick her up, he told the boys that she had been out with some sexhound, a kid named Kilgallon. So a deal was struck with the boys. Not to tell anyone. To pretend it never happened."

"Did they agree?" Walt Fennessy asked.

"Yes. Adam said when the team met afterwards back at the boulder, they all agreed."

"Who supplied the booze?" Bill Flanagan asked.

"Who else but Peter Walker!" said Harry, not at all concerned that Rick Walker sat just across the table. "And my Adam swore that they followed her only because they were afraid she was going to get hurt. Maybe stumble onto Old Montauk and get run over. Like that guy all drugged up a few years back from Mastic Beach. Flattened by a bread truck."

Paul Mumbino asked, "Did your Adam say anything inappropriate happened? I mean, to the girl?"

"The girl wasn't touched! But what Adam's worried about, and what we all should be worried about, is a rumor starting. That would tank his scholarship."

"My George's, too," added Hank Legstaff. "The next thing you know, they'll be painting our boys as a bunch of rapists in the *Long Island Press*."

After talking strategy, the fathers decided that unless the incident went public, they agreed they would not tell their sons that they had met. "We got to make them think," said Dan Hurley, "that we don't know. And, Harry, I say you tell Adam to drop the whole thing as if it never happened."

"But," Bill Flanagan warned, "there's no way we can keep this from our wives. So we've also got to drill into their skulls that they are to carry on as if nothing has happened. Our sons' reputations are at stake."

"Bill's right." Dan added. "And just hope the thing goes away."

True to their word, the fathers rushed home before their sons awoke to have that conversation with their wives. But at the Hurley's house the going got rough, Catherine calling the agreement "nauseating." She argued that there had to be more to the story, that the full truth needed to be squeezed out of Dennis. "Or else, Dan, he will carry this to his grave. Along with the other boys."

"Are you telling me that the cross-country team did something unseemly to the girl? Huh, is that what you're telling me?"

"They are adolescent boys, Dan!" she exploded. "And they were drinking, right?"

The shouted words carried upstairs and woke up Dennis, who heard angry voices below. Cindy McGallister?

He went out to the landing. But things below had gone quiet. He headed downstairs to find them sitting at the kitchen table, his father's hands dutifully clasped atop the kitchen table like an obedient schoolchild at his desk. The air thick with silent reproaches, his mother's fists were dug deep into her thighs, her head sinking in a way that for Dennis required no further explanation. They knew. They had to know.

"Well, Catherine," when waiting out the silence became unbearable for Dan Hurley, "your son's right here. Do you still want me to have that talk with him?"

Her chair scraped the floor as she stood to leave. "Sure, Dan," Catherine intoned with sarcasm, bending in an exaggerated bow. "The laundry woman, however, has work to attend to down in the basement!"

Later that night, Dennis was sitting at his desk doing homework when he heard an intense shouting match that felt like raw steel on the spine. Again going to the landing, he heard his mother mention Cindy McGallister by name before she slammed the basement door behind her. The front door opening and closing, Dennis heard the wagon pull away on Crocus. For a terrifying moment Dennis thought his father was running away from home. But later when the wagon rolled back into the drive, Dennis went downstairs under a cereal pretense and found Dan Hurley holding a glossy white bag, the Kwong Ming red dragon emblazoned on it. Opening the basement door, his father yelled down, "Fried shrimp, Cat. Egg rolls, too."

"Thanks, but no thanks," she called up.

Glancing at the abandoned bag on the kitchen table, Dennis watched his father leave for a walk on the field. But no sooner did the front door close shut than his mother returned upstairs.

Without a word to her son, she removed candles from the hutch and tore the clear plastic off with shiny white wicks.

She's relenting, Dennis thought as he headed back upstairs. He knew what the candles meant. That his father from the field's gloom would notice the tiny flames in the kitchen window and come racing home. Which is exactly what happened, and while at first the voices below were muted, there eventually came his father's queer imitations of Bogey and Jolson, each mingled with his mother's hearty laughter. Dennis went back down and found the candles burning unevenly, dappled light on the thin layer of fried rice left on their plates. The two of them stood by the sink, each holding a drink. Catherine saw her son and sighed, as if life was good again. His father, on the other hand, with puckered lips knew it was a perfect opportunity to charge the fridge for more ice cubes.

Dennis returned upstairs.

Sure, he told himself, tonight's hatchet has been buried. But Cindy McGallister is out of the bag. He'd need to tell the gang, and when they all met that next day in the alley behind the market, he told them that he had overheard his parents having an ugly argument about the incident, and that he had heard them mention Cindy by name.

"Did they confront you?" asked William.

"No, they didn't. Not sure they want me to know that they know."

"Now that you mention it," Fenny said, "my parents were real quiet yesterday. How about you, Adam?"

"Oh, maybe a bit," replied Adam, who played dumb, just as Harry had instructed.

"But how the hell could our folks have found out?" asked William. "And what do they think happened?"

"Who cares how they found out," said Legs. "And I wouldn't doubt if they're thinking that Mums almost molested Cindy."

"Hey," Bobby Mumbles yelled, "I didn't touch the merchandise. And I didn't hear any of you complaining at the time."

"Listen," William said, "what's important now is that we go about our fucking business."

"Yeah," Dennis added, "and get ready for the indoor track season, just a few weeks out."

11

When Father Mulski, years earlier, demoted Sister Jean and gave the cross-country job to Jack Hogan, in the same meeting the pastor also offered him the head job of the indoor and outdoor track seasons. But Coach Jack wanted only to work with the distance runners. So, to get around it, he said to the pastor: "I wonder, Father, if we might want to keep Sister Jean, a star college athlete in the sprints and field events, as head coach during winter and spring track." While Coach Jack felt his nose growing the length of a long jump pit, he wasn't done yet. "See, it would be a shot in the arm to work as her assistant during the track seasons to watch and learn from her while I take care of the distance guys."

Liking what he heard, Mulski agreed, and each year thereafter Coach Jack did his best to soft pedal the training of his runners during the indoor and outdoor track seasons—all in an effort to keep them injury-free in the run up to cross country. Even so, following the Watkins Glen state cross-country meet back in November, his distance runners had considerable success during indoor track. Perhaps their best day came in February, at the prestigious Bishop Loughlin Games, held on the wooden track at the Washington Heights Armory in Manhattan. Adam ran a 4:16

mile for a second-place finish. Legs nosed out a stud from Essex Catholic to win the 880 in 1:54. He followed that up with a 49 quarter leg in a distance medley victory, Peter running a 1:59 half-mile, Dennis, a 3:12 three-quarter leg, and William, a 4:23 anchor mile. Fenny's 9:41 and Mumbles' 9:43 were strong PRs in the two-mile.

None loved Coach Jack's soft approach during the track seasons more than Legs. It left him fresh for several big races. Harry questioned the limited training his Adam was receiving as well as Coach Jack's decision to enter his son in several half-mile races. But when that spring Adam ran a 1:55 half-mile at the Loucks Games, a PR by three seconds, Harry was convinced that his son's speed had dramatically improved, all of which would help him on the final straight during the upcoming cross-country season.

As for the core three, they knew full well that they lacked the talent to place in individual events in big invitationals. But with the help of Legs or Adam as a fourth man in the relays, they picked up hardware during the outdoor season. The highlight was a third-place medal in the two-mile relay at the prestigious Penn Relays in Philadelphia's Franklin Field. So, too, on the van rides home did one of the three suggest in novel ways that the upcoming cross-country title that fall was theirs for the taking. Such comments gave Coach Jack goosebumps.

ON A BRILLIANT sunny day in early May, a few weeks after the Penn Relays, a large crowd gathered on the Great Lawn for the formal announcement of Cassidy's episcopal nomination. After several dignitaries offered short but flattering speeches, the Monsignor took the stage. And as he started waxing poetic about his humble roots, the droning false modesty carried across the parish grounds to the Red Oak where Coach Jack stood among his runners, who were stretching in preparation for a workout.

"Okay, boys," said the coach glancing across to the Great Lawn, "another fucking day in paradise, and we come to find out that on the very morning this November when we run for a state title, big weeniehead will be in Rome sucking up to the Pope. But let's not allow any of this to distract us from the business at hand. For today's six-mile reservoir run, I want a slow burn. Pretend it's cross country, and you're in the hunt. Steady does it through the first two miles, torch the middle two, grind sausages the rest of the way. Got it?"

"Got it!" Peter said.

"Coach," asked Adam, "with the spring track season winding down, when are you going to decide what we are running at sectionals? It would be nice to know. Harry thinks the two-mile is my best bet. Not the mile."

"Hey, you tell your old man that he and I agreed that we'd work on speed during the track seasons. Remember we want a 4:50ish first mile at state this fall to be little more than a walk in the park. All so that you can leave the field in the dust. Got it?"

"And I," said Legs, "ain't running in the mile-relay trials at state. Got to be fresh for the 880."

To that, Coach Jack tapped the stopwatch, "Fucking set and go!"

Only Fenny and Mumbles failed at sectionals to qualify for the state outdoor championship, held the third week in May at the SUNY track in Binghamton. There Adam took third in the mile. Legs went out in 54 in the 880 and easily held on to win. In the slow heat of the two-mile, the core three came across the line together in 9:26. Given that each of the five runners had a PR, Coach Jack stopped on the way home to treat them to a meal at a Poconos steakhouse. Once back in the van and on the road again, it became clear to the boys that the cut of their choice was intended to prepare them for their coach's pearls of wisdom regarding cross-country training over the summer.

"You know, boys, that the dead period soon begins, which means I'm not allowed to hold practice until July 1st. But I fully expect you'll run during June like you did in previous summers. And don't forget, also in June you're all committed to work the Sitting Bull series every Tuesday night."

The team knew that Coach Jack, via his captain, would dictate the terms of dead-period training. The previous four summers he got his varsity part-time jobs at the local rec center where he paid the manager there, a former harrier of his, to get after the boys to run. But given that the rec center now had a new manager, Coach Jack was forced to find a new resource. He hoped he would find one with an invite to Harry Feltman for a meal at Ruby Tuesdays. And when a few days later the two of them were sitting in a booth across from each other, Coach Jack asked, "Harry, do you remember the conversation last fall about Adam's summer weight-training program? About giving him the chutzpah needed that last fifty yards at next year's state meet?"

"How can I forget? You called Adam a fucking string bean."

Coach Jack informed Harry that since the parish weight room was off limits during the dead period, he could get a killer deal on an all-in-one weight-lifting machine from a friend of his who worked at Model's Sports. "And, what if, Harry, one such machine was to mysteriously land on your doorstep. And…"

"And, goddammit, what?"

"And three afternoons a week during June's dead period, you'll volunteer your backyard as weight-training central for the team?"

Harry was incredulous. "You can't be serious!"

"And the machine will stay at your place for the rest of the school year. For Adam to use at will, donated back to the parish when he graduates. His out-of-this-world core strength will allow him in November to gap the field at state and fly down the final straight for one hell of a win."

"How often will they meet at my house?"

"Each week during June, from three to five on Monday,

Wednesday, and Friday afternoons. Each day, they will run first, lift second. In that order."

"My fucking nerves."

"And if the boys behave, they can swim in that kidney-shaped inground pool of yours afterwards. So, wadda you say?"

"I know these boys. A pack of Catholic runts. As youngsters, they were at my house all the time. Mostly behaved. But as they got older, things got way out of control. Walker, for one, is a downright ticking time bomb. And that Fennessy! You heard what he did?"

"Tell me."

"One Saturday Ida and me went to the matinee of *Bonnie and Clyde,* leaving the house to Adam and those runts. So what did Fennessy do? He jacked up the fish tank's thermostat before depth-charging Oreo cookies stolen from the kitchen jar. Each creature was floating sideways when we got home. Walt Fennessy ended up writing a two-hundred dollar check to me on the hood of a police car. From that day forward I banned Adam's friends from the house. No, Fennessy's a psychopath who belongs in the barb-wired center for juvenile delinquents in Riverhead."

"Hey, Harry, sorry to hear about your dead fish. But we got bigger fish to fry. Like a state championship." He slipped Harry a white envelope. "A hundred smackeroos inside! For the pizza over the month. And I'll kick Fenny's ass up and down the Field Six dunes if he so much as farts. C'mon, Harry, it's a small price to pay for Adam's big-time scholarship."

Feeling that he won over Harry Feltman, Coach Jack left Ruby Tuesdays and headed over to the locker room. He was still firming up the fall meet schedule. As he pulled the van into the parish, he noticed soda cans and candy wrappers thrown about the path entrance to the Sitting Bull course.

"What the hell!"

COACH JACK made his way over to clean up the mess unaware that he was being watched by Liz Pearce, who, in Vinnie's upstairs bedroom, sat by the window smoking a cigarette. Across the way, her boyfriend lounged in bed. Suddenly, he jumped up and opened the closet door. "How about a little pick-me-upper?"

"Can't, Vin. Got called into work. I close tonight."

Vinnie pushed aside a closet panel and proceeded to work a combination lock to the secret safe he had installed. He withdrew a bag of pot and pulled up a crate so that he could sit next to Liz by the window. He rolled a joint and lit it. He took a toke, then forced his girlfriend to do the same.

"I hate that guy, Liz." He motioned to Coach Jack outside raking up the litter.

"Why?"

"Because he's an asshole."

"Why's he an asshole?"

"Because the guy's everywhere. Take another hit." Which she did. "He's the kind, Liz, who's got eyes in the back of his head."

"That's why you should stop selling stuff out the back door."

"And then there are those runners of his. They're like cockroaches. Popping up at the damnedest time."

"Again, you got to stop selling stuff out of the back door."

The drowsy effects of the pot kicking in, Vinnie's hooded eyes followed his father carrying a ladder to the convent to adjust a sagging gutter.

"Did I tell you that Garland wants me to give a talk on my war experience at the parish picnic the end of August?"

"Gonna do it?"

"Why not? He told me he could get me a cushy custodial job up north, at a parish in Port Washington. Where a friend of his is the pastor."

"Port Washington?"

"Hey, you're the one who keeps telling me that we got to get out of Bellport. We can rent a place there for cheap. Plus, I can get a boat and shoot across the sound to Connecticut to buy my stuff. Safer than driving each time."

"But you promised you were quitting after you sell the current stash."

"What the fuck, Liz?"

"You also promised you'll get divorced so that we can get married. My ovaries, Vin, are getting smaller by the hour."

"How am I supposed to get the money to put a down payment on a house? Our house, Liz. Huh, you tell me?"

Standing to leave, she said, "You're a big boy, Vinnie. You figure it out. Some of us work for a living."

12

In Room 12 of the Lantern Inn, Coach Jack smoked a cigar as he paced about in his briefs. He suddenly stopped, and lifting the receiver he dialed a number.

"Hello, Harry, Jack Hogan here. You got a minute? I wanted to-" He stopped to cup the receiver after a cackling Margie Mudhank threw the bed sheet aside and spread eagle. "Hey, shut that trap of yours. And cover yourself."

Back to the phone.

"Sorry, Harry, had to turn the TV down. Anyway, this afternoon being the first weight training session, I was wondering if there was anything I could do on my end to help?"

"Yeah, say a prayer to that Christian God of yours that I don't stone to death one of your runners."

"Maybe, Harry, you can lend captain Dennis Hurley a hand. He might need a little help getting after Legstaff. Or the idiot, Fenny."

"Oh, don't you worry. I plan on making the ground rules clear right away. Rule #1, no one's to step foot in the house."

"But what if they have to piss?"

"They can use the stool in the shed."

"I love it, Harry. And do make damn sure your Adam gets

after it. No one, I mean, no one, is to outkick him at state after he benches a ton of weight over the course of the year. And remember this, not a college coach gets through your front door unless they bring you and Ida a pound of lox."

"Was that a crack?"

"Hell, no. Sure, I'm a potato head, but I'm always getting a sesame seed bagel with lox and cream cheese at Otto's. I love the shit out of it."

"But isn't it illegal for a coach to bring gifts?"

"Hey, no tickee, no washee."

"Let me ask you this, Coach Jack. Ida's been reading these articles on cross-country running. She's worried about Adam's running form. Who wouldn't? His arms swing all cockeyed across his body, chest high. And there's his legs kicking high when the experts say there should be a slight knee lift."

"Damn, Harry, he's one of the top runners in the state."

"But Ida says the best running minds think bad running form can be corrected."

"Fuck, Harry, the reality is you can't teach an old dog new tricks. Got it?"

Margie threw a pillow at Coach Jack.

"No, I don't get it Coach, not really. Then Ida shows me this magazine article called *Mind over Matter in Cross-Country Running*. It's about a New Mexico high school coach who has his runners think positive thoughts during races, even hum songs, and how it helps them. Are you familiar with this coaching philosophy?"

"Listen, Harry, from where I stand, when a kid's in the throes of a race, he's not capable of thought, no less belting out an Elvis tune. All he can do is keep his head on straight while he tries to tolerate the chaos rolling around in his brain, the pain wracking his body."

"That's an awful picture you paint, Coach Jack."

Margie threw a second pillow that missed him but knocked his drink over.

"Harry, Harry, Harry! Try looking into the eyes of your Adam a mile into any cross-country race. You'll find he's already on his death bed. At mile two, the Rabbi's giving him last rites. And coming down the final straightaway, your son knows nothing except the horror of the casket's lid coming down on him."

MEANWHILE, BACK IN BELLPORT, Dennis lounged on his bed, daydreaming of the big Van Cortlandt race that November. After cruising through a sub 5:20 first mile, he told himself he'd slow burn the shit out of the Back Hills for a 5:10, then pouring on the hot sauce, as Coach Jack likes to say, over the final mile, William and Peter running beside him the whole time.

"Dennis," his mother's voice traveled up the stairs, "it's five to three."

He jumped out of bed and hustled over to the Feltman's, where he found a handwritten sign tacked to the front door,

Go round back!
No one's to EVER enter the house!

Weaving around, Dennis was startled by the new-fangled weight machine that sat under the awning. He was the first to arrive. Moments later, Harry Feltman came out the back screen door with a jug of water and paper cups that he put on the table.

"Oh hi, Dennis Hurley. Adam just went up to change into his workout clothes. You all set for a month of weight training?"

"I am."

"And are you ready to make sure the team follows the ground rules that I will announce once everyone is here?"

"Yes, sir."

"Of course, you are. You're probably the only one among the bunch who always followed the rules, who never gave me trouble. Which is why I regret that I had to include you when I banished the whole lot from my house after Fennessy the asshole killed all my fish. If I'm not mistaken, you still had that brace thing on your leg at the time. That was also when you and Adam were playing marathon games of chess. You remember?"

"How can I forget? And I remember you taught me the game."

"You were a good student. The discipline to control the center of the board. Not going apeshit with the pawns like crazy Peter Walker."

Dennis could not help but laugh.

"So, anyway, do you think my Adam is on track? You know, do you think Coach Jack's got it right about this weight training business?"

"All I know is that when William, Peter, and I started doing pull-ups during our sophomore year in the Flanagan basement, our speed increased dramatically."

"How dramatically?"

"We could barely break 60 seconds as freshmen. But after the pull-ups, during the track season, we would run on the mile relay in dual meets, and each of us brought our times down to 53 and change. William once ran a 52."

"So you think it will help my Adam?"

"Can't imagine anyone beating him next fall once he has upper body strength."

Just then William appeared, followed shortly by the others, after which Harry, with his eyes mostly fixated on Fenny, laid out the ground rules.

The session started with an out-and-back to Mastic Beach docks, the run a sloppy one since it rained cats and dogs that morning. The team spent much of the run dodging puddles.

"Hey, Adam," said Legs, the team now running along Spring Street, "how about you get Harry to splurge and throw in a couple of calzones?"

"Never," replied Adam.

Fenny and Mumbles were making a game out of stomping puddles.

"Assholes!" William shouted at the two after getting splashed.

"So, Legs," Adam said, "you were a no-show over the weekend. You missed a total of eighteen miles."

"While resting my weary bones, I was on the phone with the Oklahoma and North Carolina coaches."

"Hey, Adam," said William, "my mom told me that Ida told her that Notre Dame is looking at you."

"Another damn Catholic institution. Don't know if I can take much more of it. Say, Denny, you think, come November, Syracuse's going to be the team to beat?"

"That's what Coach Jack keeps saying. And I think he's right."

"Maybe," Bobby Mumbles said, "we can ask Coach Jack to throw in more money for the calzones. Harry can't turn that down."

"Mums?" said Peter.

"Yeah?"

"You know if Joan Seville's still going out with Walters?"

"Who cares, Peter. I say if you want Seville, you get Seville. She's damn hot!"

"Seville, Peter?" William asked.

"Just a thought. Starting to think about the prom, right around the corner."

"So is state," said Dennis.

"I'm a big boy, Denny," replied Peter.

The round trip to the docks was followed by a weight-training circuit. When it was Adam's turn at the bench press, following Fenny lifting 150 pounds, Harry hovered about. He was not pleased that his son could not once get 120 up.

"Not to worry about it, Adam," said William, "by state, you'll be kicking Fenny's ass. You wait and see."

The pizza was delivered at 4:30, at which time Harry said, "You've got thirty minutes to eat. And if you decide to swim, don't pee in the pool."

"And don't forget," Dennis told his teammates, "tomorrow at four, at the parish for a fartlek run to the Preserve. We work the first Sitting Bull after that."

WITH AT LEAST a hundred youngsters sitting lotus style on the auditorium floor, their fathers standing behind them, Coach Jack's low-timbered voice crackled through the auditorium: "Welcome, welcome! Yes, a big hearty welcome on this, the first of four Tuesdays in the Sitting Bull Run Series during the month of June, where my varsity seven," he paused to point at the registration table, "sit right there, ready to sign up your sons." That made for an easy transition to a brief account of the "meteoric rise of St. Theresa's cross-country program." The race director then explained the details of the series, including the three age-group divisions. After which, he said, "So with all of that in mind, I'd be glad to take a few questions."

"Coach Jack," a father's hand went up. "Can you tell us a little bit about your coaching philosophy?"

"Funny you should ask," said Coach Jack. "Yes, times they are a-changing, as punk Bob Dylan likes to say. But Jack Hogan still believes in time-honored traditions, and to sum up my philosophy, I think of myself as a master teacher. And here is what I teach..." As Coach turned the overhead on, a waiting transparency shot content onto a wall.

<u>*EDUCATING THE RUNNER'S MIND*</u>

How to train and race
How to develop speed and stamina
How to rest, recover, and stay injury free
How to run on varied terrain
How to develop positive thoughts about running

"But what if," another father asked, "my son has little natural speed?"

"For those of you who are worried that your son's lack of fast-twitch muscles might interfere, forget about it. Cross country is not for speedsters. It's for the stout of heart. And keep in mind that while winning is one of our goals, I also preach fun-in-the-sun to my boys, especially to each incoming freshman class. Living so close to the ocean, my runners often train down at the beach, capped off at times with bodysurfing in balmy waters."

"Coach," another father shouted out, "I like it. I really do. But since eastern Long Island is pretty flat, how do you compensate?"

"Shoot, we got something that the upstaters, with all their hills and dales, don't got. We got the shore, which offers all the rhythm breakers a typical cross-country course throws at you. Take what I call the Lighthouse Workout."

Coach Jack's pause here was strategic. He was about to get into the weeds. "The workout starts out with a 300-yard climb up the steep inlet bridge, a veritable Mt. Everest that dwarfs any hill we run during the season. From there, my boys spill onto the soft shoulder of Ocean Parkway, the kind of thing that mimics the grueling first mile of the Bear Mountain course. That's followed by a series of ups and downs through dunes with sharp inclines. Then, and here's where it gets downright interesting, next comes a few miles in the sand that saps the life out of you, but which involves a fuller range of motion that builds up everything from ankles to hip flexors and arms. Trust me, by the time my boys U-turn at the lighthouse, they are ready for a breather."

Another strategic pause.

"But no such luck. They must retrace their steps, the workout turning into a slugfest that, to the faint of heart, is tough to watch. But when all is said and done that day, my team gets a good eight miles under their belts, eight miles that simulate the most adverse cross-country race conditions."

"So you're saying, Coach, that you are all about volume?"

"A runner myself back in the day, I have spent countless hours studying the training techniques of master coaches, starting with that of the great Arthur Lydiard, all of which has evolved into today's standard, the mix of volume and interval training."

"So how do you mix them?"

"I was hoping you'd ask that." He wheeled around to stare down his team with a look that screamed, I will annihilate anyone who doesn't maintain his poker face. Spinning back around, "In the last decade, a civil war has started. One camp mopping up the high volume approach. The other camp, whose Kool Aid I drink, pretty much follows what Roger Bannister did to prepare for May 6, 1954, when he ran the first sub four-minute mile. And that is, part volume and part progressive intervals, a notion embraced by Bill Bowerman, who coaches my hero, Steve Prefontaine, at the University of Oregon. In other words, we move from building a base with high volume in July and August to lower volume and increased speed work in September and October. After which, we then taper for a good week as we approach the state championship race the first week in November! And we are able to do so because my boys, in both mind and body, are ready! So, folks, that's it in a nutshell, and I'll end by saying that a Jack Hogan team is a community of runners, where grit, determination, and fun-in-the-sun all rule the day. Now, with my merry band of seven waiting at the registration table, why don't you-"

"Hey, Jack Hogan," interrupted a man who was short and plump. "If you believe in community so much, why is it that a good number of your runners over the years have quit the team because of a mean-spirited dictatorship where you run the boys into the ground?"

Jaws dropped. Faces, spellbound.

An enormous smile formed on Legs, smirks on Fenny and Mumbles.

The core three holding their breath, Dennis noticed Coach

Jack's tongue slipping out a bit, a tell-tale sign that some wayward muse was about to take charge.

"And your name is?" his coach asked.

"Phil Voit, uncle to one Mark Voit, your team captain last year, whose father, my brother, died three summers ago when Mark was a freshman and ran JV."

"Yes, I was sorry to hear that."

"So sorry that not so much as a card was sent to the family! A community of runners, you say? Is that why last fall you left Mark in upstate Watkins Glen after the state race?"

"Hey, buddy, your nephew, for no good reason dropped out of the race. As for me leaving him behind, he went missing in action. We searched for him. I assumed he left with the Mepham High team."

"You assumed wrong. I had to drive up and pick him up. It was after dark when I got there."

To that, Coach Jack started rubbing his forehead. Dennis hoped the delay meant that his coach was merely gauging tone before offering up a gracious apology.

"Sure, Mr. Phil Voit, I'll give you my two cents. But, dammit, we have races to run tonight. I made Mark captain because over his junior year, all the hard work of his first three years paid off. As for this past season, only he knows why his times dropped off. Or why he dropped out at state. So," said Coach Jack heading for the door, "I'll let Captain Dennis Hurley field any other questions you have. I've got this year's first Sitting Bull Run to prepare for."

Once the door slammed shut, Mark's uncle said, "So, Dennis Hurley, I see you're this season's lapdog. I mean, we all know how Jack Hogan abuses his runners. Calling Adam Feltman a hebe with fuzzy hair. And George Legstaff, a lazy bastard. And then there's his leaving James Fennessy behind in the dark after a bad practice at Wading River Park. Ain't that right, Fennessy?"

A slight smile emerging on Fenny, he slumped back and crossed his arms behind his head.

"See, everyone," Mark's uncle said, "See what I'm saying about everyone's hero, Mr. Jack Hogan?"

William Flanagan shot up, his face burning red. "Hey, Mister, you don't know the half of it. Adam Feltman and his fuzzy hair loves Coach Jack. And Coach Jack loves him back. He loves us all. Hell, you ever seen Coach bust his ass for us in every possible way? Well, I have. As for Legs and Fenny, both deserve more than a kick in the nuts for the stunts they pull. But still Coach Jack breaks his back to make each of them better runners. To make all of us better runners. As for your nephew, he was a tender prima donna who couldn't take the heat. Period!"

"What William means," said Dennis, springing to his feet.

But he didn't know what to say. It took a father to step forward and rescue him.

"Hey, all, my oldest son Andrew ran for Coach Jack, who gave him a few well-deserved tongue lashings. To this day, Andrew says that if it wasn't for Coach Jack, he wouldn't have gotten through the ROTC at Manhattan College. That's why my youngest son is here tonight."

"So, everyone," said Dennis finding his voice, "judge for yourself these next four Tuesdays. But as captain, and I'm probably biased, I know Coach Jack bleeds for us each and every day. So how about you all get up here and register your sons?"

This time, lines formed at the table, and soon the race director, as he did each summer, bullhorned directions that included following the cones and grabbing one's prize at the end of the race. "And make sure that at the turn-around point, each of you taps the plaque and shouts, Sitting Bull!"

The three races that evening went off without a hitch. The Pee Wee division, ages 7-8, saw many of the participants in a stop-and-go mode, with a parent beside them. Most participants in Junior Bantam, ages 9-10, ran the whole way, the fathers of the two top boys from Syosset given vouchers for the following week. The 11-

12 aged Bantams featured a large pack fighting desperately to the very end.

WITH DUSK EMERGING and Coach Jack talking with the last of the fathers, the core three were charged with picking up the cones. Meanwhile, over at the bungalow, Vinnie sat on a crate by his bedroom window. Opposite him, Liz sat in a chair. The room was filled with the familiar haze of pot smoke.

"See those three out there," said Vinnie.

"Yeah, Vin, what about them?"

"Those are the three who brought that drunk chick home that night. And who I scared the shit out of on my Harley."

"You what?"

"I was out for a ride with the guys on Old Montauk. Those three were running on the shoulder. They had to jump out of the way, and quick."

"Not smart, Vin."

"No harm, no foul."

"Vin?"

"Yes, Liz?"

"It's been a long day. Worked my ass off unloading boxes. How about a back rubby-dub-dub?"

"Now we're talking."

DENNIS LIE IN BED that night peering across the room at the big bold eyes before posing a question. "Say, Pre, what'd you think of Coach Jack's dog and pony show today in front of all those parents?"

Then Dennis thought, Not only getting beat up by Voit's uncle, but also how he conveniently omitted his ballbuster workouts. For example, take Coach Jack having us do thirty minutes of back-and-forth bumrushes in the sand. Or running north to south in creek water for an hour. Or when we fartlek up and down the

Rocky Point hill until we croak. Huh, Pre, what do you think? But knowing you, you'd love Coach Jack's ballbusters! If anyone loves the taste of death, it's you.

As the month of June wore on, Dennis was pleased that he didn't have to get after Legs, Fenny, or Mumbles to run before the weight sessions at the Feltman's. Yes, the three sometimes missed a weekend run. And Dennis didn't feel bad at fudging the numbers a bit when his coach called to check up. One Sunday night the captain even picked up the phone and called Coach Jack to brag about the run they did that day to Devil's Horn on the north shore.

"Damn, Dennis, how many miles is that round trip?"

"Little under sixteen."

"Shit, think I'm gonna head out for a bar burger and toast the chief."

"Don't forget to ask for an extra pickle, Coach."

"You betcha. And Dennis?"

"Yes?"

"Stay the course. The team needs you. I need you."

13

"Hey, like I've been telling you two," said Peter with his thumb out on the shoulder of Ocean Parkway, "tonight's a piece of cake. After my cousin lets us slip in through the side gate, we'll stay for just one set of songs and then return to my tent for a night of poker."

Just yards away, and sitting on the shoulder, Dennis and William barely heard their friend's words. They were too busy wondering if a car would ever pull over and give them a lift to the Neil Young concert at the Guy Lombardo Beach Theater five miles down the road. While sleepovers in the Walker's 20 X 16 backyard tent was something the three boys enjoyed during previous summers, William and Dennis tonight were leery about Peter's concert idea, feeling it smacked of trouble. But seeing that it was now the final week of June with nary a Peter Walker debacle of late, and since it had been Peter who was always pushing for weekend runs to the north shore trails, they figured they owed him for keeping the team on track.

Relieved to see a Volkswagen van finally pull over, the boys hopped in. The driver not much later dropped them off across from the theater, a tinny Neil Young already melting the sky. But on the way to the venue's side door, Peter detoured to the concession stand where unattended cases of beer, to be sold at intermission, stood beside a pallet of bagged ice. Without batting an eye, he grabbed an empty box and put two six packs in it, topped off with a bag of ice. He absconded with the load and headed across Ocean Parkway for the beach, his dazed friends trailing.

"Well," Peter said as they mounted a dune, "guess the concert will have to wait. Time to body surf." The pronouncement was capped off with his signature metallic laugh that showed back teeth. William was about to cry foul. But like Dennis, a smile emerged on him as he noticed huge waves forming in smooth precision and crashing the shore. A second set of waves came. The two followed Peter down the dune's bank and onto the beach sand. Not far along Peter stopped to pour the ice over the beer.

"Wadda you think? Humming cold beer in no time!"

He tore off his shirt and jeans, nearly falling over as he kicked them off. Finally, his briefs, whose elastic band he stretched like a rubber band and shot into the air. With powerfully loping strides, he ran over the sand and dove into the water.

"Son of a bitch, Denny! You see that?" said William, stabbed with excitement. "That fucker does it to me every time."

He stripped down and began his own dash to the water.

Dennis was next, and after diving in and surfacing chest high, he was having trouble planting his feet when the straight-armed Peter came screaming in on a wave, "Watchouuuutttttt!" The two collided, the wave tumbling them in like broken wheels. Dennis skidded along the sand, and as he gasped for breath on all fours, he saw that Peter had somehow landed on his feet next to him and was already turning back for more.

"C'mon, Denny Boy! Time to attack."

Dennis smacked an ear to dislodge the sand, dove back in, the three boys catching wave after wave.

But soon, with dusk settling in, they returned to the sand and got dressed.

"We better think about hitching a ride back to Bellport," William said.

"Yeah," Dennis agreed. "To that tent of yours, Peter. I plan to win big money."

"Damn," yelled Peter as he served up an impressive yawn and opened a beer. "I thought we were sleeping in William's yard. At least, that's what I told my mom."

Only then did the other two understand that they had once again been duped by the wily one, who went on to add, "Well, if my mom thinks I'm at your house, and both of your parents think you're at my house, we have nowhere to go but here. Besides, my dad's out of town. This time in some podunk town in Missouri. Or is it Alabamy?"

The metallic laugh.

Dennis and William looked like travelers caught in a downpour.

"Time to start a fire," Peter declared, and after washed-up wood was scavenged at the base of the dunes, he flicked a cigarette lighter magically retrieved from his pants pocket. With the flames growing, William and Dennis at first said no to the beer. But as the water turned a drab olive, they acquiesced.

Peter's chatter soon dropping off, the sun's fuzzy orange light disappeared under the horizon. With darkness upon them, the boys felt the whole force of the ocean out there. At one point Peter leaned over, blew into the fire, and fanned its red center.

"You know," he said, his feet grinding the sand, "I sometimes push the envelope. But most of the time, and I tells meself this when I'm all cooped up at home, I simply likes to be with Denny O'Hurley and Wee Willy Flanagan. Especially when we are banging out a monster pace in some big race, coming by the mile and ready to slow burn, ready to pick off one runner after another." Peter collapsed a beer can with a two-handed squeeze and looked up at the stars. "Yeah, a damned gorgeous night. I love it. I love it all."

"I hate to rain on your parade, Petey Walker," said William. "But formal practice starts up pretty quick."

"Yeah," added Dennis, "like next Monday when the dead period ends."

Peter scooped up a handful of sand and blasted the fire with it. "Damn Jack Hogan and his fucking orange cones. Stealing the summer right out from under my nose."

"I grant you that," William said. "Coach is one big hemorrhoid up my ass. But he's going to get us a state title."

"That he is," from Dennis.

"Now that I think of it," Peter said, "I'd do anything to win state."

Again the boys went silent, the surf sounding like it was miles away.

"Hey," Dennis said, "Coach called me to remind everyone to bring their dedication paper to the sacrifice ceremony. Which takes place right before the time trial." The reference was to the first day of formal practice on July 1st, when tradition called for each varsity runner to meet at the plaque and burn a piece of paper with the name of the person to whom he will dedicate the season, that followed by the first of three mile time trials over the season.

"By the way," Peter added, "gonna kick ass in the time trial. You wait and see."

From there, they turned to dissecting the teams who represented the main obstacles to a state championship, mainly Syracuse Central and Albany Hamilton.

The three soon falling asleep, Dennis awoke sometime later to an enormous starlit sky that dwarfed the mass of water. A slight wind, sounding like so many harmless rumors, drove thin dark clouds across the moon. He lifted his head briefly to see his two friends sleeping soundly. When he next awoke, a dawn fog had settled on the water.

He needed to piss.

So he climbed up on a dune, and like a wild dog he took aim

at a monster weed, that followed by a running jump off the dune, his hands paddling the air as he hit the sand. He rolled over and sat up. He saw a faint light atop the ocean's eastern horizon. He sat a while longer and soon took in the sun's brassy streaks hitting the water, the breakers gurgling whitewash.

BACK AT ST. THERESA'S, the small audience of nuns watched Monsignor Cassidy conclude early Mass with a slow solemn bow to the Crucifix high above the altar. From there he disappeared into the sacristy and consumed the unused communion hosts, which for him always felt like scraps of sticky paper on the tongue, dry and indissoluble. Not even gulps of red wine could fully rinse away the yeasty aftertaste. The pastor was always anxious to get back to the rectory for morning coffee. And after leaving the church that morning, he was well on his way to doing just that when he heard voices fast approaching. At first, he didn't know that the voices were those of the three pie-eyed beach travelers on their way home, now heading for the path. To avoid talking with whomever it was, Cassidy ducked behind a large fern. He would wait for them to pass before he went inside.

The boys now just yards from the hidden pastor, Peter stopped and looked up at the rectory. "I often wonder if any lonely nuns with good old fashioned you-know-what on their minds have ever slipped inside for a romp."

As Dennis and William laughed and smacked Peter on the back, the three resumed the trek home. The pastor stepped out. His eyes two knives, he stared the boys down before heading inside. Once back in his office swivel, he spun around for a further view of the three miscreants, now skirting the Great Lawn. His concentration remained unbroken even as Mrs. Wooten strolled in with the coffee tray and the *Bellport Citizen*.

"Good morning, Monsignor. Coffee's piping hot."

Still locked in on the boys, he said nothing as he watched them wrestling each other near a Great Lawn flower bed, a sprinkler system spraying them. As one escaped, the other two grabbed him, all three again going to the ground.

The secretary giggled.

"Mrs. Wooten finds that funny?"

"Oh, Monsignor, it's just that some years ago I caught those same three. Peter Walker, a perpetual motion machine. William Flanagan, a scrappy child with a foul mouth and temper. And Dennis Hurley, well, he's too quiet for my taste and he-"

"Mrs. Wooten! You caught those three doing what?"

The boys, now mud-splotched and dripping wet, intensified the wrestling match.

"During a rainstorm, Monsignor, romping in this terrible mud fight on the parish's north playground. After that, I called them the three little pigs." She pointed at them. "See, it still rings true today."

"Clever, Mrs. Wooten. Clever."

As she laid down saucer and cup and poured the coffee, they both saw Father Ken Garland steer his car into the parish and slow down for a friendly wave to Sister Winifred, the elderly school librarian known as the Prune. She rarely missed a morning and afternoon stroll about the grounds. It was then that Father Ken noticed the three boys entangled near a flower bed. He pressed a heavy foot to the brake, the car stopping abruptly.

Unable to hear the proceedings through the glass of Monsignor's bay window, both pastor and secretary had to rely on body language.

"Hey, you three!" yelled Father Ken from inside the car. Dripping mud, the boys unraveled themselves and stood. "Do you know that you're tearing up the Great Lawn?" The three looked at each other with mocking shrugs, which further angered the priest. "How would you like me to report you to Sister Rosaleen?"

When no answers came, Father Ken exhaled. The aggravation

not worth it, he drove away, the retreat emboldening Peter to call out, "Hey, Doughboy, honk if you love Jesus!"

Neither the priest nor the Prune heard the brazen remark.

Judging by the cocky posture of the Walker boy, Cassidy presumed the three boys had given his assistant lip. He began mulling over whether he should sic Sister Rosaleen on them. They were, after all, a nuisance going as far back as he could remember, and often after the sun went down. First, it was the Hurley boy stealing into the church for a glimpse of Mulski in his casket. Then the three of them getting caught in the grade school gym playing basketball at two in the morning. The manager of the Bellport Country Club once called to report that the three, late at night, had been skinny dipping in the club pool. As Cassidy was thinking this over, his attention was drawn to a late-twentyish woman in a slinky outfit, cigarette in hand, who passed the three boys on her way onto the grounds.

"That, Monsignor" Mrs. Wooten said, "is Vincent Malagati's girlfriend."

"But the boy's married!"

"Her name's Elizabeth Pearce. A grade school student here, but only for a few years."

"How does Mrs. Wooten know all these things?"

"So, Vincent, upon returning to Bellport last year, after leaving his wife and children behind in Florida, recently reeled in this Pearce woman. She lives just off Old Montauk Highway and works at a downtown clothing store. Apparently without a car, she uses the path to travel to the bungalow. Where she sometimes—"

"Thank you, Mrs. Wooten."

"In fact, she was here at the rectory just last week."

"She was where?"

Vinnie, in his denim vest, came outside. Liz Pearce joining him, he kissed her before the two mounted his Harley and took off.

"Vincent met with Father Ken. Something about working up another war story, this one for the *New York Times*."

"Father Ken's a buffoon! And is Charlie aware that his son is living in sin?"

"I'm sure he knows." And as she turned to leave, "Monsignor, you have quite a line-up today."

"Oh?"

"Breakfast at nine with Mr. Barnes from the bank. At the Country Club."

"And?"

"Father Ken would like to meet at eleven. To discuss his blueprints for a new prayer garden."

"I thought our beloved Casimir Mulski, before he stepped out, put that crazy notion to bed."

"And at one, there's Sisters Immaculata and Mary Gonzaga. They are not at all happy about their transfer orders."

"Do offer my apologies to Father Ken and the good sisters."

"And don't forget about the KOC black tie tomorrow night. It's in your honor, you know. To celebrate the nomination."

"Thank you, my dear woman."

Following the sprinkler brawl, the three boys washed the mud off in the creek as best they could before detouring to Oscar's Deli for a buttered roll and juice. After passing the Harley out front on its kickstand, they found Vinnie Malagati and his girlfriend waiting on an old woman at the counter who was digging through her pocketbook for money.

"C'mon, lady," Vinnie called up to her. "It can't be that hard to pick coins out of that crusty purse of yours."

William didn't like the remark. "Hey, pinhead, cool it."

"And who the fuck are you?" said Vinnie turning around for a closer look. "Hey, I remember you and you and you! That drunk girl on the couch. That was wild. And playing in the mud, I see."

Dennis tugged William's arm, indicating it was time to leave before Vinnie got more specific about the Cindy McGallister incident in front of the small crowd.

William wouldn't budge. "Listen, asshole, we were helping her."

The outraged Vinnie absorbing the insult, his girlfriend whispered to him, "C'mon Vin, we don't need any trouble."

Vinnie pulled open his denim vest, displaying a sheathed knife.

Liz again tugged on Vinnie, who shot one more look at William before leaving.

When Dennis got home from the deli, he found a note from his parents. They had taken Christine to finish up clothes shopping for college. She was being dropped off at the Stonybrook University dorm the following week. Relieved that he would not have to explain the mud stains still on him, he went upstairs and showered. He collapsed onto his bed and fell into a deep sleep, not to stir again until awakened a few hours later by the soft whacks of Mr. Gulla's nine iron out on the field.

After the deli, Vinnie and Liz took a long bike drive out to Montauk Point. On the way back they stopped at the American Legion, where after drinking beer and eating happy hour spareribs out of tins, they turned to the pool table.

"Hey, Vin," said Liz racking up the balls, "you got to cool it with that knife of yours."

"You think so?"

"I know so."

"Why doesn't Miss Smarty Pants just break the fucking balls?"

"We got a good thing going. Don't want to screw things up. Remember what you told me, the priest's gonna get you a cushy custodian's job in Port Washington."

"Not to mention some speaking gigs about the war."

With more than a tad of sarcasm, Liz said, "You mean, your POW experience?"

"Hey, don't start that shit again!" He said that yanking up his muscle shirt to show a long, jagged scar along his stomach. "In case you forgot, got this in the Quang Tri province when I got captured along with my buddies. A guke, just for the hell of it, goes down the line and slashes each of us with his bayonet. Nothing we could do. And what did I get for it after I escaped? A shitload of stitches and some lousy medal."

"That lousy medal's called the Purple Heart. And technically you weren't a POW because you escaped before they got you to a camp. Right? I mean that's what you told me when we first met. That's not what the locals read in that newspaper story."

"I never came out and told that reporter guy that I was a prisoner of war. I just said that I got captured and escaped. And that's what Father Ken wants me to say in my speech at the picnic."

"I'm only saying, Vin, that you also might want to cool it with the knife as well as the war stuff."

"Hey! Break the goddam balls!"

Some hours later, the sun low in the sky, the old custodian finished up his parish work and gestured to Rosa to jump into the bed of his truck. He drove the short distance to his place, where under the carport he parked beside his son's motorcycle. He went around back. While checking the chlorine level of his above-ground pool, he noticed a coat of pollen had blanketed his backyard grotto statues of St. Francis of Assisi and flock of animals, the saint some four-feet tall, his fauna half that. He grabbed the hose, and as he sprayed the statues clean, he watched a scruffy teen approach and knock on the back storm door. The door opened, Vincent passing along a small bag in exchange for money.

As the teen scuttled away, the old custodian felt a rumbling in his head. He knew what had just transpired. And he knew what he should do. But he felt powerless. He looked up and caught the girlfriend, smoking a cigarette and staring down at him from his son's bedroom window. A few minutes later, she came out the back door. The old man watched her pass through the gate and head for Main Street.

14

It was getting late, going on ten, when Coach Jack left the cross-country office to drive over to the post office and slide the entries for the Jersey Shore Invitational into the drop box. From there he headed over to Chief's, and grabbing his briefcase, he got out just as rain started. Hustling inside, he took a bar stool at the far end, a few over from Joe Mahoney, a handsome patron with a floating Adam's apple who some years back sold his Kodak patent for a bundle of money, and who, now, was distracted by the two broads sitting apart from each other at the bar. At the opposite end was Kerry Masterson, once taken home and routed by Joe. She looked bored, the fingers of one hand splayed on a cheek bone. She took a deep drag and exhaled the smoke in streams that alternated nose and mouth. Midway down the bar sat Angela Russo, the owner of Porter Paints. Tonight she wore a scalding hot black blouse-and-skirt combo that got Coach Jack wishing he was young again. Kerry and Angela would compete for drinks once late-night regulars trickled in.

As Billy Boyce laid a beer down in front of the coach, he said raising his voice, "Looks like Joe here, Jack, plans on playing footsie tonight with one of the two gals."

Hearing his name, Joe broke out of the spell. "You were saying, Billy?"

"Was just wondering if you are ready for another Budweiser?"

"Why, yes, and Jack's drink is on me."

"Thanks, Joe," said Coach Jack as he reached into his briefcase for a pad and pen.

"That team of yours again, Jack?" asked Joe.

"What else?"

"Can I help?"

"Perhaps. At summer's end each year, I always take my team to a clambake out in Amagansett, to reward them for a tough few months of training. I want something a little more robust this year. But I'm out of ideas."

"A fucking brothel, Jack," Joe suggested. "Your kids will love you for life."

"Hey, don't think that hasn't crossed my mind."

"The date?"

"Last Friday in August. Day before the parish picnic."

"Why not take them out to the Montauk Point Festival. Right on the water."

"You ever been?"

"Go every year. Got food trucks, not to mention that Friday morning is the women's mini triathlon. You'll have to hose down your boys after that event."

"You know what, Joe, Montauk is a hop, skip, and a jump. We could get out there early and be back in time for the tent."

"Tent?"

"Me and some Elks always put up the picnic tent the day before."

"Jack, you're a fucking animal. I don't know how you keep up with it all. And by the way, how's that team of yours getting along?"

"Joe," cried Billy Boyce, "don't you read the papers? Jack's got a top-ranked team."

"What I meant, Jack, is how's the training been coming along?"

"Pretty well. But we're still in the dead period. Only get to see them during the Sitting Bull series when they lend a hand."

"You know, Jack, I sometimes take my Sunday dinners on the deck at the country club. I see the same three kids of yours running along the beach all the time."

"The core three is what I call them. Hurley, Flanagan, and Walker. Can you guys can keep a secret?"

"Of course," Billy said.

"I've been coaching for some fifteen years now and have had some good kids. Really good kids. But those three, I love those fuckers. They run like I did back in the day."

"How's that?"

"It's complicated, Joe. Would take half the night."

"The short version, then."

After a gulp of beer, Coach Jack said, "See, I had this bad habit back in high school of going out way too fast in races. Always paid for it. My coach pulled me aside and told me that I might want to try going out at an easier clip, then surge like a wild rabbit."

"How'd it work for you?"

"Initially, hell on wheels. But over time I got good at it, winning myself some big races. I've made it my team's racing strategy, which I've nicknamed slow burn. Anyway, my core three have made an art form of it."

"I like it, Jack," said Joe slapping the bar. "In fact, I like it so much that I'm gonna mosey on down the bar and see if either of our two lovely ladies is interested in a slow burn."

"You do that, Joe. But remember it involves a sustained surge."

Over the next half hour, Coach Jack fixed his concentration on his notebook where he brainstormed the week's workouts. While he was doing that, the front door opened and in walked Vinnie Malagati and the gorilla. Sopping wet, they had pulled into Chief's on their Harleys to escape the rain.

At first Vinnie's rain-soaked eyes stared wildly around, his right hand jumping out in front of him like one finding his way through the pitch black. He wiped rain off his face. He refocused on the gleam of amber-filled liquor bottles that stood in immaculate rows against the beveled mirror.

"Hey!" he called out, his voice slurring somewhat, "beer and a chaser for me and my friend." Seeing Kerry at bar's end, "And a drink for that lovely girl." With that, Angela looked over her shoulder at Vinnie, who added, "And definitely her, too."

Billy Boyce first winked at Coach Jack as if to say, pardon me while I take care of business.

"Gentlemen, you two deserve a little something for dancing in the rain. But given that you've had too much to drink, I must ask the both of you to leave."

"Hey," replied Vinnie, "it's cats and dogs out there. The drinks! Now!"

"Yeah," said the gorilla. "Now!"

"You know, you boys might want to try Top Hat over on Ingram Drive. They sometimes look the other way."

Vinnie, with eyes slit like razors, understood what was happening. But he wasn't about to be swept out the door like a water rat. "The fucking drinks, Mister!"

"This is the last time I am going to ask you to leave."

"And what are you going to do if we don't? Huh?" Vinnie stepped forward. "And what's to say if we are forced to protect ourselves?"

No sooner had Vinnie made the threat than Billy Boyce hit a button under the counter that resulted in a loud ringing bell. Scuffling was heard above before the upstairs tenants came down. One at a time they appeared, each sporting a disgruntled look. One guy in briefs held a baseball bat. Another in a Suffolk County police uniform wielded a gun. The biggest of the three wore a bathrobe, a badge in one hand, a tire iron brandished in the other.

"Now," Billy Boyce said, "you boys can leave peacefully. Or you can get tossed out on your ears. And it won't be pretty."

Vinnie grinned cagily, and as he looked around to buy time,

he recognized Jack Hogan. "Hey! You're that coach guy, from the parish. You can vouch for me."

Billy Boyce said, "Game's over. Time to leave."

Vinnie would not take his eyes off Jack Hogan. "Go ahead, Coach, tell them who I am. That Charlie Malagati's my old man."

"Son," Coach Jack replied, "think Top Hat. They will serve you there."

"Shit, I even live with him on the parish grounds."

The guy with the baseball bat stepped up, his free hand grabbing Vinnie to move him along. The writhing Vinnie ripped away. "Don't touch me." But the cop in the bathrobe poked Vinnie with the tire iron, helping him out.

The gorilla looked as if he was about to take a swing. A jab in the stomach with the baseball bat disabused him of that notion.

No sooner were they out the door than Billy Boyce turned to Coach Jack. "I think I read about that asshole in the newspaper. A prisoner of war. You know anything about that, Jack?"

"Only that Garland was behind it. Nothing more."

The dust having settled, the jukebox in full swing, Joe Mahoney now stood next to Angela Russo at the bar. "Hey, Jack, this young lady here wants to know how you teach that coaching strategy to your runners?"

Coach Jack was about to reply. But Angela turned on her stool, and scavenging her purse for a cigarette lighter, she turned to stand when her legs fell out of her black skirt. He felt the irritable thud of longing. Angela looked up at him, her large red mouth issuing a playful scowl. He responded with a tip of the head at a jaunty angle, followed by a gulping draw. That seemed to give him the strength to indulge one more friendly leer as she lit her cigarette. With Joe at her side, she roamed over to the jukebox and plugged it with more coins.

"Huh, Jack," Joe said, "tell Angela here how you get your runners to buy into that slow burn thing?"

"I beat it into them, Angela, that's how."

Then it came, June 30th, the last day of the dead period. For Coach Jack that meant the promised land was less than twenty-four hours away. For Dennis, it meant his role as Captain Ahab was about to kick into high gear. Returning home from the final weight-training session at the Feltman's, he saw two men unloading a large hutch off a truck. His mother stood beside Alice Crimmins, who was supervising the workers. Dennis avoided them, and once inside, he found his father staring out the kitchen window.

"Yet another damn piece of old wood, Dennis, that your mother, at the behest of Alice of Wonderland, bought at some antique shop out east."

"Where's Mom going to put it?"

"Who knows? By the way, how'd it go over at the Feltman's today?"

"Good, except that we decided to skip the afternoon run, it being so hot. William and Peter and I are gonna do a night run to the Preserve."

"Not a bad idea."

"Followed by a slice at Sal's."

"Last night of freedom?"

"Yeah, Coach officially takes over tomorrow. Starting with the mile time trial."

The three boys met as planned that night, and on the return trip from the Preserve, Peter picked up the pace, which the three maintained onto Old Montauk and along the path.

"I feel good," said Peter. "How about you guys?"

"Me, too," said William.

Dennis added, "Hope we all feel this good...at tomorrow's time trial."

"Just for the heck of it," Peter added, "I'm thinking a 61 first quarter."

"Suicide," said William.

"Yeah," said Peter surging ahead, "but it will scare the shit out of Adam...and here's a preview," now shouting over his shoulder, "of how...I'm gonna leave...you two in the dust tomorrow."

William and Dennis promptly caught up to him, both yanking him by his shorts, and going right by him.

"Who's the Mary Jane now," William cried out.

"Let's keep this up through the parish," Dennis called out as they passed the plaque, each tapping the chief. "All the way to Sal's."

Which they were doing when Peter abruptly stopped as they entered the parish grounds. He bent over, hands on knees, catching his breath.

"What's wrong?" asked Dennis, stopping along with William, sweat pouring off each of them.

"It's damn hot out here," Peter replied. "That's what's wrong."

"And?" William asked.

Peter pointed in the direction of the Malagati's rear yard. "And you see that pool over there, sitting all lonely like?"

"Oh no!" said William.

"The old man, Peter!" Dennis added. "And Vinnie! And the dog!"

"And a little skinny dipping on a hot summer night. We deserve it. All the work we've put in." And starting for the bungalow, "But I'm already seeing you two ain't got what it takes."

William gave Dennis a look as if to say, we have no choice but to make sure the asshole doesn't blow up the universe.

Their trainers scuffling the pavement, they passed right by the convent. Peter carefully raised the latch and pushed open the wooden gate for his two friends to pass through. The gate creaked going back.

"See," whispered Peter, nodding at the carport. "No Harley. Vinnie's off with that Liz chick. Just the old man sawing logs in there. As for the pooch, it's anyone's guess."

The pool's filter humming in the background, the three boys

headed past the dark bungalow to the grotto, where St. Francis and his animals stood.

"I wonder," Peter said kicking off his trainers and throwing his clothes over the outstretched arm of the saint, "why Malagati keeps a goddam pool no one uses, like he's gonna throw a big party or something." Leapfrogging in, he submerged, that followed by a hard crunching sound as his feet pushed off the pool wall. His dark figure torpedoed to the other side where he resurfaced with an immense smile. Again, he went under and across.

"C'mon, you pansies," he said coming up for air. "Strip down and get in!" His two friends returned wary looks. "Besides, if anyone's awake, there'd be a light on. The dog would be barking like crazy."

The guarantee aside, Dennis knew the house's first-floor layout from his paperboy days. He pictured Mr. Malagati lying awake, whispering strategy to Rosa, ready to strike.

"C'mon, fellas, in!"

"Can't fucking believe this," said William as he undressed, clothes tossed over a concrete wolf. Dennis looked again at the bungalow before following suit.

Once in the water, Dennis and William waded, their palms lightly massaging the surface as they watched Peter, a whale in ocean frolic, go back and forth, his white buttocks bobbing along the way. Soon the two forgot themselves and moved more freely about the pool.

"Would you take a look up there!" said Peter, who pointed out a few different constellations, describing them as grand celestial events. It was moments like this that Dennis felt some sacred well inside of his friend was being filled, which once full would set the galaxies on paths of endless cavorting.

Peter mentioned the upcoming Staten Island meet. "Coach Jack told me all about the course's bad-boy hill right before the water tower. Well, I'm gonna crush that hill. And speaking of crushing it, you two going out with me in 61 at tomorrow's time trial, cruising to a 4:25 mile? And scaring the shit out of Adam in the process?"

"I like the 4:25 business," said William. "But Ole Jack will go berserk if we go out any faster than 65."

"Say," said Peter, "how about an underwater contest?"

The three going under, William held his breath the longest. Peter wanted a rematch. Yet about to submerge, they heard car doors slam over at the convent as a few nuns were being dropped off.

"Time to go, Peter!" whispered Dennis.

"Damn! Just getting warmed up."

"Now!" said William.

All three jumped out, Peter the first to grab his clothes. But his shirt snagged the saint's hand, sending the statue crashing to the ground. The right arm, severed at the shoulder, rolled some before stopping.

"Shit!" Peter cried. "Wadda we do?"

"We fucking bolt!" said William. "That's what we do."

As they moved to do just that, however, there stood Mr. Malagati, just a few feet from them. An apparition with white curving teeth, he held a long butcher's knife out in front of him. The weapon moved in Dennis' direction until its point poked his stomach.

Peter moved, the knife going to him in the same way.

Then, to William.

"You boys. Again." The knife pointed at the fallen saint, "Some men killa for their property. You know?"

"Yes," said Dennis, his two friends eking the same.

"Now, take ass outta here. Go!"

Clothes and trainers slapped back on, the boys hotfooted it like the wind, streaking over parish grounds and the path. They stopped at the plaque to catch their breath. William cursed wildly, as if a death sentence had been handed down. "Fucking Peter, you happy now?"

"Just a little hiccup, that's all."

"You think the old man's gonna overlook our busting up the saint?"

"Hey," Dennis said, "why don't we go back to the bungalow? Apologize. Tell him that we'll pay to have it fixed."

"Not a chance," said William. "Did you see that knife?"

"William's right," Peter added. "Besides, as Legs would say, Malagati's a magician who can fix anything."

15

July on Long Island is little more than the summer deepening into itself through a series of identical cycles. Each cycle begins with a hot sun that lingers for days, followed by a thick humidity that hangs about before there comes a protracted rain, not torrential, but slow and steady, on most days lasting into the afternoon. When the rain stops, water seeps through the leaves, and the air grows hot and muggy. The sun then burns away the moisture, the field's grass magically higher. For Dennis, the process always aroused a fullness that gladdened his heart. But when he awoke to the flat dawn light that first day of July, his mood was anything but high. His mind flashed to the saint, prone on the ground, its severed arm creating a divot in the lawn. Dennis' eyes traveled along the ceiling's swirled plaster over to the grey window. The curtains swelled and twisted about. He waited for a breeze to skim his face. It didn't, so he rolled over and looked at the alarm clock. 6:42 a.m. He tossed some before falling back to sleep.

A good hour later, the eastern sky now filling with light, Charlie Malagati awoke in a sofa chair. He barely slept a wink. Those same three boys, he growled to himself, who were tangled up with the drunk McGallister girl. They were given a break then. The girl's father wanted that.

"No break now," the old custodian muttered, "No, not now."

He looked at the clock. It was approaching eight, which meant that early Mass was over and the pastor was back in his office. The old man whistled to Rosa, who followed him out to the truck and jumped in the cab for the short ride over to the rectory.

The statue incident was relayed to Monsignor Cassidy.

"Okay, Charlie, thanks for bringing this to my attention. The boys will be punished. You can count on that. But did you call the police?"

"No."

"Which is probably wise. I would ask that you not breathe a word about this to anyone. Such matters call for discretion."

"Yes, Monsignor."

"Let me give the situation some thought. I'll get back to you. And just for my own information, can you somehow reattach the arm?"

"I try."

"Do try, if only to bring tranquility back to the grotto."

Once his custodian was gone, an angry Cassidy banged his desk. "Those three!"

In the old days, such a stunt by parish hooligans would lead to his phoning Sister Rosaleen and hinting at expulsion. From the sidelines, he'd watch the principal set into motion a zealous prosecution. How sweet it would be this time to watch the three little pigs sent into exile. But, and this Cassidy knew from experience, the expulsion of athletes from a star team would send shock waves, causing the newspapers to sic their lapdogs. A few years back, the *Long Island Press* had reporters dig their noses into the expulsion of the Perkins boy, the school's state tennis champ, after he stole Sister Eileen O'Shea's gradebook. A public spectacle was the last thing the pastor now wanted, especially with the archbishop coming out the next night for another black tie event, this time at the Southampton University ballroom.

But Christ, Cassidy thought, I simply cannot let those three go scot-free.

As he spun around in his swivel chair, he spotted Jack Hogan putting down orange cones. A grin emerging, the pastor turned back to his desk and moved a few items a centimeter or two, the slight repositioning confirming for him the efficacy of the delicious strategy he had just stumbled upon. A guessing-game ploy that would punish Hogan as well as the boys.

"Mrs. Wooten," he said tapping a phone line. "Please come to my office."

After he told his secretary what had transpired at the Malagati's, he told her that he wanted her not only to summon the boys to his office immediately, but also to inform the principal of the vandalism. "Do tell Sister Rosaleen, however, that for now I simply want the boys to stew. Later this fall, when the time is right, we will settle the score with those three."

"Oh, Monsignor, but you must know that Sister Rosaleen will insist on something right away."

"Mrs. Wooten!"

"Yes, Monsignor, I'll let Sister know."

CATHERINE HURLEY called up the stairs a second time. "Dennis, did you hear me? The rectory! The pastor wants to see you now!"

He winced. The old man had contacted the pastor.

"Dennis!"

"Here I come."

He dressed and went below where he was met by the angry brows of his father. "Who would have thunk, Dennis, late night training?"

"Tipping statues, honestly?" his mother added. "As if pool hopping isn't bad enough."

When Dennis reached the parish grounds, he saw Coach Jack

pulling his wagon with cones in the direction of the Sitting Bull course.

Shit, he's already setting up for the time trial this afternoon.

Dennis then looked over at the Malagati yard, the saint and his arm gone. He continued on, his two friends found waiting in front of the rectory.

"Denny," said William, "our goose is cooked."

Mrs. Wooten walked them down to the hallway bench, her only words, "It would be in your best interest to remain perfectly quiet."

Once seated, they were greeted by a portrait on the opposite wall, Mulski sneering back, his tiny eyes blazing above a pinched nose.

The wait was considerable. William continued to mutter outrage, and when Mrs. Wooten finally appeared and ushered them into the office, he whispered to both his friends, "Play dumb. Real dumb."

Cassidy stood behind his desk, sipping coffee and gazing out at the grounds. Mrs. Wooten lined the three up and left. The pastor first placed saucer and cup on the desk before lowering into the swivel. "Boys, as I'm sure you know, only serious business would have compelled me to summon you. And for your edification, I'll put things as plainly as I can." He paused to mold a small round opening with his mouth the size of a pea, a low whistle escaping. It was as if he had just discovered the act, and liking it, he looked down as if he could see his breath. His pale blue eyes jumped in the boys' direction, startling them, making everything in the room seem to expand. For the briefest of moments, Dennis saw how Cassidy had made an art form of terrorizing visitors.

"Now," the pastor began, "two crimes stand front and center. Vandalism as well as trespassing, though that shouldn't surprise me given your penchant for wreaking havoc on the parish grounds during the nighttime hours. In fact, you three-"

"Monsignor," interrupted Peter who thought a frontal assault of honesty was their best bet. "We run on the parish path at night all the time! You know, with the state championship just a few months away."

William lowered his head, sure that Peter was fucking things up and good.

"Anyway," Peter added, "we were on our way back from a barn-burner of a run. We were hot. As in sweating bullets hot. A swim seemed just the ticket. The statue was a pure accident."

"Thank you, Mr. Walker," said Cassidy trying to suppress incredulity over the brazen outburst. He turned to Dennis. "How about our Hall of Fame altar boy?"

"What Peter meant to say, Monsignor, is that we showed poor judgment."

"Mr. Flanagan?"

"The statue was an accident. The trespassing, all ours."

"I see," said Cassidy, withdrawing into his thoughts. The delay was strategic, and once resuming, he jutted out his jaw and said, "The first thing I need to remind you boys of is that the woods surrounding our parish lead young minds to a vulgar kind of existence. You've undoubtedly heard of the rout by public school students in those very woods, and the tragic events therein. To the tune of several drug overdoses in recent years. Nor should I have to recite for you the most obvious of restrictions, that parish students have no business at night on our grounds."

"It won't happen again, Monsignor," Dennis said. "As captain of the cross-country team, you have my word."

Cassidy laid his hands flat on the desk's surface, his blood rising at the boy's pat response. "All of that said, you can imagine how surprised I was when Mr. Malagati reported the late-night frolic by three renegade members of the illustrious parish cross-country team. For infractions far less, Sister Rosaleen has sent students packing to the crosstown institution. Which is why it would behoove you to keep a low profile. In other words, the freelancing comes to a grinding halt as we wait and see what punishment, what bed of nails, Sister Rosaleen will dole out. Capiche?"

"Yes, Monsignor," muttered William and Peter.

Dennis waited, then in seeming defiance he uttered a barely audible, "Yes."

The Hurley boy's less than robust response rubbed Cassidy the wrong way. He lifted his hand and waved them off. "Go, you three. Go!"

Once in the hallway, William said, "We're goners!"

"At the very least," Dennis added, "Rosaleen will suspend us."

"Freelancing," Peter said with sarcasm. "Capiche. Crosstown. Bed of nails. Big words. Cassidy playing games, is all."

As they passed Mrs. Wooten at her desk, they were unaware that she already had contacted Sister Rosaleen and informed her of the incident and the pastor's wishes. Nor did the boys know that the Prune, out for a walk, had bumped into Coach Jack putting up cones. She told him what had transpired. So when the boys left the rectory and approached the path, they thought the coast was clear. But then they saw their coach coming right at them.

"Ain't this just fucking grand," said Coach Jack reaching them. "I wake up this morning to a nice warm piss, dreaming about how I've finally got a team primed to win state. And how, with the dead period behind us, and ready for today's time trial, we're ready to get after it. All happy as a clam, I drive over to the parish, and while getting the Sitting Bull course set up, guess who I run into but the Prune. Who tells me that three of my runners last night decided to deface the Holy Roman Empire!"

"Coach," Peter blurted, "it's just a statue."

"Don't you assholes know that statues are the face of the Church? They're like rock stars!" Then noticing the rectory secretary out watering flowers on the porch, Coach Jack said, "I have no choice but to go brown-nose Wooten to find out what's going on. Who knows what kind of crap Cassidy will pull, the devious monster that he is. Or the Amazon Woman, all eight feet of her. Now, dammit, you boys get home and rest up for the time trial. See you at three."

Mrs. Wooten confirmed for the coach that his boys indeed were in hot water. But knowing that her boss would not want the details revealed, she told him only that Sister Rosaleen would be the arbiter of punishment. "And if I was a betting person, Coach Jack, I would say that the boys' fate, and perhaps that season of yours, is sealed like a vault."

"What are you saying?" Coach Jack screamed back at Mrs. Wooten, picturing himself busting open her smug face.

16

A frenzied Coach Jack over the next few hours paced about his office. He knew what a harsh disciplinary response by the principal would mean for the season. Suspension would muck it up. Expulsion, kill it. Still, he told himself that he couldn't let on to his team just how distracted he was by the stunt the core three had pulled. He must put on a front and plow ahead as he always does on the first day of summer practice when the dedication ceremony and time trial take place. And what better way to begin that process than to wave the day's sports headline in the face of his seven. Which he did with characteristic flair when they arrived at three and were sitting on the locker room benches.

St. Theresa's X-Country
Ranked Second in Pre-season State Poll
To Syracuse Central

"So, here we are on July 1st," he began. "The dead period's behind us, and the polls telling us that we are God's gift to the world. But polls don't mean shit. And now that summer fun is over, it's time to say bye-bye to those sweet tangy waves. Boys, we got a state title to chase. And to see what kind of shape we are in, today's the first of three mile time trials. To gauge where we are and where we are going. And to add to the fun, don't forget that we are to take a little road trip this Saturday to Sunken Meadow for practice."

The announcement met with groans, Coach Jack looked to his captain, who replied, "Sounds good, Coach."

"Bet your ass it sounds good. Now, before you all go to the plaque with your dedication name, look at the cross-country board. I just stapled the results from last year's time trials. Except for Mums who was too busy chasing tail, and Legs who's forever a lazy SOB, you others will see a decent progression from the first to the third. So do take a gander, and I'll see you at the plaque."

After Coach Jack left for the path, the team crowded around the board and studied the results from the previous season.

<u>1973 Mile Time Trials</u>
<u>Sitting Bull Run Course</u>

<u>July 1, 1973</u>
Feltman: 4:24
Voit: 4:26
Hurley, Flanagan, Walker: 4:27
Fenny: 4:38
Legstaff: 4:41

<u>September 15, 1973</u>
Feltman: 4:22
Hurley, Flanagan, Walker: 4:26
Voit: 4:30
Fenny: 4:35
Legstaff: 4:37

<u>October 29, 1973</u>
Feltman: 4:21
Hurley, Flanagan, Walker: 4:25
Voit: 4:29
Fenny: 4:32
Legstaff: 4:35

Some fifteen minutes later, the team and their coach stood in a circle around the plaque, each runner holding his dedicatory name.

"Okay," Coach Jack said passing a lighter to his captain. "It's time to dedicate the season, just as all my teams have done."

Dennis was the first to light his paper and drop it atop the plaque. Each of his teammates, one after another, repeated the process.

"Now, if the Chief can take a little heat," said Coach Jack, swatting ashes to the ground, "so can we. But before we toe the line, a good warm-up of stretching and bumrushes. Got to get your heart beating like hell."

As the team started stretching, Coach Jack pulled his captain aside. "Anything from the Amazon?"

"Nothing, Coach."

"Nothing?"

"Not a word."

"I've been wracking my brains thinking what's in Jimmy Boy's best interest. Logic says he has the Amazon whack you three. But I start thinking, with the big upcoming celebrations for him, he doesn't want the bad publicity. I'm hoping that's what he's thinking."

At the last second, Peter forgot all about the 61 first quarter, and instead ran with his two friends. All three struggled mightily to post an unimpressive 4:28. A disgusted Coach Jack had nothing to say afterwards.

After long junk miles the next day, the team on Wednesday ran three repeat miles on the boardwalk. The coach demanded slow burn for each repeat. Except for Adam, it was an ugly workout for all. Especially the core three who ran a horrible last mile, after which their coach let them have it: "The extracurriculars taking their toll, you three? Huh? And the rest of you! No one except Adam ran worth a damn. Maybe I should make an appointment with the rabbi at the B'nai Brith in Patchogue and see if I can't get me four more fuzzy-haired kids. The kind who got heart! The kind who can win St. Theresa's a championship! Damn, the state meet should stir a fire in your souls! To hell, I say!"

The coach kicked the ground and shouted over his shoulders as he stomped off, "Tomorrow! Nine sharp!"

Once the coach pulled away in his van, Legs cried, "the asshole forgets it's still summer."

"Legs," Adam cried out, "you should be out in front with me."

"Hey, no one hates cross country more than me! I'm only doing this to stay in shape for winter and spring track, when I plan to take dead aim at several state records."

"Wonderful!" Adam cried, "Legs announces he's using cross country as a training program for the Olympics."

"Plus, my little friend, once I give Coach Jack an inch, he'll want a yard. No, I like the current system. The only time I bust my ass for Coach Jack is the last half mile of every race. Got it?"

"Great," Adam was now visibly frustrated, "We're competing for a state title, our first meet in Staten Island right around the corner, and you guys are jerking off. How about you, Denny? What's your pleasure?"

"My pleasure is that we all take a deep breath."

"I'll take a deep breath alright," said Adam, and as he took off, he yelled over his shoulder, "I'll do it in the shower where I'll rinse off the stench of this team!"

As they started their cool down back to the parish, Fenny and Legs spent most of the time complaining how Coach Jack was once again stealing the summer. As for the core three, however, they were anxious to see what the bungalow yard looked like. Reaching the parish, they saw that the saint was back at full strength, again ministering to the animals.

"See!" said Peter. "Like I said, Merlin the Magician waved his wand and made it go away."

"How the fuck did Malagati do that?" asked William, who didn't know that the old man had spent the morning drilling, inserting rebar, and feathering mortar.

"Who cares how he did it," said Peter. "So long as we once again have an arm to hang our wardrobe on when we next go for a swim under the stars."

By Friday morning, Coach Jack was actually in a chipper mood. His team the day before slow burned an impressive eight-miler to the county wildlife museum. But equally important, his captain again told him on the phone the night before, "Nothing yet from the convent, Coach. Hoping that Peter's right. That the coast is clear."

"Peter could very well be on to something with Saint Frankie again strutting his stuff in Charlie's grotto."

So did the team like what Coach Jack had to say that Friday afternoon. "Since we leave in the morning for a Sunken Meadow workout, how about you boys, after some junk miles to Field Two and back, make a pit stop at Sal's? Rumor has it that high-carb pasta dishes will be served up on the house. See you at 9 a.m. sharp."

Fenny did a slow dance. Peter howled.

Once the boys had left for the inlet bridge, Coach Jack drove over to Sal's where he left money for the team dinner. From there he headed over to Chief's to wash down a bar burger and onion rings with several mugs of beer.

That next morning, the team passed a muttering Mr. Malagati as they went into the locker room to gather their running gear for the Sunken Meadow workout. He was working under the hood of Coach Jack's old van. By the time they came back out, the hood was down, the custodian gone, the mechanical issue apparently fixed.

"Yeah," said Coach Jack, steering out onto Main Street, "when it wouldn't start, I went a-knocking on Charlie's door."

"He answer with a meat cleaver, Coach?" William asked.

"Nah, just the same old pissed-off look. But if anyone could fix it in a jiffy, Charlie could."

"Yeah," said Legs, "One of these days Merlin's gonna march on over and have a final showdown with Chief Sitting Bull."

SITTING BULL RUN

"And who, Legs, would win that contest?" asked an amused Coach Jack.

"Merlin, of course, on Arthur's payroll as he is."

"Hey, Coach," Fenny asked, "how'd you get the Sitting Bull bug anyway?"

"Good question, James Fennessy. As a kid I read all these books about American Indian chiefs. And I came to love those crazy bastards for their guts. Their backbone. So I had the Injun bug way before I arrived in Bellport. Anyway, one night Ole Jack was on a barstool sipping on a sodi pop in Chief's and gawking at that mean-ass stare of Sitting Bull, when he gets this idea of a summer running series for the kiddies. Turned into a pot of gold for the program. The recruiting potential, for one thing. And we now had a place on parish grounds to run interval workouts. In fact, my first cycle of runners got this hard-on for Sitting Bull. Before you knew it, the chief became our battle cry. And I hope you boys cry like hell today during today's Sunken Meadow workout."

To drown out the moans, he turned on his crooner station.

For a good number of years Coach Jack entered his team in the St. John the Baptist's Invitational, held the third Saturday of September at the iconic Sunken Meadow State Park course on the north shore of Long Island. He did so to give his team an opportunity to race on the same course they would run on later in the season, in the Catholic League championship. Back in 1965, however, after one of his scorers was disqualified for running without his number, Coach Jack cursed out the St. John's coach and told him in front of a large crowd that a St. Theresa's team would never run in his lousy meet again. Instead, he started taking them to the Jersey Shore Invite at Holmdel Park.

Since then, to make up for the lost racing opportunity on the league championship course, Coach Jack had his teams work out at Sunken Meadow several times during the summer months. They always looked forward to the excursions. After the workout Coach Jack would treat them to nearby Stan's Arcade for a pork tenderloin platter as well as games. This year's team, however, dreaded the trip. The temperature that first week of July had reached 90 degrees, the air thick and soupy.

Their dread turned to horror as Coach Jack, once arriving at the park, announced the workout: "Okay, my Merry Band, last night I reached down into my bag of tricks and came up with a humdinger. Which is to run the course's second mile five times. A five-minute rest in between."

He waited for the groans to fade before he continued.

"You'll start the repeats at the mile marker, which is where the slow burn surge in actual races begins. And, dammit, for anyone who sandbags today's workout, especially Cardiac Hill, not a penny at Stan's. Got it? Good. Now, give me a good warm-up and be ready to go in forty-five minutes. And for Christ's sake, don't forget to hit the can!"

As expected, Adam had a stellar workout, averaging 5:19 for each repeat. So did the core three exceed expectations. The same with Fenny and Mums. Lazy ass George Legstaff cratered after the third repeat. Yet rather than leave well enough alone, Legs had just mounted the van for the trip to Stan's when he said, "Gem of a workout, Coach Jack."

To that, his coach gave the rear view a walloping stare. "Hey, Legs, I'd be glad to drop you off right here, and with any luck at all, the natives who hunt in these parts will cut your dick off, skillet it on low heat, and with a dash of salt have themselves a jim-dandy of a midday meal. Got it, Legsy Pooh?"

Coach Jack apparently liked what he said so much that he turned on his crooner station and started singing along. And he might have sung all the way to Stan's, but just as the van exited the park, a dull engine knocking came. It grew louder, metal hitting metal, smoke surged from the hood.

"Damn Charlie Malagati!" the coach hollered, the van swerving onto the shoulder. "Out, damn it, out! Before this thing blows up!"

The team, now on the shoulder, stood back as Coach Jack tried lifting the hood. Billowing smoke pushed him away.

"Shit!" He paced about trying to come to terms with the situation.

"Well, boys, I guess this is God's way of telling me that I'm gonna have to bust open the goddam piggy bank. Spring for a new van. But first, we got to get home. Wait here, and for fuck's sake, don't go playing in traffic."

After securing a taxi, Coach Jack returned to the van where he grabbed his toolbox in the back. First, he ripped off the license plates. Then, the battery, radio, hubcaps. Two tires. When the taxi pulled up, Coach Jack told the driver to hit the back trunk latch. The driver did so, thinking the running equipment would go there. But the van parts were also crammed in. Most of the boys knew that Coach Jack planned to sell the parts. None knew he would also report the van stolen.

"Now, get in," Coach Jack snapped at his team. He positioned himself in the front with Dennis, the other six squashed in the back on top of one another. The driver, with second thoughts about the cargo, sat stone silent.

"Hey, Mack, or whatever your name is, put this thing in drive and let's go!"

Saturday traffic was light, and the hot breeze blowing through the windows made the runners feel sticky and cramped. They knew better than to complain. Nor did Coach Jack have anything to say until they approached Bellport, where he gave the driver directions to the parish. "And once there, my man, head straight for the rectory garage that's painted asshole brown." But as the taxi pulled into the parish, the coach saw Mr. Malagati pruning rectory bushes with electric hedge clippers. "Christ, the bastard's creeping around."

The old custodian in turn, recognizing the passenger in front, turned the clippers off.

"Hey, Charlie Malagati," Coach Jack said as he got out and

lifted the door to the garage's empty fourth stall, "top of the afternoon."

Mr. Malagati didn't blink.

"Okay, Dennis, Peter, tires go in. William, the radio. Adam, the hoses."

The clippers still in hand, an angry Charlie Malagati stepped into the garage and now stood just a few yards from the coach and his varsity runners. "Hogan, this parish garage. For cars, no? Not for junk."

The clippers switch accidentally tripped back on, the serrated teeth creating a hissing clatter, the machine with a seeming mind of its own jumped in the direction of Coach Jack and his team, all of whom stepped backwards as the old man struggled to turn it off.

"Thank you, Charlie, for not cutting my hand off. Would have been hard on the boys, seeing blood shooting out of their beloved coach like a geyser.

"No, Hogan. I no play game."

"And what did you do to my van? It blew a bloody gasket on the way out of the park."

"Take stuff out! Take now!"

"Who are you anyway? The Pope?" Coach Jack's lofty contempt was cracking. His mouth sagged, his eyes a hard stare.

"I go. I go Monsignor."

As the old man lapsed into his foreign tongue while walking away, Coach Jack desperately worked his mind for a rebuke. But seeing the old man already climbing the rectory steps, he said, "Boys, your asses in the taxi. Now!"

The parts left in the garage, Coach Jack slammed its door shut and joined his runners in the taxi.

"Wow, Coach" said Fenny, "that was a close call with the clippers."

"Yeah," Legs added, "Merlin might have had a field day decapitating Coach Jack and his merry band."

"Hey, you two," Coach Jack screamed, "shut your traps and let me think."

The taxi fell quiet as the coach decided that he would personally deliver each boy to his front door, a glowing report of the practice given to one or both parents. With 32 Crocus the last stop, the coach paid the driver and accompanied Dennis up the drive, where on the front porch and over a few cold beers, he described for Dan and Catherine the van's "demise" as well as the "team's monster workout." He spoke in the easy way of a well-fed man.

"Well," he stood after finishing a second beer. "Time to head home. Kick off my shoes and take it all in."

"Can I give you a ride?" Dan asked.

"Nah, a neighborhood stroll is just the ticket."

After waving good-bye to Coach Jack, Dennis and his parents from the front porch watched him striding down Crocus in the late afternoon sun. His was a bracing walk, as if cleaning the town of cobwebs. Little did they know that he was on his way to the parish rectory, where he'd present his side of the incident to Cassidy. What Coach Jack didn't know was that after Cassidy had given Charlie permission to dispose of the van parts, the pastor had been picked up by District Attorney Nick Lambert and chauffeured to the Southampton Galleria. The well-known sculptor, Piero Montana, was now giving shape to his subject with chisel and hammer. Cassidy, adorned in regalia, stood in a studied calm.

"Fuck," Coach Jack muttered after the smug Mrs. Wooten told him that the pastor was preoccupied elsewhere. On a hunch, the coach went to the rectory garage and found that everything was gone.

LATER THAT NIGHT Dennis came down for cereal and found his parents at the table. A low moan escaped his mother working a needle into a double pleat. Dennis thought she had pricked herself.

But the moan was an exaggerated sigh meant to ready her son for the conversation about to be had.

"So, Dennis, Ida Feltman called to report that Charlie Malagati and Coach Jack had words over van parts left behind at the parish. In fact, Adam told her that there was a moment when Charlie's hedge clippers got too close for comfort. That's something your father's favorite coach in the universe never mentioned to us when he was being spoon-fed beer on our front porch."

"Adam exaggerating, is all, Mom."

"Your mother, the cynic," his father chimed in. "If not ragging on Coach Jack, it's Cassidy. Or Sister Rosaleen. Or for Christ's sake, even on your mom's best day she has unkind things to say about poor Charlie Malagati."

"It's just that Charlie's always got this scowl on him. And he finds it hard to look a person in the eye."

"Cat, stop while you're behind."

"Dennis, do you remember growing up and being afraid of Mr. Malagati?"

"A little bit."

"See, Dan. And to be honest, it has only gotten worse since his Loretta passed."

"What do you expect? The guy was married for over fifty years. But he didn't go into hiding. In fact, in the weeks that followed her death, everyone in the parish knows that he never missed a day of work. Not one."

"You remember Mrs. Malagati, Dennis, don't you?"

"Of course, he does, Cat. He's practically lived at the parish all these years."

"You know, Dennis," his mother worked up a nostalgic tone, "I never take for granted the rich history you have had with St. Theresa's. Altar boy. Paper boy. Not to mention the volunteer work."

"And let's not forget," Dan with a chuckle added, "the various parish gaffes. Pool hopping the most recent one." Then with a wide grin, "Though none of us will ever forget the Mulski coffin incident from some years ago."

"Be nice, Dan."

"Be nice! You're the one who started us down memory lane."

Dennis responded by shoving a spoon full of cereal into his mouth before heading up to his bedroom. Plopping into bed, he felt agitated by his father's mention of the visitation debacle. But shaking it off, his mind drifted to his mother's mention of Mrs. Malagati. Dennis had a keen recall of the last time he saw her. It was one Friday back in seventh grade, when as a newspaper delivery boy he went on his bike to collect the sixty-five cents owed by each customer for the week, the tip money inevitably leading to a slice at Sal's. The route itself ran through downtown and concluded at the parish mailboxes. More than a few of his customers waited at the front door in terror each day, hoping that their soldier son was not among the military portraits, the day's casualties, displayed in the bottom right corner of the front page. None stood by with greater fear than Mrs. Malagati.

Approaching the bungalow that spring afternoon, Dennis suspended peddling and glided over the drive. He knocked and waited for her to answer. He wasn't surprised that she didn't come right away. In recent months, the circulation problem in her legs had slowed her down. After knocking a second time, her muffled voice came, "Dennis, Dennis, let yourself in."

He opened the front door and shouted, "Hello? Mrs. Malagati?"

"I'm back here. Come."

A bit nervous, he stepped into the foyer, which was as far as he had ever been.

"Come, Dennis."

As he passed into the small living room, it all reminded him of Grandma Nellie's house in the city. The old round furniture. The throw rugs. The smell of floor polish.

"Here I am. Back here."

Walking through the kitchen, he was struck by the oil painting of Jesus that hung by a small exhaust fan. He might have stopped to inspect the pink facial tones, but Rosa was sitting in the hallway and gazing up at him.

"Dennis? You there?"

"Is Rosa friendly?"

Mrs. Malagati laughed. "Rosa, honey, come to Momma."

The dog obeyed, and as Dennis moved down the hall, he spied a room on the left, its bed covered in layers of quilts. On the dresser was a foot-high statue of the Blessed Virgin Mary, flanked on both sides by piles of folded clothes.

He found Mrs. Malagati in the far room. She was in her bathrobe and sat in a sofa chair, her frizzy gray hair tied in a bow. One hand petted Rosa on her haunches. The other hand, a gnarled fist tucked under her chin, unfurled and reached for the newspaper. As her wary eyes searched through the day's war casualties, Dennis took note of the room bolstered with streaks of natural light that passed through blinds. She must have spent her days there, he thought. The television across from her, newspapers on the floor. On an end table, prescription bottles, a water pitcher, a small glass.

Her son not among the casualties, she looked up at Dennis with a reassuring smile and said, "My legs, they no good anymore. Charles, he worry. I tell him I not go anywhere until I see my grandchildren. There," she said pointing to the framed picture, which Dennis handed to her. "That my Vincent and wife, Susan. And grandchildren, Carol and baby Charlie. They all live in Florida. Vincent promise to bring them up to see me. Poor Charles, he buy pool. He break back each year getting it ready for them."

She next nodded at Vinnie's formal army portrait. "You know, this Vincent's room as a baby. His crib, there. So long ago."

She would have had more to say about her son but that the front door opened.

"Papa, that you?"

"Yes, Momma."

"Come see Dennis Hurley. He collect. Newspaper. I invite to see picture of Vincent."

The old man replied in Italian.

His wife answered, "Yes, I pay him." She tried to stand but fell back into the armchair. She gestured toward the leather change purse on the television. Dennis handed it to her.

The door opened and closed again. Mr. Malagati was gone.

"My Charles a funny man. Each day he come back from parish. Check on me. But also to water flowers. Such a funny man."

With that she picked four quarters out of the bag as she always did. That included a generous tip.

"Until I get better, Dennis, I spend much time here. I hope-"

Gurgling sounds were heard in the wall, intense water surges leading to the outside spigot.

Mrs. Malagati smiled. "There he goes again. Until I get better, you come back here."

"I will."

Remounting his bicycle, Dennis pedaled down the drive. Before disappearing, he looked over his shoulders and saw the gruff and sweaty seriousness oozing out of the old man. Dennis knew the pose well. Mr. Malagati was never more at home than when he was working his well-manicured property. Whether that meant trimming lattice vine, or pruning, or dropping more grass seed on an already plush lawn. Or simply watering the array of flowers, as he did today.

Once back on Main Street, Dennis' thoughts returned to Mrs. Malagati. As he made his way that Friday through downtown, however, he had no idea that he had seen her for the last time. The ambulance came a few days later. She lasted less than two weeks at Good Samaritan Hospital.

17

The week following the junking of the van, the team returned to Sunken Meadow for another grueling workout, this time cramming into a station wagon rental from Hertz, which Coach Jack would use while he looked for a deal at different dealerships. Today he had them twice run the course without stopping, each time demanding a slow-burn surge from mile one to mile two. Extra coins for Stan's Arcade went to those who met the coach's assigned goal time. Only Legs failed to satisfy the goal set for him.

The next day the team was sent on a long out-and-back to Field Nine's bird sanctuary. On the way out of the parish grounds, the team passed by the marquee, which read,

Sign Up Now!
St. Theresa's End of the Summer Picnic
Saturday, August 30th

"Hey," said Fenny, "Can't wait for the picnic weekend. The Montauk Point Festival on Friday, parish picnic the next day. No running either day!"

"All I know," said Legs, "is that Ole Jack had better get a new van soon. King Arthur can't squeeze his balls into that rental again."

"Not to worry, Legs," said Dennis, "that's what he's doing today. Looking for a new van."

"Hey, with Coach Jack missing in action," said Fenny, "I say we pass on the run and catch a few waves."

"I'm in," Bobby Mumbles said, "especially with all the babes out there."

From Legs, "Arthur's on board."

"Fuck, no," said William. "First we get this run over with. Then swim."

"Agreed," said Dennis as the team mounted the boardwalk. "And let's keep the pace under six minutes."

A week later, on July 24th, the temperature hit 104 degrees, a Long Island record for the day. The summer solstice brought with it a row of unbearably hot days that softened the tar of main roads and sent most of Bellport behind closed doors. Lasting a solid week, the heat wave radiated down from a blue sky and turned grass a creamy brown. Dusty, wilting leaves hung from trees like dead fish on trotlines. Neighborhood dogs, irritable and hot, barked their respective cases that were heard for square blocks. Even the coke cans that the Dunn brothers sent heavenward via bottle rockets had an unimpressive descent, lazy and whirling.

As for the team that week, Coach Jack moved practice to 7 p.m. when it was not so hot. Things were different for the team during the day. Legs rarely came out of his bedroom, the window unit blowing cold air across his face. Fenny and Mumbles roamed the new indoor mall on the western edge of Bellport, a swirl of eager young ladies about them. To the hum of an outdoor fan, Adam played chess with Harry under their backyard awning, stopping only to take dips in their pool. To mostly still beach flags, William, Peter, and Dennis waded in the ocean, its sea-green surface hardly moving. But one day, when a north wind picked up and waves formed in large mounds, the three boys bodysurfed for hours. Collapsing afterwards on the warm sand, they cradled their faces in the soft bends of their arms and gazed out over the water. Before long, however, Peter and William were back riding waves. Dennis decided to stay behind to relax on his towel.

Not much later, he noticed a classmate, beach bag in hand, walking along the shore in his direction. Her heels swishing the sand, Dennis knew Eleanor Fenwick, classmate and all-county swimmer, as a voice throaty with desire. After school she might dress in a T-shirt and shorts and saunter past the boys to the tennis courts for elaborate stretching exercises, only to return to the girls' locker room in a steady trot, cheeks red, full bosom heaving under the sweat-stained shirt. That's why at night Dennis sometimes found himself gazing out his bedroom window and borrowing from George Legstaff's palette to draw Eleanor Fenwick as the fair daughter of an English monarch. High but slightly rounded cheek bones, full trembling lips, light brown eyes, flowing chestnut hair.

"Hey, Dennis Hurley," Eleanor said when she reached him. "How about you grab that towel of yours and take a walk with me along the shore?"

"Sure." He replied, now standing and waving goodbye to his two friends out in the water. They in turn flipped him the bird, even as a white-winged gannet out past the breakers dove dagger-like into the water for food.

Dennis and Eleanor walked a good ways, both occasionally looking up at the dunes where scattered lovers, all men, ranged about. Just when Dennis thought it was safe to stop, she looked at him as if to say it's not private enough, that the small handful of bodies on towels are a handful too many. When Eleanor felt they were far enough along, she whipped her beach towel out over the sand. She wiggled her hips and lowered her shorts. She cross-armed her shirt off, exposing a silky black one-piecer.

Dennis watched her take off running, her feet kicking and slashing high, and diving in. She resurfaced waist high, her outstretched hands shaking over the water, as if to calm it. She trudged some until the sea floor dropped, at which point she swam out past the breakers. Now wading, she turned and beckoned

Dennis. He took off and dove in, and reaching her, the two swam out further. Dennis at one point looked toward the shore, the dunes now small mounds with feathery caps. Turning to Eleanor, he noticed that she had lowered her top and was floating on her back, her hair spreading like tendrils. Tilting her head some, she smiled at him, then submerged. She resurfaced, the suit restored to its former position.

Soon back on their towels, she shook her long hair to help dry it in the sun. Dennis stole a look. Her hair was no longer fine and silky but sagged in coarse wet fibers. He pictured his fingers running through them and inspecting the strands along her neck.

Eleanor asked him about the team. She kept grabbing his arm and guffawing as he tried to explain the dynamics of a Jack Hogan cross-country program.

"That's simply wild, Dennis. I had no idea your coach is such a horrible human being."

"Oh, but he's not. Strange at times, but not horrible. Plus, I really like to run for him. He's a great coach."

Feeling somehow slighted, Eleanor deflected, "There I was, minding my own business after school one day when you guys came running by. Hogan was screaming at you all. He called George Legstaff, and I quote, 'a lazy-ass motherfucker.' I heard other things, too, Dennis. Real whoppers. And if that wasn't bad enough, you now tell me he makes you guys run in beach sand. That must feel awful on your legs."

"Which is why he makes us do it."

"But why in the world would anyone want to run, especially in the sand?"

"Actually, Eleanor, I love to run. It's the only time things feel right for me. Especially when I run along the water, when the sand's packed down and level. Gulls drifting about, too. Doesn't get any better than that."

"You're starting to scare me, Denny Boy. That's how your friends address you, right?"

"Sometimes."

"Well, Denny Boy, today's as good a day as any to begin the big search."

"For what?"

"My senior prom date. Nine short months away. I might have waited until the parish picnic, right around the corner, to start the process. By the way, you're going to the picnic, aren't you? I mean, it's only a few weeks away."

"Wouldn't miss it for the world."

"Do you dance?"

"Do I dance, you ask?"

"Yes, at the picnic I'll be keeping an eye on who can dance and who can't. Gotta have someone who can really boogie woogie on prom night. C'mon, let's go back into the water."

This time they bodysurfed. Dennis marveled at her snapping back and diving in after each ride. Reminded him of Peter. They eventually made it back to their towels. Flat on their backs in the mid-afternoon sun, she rolled over, her arm falling across his stomach, her feet digging the sand like a sea crab burrowing under.

Dennis saw Eleanor a few days later. This time, a passenger in a fast-moving convertible driven by Skip Kincade, a Dartmouth freshman home for the summer.

18

As July moved into August, so did a cold front from Canada push the miserably hot and humid air of midsummer out to sea. Coach Jack was tinkled pink when the weatherman with a jet-black toupee on the nightly news reported that a more reasonable daytime temperature in the low eighties would linger for several weeks. A milder air would make it easier on his seven during the month of August when he'd take them to practice on some of the major courses they'd compete on during the fall. Each time his seven would confront a vintage Jack Hogan workout that simulated the more challenging sections of each course. This year at the Holmdel Park, they ran an hour's worth of the notoriously steep uphill portion of the Bowl, the course's signature feature. The next week at Bear Mountain, they ran a ninety-minute fartlek over the middle mile, which features two back-breaking hills, called the Beast and Upchuck, respectively. Back at Sunken Meadow, Coach Jack had his seven do countless bumrushes over the course's start, the sandy sections, and the final straight, followed by a tempo run over the entire course. The last of the summer road trips, at Van Cortlandt, saw his team do grueling mile repeats on the Back Hills.

Soon, though, with the summer drawing to a close, the

coach reminded his team that two months of progressive interval training was about to begin in earnest once the racing season got underway the first week of September. But, first, Coach Jack had to prepare for the biggest money maker of the year, the parish picnic, the serious financial crumbs of which went into his pocket. Picnic chairman for over a decade, he would need to spend the better part of that week preparing for the event. As far as his team was concerned, except for Tuesday's dune workout, he sent them out for long runs on the roads. To motivate his seven, he often mentioned the women's triathlon at Friday's Montauk Point Festival.

As HIS VARSITY in beach garb arrived at the parish the morning of the festival, the marquee read,

Tomorrow's Parish Picnic
Starts at 2 p.m.

Outside the locker room they found Coach Jack standing beside the Hertz station wagon that he continued to use as he waited on a special-order van to arrive from Detroit. White zinc painted on his nose, he wore a plaid button-down shirt and a large, baggy bathing suit that dropped past his knees, stopping just short of large muscular calves made larger by the flip-flops he wore.

"Ok, boys, get in and don't yuck it all up."

"Hey, Coach," asked Adam once the wagon turned onto Main Street. "Do you really think Malagati sabotaged your old van, like you said?"

"Malagati," said Mumbles, "hates Coach."

Fenny added, "And Coach hates Malagati."

That must have hit a nerve, for Coach Jack had no response. The wagon grew quiet, and only after the stop at Otto's Deli for take-out breakfast sandwiches did the chatter resume.

"Okay, boys," Coach Jack said as the team began to devour the sandwiches, "once we reach Montauk Point, throw the wrappers and any other shit away. Got to keep this rental spotless. And for Christ's sake, let's behave on the beach. Especially when the chug-a-lug gals come running by."

"When do we eat lunch?" Legs asked.

"Noon. Then we head back to the parish. Got a ton of work to do for tomorrow's picnic."

Once down by the water, Coach Jack drove his beach umbrella pole into the sand and unfolded his reclining beach chair. There, he thought to himself, my seven Mary Janes should have no problem staying out of my hair. He looked out over the water and smiled at the breakers rolling in, a whispering of breeze everywhere. Down past the red flag, surfers kicked high in the spray. Coach Jack laughed out loud when he saw a meet official putting up markers along the shore for the women's mini triathlon. His boys would soon salivate over the skimpy outfits.

"C'mon, you guys," Peter yelled at his teammates, who one by one lined up for a short foot race down to the water. "Set and go!"

"Crazy fuckers!" Coach Jack cackled over his boys pulling and tugging each other in the charge down. Once they were all in the water, he got a kick out of watching them catching wave after wave. He eventually nodded off in his chair, and he might have slept longer but for the shrill voices of Fenny and Mums, who were plucking wings off captive flies and dropping them into a sand pit they dug. Coach Jack stood and plodded over for a look-see into the pit, where he counted six poor creatures down there in a slow death march.

"Hey, you two, knock it off or no lunch money. I'm going for a long walk."

He grabbed his straw hat and left, his heels throwing up squirts of sand. He walked a good way before mounting the first jetty and stepping down over boulders to the end. Lowering his shirt and hat onto the last boulder, he dove off, and as he waded in the choppy water, his mind drifted to the first Saturday in November. He pictured Adam gapping the lead pack in the Back

Hills. The negative second-mile split of the core three would move them into the top twenty as they descended down to the Flats, bumrushing a ton of bums on the final stretch. Of course, damn Legstaff would have blown by the core three with exactly a half mile left, mowing down enough runners for a top-five spot. All of which would ensure a mouthwatering, ass-whipping of the Syracuse Central team.

Coach Jack returned to his umbrella in time to join his team and other beachgoers watch the mini triathletes come running by. Mumbles exchanged lewd comments with Fenny and Adam. But they did so in hushed terms. Once the field had passed, Coach Jack announced that he would give them five bucks apiece for the food truck. But only after they all had showered and changed in the outdoor facility.

"Ain't going there," Fenny said. "It's filled with queers."

Coach Jack's eyes gleaming, how sweet it would be to force the imp into the showers. "If that's the case, Fenny, no food truck for you. Not to mention that you'll have to call your parents for a ride home."

The open-roofed facility was packed with men waiting in lines, three to four deep. Coach Jack took off his suit and wasted little time getting his team to do the same. "And don't forget to rinse your cracks. No sand in my rental."

The unabashed Adam, the first of the team to slide off his suit, yelled out, "Let's go, Fenny, strip down. Let's see them crown jewels."

Coach Jack smiled and left for a line, Fenny the last to take off his suit.

"Hey!" said Adam pointing. "Seaweed's pasted on Fenny's pecker." The others looked, and sure enough, a green sliver. They all laughed as the seaweed was picked off, a sullen Fenny turning for the far line.

Afterwards, the team grabbed a table beside *Barbecue Bob's* truck, the menu of choice. While cueing up to order, Adam became the target of an antisemitic slur by a member of the Longwood

High cross-country team who, proudly donning his singlet, called over, "Hey, Moses, won't the non-kosher food slow you down?"

No sooner did his Longwood teammates, also in their singlets, erupt in laughter than William Flanagan barreled into the gang leader and knocked him to the ground.

"You gonna apologize to my friend, Adam Feltman?" William said, pointing down at him. "Or am I gonna have to beat you to a bloody pulp?"

Unwilling to take on William, whose neck veins were popping out, the loudmouth stood and muttered, "Sorry."

"Sorry, Adam Feltman," William insisted. "Say it!"

"Sorry, Adam Feltman."

Stepping between the two, Dennis stole a look over at the beer tent where Coach Jack was laughing it up with others.

Some thirty minutes later, with his seven back in the rental, their coach said, "Boys, I'd say that with the exception of Fenny's premeditated murder of those poor creatures, this morning's outing was a tremendous success. And even though there's still a good half day's picnic preparation waiting for me when we get back, Ole Coach got slow burn in his bones, ready to surge at mile marker one, crushing anything in the way."

"I like the attitude, Coach Jack," said Peter.

"And I like Peter Walker," his coach replied.

"What Arthur likes," said Legs, "is that there's no running today."

"Or tomorrow," Fenny added. "We never run on picnic day."

Their coach replied, "Enjoy it while you can, boys. Cause you ain't gonna see a stretch of easy days again until we taper for state."

The rental took off, and as it passed over the Montauk Inlet, Dennis took in a flock of gulls diving after the innards that the mates on a charter boat threw overboard. He also noticed that Coach Jack must have enjoyed his time in the beer tent. His whistling of *Beautiful Dreamer* was vivid, loud. The coach's mood changed, though, when the rental pulled into the parish a little after two p.m. There on the north lot, the old custodian, along with a dozen Elks, were adjusting the ropes of the enormous white canopy tent, already raised into position.

"Damn Charlie Malagati!" cried Coach Jack, slapping the dashboard. "And damn those Elks! The tent's backside is too close to the school. They were supposed to wait for me to get back before the tent went up!" He detoured over and yelled out to an Elk, "Hey, why didn't you wait for me?"

"All I know is that Garland told Charlie to get the tent up."

"Fucking Doughboy!"

The rental sped off in the direction of the locker room. There he told the team they'd have to wait until Monday to discuss the week's training cycle for the first meet in Staten Island the following Saturday. Coach Jack did pull the core three aside to ask if there were any developments on the pool hopping front.

When each boy said there was not, Coach Jack said, "Okay, from here on, that business is history. Got it?"

All three nodded.

Dennis arrived home just as Aunt Pearl pulled up in her green Nova. She jumped out with a grocery bag and made her way up while Uncle John leveraged himself out with his cane.

"Hi, Dennis," she said as they met on the drive. "Your mother and I are making salads for the picnic tomorrow. Something to go with the greasy fried chicken Hogan serves up every year. Any ideas?"

"Anything will work, Aunt Pearl."

"Oh, and your mother and I are each gonna enter a dish in the casserole contest. She's doing a creamy vegetable and cheese. I'm thinking about a chipped beef gizmo."

"Uncle John going to the picnic?"

"Think Old Polack Face would miss all the potato salad and beans? God, the beans." With that she turned and looked back at her husband closing the passenger door. "Call 911, Dennis, if he keels over on the way in."

As darkness gathered later that day, the shiny Hertz rental stood out in the mostly empty parking lot of the Lantern Inn. Inside Room #12, Coach Jack paced about in his briefs, a cigar in one hand, a can of beer in the other.

"And the kicker, Marge, is that Charlie was off by a good twenty feet. The goddam tent now butts right up to the classrooms. Leaves almost no room for the fryers or the tanks! And, shit, I've got to be over at the parish at the break of dawn to finish up."

"Come to mama, Jack."

"He had no goddam business putting that tent up. None!"

"Mama, Jack. Come to her."

"You are a great gal, Marge, and God knows you got an ass to die for. But I'm pissed. It's not only Charlie sticking his nose where it don't belong. I also come to find out that Cassidy put the Doughboy in charge of designing a picnic program. Shit, we never have a program. Worse, he's having Charlie's punk kid as a guest speaker."

"No!"

"Yes. And all week Rosaleen's breathing down my neck about renting white tablecloths."

"Under whose orders?"

"Who else!"

"Fuck, Jack, you don't think Cassidy will make an appearance, do you?"

"Hell, no. It's the parish picnic for God's sake. Where folk use sleeves to wipe shit off their mouths. Get good and drunk so that they can make asses of themselves on the dance floor. You know, I never thought in a thousand years I would think what I'm now thinking."

"And that is?"

"That last year I should have handed the picnic over to someone else. For good. I've got a state championship just a few short months away. And more to come, hopefully."

"Nonsense, Jack. The picnic would die without you. You keep it alive each summer, changing it up with something new that folks like. Take the Macarena contest that one year. Or the water-balloon throw for seniors. Or for fuck's sake, those belly dancers. Rosaleen shit her pants. By the way, what've you got planned for this year?"

"You know what, it's been so crazy looking for a new van that it got away from me."

No sooner did he say that than his mouth opened, eyes grew big.

"What, Jack?"

He took a drag of his cigar and slowly blew out a long line of smoke.

"Tell me, Jack, or Room #12 ain't gonna see any action tonight."

"Yes, my cuddly Margaret Mudhank," a smile emerging. "I got a big picnic idea."

"Shit, Jack, what is it?"

With that, he took a swig and lowered his beer down. He set his cigar in the ash tray and moved toward the bed. "Be glad to share my idea with you. But first, of course, you got to slow burn a lighthouse run with me."

19

It was approaching noon the next day when Cassidy spun around in time to watch the tent's entrance banner being raised.

St. Theresa's Parish
End of the Summer Picnic

The pastor glimpsed other activities as well. Hogan snarling orders at a vendor. The band stage being assembled. Charlie throwing carpet over an extension cord. A food-distribution outfit dropping boxes out of a truck. Elks pulling kegs of beer on hand dollies.

Mrs. Wooten entered the office to retrieve the pastor's lunch plate. She looked over his shoulder and saw what Cassidy was fixed on, the bustle of nuns arranging bouquets atop the white tablecloths.

"My, my, Monsignor. Wonder what all the fuss is about this year?"

"Not a clue."

She spotted the *Malagati Landscaping* truck, three men raking mulch around the St. Theresa statue on the Great Lawn. "I see Charlie's once again hired his three nephews for the picnic."

"One assumes that to be the case, Mrs. Wooten."

It was after one-thirty when cars started pulling into the parish parking lot, the Hurley wagon among them. From the front seat Tommy watched parishioners of all ages and all sizes file in under the tent. Most lugged in family coolers filled with salads and desserts.

"Look, Daddy, look!" Tommy said in excitement.

"Yes, sirree," replied Dan Hurley. "The big parish picnic!"

"Whoopie!" said Aunt Pearl who sat in the middle seat next to Uncle John. Dennis was in the way back guarding the cooler.

As was the case with most parish families, it took some time for the Hurleys to claim a table and settle in. Yet after all the hubbub surrounding that, Dennis thought it odd when the two o'clock starting time finally arrived and the prior bustle dropped off to a confounding inertia, the picnic stalling with labored smiles and half nods. Picnic chairman, Jack Hogan, also saw it. He wasted no time snapping orders at the band to begin, the Elks to carry pitchers of beer around the tent and fill empty cups at no charge. A groundswell arose, the first round of parishioners making their way to the dance floor. Soon dancers were hoofing it up to the music while paying customers waited on the beer line. After a respectable amount of time was allowed for frivolity, Cassidy, with Nick Lambert at his side, stepped out onto the rectory porch, pausing to command all eyes.

Moses-like before the Red Sea, the pastor headed for the tent, parting all that stood in the way of his path. A nervous Sister Rosaleen, privy to Cassidy's intentions, had already signaled that the band stop. Dancers returned to their seats. The crowd continued to gawk at the Monsignor, who, upon entering the tent, struggled to maintain an outward cheerfulness. Once or twice he lifted a hand to wave. When he finally took his seat at the head table with a handful of prominent parishioners, he signaled to Lambert who went to the band's microphone.

"Greetings, everyone, greetings. As most of you know, back

in the spring the parish learned that Pope Paul VI will personally consecrate, on the first Saturday in November, a select group of clergy at St. Peter's Basilica in Rome. The group to include Bellport's favorite son, James Francis Cassidy, the next Bishop of the Diocese of Rockville Centre."

Soft applause.

"All that said, we will be lucky to have the new diocesan bishop living with us right here through graduation next May, at which time he will leave for the chancery. Knowing that his departure will be a sad day, Monsignor in the meantime will make it a priority to take full advantage of as many opportunities as he can to break bread with the parish community. Thus, his presence today, which will include a reception line."

After Lambert finished up, Sister Grace Corde rushed two chicken dinners to the head table. Cassidy started on the meal even as he stole disdainful glances at parish girls who, out of uniform, impersonated hippies in shredded jeans. Others came as gypsies in flouncy skirts, some donning necklaces that dangled seashells and shark teeth. Unable to finish his meal, Cassidy again signaled Lambert, who pulled out the pastor's chair, the two proceeding to the front of the stage to initiate a receiving line.

Aunt Pearl saw all of this, and as she tore at a chicken leg, she sneered at the fawning parishioners rushing up to the line. "I, for one," she said to her sister, "will be glad to see him gone for good."

"Yes, Pearl, he'll make a fine bishop as he brings the diocese to heel in no time at all. As for today, we can see what His Highness is up to, hobnobbing with the big shots. All so that they remain donors to the diocese."

"Girls," said Dan, "be nice, now."

When it became obvious to Cassidy that parishioners wanted to get back on the dance floor, he looked for an opening to take flight back to the rectory. He found one when the collarless Father Ken, out in the parking lot, drew the attention of many by laughing violently after a fall in the burlap bag race. Within minutes of the pastor's departure, the band resumed, and over the next hour, the dance floor again moved with great energy. Aunt Pearl, in her pumps and A-line skirt, snatched the bandana that the drummer had tossed out, and to the roar of the crowd, wrapped it around her head. Not to be outdone, Uncle John with his cane ambled out to the dance floor. Grinning at a bevy of young ladies careening round him, he tossed his cane aside and improvised slow jazzy movements to the music. He swayed his hips and waggled his fingers, the dance floor all but losing its mind.

Standing off and taking it all in, Dennis felt a tap on his shoulder.

"Denny Boy, would you like to dance?"

His eyes skipped past the wet lips to her midriff, then to cut-off shorts and bare feet, toenails painted a loud red. With a laugh, Eleanor Fenwick slipped one arm around his and said, "That's okay. We can just watch." And watch they did until a local stud asked her to dance. Dennis retreated to his family's table just as his aunt and uncle returned to their seats.

Sometime later Peter and William appeared, hands jingling coins. "Let's go, Denny," Peter said. "Off to win big at the roulette table."

"Not so fast!" said Aunt Pearl. "I never got to ask you guys what the Horse's Ass had to say to you three at the rectory a few weeks back. You know, about getting caught in the buff?"

"Pearl Girl," said Uncle John, "watch that smutty mouth of yours."

"Hey, Old Man, finish your beans and play dead. Huh, did he spank your hineys and good?"

"Classified, Aunt Pearl. Gotta go."

Each boy won a round at the roulette table. They placed another bet just as Vinnie approached in his army fatigues, Liz Pearce at his side. Vinnie put his dime on number eight as the wheel was spun. With the winning number being nineteen, Vinnie nudged his coin there. "Hey, look, my lucky day."

"Nice try," said William pushing the dime back to eight. "But God hates a cheater."

"Damn, not you three again."

"Yes, Mr. Army man, us three again."

As Dennis yanked on William, and Liz did the same to Vinnie, Father Ken arrived with a prize he had just won, a goldfish swimming in a plastic bag.

"Hello, hello, Vincent and Liz. I see you've met the three parish vandals who, so I'm told, recently practiced their craft at your house, and now only await the principal's retribution." Handing the bag to Dennis, "Here, Mr. Hurley, a reward for those who swim in the backwaters. Anyway, Vincent," he paused to wink at him, "I'll be seeing you in a bit."

As the priest left, Vinnie exposed the sheathed knife at his side. "If any of you dare step foot on my property again, I'll do what my old man ain't got the stones to do. Skin each of you alive. Bury you in the woods."

"Not," William poked Vinnie with a finger, "if we bury you there first."

Both Peter and Dennis, now tugging hard on William, were able to pull him away, Vinnie left behind to stare them down.

"Damn, William," said Dennis, "we can hardly afford any more trouble. Remember what the Doughboy just said, Rosaleen deliberating our fate."

"Smoke out of his ass, is all," Peter answered for William.

The sun low in the sky, Father Ken mounted the stage and interrupted the music by tapping the microphone, unhappy dancers sent back to their seats.

"Ladies and gentlemen, I'd like to conclude this year's picnic by inviting up to the podium a very special guest speaker, Mr. Vincent Malagati, son of our esteemed custodian of some forty years."

Dennis looked over and saw Mr. Malagati, who paused from adjusting a concession pressure gauge to look up at his son. The old custodian's face hot like a stone, he shook his head in disgust. He spat at the ground.

"Lucky enough to escape as a prisoner in Vietnam, and now man enough to talk about the quagmire we call war, Vincent has become a regular at local American Legion events. He represents a dream we all have about growth at St. Theresa's."

The priest pausing to wink at Vinnie, some in the audience looked intrigued. Still others, remembering Vinnie as a town bully, were in no mood. Among them was Jack Hogan who had other plans to conclude the picnic.

"Growth," Father Ken's voice turned strident, "that someday comes in the form of a new parish prayer garden. Where we all can find tranquility and peace when we speak with God. So, a big round of applause for Vincent Malagati."

No sooner was that said than the cross-country coach mounted the stage and stepped in front of Vinnie. Coach Jack announced the grand idea he had withheld from Margie Mudhank the previous night at the Lantern Inn: "Yup, Father Ken. A new prayer garden. An idea for the ages. In addition, Ole Jack Hogan wants everyone to know that after the speech, and to conclude this year's picnic, there'll be a special foot race on our very own Sitting Bull Run course for the youngsters of our parish. A short mile. Prizes for all who finish. And the icing on the cake is that our very own state-ranked parish team will take part in the race."

From his table, Dennis exchanged a stunned look with his two friends, each with their own families.

"Now, as Father Ken said, a big, fat welcome for Private First Class Vincent Malagati."

Vinnie stepped up on the stage to applause and flattened the sheets of paper awaiting him on the lectern. "Sitting down last night to ponder my heartfelt experiences in Vietnam, I asked myself what in God's name went wrong? Now, I'd be the last one to take umbrage with the elected leaders of our country, for the ambiv- ambiv-" As Vinnie choked on the word, it became apparent to anyone who had sat through one of Father Ken's homilies that the guest speaker had help with his speech.

With Vinnie soldiering on, Jack Hogan outside the tent had gathered his varsity seven, who were not at all happy that they were being forced to take part in the race.

"But it's the parish picnic," Legs moaned. "We've been eating all afternoon."

"I'm practically bloated," Adam added.

"And I'm in sandals," from Fenny.

"Me, too," said Mumbles.

Jack Hogan exploded. "I don't give a flying fuck if you've just eaten six bratwursts and a bucket of coleslaw. Puke your brains out for all I care. But make damn sure that you and your bare feet are on the starting line when the gun goes off. Or else! And, Legs, be my guest! Make an ass out of yourself by finishing dead last! The *Bellport Citizen* would love that picture."

Jack Hogan returned under the tent and mounted the stage, now standing with arms folded just feet from the guest speaker. Clearly rattled, Vinnie awkwardly concluded his speech with, "You're good people. Peace."

"Race time!" shouted the coach.

With a mob of young participants crowded along the starting line, the barefoot varsity team stood sandwiched in the middle. Coach Jack raised his bullhorn and offered a few directions, which included tapping the plaque at the halfway point and shouting, Sitting Bull.

"Okay, all you huckleberries! It's time." The starting pistol raised, "Runners, set, and...."

The pistol's crack, the field took off.

Coach Jack waited just a short time before he again raised the bullhorn. "Folks, while we wait for my varsity to loop the tennis courts and head down the path to the turn-around point, the plaque of the famous chief, keep in mind that St. Theresa's returns six runners from last year's third-place state finish. Pundits say we're the team to beat this November."

However, while lavishing more praise, he noticed that his team was trapped in the middle of the field. He lowered the bullhorn and charged over to the race trail, in time to get directly in their faces. "Break now, I say. Break now, or else!"

Adam took off, dragging with him Legs, who blurted, "Slow down, asshole."

"Damn you, Legs," yelled Adam, forcing his teammate to go with him. Dennis saw this and surged, pulling along Peter and William. Fenny and Mumbles waited a bit before they also took off.

To Coach Jack's great relief, his team entered the path ahead of the field in packs of two, three, and two. "Yep, folks," the bullhorn again, "I love these boys! I truly do. And pardon my French, but they've been training like hell all summer long. Right now, they're running in the same formation they'll run this November when they hope to win state."

The three packs reemerging from the path wowed the crowd with the gulf between Jack Hogan's varsity and all others. The gulf grew larger as they circled the tennis courts and motored down the final stretch. To rousing cheers, each exhausted pack crossed the finish line, one after the other, not at all sorry that Coach Jack's damn show-and-tell was over.

Soon the long line of runners trickled in. Sister Jean reached into a canvas bag and passed along a small door prize to each.

As the final stragglers, some walking, finished the race, the bullhorn was raised a last time. "Well, folks, another annual parish picnic has come and gone. Hope you had a damn good time. And do have a safe drive home."

Dusk gathering strength, the families started to pack their belongings and make their way to their cars. The Walkers were among the first to leave. Peter, with the family cooler in tow, detoured over to William and Dennis, still dragging from the race.

"Hey, I just passed Mary Gonzaga talking with the Prune."

"About?" asked Dennis.

"The saint's busted arm. And you're not gonna believe what I overheard!"

"I fucking knew it," said William. "Expulsion?"

"It's not good," Peter replied with pursed lips.

"What do you mean it's not good? Tell us."

"Gotta go. My dad's waiting. Meet me at the boulder at ten. Tell you then."

"Suspension?" Dennis yelled after him.

"Make it eleven," Peter shouted back. "My dad will be asleep by then."

Soon, as the Hurley wagon merged into the line of cars heading out of the parish and onto Main Street, Uncle John let it be known that he didn't like Vinnie's speech. "Chicken noodle soup. Canned."

"John," Aunt Pearl said, "everyone has their opinion about the war."

"I didn't know Ginger Rogers talks politics."

Aunt Pearl was too tired to argue, and by the time Dan turned onto Crocus, Tommy had fallen asleep in his mother's arms. Dennis, in the back of the wagon, closed his eyes and pictured running along the shore, the day's heat all but gone, waves curling and dropping in thuds. He couldn't help but feel a tenderness for the day, which had finally come to an end. But then his eyes snapped back open. Rosaleen came to mind. And what Peter had learned. And the meeting at the boulder at eleven.

Damn, he muttered, the day's not over yet. Not by a long shot.

A BOURBON IN HAND, Cassidy turned off the desk lamp and sat in the darkness watching what remained of the clean-up crew finish its work. In less than an hour, the concession stands had disappeared. Tables and chairs whisked away. Only the picnic tent remained intact, to be taken down in the morning.

The pastor waited for the last vehicle to leave the grounds, Hogan in his new van, before swiveling around and turning his desk lamp back on. The wall clock nearing ten, he lowered his drink and unlocked the desk drawer. He withdrew the *Memorandum*. He skimmed through its annual lists until he reached the current year, *Jack Hogan* the last target on the list. Cassidy penciled in *Father Ken*.

Satisfied, he returned the book to the desk drawer, locked it, and retired upstairs to his apartment.

20

It was after eleven, 32 Crocus dark throughout, when Dennis felt safe slipping outside. Once on the field, he bumped into William, who said, "Here goes nothing, Denny, judgment day."

The two passed through the woods and bounded the creek rocks. They found Peter sitting on the boulder.

"Okay, Chief Wrecking Ball," William said. "What's the big news?"

"Yeah, Peter. Let's have it. What did you hear?"

Peter jumped off the boulder and reached into a cardboard box filled with six cans of beer. He pulled out three and placed them on the boulder. He opened them, and after handing one to each of his friends, he lifted his own high in the air and said, "A bon voyage party, that's the big news. You know, to toast the summer goodbye!"

William looked at Dennis. "Is it possible we've been fucking duped again?"

Peter said, "C'mon, you two. I heard nothing. No expulsion. No suspension. You both know we would have heard something by now. So I grabbed a six-pack of my Dad's favorite brew. Schlitz! The beer that made Milwaukee famous."

William looked out into the woods. "What do you think, Denny?"

"Hard to say, though it has been a good week since the St. Frankie incident, and still nothing. Maybe we dodged a bullet after all."

"We always do!" said Peter, again lifting his beer for the toast. "To the Summer of 1974! May she rest in peace."

Dennis added, "And may the fall season bring us good luck each and every Saturday."

"On some bad-ass race trail," said William.

"Heck, yeah, now we're talking," Peter said. "Hey, why not go through the season, one meet at a time, each of us tossing out predictions."

That's what the three started to do, beginning with the Staten Island meet to be held that next Saturday, each one calling out mile splits, place, and final time. Yet as they turned to handicap the next meet, the Cardinal Hayes Invitational at Van Cortlandt, Peter nudged his two friends. A dull bemusement spread over the faces as through the trees they recognized the slow gait passing through the cemetery. Peter waited until the old custodian had disappeared before he said, "Enough of Malagati. Let's get at Cardinal Hayes! Where a 5:10 first mile ought to do the trick! Huh, Denny, what do you think?

Dennis did not answer. He was too busy peering out into the night, as if smitten by the leaves that twirled and shined with dew and rustled the mind with vague promises of running glory. But he wasn't daydreaming about the first-mile split. Rather his mind was still fixed on the old man and his dog, even though they had moved deeper into the cemetery and were lost from view.

"Huh, Denny?"

"What Denny thinks, Peter," said William, "is that a 5:10 first mile at Vanny is crazy, especially with the damn cow path and Freshman Hill. And if we tag along, we'll all die like dogs. Pure madness, just like you dragging Denny and I out here tonight for no good reason."

"Maybe, though," said Dennis as he continued to study the woods, "mad Peter Walker has managed to pull off a quiet evening."

"Hey, the night's still young," quipped Peter who took a swig.

"Not for me, it ain't," said William. "I'm all for finishing our predictions. But I'll be heading home the moment we're done."

Smacking of hubris, the three boys over the next hour resumed their analysis of each meet. Peter, of course, led the way with wildly outlandish projections that nonetheless brought goosebumps to his two friends. But when it came time to predict sectional splits at Sunken Meadow, Dennis again looked toward the cemetery and said, "You know, Mr. Malagati didn't look all that pleased at the picnic when Vinnie took the stage. Wouldn't be surprised if the two of them got into it when they both got home tonight."

"Damn!" said William, "wish I had a front row seat for them fireworks."

"Hey!" cried Peter, the flash of a smile on his face. "I know where just such a seat can be found!"

He chugged the rest of the beer, tossed the empty in the box, and took off running in the direction of the parish. His two friends did the same, both shouting ahead to Peter that he stop. But he continued on, even after reaching the dark grounds where the empty picnic tent stood. He passed the convent and finally came to a hard stop some ten yards from the bungalow fence, the pool just ahead.

The other two reached him moments later.

"Fuck, Peter!" hissed the out-of-breath William.

"Tell me," said Dennis, "you're not thinking of another swim?"

"Nah. Something far more sublime!" Peter said this pointing directly to the right and to the convent's flat-roof garage, less than ten yards away.

"Dammit, Peter," William said. "Not a joy ride?"

"Warm to hot," said Peter making his way to the side of the

garage, where he grabbed a low-lying tree limb. Pulling himself up, he stepped over onto the flat roof and said, "C'mon up!"

"What the fuck!" William said.

"C'mon up, and I'll tell you all about it."

Dennis looked at William. "We better go up there and talk him down!"

Soon all three boys were sitting atop the roof.

"It's like this," Peter began. "Once when I was heading downtown, the windows caught my attention. So I jumped up here."

"What windows?" Dennis asked.

"Them," said Peter pointing at the second-floor convent windows across the way. In plain view was a small handful of nuns in a social room of sorts that spanned the building's west side. Stripped of habits and veils, some were in civies, others in bathrobes. The faces of William and Dennis went blank when they looked at the floor above, where behind drawn curtains silhouettes were preparing for bed.

"Aw, we ain't going to Hell," Peter said. "Besides, do you hear the convent's central AC?" He paused to allow his friends to listen to the system humming in the distance. "We could belt out a Beatles tune, and no one would hear."

"Shoeless fucking Peter!" William said. "You're out of your mind. Just a few weeks ago we got caught swimming right over there." He pointed at the Malagati pool. "Tonight, we're Peeping Toms on the convent garage!"

"Hey, you two said you wanted front row seats for the fireworks," said Peter, gesturing to the Malagati's. "Sometimes when I'm up here, I hear commotion over there. The old man and Vinnie going at it. All seems quiet tonight. But, and here's the real reason I brought you here, take a look up there."

All three arched their necks to see an opening in the trees that framed a night sky dusted with bright stars.

"Ain't that a sight for sore eyes," said Peter, who reached into a gutter and pulled out a bottle of Seagram's. He took a swig and offered it to his two friends.

Both shook their heads, an emphatic no.

William added, "Time to go! Now!"

"Okay, William," said Peter who took another swig before slipping the bottle into the gutter. He lay flat on his back. "But first, three questions and we're out of here. Promise. So to win state, where do our top five scorers have to finish? I say Adam takes third place behind upstaters Bronson and Galloway. And Legs, he must-"

The rattling of the bungalow's rear storm door caused the boys to crawl over to the edge of the roof for a better look. Liz Pearce had come outside and now stood, shoes in hand, with a panicked look. She started for the gate where she stopped to put her shoes on. Once through the gate, she stumbled and fell before scrambling up again to start running in the direction of Main Street.

"What's going on?" whispered William to his two friends.

The storm door again opened. Out came the bare-chested Vinnie in his jeans. "Hey, Lizzie," he called out looking around the yard, "where'd you go?"

Mr. Malagati came out, a gun in hand.

"Look what you did, old man!" yelled Vinnie, whose angry words, somewhat muted by the distance, could still be made out by the boys. "You scared the shit out of Lizzie. Now she's nowhere to be found!"

His father in response went over to the picnic table and pulled a white sheet off Rosa. The boys saw the lifeless dog for the first time.

"Our Rosa, Vincent," Mr. Malagati asked, "why?"

"You mess with my shit. I mess with yours."

The custodian swung the gun in an arc to point directly at Vinnie, whose initial fright turned to bravado as he moved toward his father. "Go ahead, old man, shoot me! Do it for Rosa! Do it for Momma! Neither's ever coming home again!"

Vinnie charged and knocked his father off his feet, dislodging the gun. Vinnie started kicking him all over.

William, the first to jump off the garage, his two friends right behind him, charged Vinnie and rammed him into the storm door, glass shattering, shards falling atop the patio. Vinnie bounced back and grabbed a stray shovel and pitched it at William's stomach, then Peter's. The blows caused the two boys to slump to the ground in writhing pain. Vinnie then turned on Dennis who, after deflecting the first blow, tripped and fell on his back. Dennis gasped at the shovel raised high in the air, a guillotine that might have dropped down on him but for the gun blast, the bullet striking Vinnie in the side. He shrieked in pain but managed to stay standing with the support of the shovel.

The hot gun in his father's hand, Vinnie staggered forward and swatted it free into the air with the shovel, which he then used to smash his father on the skull. The old man, falling to the ground, did his best to fend off one blow after another.

"Die, you bastard. Die!" screamed Vinnie.

But as he wound up for another swing, a second blast came. The bullet this time hit him square in the back, causing him to spin about some before dropping to his knees. He looked up and saw Dennis pointing the gun.

With dull eyes, Vinnie hissed at the shooter, "I will kill you...I will kill your family."

The threat unmistakable, a crazed Dennis bound forward and cracked Vinnie across the side of the head with the barrel of the gun. Vinnie fell face first to the ground.

Flat on his stomach, Vinnie raised his head some, his mouth a wet rattle of teeth and blood as he tried to say something else to Dennis. A convulsing came instead.

Then nothing. Vinnie's head dropped for the last time.

PART 2

21

On most summer nights, the Malagati property seemed an enchanting retreat. Moon-soaked flowerbeds. The air, fragrant and slow-moving. The pool shimmering, as if a hand from heaven had dropped diamonds on its surface. But tonight, things were different. Those on the lawn held their position as if frozen in time. Dennis, the fisted gun dangling at his side. William and Peter, crouched on the ground. The old custodian on a knee, his son sprawled dead just across the way. It stayed this way a good while.

Mr. Malagati was the first to move. He stepped over to Vinnie and yanked him over onto his back. The old man again went to a knee, and with the boys looking on in a state of shock, he took a heart-wrenching inventory of his son.

Slowly nodding his head, he stood. He went to the patio's enormous wooden planter, some two-and-a-half-feet tall and stretching about six feet long.

He looked to the boys, "Help now, please."

Dennis tossed the gun to the ground before joining his two friends to help Mr. Malagati push the planter up and over, flowers and dirt spilling out. The planter pulled upright, the boys stole looks at each other. They knew what to do. They lifted the planter and followed the old man inside the shed. They placed it on the far side, leaving room on the wooden floor for a tarp that the old man laid out.

Mr. Malagati pointed to his son out in the yard.

Without a word, the boys retrieved the body and laid it atop the tarp.

The old man grabbed a cloth rag, and, as best he could, rubbed his son's face clean of blood and grime. He took one last look before wrapping him. He stood, backstepped, and again gestured to the boys. They lowered Vinnie into what had become a makeshift coffin. Mr. Malagati pulled plywood from the rafters and nailed the coffin shut.

"We bury. In woods."

The three boys avoided eye contact with each other as they took position. William at the front, Peter and Dennis, each on a rear side. They strained to lift the load, but once out in the yard, it became more manageable.

They followed the old man who, holding three shovels, held the gate open for them. He looked askance at the convent before scampering ahead of the pallbearers. The shovels jostling about, he led the boys across the grounds in the direction of the path, his scuffling steps bringing to mind a bear dragging prey to its lair.

Once on the path, the chorus of night sounds grew louder, crickets moaning dull-snapping sounds. At one point, William's foot caught a low spot. Nearly falling, he regained his balance, the bundle inside moving around like a bag of sand. At the Sitting Bull plaque, the processional turned and weaved a good way through trees in a northeast direction. Mr. Malagati stopped and pointed down at the desired spot, still in the woods but not far from the bottom row of graves. Nothing needed to be said as the boys lowered the coffin to the ground.

The three shovels dropped, the old man retreated to a nearby tree to stare into the night.

The boys started digging, stopping only to take brief breaks. They tried not to look at each other. Every so often they did.

The digging remained fierce, each boy at times startled by his own panting breath.

As the hole grew deeper, they took turns dropping in to continue digging while the other two stood above and watched.

When the hole seemed deep enough, William yelled over, "This do, Mr. Malagati?"

The old man refused to respond.

Dennis jumped into the hole to help with the maneuvering. No sooner was the box below ground than William and Peter started shoveling dirt back in, their friend sprayed with it as he pushed himself out of the hole.

Dennis remained on his knees, and as if a flood started in him, his arms plowed dirt at a feverish pitch, this as the other two heaved shovelfuls.

The hole soon filled, a mound emerged above it.

The boys dropped the shovels, a brisk walk turning into a mad dash. Like wild dogs they tore back through the trees and past the plaque, down the creek's bank, splashing water above their heads. On the other side they ran to the wood's edge, where they stopped and paced about. Nothing but terror on their faces, the intractable night emptying their lungs of air.

"Holy, holy shit!" cried Peter. "We just buried Vinnie Malagati!"

"After fucking killing him!" said William. He cried out as he took off running, "Get rid of everything. Burn it all, including shoes."

Peter started running, too.

Dennis shouted after his friends. He wanted them to go over what had just happened. But they ignored his calls and soon exited the woods. He looked back and through the trees spotted the distant figure of Mr. Malagati, again on a knee. Dennis shook his head and took off for the field. His friends had already crossed it and were now heading down Dahlia Lane to their homes. He took dead aim at 32 Crocus.

Once in his room, he undressed in the dark. He nudged his clothes and trainers under his bed. At the window he peered across at the woods. He closed his eyes. Rocked by the images that flashed through his brain, he collapsed onto his bed. He tossed about and struggled to sleep. But then came the town's foghorn. It was the last thing he remembered.

Soon, the winds picked up and a storm rolled into Bellport. Rain flashed down, black and silver. Tree boughs whipped houses and scratched gutters. A spectacular thunderclap awakened Dennis, the percussive roll shaking his house. He went to the window. Rain misted through the screen. Shrieking white flashes lit up the field and woods. He fell back to bed and curled the pillow around his head. He waited for sleep to return.

A DRENCHED MR. MALAGATI had fought the gusting rain as he finished spreading foliage over the mound. The three shovels in hand, he left for home, rainwater dissolving footprints. Reaching the bungalow, the old man, with wheezing gasps, dug a hole in the rear of the yard for his beloved Rosa. He wrapped her, and after lowering her, he filled in the hole. He dropped to a knee and stayed that way a while.

He then turned to the mound of planter mud, grunting shovelfuls into the yard, spreading it out as best he could. He took the shovels into the shed and wiped each one down. He retrieved the gun and placed it on the picnic table. He ran his hands through the wet grass until he located the two gun shells, which along with the gun, he took into the shed. He hid them in a secret workbench compartment that held other keepsakes. Only then did he retreat inside. After toweling off mud, he lifted a framed photo of his Loretta and slumped onto a chair.

SITTING BULL RUN

THE STORM HAVING BLOWN out to sea, Dennis awoke at dawn to the cries of land birds. He looked over at the poster. Pre's dark, vexing eyes now seemed to be saying that he, too, was on the run from some terrible wrong he had committed. Dennis got out of bed and went to the grey window. The field looked like it did whenever a summer squall had passed. Strong slow winds, cool and moist, shouldering their way, treetops swaying back and forth. Somewhere out there in the woods a box was sinking in newly dug earth.

Good God! If we had just left well enough alone after the picnic. If we had just stayed home!

SISTER GRACE CORDE looked into her bedroom mirror. Her habit in place, a strand of red hair slipped out of her headpiece. She frowned some before tucking it back under.

"There."

Ready for early Mass, she'd join Sister Mary Clotilda waiting below. But as she turned to leave, out the window she noticed Charlie retrieving the newspaper from his drive. He seemed in a rush. Scurrying, in fact, which surprised her. Charlie never scurried.

A FEW HOURS had passed. Catherine tapped her son's bedroom door before opening it.

"Dennis, Dennis," she nudged him awake. "We're leaving for nine-thirty Mass." She pulled apart the curtains, the room filling with light.

"My stomach's bothering me, Mom. I'll go later. Okay?"

"Your father won't be happy. But okay."

Once the wagon had pulled away, Dennis got up and looked out at the puddles on Crocus and across at treetops no longer swaying. He drew the curtain closed and fell back into bed, not to wake up again until his mother, returning from Mass, called up to ask how he was doing.

"Stomach still hurts," he shouted back. "About to shower."

Burn everything is what William had said. So he pulled it all out from under his bed. He saw red splatter on his shirt and jeans and sneakers. As he stuffed it all into an old gym bag, he discovered congealed blood and dirt on his arms. In the second-floor shower, he scrubbed and scrubbed, reddish brown streams flowing down his legs into swirls around the drain. The ceiling light grew dim in the mist, then indiscernible.

Fully dressed, he went below and slipped out the side door. He burrowed his gym bag deep down into a pocket of trash inside the garbage can.

Back inside, he found his parents at the table.

"So you're feeling better?" his mother asked as he poured himself a glass of juice.

"A little."

"Hey, Dennis," said his father holding up a newspaper photo of the core three on the final straight of the picnic race. "Coach Jack Hogan must have been tinkled pink."

His mother asked, "What time is practice today?"

"Run-on-your-own day. Think I'm gonna go back upstairs and lay down."

"The picnic race get to you?" his father asked.

"Think so. Is it okay if I skip Mass today?"

"Better not be faking it."

"Before you head back up," his mother said, "please go through the box of clothes in the den. And tell me what fits and what doesn't. School starts on Wednesday, you know."

He did just that. But he also made a hushed phone call to William, who told him not to call anymore that day unless something came up. Peter had little more to say than "what's done is done."

SITTING BULL RUN

A few hours later, Dennis again phoned his two friends. He asked each to go out for a night run and discuss what happened.

Not tonight, both replied.

What the fuck, Dennis thought as he headed up the stairs to his room where over the next several hours he paced about. William in his basement attacked a punching bag. Peter took a long bike ride. On the way back, he stopped to scoop up the box of empty beer cans at the boulder.

The old custodian waited until the sun set before he hosed down puddles in the grass that reflected blood. He swept up glass and taped plastic over the storm door. He hosed excess planter dirt off the surface of the patio. He looked around and went inside.

During the day, Liz Pearce failed several times to reach Vinnie by phone. She didn't know that the old man had stood by unwilling to pick up. She had a bad feeling. Late that night she set out for the bungalow and found both the motorcycle and the truck under the carport. Light bled through the edges of drawn shades. She went around back and noticed plastic taped over the storm door's ragged edges of glass. She knocked on it several times. No one came.

She stepped back and called up to the bedroom window. "Vin! Vin! You there?"

Nothing.

"C'mon, Vin."

Still nothing.

She left for Main Street where over the next few hours she drank heavily at the Branding Iron. Eventually, the bartender said to her, "It's nearing one-thirty, Miss. Can I get you a taxi?"

"Sure, why not."

It took a while for the taxi to arrive, and once back at her house on Fountain Lane, she phoned the bungalow over and over again. Still, no one picked up. She looked at the clock. When she saw that it was nearing three, she felt herself reaching the boiling point. She left her house and headed for a phone booth at a nearby gas station to dial 911.

"What is your emergency?"

"You need to send someone over to St. Theresa's parish. To search the Malagati place."

"Your name, please?"

"Something's really wrong there. Send someone now."

Liz hung up and returned home, where she curled up in a blanket and cursed herself to sleep.

22

A dawn fog covered all of Bellport as police continued fanning the parish grounds with flashlights. A Suffolk County government vehicle driven by D.A. Lambert left the rectory with Cassidy in the passenger seat and crawled in the direction of the bungalow. As the vehicle neared, the pastor recoiled at the sight of a detective putting a handcuffed Charlie into the back seat of a squad car.

"Like I said, Monsignor, an anonymous call came in a few hours ago. Charlie without any prodding admitted to it right away. He even told us where he buried the body. But nothing more. Nothing at all. Now we got to get him to tell us what happened."

Lambert steered the vehicle into the cemetery and over to the cordoned-off area. A large police presence stood by the planter, the top pried off and resting beside the hole cleared of dirt. The pastor, in a bathrobe and rain boots, stepped out of the vehicle. He flinched at the body being lifted out of the makeshift coffin and transferred onto a gurney. A journalist across the creek snapped photos.

Waking later, Dennis went below and found his father dunking a tea bag.

"Where's Mom?"

"Out front getting the paper."

He turned and saw her out by the curb retrieving the *Bellport Citizen* from the mailbox. Starting back up, she stopped when something on the front page caught her attention. Her head bobbing, she looked up, and as if the house was on fire, she nearly tripped racing up the drive.

"My God, Dan," she cried out entering the kitchen.

Her husband stood. "My God, what?"

She dropped the paper on the table. Dan lurched at the headline. Dennis, too.

*St. Theresa Custodian
Confesses to the Murder of Soldier Son
Found Buried Near Parish Cemetery*

The article included three photos: the handcuffed Charlie being led into the courthouse, the makeshift coffin beside the hole, and the disheveled Cassidy in bathrobe and rainboots.

"And look here, Dan, it says, *Police know little at this point except that Vincent Malagati received multiple gunshot wounds. Blood splatter collected in the bungalow's backyard indicates that the shooting most likely occurred there, the body then transported to the cemetery. An anonymous 911 tip is what led police to scour the parish woods where the fresh grave was discovered.*"

Dan pointed to another line. "And there's this, Cat. *Sources say that Malagati is not cooperating with police other than admitting to the shooting.*"

The phone rang. Catherine picked it up and listened before saying, "Yes, Pearl, we're just now reading it. Let me call you back."

Seconds later, the phone rang again. This time she handed the receiver to Dennis. "It's Coach Jack."

"Coach?"

"For Christ's sake, Dennis, nightmare on Elm Street. Gonna need to cancel practice today until I find out just what's going on. I need you to call around and tell the others that I want everyone to make sure they run on their own today. And I mean, run."

"I will, Coach."

"That's not to say we won't resume practice tomorrow. Tell everyone that we'll meet tomorrow at three o'clock in my office. Got it?"

"Got it."

"You do know school starts on Wednesday and we have our first meet this Saturday?"

"Yeah, Coach."

"Remind them of that, too."

"I will."

Dennis went into the den to make the calls, the last two going to Peter and William. The three agreed to meet downtown right away.

A FEW MILES NORTH in Yaphank, waiting journalists and television cameras converged on the steps of the county jail. Except for the initial reporting, little else had been revealed since the discovery of the body some hours earlier. Editors sent their best people to dig up whatever they could. A sensational story about the custodian of the prestigious St. Theresa's parish killing his decorated veteran son would easily sustain itself for days on end.

In an interrogation room, a detective named Watts sat opposite Charlie Malagati, whose forehead and cheekbone appeared hollowed out by angry purple bruises. Lambert looked in on the interview through the one-way mirror. This was the second time this morning that the old man had been pulled from his cell.

"Dammit, Charlie," said Watts, "you admitted to pulling the trigger, right?"

"Yes."

"Why not tell us what started it? And where's the gun? And

how the heck you managed afterwards, all on your own, if that's what happened?"

Charlie shook his head back and forth. He would not say.

FLANKED BY WILLIAM AND PETER outside Whelan's Drug Store, Dennis lowered the *Long Island Press*. The account there was much more thorough than that of the *Bellport Citizen,* starting with Charlie Malagati confessing only to the shooting. The article also reported two bullet wounds to the victim's back and side. Other information included that the family dog was found buried in the yard and that Elizabeth Pearce was seen riding on Main Street with Vinnie on his Harley around ten that night.

"The only thing that's missing," Dennis said, "is that I finished Vinnie off."

"And that we buried him," from Peter.

"Thank God the old man's not talking," William added. "And thank God for the rain that hopefully washed away any tracks we left. You two did get rid of everything, right?"

Both nodded.

Dennis said, "Why won't the old man just tell them what happened?"

"We fucked up," William shot back. "That's what happened."

"What I mean is, why doesn't he tell the police he was protecting me from Vinnie, who was about to slice me open with that shovel."

"He won't," said William. "The only thing Malagati cares about is that his son is dead."

"And that I followed up with a second shot. And a whack to the head."

"Hey, there's enough blame to go around. I was the idiot who first jumped off the roof."

"And I led us there," Peter added. "Let's just pray the old man continues to keep his mouth shut."

"Rosa," said Dennis. "Vinnie probably killed her. You heard what he said about the old man *messing with his shit* stuff?"

"We don't know that," Peter said. "The dog could have croaked on its own. In fact, what's to say that's not what caused the old man to go psycho in the first place."

Dennis would not let go. "What about the girlfriend? We saw her fleeing. What if she knows what happened before we got there? What if she knows what caused it?"

"What if, Denny," William cried, "the goddam queen has balls!"

A sheriff's car pulled into the parking lot, prompting the boys to start in the other direction.

"At least," Dennis said, "let's get our stories straight. So that when detectives come knocking at our doors, the three of us will know what to tell them."

William and Peter stopped in their tracks. They turned and stared down their friend.

"When the time comes!" William shouted. "You know how many laws we broke?"

"So what are we going to do?"

William poked Dennis in the chest. "What we always do."

"And that is?"

"We run. We eat. We sleep. That's what we do."

"Are you serious?"

"As a fucking heart attack!"

"No one, Denny, can ever know that we were involved," said Peter.

"Not our parents! Not anyone!" William reaffirmed. "Got it?"

When Dennis would not answer, an angry William repeated his question, "I said, Denny, you got it?"

With reluctance, Dennis said, "Got it."

As William and Peter resumed walking, Dennis was about to catch up when he heard a horn blast. Aunt Pearl in the green Nova pulled up beside him. "Quick, get in. I'll give you a ride home."

He got in, the Nova taking off.

"With his wife dead and gone, Dennis, I'm thinking that Ole Charlie got the itch for Dizzy Lizzy. I'm off to see what your mother thinks. You wait and see. Auntie Pearl will get to the bottom of this."

Up in his room, Dennis heard his aunt's bellowing voice below, at one point calling for the death penalty.

Later that night, William phoned to remind Dennis about what was at stake if their parents were to find out. "They'd lose their minds, Denny. Start poking around. Wanting answers. Before you know it, police would catch wind and shit would hit the fan. We'd all go down in flames. No, dammit, our parents are never to know. Never!"

William hung up without waiting for a response.

Over at the Bellport Country Club, Nick Lambert hurried into the dining room where he found Cassidy sitting in a far corner.

"Sorry to keep you waiting, Monsignor."

"Not at all, Nick."

"So, where to begin?"

"Obviously, not with that hideous photo of me in the morning paper."

"Awfully sorry that was taken."

"What do we know, Nick?"

"At this point only that the two knocked the stuffing out of each other in their backyard before Charlie shot him. Found blood as well inside the shed."

"Sure it was Charlie who shot him?"

"We are. The blood matches. Traces of gunpowder. And, of course, he confessed to the shooting. But he'll say nothing else. He won't budge."

"What about the girlfriend? I read she was seen with Vincent after the picnic."

"Yes, my men already tracked her down at her place on Fountain Lane. She admitted to being at the bungalow. But when

Vinnie and his father got into what she called a nasty argument, she said she left. She admitted to contacting 911 the next night after she repeatedly called the Malagati place throughout the day. But no one answered."

"The source of the argument?"

"She said it concerned borrowed money. We plan on giving her a lie detector test."

"And the burial, Nick? Nothing definite there, you're saying?"

"Had Charlie used his truck to transport the body, even with the rain that washed away all tracks, there still would have been mud splatter on wheel wells. But nothing. Leaving us to believe..."

"Yes?"

"That Charlie might have had help."

Cassidy shuddered.

"Monsignor, we found three shovels in the shed, the handles still damp, the blades with traces of wet mud. I immediately thought of Charlie's nephews. After all, we learned that they shoveled mulch on the parish grounds the day of the picnic, which they also attended."

"Have you contacted them?"

"Yes. We spoke to each on the phone. They said that after the picnic they went out on a night fishing charter. Off Fire Island. My best man's driving there as we speak to check out the story."

"What do you think he'll find?"

"To be honest, I think we'll find that their story holds."

"I see."

"Monsignor, does Charlie have any acquaintances we're not aware of? Maybe three poker buddies?"

"Charlie! The man's a loner..." The pastor's voice trailed off as the three little pigs came to mind. After all, they had just recently vandalized the bungalow grotto, and they were forever prowling about the grounds in nocturnal frolic. But no sooner did that thought emerge than Cassidy dismissed it, if only because the involvement of parish youth in such a horrible crime was more than his sensibility could handle. The far more likely scenario was the unique resourcefulness of his custodian, who was notorious for working solo on all parish fixes over the years. "In fact, Nick, I don't know if Charlie has a single friend."

"That's what I thought."

"Nick, where might we be going with all of this?"

"At this point we are obligated to exhaust all possibilities. It could get ugly if others are involved."

"A hornet's nest of reporters is what you're saying. The newspapers, the TV stations, they'll all have a field day."

"You know, Monsignor, if the old man would just tell us what happened, and where the gun is, I could move things along quickly. Get things wrapped up in fairly short order."

"Before Rome?"

"I like to think so."

"From time to time, Nick, Charlie's opened up to me. He trusts me. I'm thinking out loud here, but if I could just have a few minutes alone with him. Of course, I doubt very much that the Vatican would want to see another front-page photo of me. This time, climbing the steps of a police lock-up."

"Listen, Charlie hasn't been charged yet. After the sun goes down tonight, I could have my men slip him out and drop him off back at his place. Maybe you can get the full story out of him there."

"I can try."

"Something rock solid that will allow my office to put this case to bed. But, Monsignor, let me caution you. In my day, I've seen lots of broken men like Charlie Malagati."

"Oh?"

"Yes, and for some of them, well, they just don't last, if you know what I mean."

"I'll be careful, Nick. I'll tread lightly."

It was after nine that night when a winded Dan Hurley entered the kitchen, Dennis and his mother at the table. "Not going to believe what I just heard at the gas station. Charlie's home!"

"Home?" cried his wife.

"Word is charges will come in a day or two."

As his parents went on to express disbelief, Dennis headed to the den phone.

Less than twenty minutes later, Peter and William crossed over creek rocks and found their friend at the boulder.

"Okay, Denny," asked Peter, "what's so important?"

"My father just heard that the police dropped Mr. Malagati off at the bungalow, but that charges are coming."

"And?" said William.

"And I'm off to see him."

"Like hell, you are."

"You're not serious," Peter said.

"You guys were there. Vinnie was about to open me up with that shovel, kill me in the process. And had he gotten his hands on the gun, he would have turned it on you, too. We need to convince Mr. Malagati to tell the police what happened. We can back him up. You can come. Or not!"

William jumping in front of him, "You're gonna get us thrown in jail!"

Dennis broke away and took off running, his friends trailing him along the path and over the grounds. All three stopped to catch their breath when they reached the bottom of the drive. The pickup and motorcycle were still under the carport. The bungalow was dark throughout.

AT FIRST, CASSIDY was unable to make out the three figures in the night. Turning off his desk lamp, he leaned forward in his swivel and refocused. He now recognized Hurley, Walker, and Flanagan. They seemed to be arguing amongst themselves. At one point, Flanagan prevented Hurley from heading up the drive.

So did Walker. But Hurley, having none of it, pushed them aside and approached the front door. He knocked. Then a second time. Cassidy pictured Charlie refusing to answer.

The boy circled the bungalow, stopping at each window. But finding curtains drawn, he returned to his friends. It was only after the three again started arguing with each other that Cassidy smacked the desk and muttered, "That's got to be it!" And as Flanagan and Walker pulled a reluctant Hurley away and disappeared on the path, Cassidy said in surprised disbelief, "Three shovels, three little pigs!"

For a brief moment, he silently congratulated himself on solving the mystery that had consumed the town all day, namely, who else was involved in the incident. When talking with Nick Lambert at the country club, he had initially dismissed the possibility of their involvement. But now, having just watched the boys at odds with each other, and well after dark, he knew better. While he did not know to what degree they were involved—the killing itself? the burial? both?—at the moment he didn't care about a precise answer. Just that these three, happily joined at the hip since birth, were now rejecting each other with the rawest of emotions, and at the bottom of the bungalow drive.

But another thought. What if word was to leak out that parish youth had taken part? The incident had already caused damage enough to St. Theresa's. The coverage would escalate into a national story. The Vatican would be left to wonder if this Cassidy fellow was indeed the right man for the job.

His nimble mind going to work, he right there and then settled on a strategy that, for all its chilling effects, would nonetheless bring closure to the affair without involving the boys, whom he would later take care of in-house. But first, to confirm his hunch, he tapped a phone line.

"Nick, this is Monsignor. Just calling to let you know that I'll soon be making my way over to see Charlie. I just got off the phone with the archbishop who understandably wants details. Anything new I can tell him? Say, on the nephews?"

"There is. The captain of the charter confirmed that they were on board when the boat left at ten, not getting back till eight that next morning."

"Your thoughts now?"

"Maybe the three shovels were just a coincidence. Maybe they had been outside when the rain started. And that Charlie put them back in the shed. And maybe, just maybe, he somehow pulled it off on his own. In any event, our best hope is that you can squeeze information out of him, especially the location of the gun. Something that will bring a swift resolution to the affair."

"I'll give it the old college try, Nick. And as mentioned to you at the club, I'll be sure to tread lightly."

His hunch confirmed, Cassidy swiveled around to take in the dark parish grounds. He'd wait until the few remaining convent lights went out before he headed over to the bungalow.

After watching the lights go out one by one, Cassidy put on his waistcoat, grabbed his top hat, and left for the bungalow. But he decided against the most direct route, past the convent. A pesky nun from her bedroom, unable to sleep, might see him if he went right by. So he scurried the long way around the perimeter of the Great Lawn.

23

The old custodian shook some when the knocks came. The Hurley boy again, he thought. More knocks, his name called out. Recognizing the voice, he turned on a light and held open the door for Monsignor Cassidy, who said, "However damnable their role was in it all, Charlie, the souls of three boys are at stake. Three parish boys. May I come in?"

The pastor didn't wait for an answer but stepped past the custodian and hung his top hat on a wall peg.

"Now, Charlie, please, do sit."

After the old man lowered onto a chair, Cassidy saw firsthand the anguish and torment that Lambert had mentioned, and of which he had no choice but to take full advantage. "For starters, you must know that I, as your pastor of many years, have your best interest at heart. And if it will also help, think of this as a private conversation, akin to the sacred seal of Holy Confession. But your story tonight must be truthful. Above all, it must include the role of the three parish boys."

The old man slowly nodded.

"Charlie, as I see it, all signs point to Hurley, Walker, and Flanagan. Those three practically live on the grounds. And how they know the night. So, go ahead, tell me what happened late Saturday evening. And please start at the very beginning."

It took the old man a while to collect himself.

But when he did, he began by describing one of his son's several financial transactions he witnessed at the back door, concluding that drugs were involved. The old man then told the pastor how his son's picnic speech made him so uncomfortable that afterwards he broke open Vincent's secret safe in his upstairs bedroom where he discovered drugs, money, and a handgun. All of this led to a halting summary of the violent confrontation in the yard that involved, yes, the three boys. He omitted that Vincent had killed Rosa, a thought too horrible to express. He finished up with the boys' additional hand in the burial.

Stunned by the details, Cassidy then asked, "Charlie, have you told any of this to the police?"

"No."

"None of it?"

"None."

"But you did confess to shooting Vincent?"

"Yes."

"And you still have the gun?"

"I hide in shed."

Cassidy took a moment to walk about the room inspecting trinkets.

"Until now, Charlie, God in his mercy has been good to you, blessing you with many productive years. Carrying an entire parish on your shoulders as you have. Now the unspeakable has befallen you, and you have things to sort out. Am I right?"

The old man nodded.

"Charlie, I find no pleasure in this. But what if the boys' role in it came out in the newspapers? Everything from their trespassing on parish grounds to their hand in Vincent's death as well as their carrying him to the cemetery and burying him? Have you thought what would happen if the police, if the public, learned of it?"

"Yes."

"And?"

"Not good."

"Yes, the three did break laws. Especially Hurley. Laws that the police could not ignore. And while I know little of these things, I imagine each boy would be rounded up, charged, and thrown in some prison for a long period of time. Ruin what's left of their lives. Their families, too."

Cassidy paused to let the image sink in.

"Which is why it is noble of you, if I am reading you correctly, to want to shield the three, and ultimately the parish family."

Before the old man had time to fully absorb the thought, the pastor went to a window and, pushing the curtain aside, looked out into the cemetery. "Speaking of the parish family, Charlie, your poor wife's been out there how long?"

"Six years."

"I miss Loretta. I miss her smile. Her gentle way. And now, Vincent."

The old man looked up, the terrible anguish again in full view, eyes wailing grief.

As the pastor retrieved his hat, he spoke words he had rehearsed in his office over the last hour, words intended to unleash the demons in his custodian: "Yes, it's enough to break a man. It would break me." Then opening the back door for the final volley, "You've led a good life, Charlie Malagati. Don't let anyone tell you otherwise."

Cassidy closed the door behind him and headed back into the night, the seeds left to take root.

Briskly retracing his steps around the Great Lawn, the pastor looked around like a burglar who had just stolen a golden chalice from the church. As he passed by the St. Theresa statue, however, he had no idea that hiding behind it was the Hurley boy, who stepped out and watched Cassidy make his way over to a side rectory door. After the earlier attempt to question Mr. Malagati had failed, Dennis had decided to wait until his parents had gone to bed and try again to gain access to the old man. He would talk sense into him. He would tell him to go to the police and tell all.

Reaching the grounds, however, Dennis had seen the pastor entering the bungalow. He waited some before he stole up to a side window. The shades drawn, he could not make out the words, only somber tones. He retreated back to the statue where he'd wait until the pastor had left before taking on the old man. While he waited, his initial thought was that Cassidy, in his priestly role, had been consoling the old man.

But now Dennis didn't know what to make of the pastor scurrying right by him. As he searched for an answer, Mr. Malagati came out and headed for the cemetery.

He's off to see his wife, Dennis thought. The moment's not right. I'll try again in the morning.

Less than an hour later, Dennis lay in bed thinking about the old man out there in miserable grief, undoubtedly on his knees, telling his wife that the police would be by the next day to take him away for good. Dennis wondered if Mr. Malagati would tell them that his son had it coming to him and that the Hurley boy was the one who finished him off.

The shore and its crashing breakers came to mind. The gulls drifting in and out of night clouds that were black and creeping low. That triggered another image, that of the future diocesan bishop creeping around the Great Lawn and back to the rectory. Dennis again wondered what that was all about.

AFTER THE TRIP to the bungalow, the pastor had left his office lights off, the moon filtering into the room and opening up a path to the decanter. He poured a half glass and drained it. He poured another and returned to his swivel. He spun around and peered out. He waited.

It's just a matter of time, he told himself, unaware that Charlie had left for the cemetery.

With the help of a third glass, the wait became bearable.

Finally, in the distance he saw his custodian returning from the cemetery. Before going back into his home, however, the old man detoured into the shed. Moments later, Charlie came out of the shed and went inside, where the lights remained off.

Cassidy again waited.

When, not much later, the gunshot came—the dark bungalow electrocuted—the pastor ever so slowly made the Sign of the Cross. He would stay put for a while. He needed to be sure that no convent lights went on.

No lights appeared. He retired up to his apartment for a much needed sleep.

24

A number of hours later, well past dawn, the parish grounds for the second time in three days were filled with a police presence. So was a gurney in play, the body being rolled out and put into the coroner's van. Seeing all this from his office, Cassidy spun around and tapped the archbishop's phone line.

His private secretary answering, "Father Zeitler speaking."

"Yes, Father, sorry to call so early. This is Jim Cassidy, out at St. Theresa's."

"Oh, Monsignor, yes?"

"Father, we've had another incident here in Bellport. Can you pencil me in for late morning coffee with Archbishop Nellenberger? It's quite urgent."

The appointment secured, Cassidy next called the limo service. He rose and stepped over to the mirror, and with as somber a face as he could muster, "After all that's happened out my way, John…."

Less than thirty minutes later, the limo driver held open the door for the pastor and drove over to the bungalow, where it stopped. As Lambert made his way, the back window lowered.

"I was just about to come see you, Monsignor."

"The archbishop, Nick. I'm off to the city."

"You can tell him that Sister Agnes Rose, who thought it

strange the morning paper had not been retrieved, peeked in a window and saw the body. We found the gun beside him. Most likely a suicide."

"I feel tremendous guilt. I was all set to go over last night. But at the last second, I got cold feet."

"I understand, Monsignor. I really put you on the spot."

"The suicide, Nick? Does it complicate matters?"

"As long as we don't find that Charlie was part of a killer drug ring, what's happened here, oddly enough, will only speed up the process. Especially if it turns out that the gun is the same one used in Vinnie's death, which I'm sure it is."

"Nick, I'd like to do a funeral Mass for both Charlie and Vincent as soon as we can. This Friday, if that's possible?"

"Yes, it is. I can get the coroner to release the bodies within forty-eight hours."

"And not to worry about a legion of young faces around here. I've instructed Sister Rosaleen to push the first day of school back to next Monday."

HOT AND SWEATY, that's how Dennis felt when he woke up. This time, he muttered to himself, he'd gain access to Mr. Malagati. He needed to do so before the police, as his father indicated the night before, came and arrested the old man. But Dennis wondered if he was asking for trouble. He tossed his blanket aside and reached for an old copy of *Sports Illustrated*. On the front cover, a photo of Marty Liquori grinding Jim Ryan out in the Dream Mile at Franklin Field. He fingered through the issue, stopping at a picture of Harmon Killebrew sliding into third base under Clete Boyer, a cloud of dirt obscuring the tag. Dennis threw the magazine aside and got dressed. Going below, Dennis found both his parents sitting in silence at the kitchen table.

"Dennis," his mother finally spoke. "More news from the parish."

She looked away, his father left to explain. "Sometime late last night, Charlie Malagati committed suicide. He shot himself."

"No..." was all Dennis could manage.

"Yes," his mother replied, and as his parents went on to discuss just how the suicide must have been the result of the old custodian's guilt for what he had done to his son, Dennis left for the den to phone William and Peter, to ask them to meet. Both replied in the same way, that they were to stick to the previous strategy to not discuss the matter with anyone, particularly their parents.

"But what about Mr. Malagati?" Dennis asked.

His two friends again had the same answer, that the suicide had put all bungalow questions to rest. It was time to move on. Neither friend would say anything beyond that.

Back up in his room, an angry Dennis banged his desk. He was sure that William and Peter had talked amongst themselves.

The Hurley kitchen was just one of many hot with conjecture about the second parish death in just a few short days. The consensus was that the old custodian could not face the thought of having shot his own son multiple times. More than a few believed that the shooting was premeditated, this based on little more than the town's prevailing bias that the custodian was a shadowy character. One local was taking the whole thing personally. Jack Hogan, a cup of coffee in hand, had been out on his driveway admiring his new van when his next-door neighbor informed him of the suicide. He grabbed the *Bellport Citizen* from his mailbox and stormed inside.

"Damn Charlie Malagati!" cried Coach Jack as he read through the article. His initial knee-jerk reaction was that the old man killed himself for no other reason than to destroy his team's cross-country season. But after the news started to sink in, he knew he had to be smart about this. His only job at this point must be to shield his runners from all the bullshit that was about to fall from the sky.

I'll tell them, he murmured, that they can't let the killing fields drag them down. But first, I'll head over to the parish. The lay of the land, that's what I need.

SOME FORTY MILES AWAY in the heart of Manhattan, Archbishop Nellenberger entered a Tudor-style dining room where a burning candelabra competed with the natural light of the stained-glass windows. He took a seat at a long mahogany table across from his guest. The butler poured coffee and left.

"My secretary, Jim, conveyed the grisly details. A phone call would have sufficed."

"I needed to meet in person."

"Of course."

"After all that's happened out my way, John, first Charlie taking his son's life, then his own late last night, I just don't think I'm the right man for the diocesan job."

"Nonsense, Jim. Your public response thus far has been beyond reproach. Any other pastor would have folded."

"Perhaps. But my concern is not so much my standing. It's how the tragic affair reflects on your office. You were, after all, the driving force behind my nomination."

"Hell, Jim, as long as the legal side of any case under my care is airtight, I sleep at night with a clear conscience."

"Which is exactly why I came in person. The legal side."

The archbishop shot a look. "Am I not correct in thinking that this case is nothing more than a private family matter?"

"I learned late last night from Charlie himself that he did not work alone. Three parish boys, members of the cross-country team, had a hand in the matter. A peripheral hand, but a hand nonetheless."

"Please, God, no!"

"After the police dropped off a distraught Charlie at his place yesterday, he asked me to hear his confession. I naturally obliged. But now with the Holy Seal preventing me from discussing the matter in any detail, I am left to carry the particulars around in my head." The archbishop nodded as Cassidy continued. "It gets worse. Earlier in the evening I saw the three boys arguing with each other on the bungalow's drive. These boys are close friends, joined at the hip since birth. They're now rejecting each other, the emotions between them raw."

Nellenberger closed his eyes.

"My point exactly, John. Which is why I come to you. I'm at a loss as to how to proceed."

The archbishop now joined hands as if in prayer. "For starters, Jim, the Church simply cannot allow renegade angels to fly down and pinprick parishes."

"Agreed."

"But just how to banish those three without violating the Seal? Perhaps more importantly, without bringing any more public attention to the matter at hand. Neither St. Theresa's nor your nomination can afford that."

"I wonder, John..."

"Yes?"

"You surely know how it is when guilt festers in the soul of a boy?"

"Like a cancer, Jim, it spreads."

"In the case of these boys, their guilt is so deep that their behavior has turned erratic. Predictably so. It's only a matter of time before..."

"Before each forgets himself, resulting in small implosions?"

"Yes, John, implosions that nonetheless break school policy. Which would leave me no choice but to ship each one off to, say, a well-meaning public school. A crosstown institution where like-minded peers can be found."

"And where such a boy would find it easier to get on with his life. But remember this. The Vatican hardly wants a front-page photo of one of its future bishops lugging around mop and pail. Perhaps some trusted minion could be enlisted to do the purging?"

Cassidy raised his coffee cup, as if to toast the idea.

The archbishop added, "When I was last in Bellport, Jim, and brought up the possibility of your immediate departure for the chancery once installed, you rejected it. I again raise the possibility."

"Don't think I haven't thought about it. But the exile of parish students to a public school never being a pretty thing, I doubt very much the boys, or their families, will go quietly into the night. No, I must stay in Bellport and see this thing through. Even if it's from the sidelines. It's my sacred duty."

"Very well. I trust your instincts." As he stood to close the meeting, the archbishop added, "Say, do join me for lunch before you head back to Bellport. Your ordination in Rome is still months away. But perhaps a preliminary chat about our itinerary?"

"Oh?"

"Yes, Jim, I wouldn't miss it for the world."

Back at the parish, Sister Rosaleen approached Coach Jack, who in the shadows of the Red Oak was toweling off the new cross-country van after a wash.

"Sister," he said, "to what do I owe the honor?"

"Coach," she said rubbing her hand along the van's sheen, "you may have missed your calling."

"Sister, you had something to say?"

"It's about your team."

"All ears."

"I'm sure you've heard all about the stunt three of your runners pulled last week."

"Not sure what you're talking about."

"Come, come. A leisurely swim. In the flesh, as they say. Followed by the destruction of private property. Ring a bell?" Coach Jack rubbed away a phantom smudge on the van as she continued, "Well, have you at least heard about the more recent parish news? That regarding father and son?"

"Half of New York, Sister, has heard."

"Which is what brings me here. To protect our students from

the media circus of the next few days, especially with the funeral Mass set for this Friday, the start of school will be pushed back to next Monday. The parish needs time to bury its own. And we will complete the healing process with a special liturgy the first day of school."

"My runners, Sister?"

"Unfortunately, fall sports teams will not be allowed to practice until school begins next week. We want to keep the parish grounds clear of all unnecessary traffic."

"That ain't gonna work. We have a meet this Saturday. In Staten Island."

"Your team, Coach Hogan, can run its meet. But your team cannot and will not practice until next Monday."

"You're not suggesting my boys take off, let's see," now counting fingers, "one, two, three, four days?"

"I never doubted Jack Hogan's prowess at basic math!"

"We have a state championship, Sister, to train for."

"Coach Jack!" she cried. "Can you not see the black cloud that hovers above the parish? Does not the pall of death mean anything to you?"

"People die. I got a team to train."

"Did you even hear what I said?"

"I hear you, Sister. I'm not sure you hear me. My boys must train. They will train."

Turning to leave, she said, "I don't know what the pastor sees in you. I would have asked for your resignation long ago. But rest assured, this time the repercussions will be severe should you ignore my direct order."

As she walked away and heard Coach Jack shout, "Goddammit," a grin emerged on her face, the man left to stew. She told herself that this essentially stupid coach, who thus far has gone through life unhampered by any moral principle, has finally felt the sharp sting of imminent retribution.

Coach Jack was indeed seething. Which is why not long after

the Amazon strolled away in seeming victory he settled on a course of action, which began with a phone call.

"Mrs. Hurley, Coach Jack here, over at the cross-country office. Is Dennis there?"

"No, he's not, Coach." Her son was up in his room, but his mother could hardly believe that Jack Hogan had the nerve to phone with all that was going on. "Can I take a message?"

"Yes, you can. Could you tell him to call around and tell the varsity runners that we are still going to meet today? At three in my office."

"For practice?"

"Not a chance at a time like this, Mrs. Hurley, when a black cloud hovers above the parish. The pall of death, you see. Which is probably why Sister Rosaleen, in her infinite wisdom, is pushing back the beginning of school until Monday."

"Oh?"

"And why she has asked all coaches to suspend formal practice for the remainder of the week as we prepare for the funeral Mass for both father and son Friday morning."

"So soon?"

"That's what the good sister just told me."

"I see."

"Yes, the meeting today with the team will be more of a talk-around. You know, to give the boys a chance to express their feelings. Sure, Charlie was a crusty old guy. But my runners, like me, have crossed paths with him many times. A strange kind of kinship, but a kinship nonetheless. So you'll pass on my message to Dennis? And make sure he phones around? Again, my office, at three."

"I can do that, Coach. And I must say I like it when your team participates in the spiritual side of things. Perhaps more of that in the future."

"Most certainly something to think about, Mrs. Hurley."

25

A few minutes past three, the varsity seven waited in the cross-country office for their coach. Some were on crates, others mulled about taking in thumbtacked newspaper clippings that testified to the school's status as a running powerhouse.

"What the hell, Denny," said Legs. "We're not even supposed to be practicing."

Fenny agreed. "Yeah, Rosaleen put the kibosh on it all this week."

"Hey," Dennis said, "I don't make the rules."

Coach Jack arrived with a deli sandwich and a pint carton of chocolate milk just as Fenny retrieved an old uniform singlet from a box, the image of Sitting Bull on its front.

"Hey, Coach, how come we don't use this top for meets? There's plenty in the box."

Taking a bite of his sandwich, Coach Jack grabbed the singlet and threw it back in the box. "Used to. Then the Amazon woman started whining that it exploits the Injun nation. What a crock."

"We all thought," Legs said, "you might have brought some edible delights for the team. After all, I heard through the grapevine that this was a healing meeting."

"And meetings," Fenny added, "need grub."

"Wrong! I'm only munching on this roast beef on white with tomato and mayo, a dash of black pepper, for the energy needed to call out your splits at today's beach workout."

"What," Legs cried, "you want us to run with the blood still drying over at the bungalow?"

The notion catching Jack Hogan off guard, he looked away, seemingly lost in thought.

"You okay, Coach?" Dennis asked.

"Yeah, but who would have thought, the old man killing himself like he did. This after gunning down that lousy kid of his. Is it really possible the old bastard's gone? I mean, who's gonna throw down rock salt? Or open buildings? Or cry foul whenever we put up cones?" As Coach Jack paused to take it all in, the core three stole fidgety looks at each other. "Anyway, enough said. Back to the business at hand. Practice."

Legs cried, "But the Amazon?"

"Hey, we weren't the ones who went on a killing rampage. Right?"

He waited for the team to take that in, the core three again stealing looks.

"Damn right! It's time, boys. We got a state championship season breathing down our necks, our first meet this Saturday in Staten Island. So, over the next few days, we'll get in a few good practices down at the beach. On Friday, we'll run an easy four. We want to be nice and loosey-goosey for Saturday's race. Got it? Good. Now, today we'll do mile repeats. Three of them, on the boardwalk, with a five-minute rest. And remember, slow burn the living shit out of the middle 880 on each. And if anyone asks, you tell them that you are running on your own. Or I'll bench your sorry ass."

"We got it, Coach," said William with fire in his voice that surprised his teammates.

"Yeah," Peter added. "Let's all get dressed and get down to the beach."

Given William's command that they don't do anything out of the ordinary, Dennis was surprised when his two friends led the team in a super quick warm-up over the inlet bridge to Field Six, where Jack Hogan was waiting by his new van. What Dennis didn't know is that the two had privately agreed that an aggressive approach to all things running, and only that, would be just the medicine needed to get their minds back on track.

As the first repeat mile got underway, William and Peter shot out with Adam. Dennis was unable to stay up with them. His two friends hammered a fast 4:32, just seconds behind Adam. Coach Jack didn't know what to make of the core three breaking up. That rarely happened. But he wasn't about to fault William and Peter, especially since they ran negative splits. So when the team lined up for the second repeat, the coach looked to his captain and said, "Let's get at it, Dennis!"

William added, "Yeah, time for Denny Boy to put on his big boy pants."

His two friends maintaining the same gangbuster approach on the second repeat, Dennis again was unable to stay up with them. On the third repeat, however, with William and Peter experiencing fatigue, the team captain caught them.

Before the team began their cool down, Coach Jack reissued his earlier warning. "We meet here tomorrow at three. And for Christ's sake, get dressed at home, avoid the parish grounds. Of course today, you'll need to sneak back into the locker room to shower. If the Amazon, or one of her lady friends, questions you, remember to tell them you're running on your own. Got it?"

"Loud and clear," said Peter.

During the team's jog back to town, William and Peter went to the lead. Dennis remained back with the others.

Once in the locker room, Legs called out to his teammates. "Just think of it, boys, Vinnie Malagati and Papa Merlin, as we speak, are being primped by the mortician. Readying them for Mother Earth."

"Magic ball say anything else?" Dennis asked with some rancor.

"Just that Vinnie's lava hot girlfriend, the lovely Eliza, has gone missing."

BACK AT THE MANHATTAN chancery, Cassidy was resting his napkin in his lap after an exquisite meal of braised lamb shanks and summer fruit. So, too, had the two clerics settled on an itinerary for November's travel to Italy. To accommodate the archbishop's busy schedule, they decided on a red eye out of JFK Friday night and a return flight early Sunday. The short back and forth across the pond suited Cassidy just fine. Never a big fan of Rome, he thought the city on the slovenly side.

So for the bishop-elect, the trip today into the city was a success, and on the limo ride home he felt the full glow of grace. With just a small bit of prodding, the Archbishop of New York had just bestowed his blessing on what was essentially an ambush of the three parish renegades. Yet the pastor knew his friend's blessing was not needed. The ambush was pretty much settled the moment Cassidy saw them arguing at the bottom of the bungalow drive. Still, there was no denying that the glow he continued to feel as the limo glided along the Long Island Expressway was proof enough that the trip had been well worth it. He had only to return to Bellport, the ousting of the boys to begin in earnest.

"Well, you don't say," he muttered as the limo pulled back into town. Out the window he saw the team on their cool down from the beach workout. They were running along Main Street, the Hurley boy in the rear, his two cohorts way ahead in the lead. The hostility between the boys that he mentioned earlier to the archbishop seemed to be on full display and ready to be exploited.

Reaching the rectory, the driver rushed to open the door for

Cassidy, who getting out, heard a familiar tenor voice accompanied by a guitar filter through the church windows just across the way. He headed there, and once inside the sacristy, he pushed a New Testament bible off a bureau to the floor for a thud. The music out on the altar stopped. In rushed Father Ken, guitar in hand.

"Oh, Monsignor, you're back. Mrs. Wooten said you went to the city. Everything okay?"

Lifting the Bible up, the pastor said, "I'm so clumsy, Ken."

"I was just prepping for the Healing Mass that Sister Rosaleen and I are planning for the first day of school on Monday. I intended to ask if you might want to concelebrate."

"Funny you should ask. I came here to prep for Friday's funeral Mass. It looks like it will be a father-son send off. You'll join me on the altar for that, too?"

"I'd love to."

Cassidy, knowing the team would soon be appearing, beckoned his assistant over to the window. "Ken, take a look out there. What do you see?"

"Why, Monsignor, the parish grounds."

"Exactly, the parish grounds. I just returned from the archdiocese, where the archbishop and I delved into the sorry state of parish affairs. I recommended that you be appointed associate pastor of St. Theresa's. Effective immediately. All with the expectation that the parish will be yours when I take leave for good." The stunned assistant tried to speak but couldn't. "And with Rome in the not-too-distant-future, Ken, as well as what's happened here, I need you to take over brick and mortar. To steer St. Theresa's out of this crisis."

"It's been a dream of mine, Monsignor, to have my own parish."

"And indeed, St. Theresa's will be yours if I have anything to say about it."

William and Peter, finishing their cool-down, came into view.

"But don't kid yourself, Ken, hard decisions abound. Parish

politics, for one thing. Vandalism, for another, which requires that we sometimes call in the authorities. That should have been the case," nodding to Flanagan and Walker passing into the locker room, "for our petty hoodlums over there. But Charlie froze when I raised the possibility of pressing charges. He wanted nothing to do with it."

"I wonder where the third hoodlum is, Monsignor?" asked Father Ken with animus. His history with those three, like Cassidy's, was wrought with antagonism.

"The third?"

"Hurley."

"Yes, Hurley. I had forgotten all about him."

"Oh, there he is, Monsignor." Dennis arrived with the other runners. "Perhaps my first official act, once school starts, will be to take each of those three to the woodshed."

"Like I should have, Ken, any number of times. In fact, I now regret not having sent the renegade angels into exile after their latest pool hopping escapade. Thick as thieves, they are left to wreak more havoc for the remainder of the school year."

"Not if we send them packing beforehand. I know those three well."

"Now that I think about it, Ken, that's exactly the attitude the church brass will want to see. Perhaps each boy sent over to the crosstown institution to get on with his life. Say, why don't you meet me at the country club for dinner after you finish arranging the music for the Healing Mass? At six?"

"I'd like that."

"We'll have some privacy there. I'll also want to hear all about the magnificent parish project you've been mulling over. The new prayer garden. Yes, I'd like to hear all about it."

Father Ken beamed.

Whatever confidence Cassidy was feeling as he left the church faded when he entered the rectory lobby and lifted the newspaper off Mrs. Wooten's desk.

SITTING BULL RUN

More Bloodshed at St. Theresa's
Parish Custodian Takes His Own Life

When he first hatched the strategy to take Charlie out, he knew there would be fast and furious media fallout. However, he wasn't quite ready for such a stark reminder of it, much less that the article included a photo of the gurney being rolled out of the bungalow. But still, once the issue was put to bed, his nomination no longer would be up for question. All that would be left was the small bit of mopping up. And to put a stamp on the process, Cassidy unlocked the top drawer and retrieved the *Memorandum*. He opened to the current Spring-Cleaning list, the last two entries, those of Hogan and Garland. He penciled in three more: *Hurley, Walker, Flanagan*. In the margin, he scribbled, *The Three Little Pigs*.

As the pastor locked the *Memorandum* back in the drawer, over in the locker room the core three were the last ones left in the showers. Shrouded in mist, they stood slack in exhaustion, hot water beating their backs.

Dennis was the first to speak. "I see that you two decided to showboat it in today's repeats."

"Doing all we can," said Peter, "to prep the all-important race muscles for state."

"Funny you should mention state," Dennis said. "I used to dream about state, night and day. Now I dream-"

"Drop it! Just drop it!" shouted William, who grabbed his towel and left.

Peter added, "We have an agreement, Denny, right? An agreement that we keep our traps shut and focus on state and nothing else."

When Dennis got home that day, still agitated by his friends' seeming indifference, he had to face the tiresome Alice Crimmins, whom he found sitting at the kitchen table with his parents.

"Why, hello, Dennis!"

"Hi, Mrs. Crimmins," he replied even as his attention was diverted to an old bookshelf that stood up against the wall.

"Dennis," his mother said, "Alice and I went up north to our favorite antique shop and retrieved that bookshelf. It's from the Revolutionary Period."

Dan rattled the newspaper.

"Ignore the old grouch," his mother said.

"Anyway, Dennis," Alice added, "since I missed your mother's birthday last month, I gave it to her as a gift."

"I think, Dennis," Catherine said as she moved toward the bookshelf, "I'm in heaven." She rubbed one of its shelves, varnished and full of primitive nicks.

"And look," Alice said, "what I treated myself to." She pointed at the several items on the kitchen table, identifying one at a time: "First, a stack of yummy pocket-size books of poetry that I will cuddle up to on a winter's night. Next, a miniature Manet reproduction of two men in banker suits and a disrobed woman, all three sitting atop a blanket in an expansive public park. And, Dennis, I save the best for last. An autographed photo of my favorite human being in the whole wide world. See, the dashed handwriting reads, *Best Wishes in this Screwed Up World. Fondly, Al Ginsberg.* Never met him. But I wish I had."

As Dennis looked down on the photo, Dan Hurley rattled the newspaper and said, "Yes, the bearded wonder! An American icon."

"Anyway, Dennis," Alice replied, "your mother tells me that that coach of yours had your team in for a spiritual awakening about the high crimes over at the parish. Tell us, how did it go?"

"Good."

"Oh?"

"We talked about moving forward as a team."

"And practice?"

"Sister Rosaleen called it off."

"You know, Alice," his mother said, "most think that even with all the rain, they still should have found tire tracks in the cemetery, if that's, in fact, how Charlie pulled it off."

"And yet, Catherine, a fair number are leaning towards his nephews, my own first cousins I'm embarrassed to say, as accomplices. Still, there's no reason why sly Uncle Charlie couldn't have managed all on his own. That's how he's operated all these years."

The phone rang. Dan reached for it, and knowing who it was, he handed the receiver to his wife who listened to what her sister had to say.

"Pearl, can I call you right back?"

Her sister said something else before Catherine hung up.

"So, what did Pearl have to say?" Alice asked.

"Oh, just that she phoned Ginny Wooten and got the scoop. It appears that our pastor has already pressured the coroner to complete the autopsies and release both bodies, in time for a Friday funeral Mass. For both. And the burial not in the parish cemetery, but in the same Brooklyn cemetery where two of Charlie's brothers are buried."

"Pearl girl," Dan looked out from behind the newspaper, "sticking her nose where it don't belong. And Cassidy's smart. It's in the best interest of the parish that we put this thing behind us as quickly as we can."

"Let's not forget, Dan," Alice fired back, "that the pastor, the snake that he is, did the same thing some years ago when a mobster came out from the city and tossed Lester Lowell, parish math teacher extraordinaire, off the inlet bridge for bedding his wife. That was followed by Lester's own wife hanging herself in the attic. The dear Monsignor had the Lowell bodies shipped to a Connecticut cemetery where Lester grew up. Yup. Cassidy's doing the same thing here. He wants the story out of Bellport. Although there's something to be said for wanting my uncle out of town."

Again the phone rang, and as Dennis slipped upstairs, he

heard his mother greet her Aunt Dorothy, who had called from Weehawken after reading about the event in the *New York Times*.

That night, his mother called him down from his bedroom.

"Listen, Dennis, your father took Tommy for a walk downtown to get some Baskin Robbins. Can you help me move the bookshelf into the den before he gets home?"

With the shelf moved into place, he retreated back upstairs. From his side window he spotted his father and brother walking briskly in a sloping rain that had started and that was now pelting quarter-size droplets on Crocus. A large piece of cardboard was used as an umbrella. Dennis pictured his father lifting it out of a downtown dumpster.

When the front door opened below, it took a while before he heard his parents. First in mannered tones, then in laughter. His father must have put Tommy to bed and talked his mother into a drink.

Dennis had trouble falling asleep that night. He kept adjusting his head on the pillow.

Finally, he looked to the wall poster. "Hey, Pre, you ever shot a guy and then pistol-whip him across the face?"

26

"Damn!" said Coach Jack the next day after his seven had stretched and bumrushed on the boardwalk. "It's gonna be damn ticklish around town the next few days, reporters crawling all over the place. I was thinking, just for the heck of it, about my Mary Janes going out today and smoking the shit out of a round tripper to the lighthouse. You know, a little something to pick up Ole Jack's spirits."

"We can do that, Coach," said William.

"Start your slow burn at the second jetty. And get after it all the way back in."

"Yeah, Coach," Peter added, "we can do that. We've got state on our minds."

"That's what I like to hear." Clicking his stopwatch, "Now beat it."

The team took off running along the shore, Adam surging to the lead. Soon the core three broke ahead of Fenny and Mumbles, Legs pulling up the rear. As Coach Jack had demanded, the slow burn surge started at the second jetty, the hot pace maintained. As the U-turn started around the lighthouse, however, Dennis called over to his two friends, "What do you say we finally meet? And talk!"

To that, William accelerated, Peter right on his heels.

Dennis stopped and yelled ahead, "We just gonna let the old man kill himself? Pretend it didn't happen?"

He picked up a seashell and side-armed it at a post. The shell shattered upon impact, a gaggle of birds springing to life above the bracken.

Fenny and Mums soon passed Dennis, who didn't resume running until Legs approached. As the two finished the workout, Coach Jack looked on in disbelief. He didn't bother to look at his stopwatch. He kicked the ground and set out for Chief's.

Later that night, Catherine shouted up the stairs to Dennis that Adam Feltman was on the phone.

"Hi, Adam."

"Denny. I'm in my kitchen with Harry and Ida. We have a question."

"Have at it."

"What we want to know is that since Malagati caused his own spucking out, will the Pope allow him to be buried tomorrow in a Catholic cemetery? I thought you'd be able to answer that, you being the only ex-altar boy I know."

Dennis knew it was allowed. But he was in no mood to explain. "Adam, can I call you back?"

"Sure, Denny. You call me back. But don't forget."

After Dennis hung up, his mother asked, "What did Adam want?"

"Oh, just what time the funeral Mass is tomorrow. I didn't know."

"It's at nine. Your father and I are still deciding whether to go."

Dennis said nothing.

Back in his room, he soon turned off the lights and fell asleep, unaware that a doozy of a dream was about to take place. Vinnie Malagati and Alice Crimmins in sordid lovemaking on the den couch. The nightmare awoke him in a stir, his left forearm knocking the alarm clock off the nightstand. Unable to fall back to sleep for a good while, Dennis felt the dream's horror slowly fade to bouts of lingering dread.

When he awoke the next morning, he rolled over and saw that it was nearing nine, that followed by the sound of the station wagon rolling down the drive and taking off. The funeral Mass. His parents had decided to go after all. He suddenly felt himself fighting the urge to attend, a notion he was hoping a long hot shower would quell. But no sooner had he showered and dressed than he took off down Crocus for downtown. Once on the parish grounds, he hurried along the church's north wall and slipped through the rear door.

Cassidy's eulogy was in progress. The Doughboy sat off to the side on an altar bench. Dennis tip-toed up the stairs to the empty balcony. He ducked below the railing and closed his eyes to gather the strength needed to raise his head. When he did, the first thing he saw was the two caskets, front and center. Nuns and lay teachers were in the front pews. A modest congregation that included his parents and Tommy was scattered about.

As Dennis looked down at Coach Jack in a rear pew, he was noticed by Cassidy, who didn't break stride: "So, yes, sadness overwhelms us all, Charles and Vincent taking leave of this world under the most tragic of circumstances. Still, we must ask God to help us bring a measure of peace back to the parish. And to do so, each of us must dedicate ourselves to devotions and novenas. And to holy confession!" The pastor paused to make direct eye contact with Dennis, who shuddered at what seemed an intentional strike. The pastor would not relent. "While some with great humility ask God to forgive a transgression, others try, without much success, to keep hidden a dark secret in their hearts."

Dennis bolted down the stairs and out of the church. And once on Main Street, he peered around as if the police, any second, would descend on him.

Turning for the market, he knew that with school being canceled, William had picked up a morning shift. He found his friend in his work apron stocking soda bottles. He wasted no time explaining how Cassidy's eulogy targeted him, to which William replied, "What kind of asshole sneaks up to the balcony during a funeral Mass?"

"All I'm saying is Cassidy knows."

"You're telling me that Cassidy was hiding in a tree like a goddam monkey and saw it all? Is that what you're telling me?"

"What I'm telling you is that out of nowhere he darted this look up at me, all the while talking of hiding a dark secret. Who talks like that?"

"A fucking priest is who talks like that."

"But there's more. On the night before the suicide, I went-"

"Like hell, there's more!" said William slamming a fist on a crate, bottles sent crashing to the floor.

Amid broken glass and soda forming a large puddle on the floor, the store manager appeared. "William!"

"Sorry, Mr. Rupp. I'll get it cleaned up right away."

"Stay here and keep the customers away. I'll get you some help."

After the manager left, William turned to Dennis, "Lambert would be all over us if Cassidy knew anything. Cassidy knows shit! Go home, Denny, go! Just be ready for practice this afternoon."

Once outside, Dennis saw two black hearses stopped at a red light. His head already a muddle from the eulogy ambush, he was now confronted by the sight of the hearses fleeing out of town to Brooklyn, which he knew, as Alice Crimmins had said, was Cassidy's handiwork. Dennis started jogging, the pace increasing until he reached Crocus where he slowed to a walk.

"Where have you been?" his mother asked as he entered the kitchen. His father was writing out checks for bills.

"Needed a binder for science. But they were out."

"We just got home. Went to the funeral Mass after all."

"Think I'm going to head up to stretch. Got our first meet tomorrow in Staten Island. Might even go out for a run."

SITTING BULL RUN

COACH JACK MET THE TEAM at Field Six. As promised, he sent them out for some easy miles. William and Peter again at the onset separated themselves from the team, though Adam quickly caught up to them. After the run, the coach gave an upbeat talk. He reminded his varsity that since the next day's competition involved a handful of middling teams, he expected nothing less than a sweep.

"See, there's no reason," his eyes squarely on the core three, "that we can't run the board. We owe it to ourselves after all the slogging this summer. Not to mention the bullshit the Amazon dumped on us this week."

As Dennis approached his house after practice, he saw his father ahead on the sidewalk talking with his garrulous neighbor.

"Good luck, Dennis," Roger Greer said, "in your first race tomorrow. Your father tells me it should be a big year."

"Hope so, Mr. Greer."

"Well, Roger," said Dan, starting to walk away with his son, "great chatting with you."

"And don't you forget what I just said. I wouldn't put it past Cassidy."

"Indeed, food for thought."

Once back in the house, Dennis asked his father, "What wouldn't Mr. Greer put past Cassidy?"

"Oh, nothing really."

"Dan?" Catherine was intrigued. "So, what did he say?"

"Roger heard rumors that Brooklyn was not far enough away for the pastor's taste. And that the hearses actually took them somewhere upstate New York."

"Doesn't Roger know that Charlie's brothers are buried in Brooklyn?"

"Oh, you know Roger. He loves rumors."

"Roger have any other doozies?"

"Only that at the barber shop years ago, he witnessed Charlie grab young Vinnie by the arm and shake him into submission. Roger used his own hands to simulate the incident. And it wasn't pretty."

"I'm hearing things like that, too."

"Hey, Cat," said Dan who noticed today's front-page photo. "Look at that." He pointed at a night shot of the pool. The caption read, *All's Quiet on the Parish Grounds.*

"Anything in the article about the girlfriend? We can't forget her."

"No, we can't. We know she was there at one point. She says she left before it got ugly. As one would expect, Pearl has her own theory about her."

"Who knows if we'll ever learn what happened."

That night Dennis lay in bed thinking how everyone, including his own parents, was adding fuel to the town's rumor mill. Minds cast back, memories ransacked in search of clues that further confirmed Mr. Malagati's fallen nature. It wasn't hard to find a local who wasn't prepared to write a line into the narrative. Dennis wrapped his head with the pillow, but it didn't help. He would have to wait it out, the bungalow disaster rolling back and forth in his skull like a bowling ball.

When he awoke that next morning, the windows were still black. The clock indicated that he had a good hour of sleep before the alarm would go off and send him into preparation mode for today's trip into Staten Island. He got up to piss, and on the way back to bed, out the window he saw flickers of light through the wall of trees. He wondered if the police were looking for more evidence? He dressed and slipped out of the house.

Once across the creek, he cut through the woods in the same northeast direction, dark and forbidden, that he and the other two pallbearers took. Soon close enough to see, he discovered that the flickering lights from his bedroom were the result of the Gise Nursery workers crisscrossing in front of truck headlights as they planted shrubs over and around the makeshift burial spot.

The Doughboy was barking orders at workers that they finish up before daybreak.

A pre-dawn raid, Dennis muttered, to disguise the area.

Dennis waited for Garland and the crew to finish and leave. When they did, he stepped out of the woods and onto the cemetery proper. The grounds made stark by the gleam of dawn, he felt the breeze just stiff enough to water his eyes. He walked over to the closest rows of headstones. He had no doubt that he would find a particular headstone. It took several back and forths before he found it.

Loretta Malagati
Loving Wife and Mother
December 24, 1899
May 8, 1968

The old custodian, and Dennis assumed this to be the case, had dreamed of joining his wife there. How Dennis wished he had gotten to him before Cassidy did.

He waited a bit longer and started back.

The house quiet throughout, he showered, and after bagging race gear, he went below and found his mother in her bathrobe heating the kettle.

"I don't know why," she said, "Coach Jack doesn't want parents at the early meets."

"He likes to say that the early ones give us a chance to shake off the cobwebs."

"Listen to you! Anyway, why Staten Island to shake off the cobwebs?"

"Something new, I guess."

27

When Coach Jack took over the cross-country reigns at St. Theresa's, he decided that each year he would schedule a first meet where his team would breeze to an easy victory. For a few seasons, it was a small invitational in Center Moriches, a few towns over. Then it became the Sag Harbor Invite, comprised of a dozen mediocre teams. St. Theresa's easily dominated Sag Harbor, most years running the tables for a perfect score. However, not long after the Watkins Glen podium finish the previous season, Coach Jack had been contacted by Andy Sullivan, the young cross-country coach of St. Peter's, his alma mater. Coach Sullivan thought there was no better way to rekindle the once prestigious Silver Lake Invitational, hosted by St. Peter's, than to invite St. Theresa's, one of the more powerful programs in the state, coached by famous alum, Jack Hogan.

Coach Jack accepted the invitation, and so assured was he of his top five hammering a sweep that he didn't blow a gasket when Legs blurted out in the van ride to Staten Island, "Hey, Coach, why are we going all the way into the garbage dump of the world?"

"Because it's high time Ole Jack paid back his alma mater, that's why. After all, St. Peter's offered me the opportunity of a lifetime to run for the school."

"My Dad, Coach," Adam said, "told me you were pretty good. Winning a bunch of races."

"I could hold my own back in the day."

"How'd you get the running bug anyway?"

"Well, my little friend, it's not much of a story. But about once a month, Pops drove me and my older brother, Michael, in an old box truck to Joe Kennedy's operation up in Boston, there to load crates of cheap booze for the tavern that Pops owned."

Fenny asked, "Who's Pops? And who's Joe Kennedy?"

"Pops is my dad. And Joe Kennedy is the father of JFK. You know, the president who got whacked. Anyway, after we got back from Boston and unloaded the truck, my brother always stuck around to work the kitchen, deep-frying lots of fish for the regulars during happy hour. And-"

"And," Legs interrupted, "we're still waiting on the origins of Coach Jack's running career."

"Ignore the asshole, Coach," William said.

"And since my brother would stick around the tavern and help out until closing, Pops always told me to get home before the sun went down. Without any bus route to speak of, I got in this habit of running all the way back to my house. Thought I was hot stuff weaving through the Richmond section and even up and over the hills of Silver Lake. It was roughly two miles from the tavern to my front doorstep. I started timing myself with a wristwatch, and dammit, no matter how hard I tried, I could never break eleven minutes. A year later I joined the St. Peter's team. There were no cross-country leagues back when I was in high school. Or a New York state championship. Just races sponsored by schools such as St. Peter's. And organizations like the Spike Shoe Club hosted races all over the city, a bunch at Van Cortlandt."

"Yeah, so how'd you get to be so good?" Adam asked.

"Well, I was shit my freshman and sophomore years. Went out too fast in races. My coach suggested that I try a new racing strategy."

"Let me guess," said Legs. "Slow burn."

"Yes, that, and much higher volume."

"How high?" asked Adam.

"Every Sunday I'd beat the crap out of a ninety-minute monster run around the streets and hills of Staten Island."

Adam asked, "So that's why you have us do at least one killer run per week."

"Anyway, while my brother was busy drinking himself to death at the tavern, cross country saved my ass. I loved running. I loved the fucking balls it took. Especially clawing my way through races. Not to mention the goddam discipline, which probably is what got me through the army. Now that you know the story of my life, wadda you say we all kick back and take in a little music to pass the time." With that, he turned on his station.

But he was not quite done, and as the van crossed over the Verrazzano Bridge, he shouted over Nat King Cole's golden voice: "The moment we arrive, I want you to walk the course. After which time Captain Denny will lead you through the pre-race rituals well ahead of the eleven o'clock gun." With that, he looked in the rear view and glimpsed his core three sitting in the back bench, each looking out the window in a blank stare.

Shit, that pool hopping thing is still eating at them.

A few hours later inside the team tent, Coach Jack's pep talk was winding down. "So, my Merry Band, you damn well better not forget what I've been preaching all week. Silver Lake's opening stretch is two hundred yards of slight downhill, which means that a ton of kids will get out too fast and pay dearly. But not us. Sure, we'll bumrush the first hundred yards for position, but after that, we settle in and bide our time. And don't forget the course's big hill follows on the heels of the small hill, all before the first mile. And that's followed by the third much shorter hill right before mile two. So, beware! And it won't mean squat if Adam and Legs place one-two, while our core three," he paused to stare at them, "hit the skids. And our five scorers had better nail a thirty-second spread!

Got it? Good!" He briefly scanned faces. "So, boys, it's the season opener of a championship season. Time to hold your feet to the fire and get a wild hair up those bony asses of yours! And stick a fist down your throats and pump your hearts for guts! Slow burn is not just a fancy term in Jack Hogan's lexicon. It's our war cry! And it means, Denny Boy?"

"A no-nonsense first mile."

"From there, Peter?"

"We surge the second mile, grinding sausages one runner at a time."

"And the third mile, William?"

"Shit hits the fan, Coach, and hits it good."

"Better believe it! Now, show me them bare knuckles!"

Coach Jack put out his hand, the seven following suit and shouting, "Sitting Bull."

Lit up like firecrackers, his varsity with a rush of adrenaline left the tent and headed to the starting line. There, all nine teams engaged in the usual mix of stretching, bumrushes, and jumping up and down like pogo sticks. A skittish look on most, only the brave ones dared to look into the eyes of runners from other teams.

Coach Sullivan took a moment to speak into the bullhorn and introduce the famous alum to the crowd. Coach Jack returned a wave.

"Okay," the young coach then said, "let the St. Peter's Invitational begin. All runners, on the line."

After Coach Sullivan looked up and down the starting line, he blew the final whistle. The once bustling crowd fell silent, the faces of fans along the ropes reflecting great excitement in the sudden quiet. But not so with each runner on the line, the silence bringing with it a moment of intense anxiety as they snatched a last breath of air.

Coach Sullivan aimed the starter's pistol at the sky, followed by the shout of set commands, the pistol crack bringing with it the stampede over the early stretch. The elbows, the bumping, the glint of spiked shoes. From there, the field fell into its usual arrow formation. Adam Feltman having already made his way to its tip, his six teammates packed themselves into the front quadrant.

By the time Adam made a hairpin turn at a large red flag, Jack Hogan liked what he saw, his top guy with a commanding lead heading for the bigger of the two hills. The core three, in the top fifteen, were led by Peter who busted through a pack of runners from Wagner High, wedging just enough room for Dennis and William to follow.

"Asshole," shouted a Wagner runner.

"Asshole, yourself," William shouted back over his shoulder.

The core three picked off a handful of runners as they fought their way up the course's first hill, whose treacherous backside left a Brooklyn Tech runner tumbling over like a cartwheel. The three sidestepped the runner, and once down the hill, Dennis felt the temporary relief of level ground as he tucked in behind his two friends before the second hill reared its head. As they started yet another climb, Dennis looked up and saw Adam nearing the crest. He took a crash count of the field ahead.

"Looks like," he shouted to his two teammates, "we're mid-teens."

The three flying down the back side looked ahead to the mile mark, just ahead. "Okay," Peter gasped, "you two ready to slow burn?"

"Hell, yeah," William returned.

But Dennis was feeling anything but ready. His arms and legs felt way too heavy this soon into the race. The culprit, he muttered, the early morning trip to the cemetery.

When a meet official called out, "5:23, 5:24," as the boys passed, Peter initiated the surge. The three passed a cluster, and after a few hundred yards they flew by more runners, climbing a very short but very steep hill that reminded all three of Sunken Meadow's Snake Hill.

"Heads down," William cried. "Short steps."

After the backside, and as the three began a long flat stretch around the water plant, Dennis struggled to stay with his two friends. He could see Coach Jack ahead at the two-mile mark cheering on Adam, now with an insurmountable lead. And when they reached the mark in 10:39, their coach shouted, "All hands on deck!"

Coach Jack now waited on Legs, who a good hundred yards behind the core three struck his typical nonchalant pose when he came by in a breezy 10:47. Fenny and Mumbles not far behind, their coach didn't wait for them to pass. Instead, he cut diagonally in the direction of the finish line, the whole time keeping an eye on the race, Adam turning at the red flag for the final stretch.

As Coach Jack made it to the finish line, he could see that Legs had kicked it into gear and was fast approaching the core three. Legs caught them in due course, and with the four now running side by side, Coach Jack counted a total of five runners in front of them.

"Wadda you say," said the panting Legs to his three teammates as they all turned at the red flag. "With Ole Charlie and his kid... stalled...at...pearly gates...it's our time to shine."

In a tortured response to Legs' outrageous comment, Dennis surged and left his startled teammates behind.

Coach Jack jumped out of his skin seeing this, his captain having just committed the unthinkable, an all-out bumrush with hundreds of yards still left in the race.

Only Legs was able to react, and soon catching Dennis, he gasped, "I'm getting second place...Denny...you get third."

As Legs turned on the burners, Dennis found himself under siege. His lungs burned. A splintering pain all over.

With roughly fifty yards left, William and Peter caught him, the three passing all runners, save Adam and Legs.

For the moment, that put to rest the misgiving Coach Jack had about his captain's premature sprint. After Adam finished in first place, however, and Legs in second, Coach Jack suddenly saw that the core three were in trouble, his captain looking the worst, his gait anything but steady. The other two were also failing. Arms punching the air, knees rising too high, contorted faces that screamed an inner hell.

The finish line less than ten yards away, two runners from Van Buren High passed all three, the sweep and perfect score dashed.

Stumbling along in the chute, William turned to Dennis and shouted, "What's wrong with you, fucking sprinting like you did!"

"Yeah, Denny," Peter groaned, "caused us to go after you. Died in the process."

At the awards ceremony, the St. Peter's coach handed out the second- and third-place trophies to the teams from Brooklyn Tech and Van Buren. After which, "And the winning team by a landslide, with twenty-one points, is the powerhouse program from eastern Long Island, the state-ranked St. Theresa High School."

Adam accepted the enormous trophy, though once the awards ceremony was over, Coach Jack grabbed it from him and stomped off. The team followed him, and once everyone was inside the tent, their coach tossed the trophy to the ground.

"Shit! I scheduled this cupcake of a race to give us a chance to flex our muscles before the season really gets going. Which we might have done had our captain not screwed it all up with an unbelievably crazy decision to bumrush with a ton of ground still left, pulling his two pool-hopping buddies with him. And in the process throwing a monkey wrench at a perfect score. This was not the Olympic trials! It was a fucking race for toddlers!"

WHEN THE VAN GOT BACK to the parish that day, Coach Jack announced what had been gnawing at him the whole ride home. "Boys, not sure why some of you decided to play musical chairs out there today. But you did, and we paid big time. Anyway, this week we're gonna run long miles in the sand until we croak."

That night an exhausted Dennis dropped like a rock into his

bed, which is why he was in a deep sleep the next morning when Aunt Pearl's voice at the bottom of the stairs jolted him awake.

"Dennis, can you hear me? I said, Hogan's on the phone."

"Damn," Dennis yelled back.

"Hey, Buster!" his offended aunt replied.

At the bottom landing, his aunt's wide frame made it impossible for him to pass. "Well, what do you have to say for yourself?" Her thick ankle bones jutted out like doorknobs.

"Sorry, Aunt Pearl. It's just that Coach Hogan's always wanting something!"

"I forgive you, Dennis. We all know Hogan's a big shit. Anyway, your mother invited us over after Mass for breakfast." She moved just enough for Dennis to squeeze by her. "Better go see what he wants."

Dan Hurley at the table handed the receiver to his son.

"Hi, Coach."

"Can you talk?"

"Yes."

"Dennis, I'm worried about you. First, falling behind in practice. Not staying up with Peter and William. And yesterday at Staten Island, you bumrushed way too early. As if fleeing the firing squad. What happened?"

"Probably overdid it, Coach, it being the first meet and all."

"I'd say you overdid it. Dammit, son, you'll let me know if anything's wrong?"

"I will."

"I mean really wrong. Like the pool hopping thing, if that's what's screwing up your head."

"I will."

"Promise?"

"Yes."

"Okay. So why not get the team together today. The Amityville Preserve at threshold pace. And remind them that with school starting tomorrow, and the Malagati boys put out to pasture, practice begins every day exactly fifteen minutes after the last bell rings. Under the Red Oak."

"Will do."

After he hung up, Aunt Pearl asked, "So what did King Tut have to say?"

"Oh, just a bit of strategy for the next race. Some of us didn't run smart yesterday."

"But I thought," his mother asked, "your team ran away with the race?"

"We did, though Coach was hoping for a perfect score."

"You hear that, Pearl? The man's possessed."

"That's why," said Dan, "Dennis has no time for small talk. He's got to get back upstairs and get dressed in time for the eleven o'clock Mass. It's Sunday, remember?"

Which Dennis made in time.

But today he wished he hadn't, the Doughboy's homily veering as it did into reflections on the "darkest of human tragedies." That prompted Dennis to leave midway through to head for the 5 & 10, where he'd loiter until it was safe to go home. And once there, he called around to gather a group to run. Ida said Adam ran first thing this morning. Legs and Fenny said, No! Grandmother Mumbino said her grandson was at a cousin's birthday party. Mrs. Flanagan told Dennis that her husband took William to help move an uncle into a facility in Jamaica Heights. Mrs. Walker reported that Peter left on his bike. She did mention, however, that William and Peter ran earlier in the day.

Damn those two, Dennis thought hanging up the phone. They ran without me.

He'd get back at them that night by unleashing a kick-ass round tripper to the Preserve. So when he finally set out later that evening, he was surprised how good he felt running in the cool night air. With his sweatshirt growing damp, he maintained a brisk pace all the way to the Preserve. Returning along Old Montauk, he thought how Legs' crack about the Malagati boys stalling at the pearly gates prompted the premature kick at Silver Lake, a kick that depleted his reserves and cost the team a perfect score.

But I'm not about to let the bungalow thing, he told himself, get the better of me, a thought that bolstered the pace. He jumped off the shoulder and onto Old Montauk's empty westbound lane. His heart now pounding like a drum, a wild animal came to mind, a cougar on a night hunt gaining on prey. And once turning back onto the path, he fell into an all-out sprint, the moonlight torching the open sections of woods around him. Maintaining the furious pace, Dennis envisioned Vanny's final straight, a burning spirit deep within carrying him along. He thrust his chin out, defiantly, his stride, long and firm and fast.

After he crossed the phantom line at the plaque, he shouted, "Hell, yeah," and pumped his fists to the sky. He had just beaten Viren in the Munich 5000 meters. A terrific accomplishment, that's what he had pulled off. Minutes later, however, after catching his breath and recrossing the creek, the impulse came to turn around as he did that night, when through the trees he saw the old custodian kneeling at the makeshift grave. This time, however, he saw only a tunnel of dark shadows through the woods. He breathed in and made his way home.

A few hours had passed before his mother called up. "Dennis? You all set? Clothes, books, running gear?"

"Yes, Mom," he shouted back down. "I'm all set."

Ready for sleep, he turned off the lights and dropped into bed, which triggered William's soda bottles crashing to the floor. If not for that, Dennis would have told his friend all about Cassidy's late-night visit to the bungalow, shortly before the old man put a bullet in his head. He might even have confided in William the ghastly thought that had been gaining traction in him: that Cassidy's visit to the bungalow was meant to nudge Mr. Malagati toward the cliff's edge, from which the old man had no choice but to jump. How else might one interpret Cassidy's cagey retreat back to the rectory?

Dennis shuddered.

He had no idea that this thought would harden into conviction over the coming weeks.

Over on Azalea Lane, Jack Hogan sat on a lawn chair in his back yard. The stars out in force, he had a stogie in one hand, a beer in the other. He was in a much better mood than the previous day in Staten Island. He was convinced that with school starting the next day, and with the Malagati business over, he'd show up to practice all invigorated. Sure, he'd ram smart running down the throats of the core three. But he also told himself that during practice that week he'd inspire the shit out of his seven. He'd ready them to bloody kick ass Saturday at the first big meet of the season, the Cardinal Hayes Invitational at Van Cortlandt Park, the site of the state championship in November.

"Heck, yeah," he called out to the night sky. "I'll go sell a washer-dryer combo in the morning. Then head over to the parish in the afternoon and sell a championship title to the boys. That's what I'll do."

28

"Good morning, everyone," came the intercom voice of senior class president, Diane Kramer, "and welcome back to St. Theresa's for what will be a wonderful school year!"

Dennis barely heard the words. He was still breathing heavily in his chair after running up the school steps to avoid being late for the homeroom bell. The announcements delivered flawlessly, the speaker concluded with mention of the all-school healing Mass that was to take place during the last two periods. But as students now waited for the first-period bell to ring, the intercom returned. "Please excuse the interruption. Would Dennis Hurley report to the principal's office, right away? Thank you, and again, do have a blessed day."

The bell sounding, everyone made a mad dash for the door. Everyone except Dennis. His initial thought that Rosaleen's pool hopping verdict was finally coming down. But moments later, a more likely scenario came to mind: Cassidy having relayed our role in Vinnie's death to the principal, she would now initiate her own investigation. She would grill me first before handing me over to the authorities.

All of this is why Dennis was startled when he learned the

real reason he was summoned. "It's anyone's guess, Dennis," Sister Rosaleen said with the brightest of wry smiles as she filled out a hall pass for him, "why Monsignor asked for you, a retired altar boy, to serve the Healing Mass. But who am I to question our fearless leader, even though Father Ken already had a server picked out." She paused to shake her head, making Dennis think she was having a conversation with herself. "Anyway," she said handing him the pass, "please get to the sacristy towards the end of sixth period. Say, at 1:15?"

"Yes, Sister."

He went to first period feeling way out of sync, and as the morning wore on, the altar boy assignment consumed him. Just what does Cassidy have up his sleeve, he kept wondering.

Dennis ended up skipping lunch to sit at a corner library table. There he absently turned the pages of a *National Geographic*. At the time, he didn't know that in the coming weeks the library would become a sanctuary of sorts, where he'd learn how to pass the time for long periods. Nor did he know that he'd stumble onto Alan Sillitoe's *The Loneliness of the Long-Distance Runner*, which he'd devour in a few evenings. Dennis was sympathetic to the isolation of protagonist Colin Smith, a young gifted runner who, after being sent to a reform school for robbing a store, refused to compete in a cross-country race against a prestigious school. Today, however, Dennis had something else on his mind, namely his altar-boy assignment.

After spending half of lunch period staring at the magazine, he stood and went to a window. He saw classmates strolling about the south lot, the loose-jointed shuffles of boys, the tight self-consciousness of girls. On a retaining wall, Hawkes and Eberhardt were doing their clown act, each dangling a foot over the side. Dennis made excuses to himself for not being out there. He did so even as the early September air was helping Bellport retain much of its summer splendor, the edge of autumn colors still weeks away.

Returning to the corner table, he found that an article on the Zimbabwean kingship ritual failed to engage him. The clock read half past twelve. The library oozed quietness. Images surfaced, bounding and multiplying, dissolving into one another. Vinnie's girlfriend stumbling and falling. The three of them jumping off the convent garage. The first gun blast. The second one. Vinnie pistol-whipped on his knees. A thud. Dennis pictured squad cars tearing into the school's parking lot. Spilling out were the bloated sheriffs who each morning enjoyed coffee and donuts at Henry's Cafe on Old Montauk. Next to arrive, National Guard units jumping out of trucks with canopied backs and darting into every corner of the school. Dennis knew that if he tried to run, his shoes would stick to the floor like glue. They'd loop a slipknot around his neck, the rope yanking him across school grounds, the student body cheering on the arrest.

On the way to Garland's sixth-period religion class, Dennis stopped to take a piss. Just his luck, Legs was at the next urinal. "What we have here, Denny, is high drama. I just had chemistry with Rose Albert who began class with a prayer for Vinnie the dirt bag! I can't wait to see what the Doughboy has in store for us. Perhaps a séance to bring young Malagati back from the dead."

Taking a seat in the back of the classroom, Dennis was equally unprepared for the specter of Garland arranging index cards in neat rows on his desk. To make matters worse, Peter and William, just arriving, took seats apart from one another and away from Dennis. That made the three of them an easy target for the priest, who now chalking *Healing Mass* on the board called out, "I hope that this is not a lover's quarrel among the parish vandals. If it is, I might suggest-"

"How about, Father," Dennis snapped, "you stick to the subject!"

Startled classmates looked to Father Ken, who grinned as he wiped clean his eyeglasses. "My, my, Dennis Hurley, usually the measured one, do tell us what that subject is?"

"Religion, last I looked."

"Well, if it's religion our renegade angel wants, it's religion he'll get." Dennis shot a look at the priest who had just mimicked the same bullshit language used by Cassidy in his office. "So, everyone," the priest continued, "let's begin by taking a look at that."

Father Ken then pointed to a large quilt hanging on the side wall with the map of the world stitched on it, only a few countries thus identified. "That quilt invites a brainstorming exercise." He scooped up one felt letter at a time and velcro'd each to the quilt's Southeast Asia region until *Vietnam* emerged.

"Yep, we'll do some soul searching today. After all, Vincent Malagati was a proud veteran with strong, if not ambivalent, ties to the war."

Dennis noticed William's shoulders sinking.

"So in the spirit of today's healing Mass, let's begin by jotting down an inspired phrase or two that describes the Vietnamese as real, live human beings."

After the class had settled into their notebooks, Father Ken asked, "Anyone?"

Legs gleaming with frolic shouted out, "Hey, Father, I'm thinking about steamy cauldrons cooking up a stew de jour of cats, dogs, and field mice."

"Funny, Legstaff," said the priest who, like a black statue of vengeance, contemplated vaporizing the boy.

Another hand went up.

"Yes, Nancy Rupp?"

"Farmers, Father. I wrote down, farmers who work the land."

"Very good. A clear sense of the soil. Of purpose. Anyone else?"

"Paddy fields," from Elaine McBride.

"Perfect. Just perfect."

The blond-haired Paul Schneider raised his hand. "The two H's, Father. Hunger and homelessness."

"Excellent! Apart from small pockets of wealth in the world, what you're describing is mankind's universal condition."

Spittle shining on his lips, the priest spun the globe on his desk. He was thinking of bricks and mortar, of the prayer garden he would build, of the parish that would soon be his. And, of course, just how pleased the Monsignor would be when sometime in the very near future he would convey to him in person that the three boys had indeed been sent packing.

"Now, there must be others with equally inspiring thoughts. How about you, Peter Walker?"

"Still thinking."

"Odd for someone who's always wagging his tongue. Mr. Hurley, you?"

Dennis refused to look up.

"Well, that leaves the third partner in crime, William Flanagan. Do tell us what you are thinking, William? What you wrote down?"

"I wrote down nothing."

"Come, now, William, what leaps off the page when you think of, say, the Vietnamese as people?"

"Which Vietnamese do you mean? The killers from the North?"

Only Dennis and Peter knew that William was taking on his father's hatred for the northern combatants.

"Ahhhh, young William, I see, you want to play that game..." The priest's voice trailing off, his right hand went to his head, rubbing it in small circles as if tiny rocks bubbled just below his scalp. It was obvious to Dennis that the Doughboy, hurly-burly on peace but short on human suffering, didn't quite know how to proceed. But then, "If you're so clever, William, do take a stab at what comes to your mind when you think of the North Vietnamese as people."

"That's easy. Animals who maim and kill."

A clammy deference might have commended William to

Father Ken, who now was sure that the Flanagan boy had left himself exposed. "Class, your thoughts about William's gem of a contribution?"

Schneider's hand shot up. "What's his proof, Father?"

"William?"

He refused to answer, which prompted Schneider to say, "If Flanagan doesn't have proof, how can he say that?"

"Because, asshole," William turned to Schneider, "that's how the jungle works."

For comic relief, Father Ken mimed Christ crucified to the cross, arms plastered to the chalkboard, and called out, "Mr. Flanagan, that kind of language can land one in a crosstown institution, where like-minded peers can be found."

Parroting Cassidy again, Dennis thought.

William waited a moment before saying, "Make no mistake, Schneider's a fool who has been led by the nose."

"And who, Mr. Flanagan, has led you?"

"My father, that's who. He saw skulls blown off in World War II."

"I see, I see. But do you actually know anyone who has fought in the jungle, as you say?"

Father Ken paused to allow a few sympathetic murmurs from classmates to take effect.

Dennis and Peter exchanged worried looks.

"Well, I do," the priest proudly asserted, "Vincent Malagati was a soldier who once held a dying comrade in his arms. Who fought, was captured, bled, and who finally returned home to Bellport with a Purple Heart medal. Now tell me. What exactly does Mr. William Flanagan Senior know about the sufferings of the Vietnamese people?"

When again William failed to respond to the taunt, Dennis knew that his friend, not one to quietly surrender, was moments away from erupting.

"Oh, please, William Flanagan, do help us understand those

patriotic thoughts of yours, inspired as they are by your soldiering father."

William sprang to his feet. "You want to know what I think, Garland? Huh? Is that what you want?"

"William!" shouted Dennis.

But his friend, not to be deterred, stepped right up to Father Ken. Chests bumping, William poked the Doughboy several times with an index finger as he screamed in the face of the frightened priest, "Well, I'll tell you, you round-bellied, worthless piece of shit! You know nothing about war. You know nothing about peace. And you sure as hell don't know a fucking goddam thing about Vinnie Malagati, the phony that he was."

Even as Dennis and Peter jumped up and pulled their friend toward the door, the lips of the battered Father Ken moved. But no sound came out.

"And one more thing, Garland," William screamed from the back of the room. "Vinnie Malagati was a cocky little monster who deserved to die!"

His two friends shoved him out into the hallway just as several nuns arrived on the scene. Sister Anne Monica and Sister Miriam pulled William toward the main office. Sister Grace Corde went right up to the priest who, having bitten off more than he could chew, was slumping against the chalk board.

Dennis looked at a hallway clock. He took off for the sacristy.

The room that he once occupied a few mornings a week as an altar boy looked vaguely familiar. The low ceiling, the Eucharistic vessels, the small, brilliant crosses about paneled walls. It all came back, and as he passed onto the altar and genuflected, he noticed Cassidy at the lectern turning Gospel pages. He hurried into the vestibule, where he slipped on cassock and surplice. He pulled open a drawer stacked with candles. Cassidy always demanded fresh ones for every liturgy. Dennis concluded the various altar tasks and returned to the sacristy. He stood by watching the pastor breaking communion wafers into small pieces to accommodate the waves of students starting to file into the church.

A knock at the sacristy door.

Cassidy gestured to Dennis that he open it. Sister Rosaleen stepped in, followed by Father Ken, still dazed by what had just happened.

"Monsignor," the principal said in a soft voice. "Can I, can we, speak with you? Something has come up."

"Why, yes, Sister. What is it?"

Dennis knew to leave for the altar bench, where one could hear everything being said in the sacristy.

"A senior boy, Monsignor, the one and only William Flanagan, used grossly perverse language in Father Ken's religion class. In a manner unheard of since I have been at the helm of St. Theresa's."

The Monsignor gazed at his assistant. "Go on, Sister."

The principal was unwilling to utter the actual language used by William. So she generalized, her hands delicately sculpting the terms, after which the pastor turned to his assistant, "To what topic, Father Ken, may I ask, did young Flanagan react in such a vulgar way?"

Before the young priest could respond, Sister Rosaleen said, "The Vietnam War, Monsignor. Several classmates even testified that the boy, with malice in his heart, bumped Father Ken before he started poking him. I thought it best to bring the matter to your attention before Mass started."

To that, the pastor spun around and laid his hands flat on the bureau. He knew his principal would interpret his reaction as a somber response even though he was actually celebrating the first of three implosions. Such success, and so soon, promised the same to come in short order with the other two. He put his game face on and turned back around.

"A vitally important topic. Where is Flanagan now?"

Father Ken finding his voice, "The main office, Monsignor. One of the secretaries is keeping an eye on him."

"And the boy's parents?"

"A call's already gone out."

"And they will be told?"

Father Ken drawing himself up to his full height, "Regrettably, Sister Rosaleen has no choice but expulsion."

"I understand, this kind of thing never being easy. Well, thank you, Sister. And, Ken, while you might want to sit this one out, could you stop by my office later for a follow-up?"

"Be glad to, Monsignor."

After they left, Dennis returned to the sacristy and found the pastor patting down his vestments.

"So, Dennis Hurley, it seems there was a little disturbance over in the school building. Starring Father Ken and William Flanagan. Were you among the lucky few who had a ticket for the main event?"

Dennis with some reluctance nodded.

"Quite a doozy from what Sister Rosaleen just said, though young Flanagan has always been a stormy petrol of a boy. Oh, well, let us not worry about poor William and his potty mouth. St. Theresa's has had enough excitement to last a lifetime. Sacred liturgy beckons."

That was the cue for Dennis to grab the large golden cross used for special services. He now held it out in front of him as Cassidy followed him onto the altar. The organ bellowed and the student body stood, hymnals in hand.

Not long after the Healing Mass concluded, Cassidy was back in his swivel when he heard shouting in the lobby. He stood and cracked open the door. He spied Mrs. Wooten blocking an apoplectic Bill Flanagan.

"Like I said, Mr. Flanagan, Monsignor is no longer responsible for disciplinary matters. That responsibility is now the purview of Sister Rosaleen, under Father Ken's direct oversight."

"Well, you tell the mighty pastor, coward that he is, that I'll be back! One way or the other."

Bill Flanagan stormed off.

Returning to his chair, Cassidy looked outside and watched the boy's father, who stopped to glimpse a large sign.

Tobin Brothers Construction
Future Home of the Parish Prayer Garden

While Bill Flanagan was doing so, he was nearly clipped by a backhoe tearing up an old sidewalk. He cursed the operator, and as he got in his car and pulled away, he noticed Father Garland in an animated discussion with Richard Tobin.

"Hey, Garland," Bill Flanagan slowed the car to shout out the window, "you fat fucking lackey. Doesn't Cassidy know that he could goddam level Bellport with a nuclear bomb, and the dust particles would still reflect the bloody mess! Which is what you will look like after I catch you alone someday. You're a damn embarrassment! That's what you are."

As Bill Flanagan tore out of the parish, he passed the new cross-country van on its way in, Coach Jack accompanying Frank Sinatra's singing *You Make Me Feel So Young* on the radio. Jack Hogan wasn't able to sell a washer-dryer combo that morning. But he didn't care. He was all jacked up for afternoon practice. Pulling the van up to the locker room, however, he found a too-quiet team stretching under the Red Oak.

"Why the faces?" he shouted out the window, unaware that Mrs. Wooten was waddling over. As he got out, she whispered to him.

He froze, eye contact made with Dennis and Peter. "You two! In my office, now!"

Once alone inside with the boys, he demanded, "Just tell me that damn Flanagan didn't fucking bump Garland?" The boys looking away, Coach Jack grabbed a wooden chair and smashed it into pieces on his desk. Spitting mad, he paced about and cursed,

Dennis and Peter slinking away. When he finally emerged from his office, he sent the team out for a long run.

Over the next few hours, he stood at the far end of the bar and drained shooters. Billy Boyce and the regulars knew to keep their distance from him.

When Coach Jack finally made it home, he poured another drink and phoned his captain, who would quickly learn that his coach was sloshed.

"Listen, Dennis, no choice but to bring one of the Peter...ssson twins up to varsity. Who elz, but flat-footed Carl? He'll be part... of the Fenny-Mumbles pack. Our only hope iz that one of those three step up over the season. Be a goddam son-of-a-bitch solid fifth man for us. In time for...ssssectionals. Anyway, can you give all three a good kkk...kick in the ass? Suck up to them, K?"

"Sure, Coach, I can do that."

"Shit, the universe ain't looking so good right now. Flanagan in the crapper. Team sss...ucking wind. Cardinal Hayezzz Invite a short six days away. Guess all that's left to do is gah..get after it. That's all we can do. Gah...after it."

Nothing about practice that week offered Coach Jack much hope. While Adam shined, Dennis and Peter traded bad days. Fenny and Mumbles ran like shit. Legs, worse than that. And Carl Peterson and his clunky stride, well, Coach Jack thought about taking a hammer to the boy's big toe. By Friday, the coach was so distracted that he forgot he was in the barber's chair when he shouted out, "Damn Flanagan and his damn mouth!"

Patrons stole looks at one another.

Try as Coach Jack might, it was impossible for him to put William out of his mind. The boy would be sorely missed the next day at Van Cortlandt.

29

After a rough night of tossing and turning, Dennis found himself alone the next morning in the locker room, his teammates already out in the van and ready for the trip into the Bronx. A stream of sunlight broke through the window high on the wall, bringing with it a floating colony of dust particles. He sat sideways on the bench hugging his knees, his chin dug into a thigh. He was experiencing a loud, brutal daydream. His hysterical mother punching the arm of a detective who was leading her son away in handcuffs. His father having already retreated to his bedroom after being told that Dennis was being arrested for murder.

"Hey, you!" Dennis looked up at Coach Jack standing over him. "You goddam bag of bones, I'm not quite sure what's wrong here. But your life's little problems, whatever they are, pale in comparison to a lot of other people. Like people with brain cancer. Or the downtrodden. Or, for Christ's sake, the Malagati boys, pushing up daisies in a Brooklyn graveyard. Now, if you're fine, and you are fine?"

"I am."

"Good! Now get your ass out in the van and get ready to run!"

Dennis gave Coach Jack a weak smile and hustled outside.

"Okay, you fuckers," Coach Jack said minutes later as he revved the engine. "Off to Vanny for our first big test of the season."

"Hey, Coach," Adam asked, "where's Fenny?"

To that, the coach looked in the rear view. After realizing the asshole was missing, a fuming Jack Hogan peeled over to 159 Duckpond Drive and pounded the horn several times. Mrs. Fennessy opened the front door with a nervous wave and disappeared. A sleepy Fenny, with nothing on except briefs, finally came to the door. Mirth flashing in his eyes, he lowered a hand into his briefs and swashed around in there as if he was rearranging large parts.

"To the fucking moon!" screamed Coach Jack as he smacked the steering wheel, this time holding down the horn and waking up the neighborhood. It took Mrs. Fennessy no time at all to get her son dressed and out the door.

Each year the Cardinal Hayes Invitational was held the second weekend in September on the Van Cortlandt Park course, considered by most the crown jewel of high school cross-country running in the United States. This particular meet was the annual qualifying competition for Catholic high schools in the Northeast. The winning squad was invited in mid-October to an all-expense paid trip to Washington D.C., there to compete against the country's best parochial teams at Georgetown University. To win that race, Jack Hogan knew, would put him over the top. The national publicity. The congrats all over town. Best of all, he'd have Cassidy by the balls given that the race featured the country's best Catholic schools.

Naturally, the pastor had never attended the Cardinal Hayes Invite despite that each year the race director sent formal invitations to all clergy associated with participating schools. On race day, a good dozen or so clergy would stand proudly by at the mile mark and cheer on the runners as they came by. From there they'd hustle back to the finish line, in time to pat the backs of exhausted runners stumbling through the chute. It was all part of a grand tradition going back many years, of which Coach Jack was damn glad Cassidy wanted no part, for St. Theresa's had never scored higher than fourth in the meet. The same powerhouse programs from New Jersey, Maine, and Massachusetts always dominated. But crunching the numbers all summer long, Coach Jack was sure that this was the winning year. That is, until damn Flanagan jumped Garland. To calm his nerves that day as he drove into the Bronx, he sang along with the crooners on his radio station. At one point, he forgot himself and took to weaving in and out of the lanes on the Grand Central Expressway.

When some hours later the first whistle blew, most of the meet's sixteen teams left their tents for the starting line. There the runners, after taking off their sweats, took stock of the air on their skin, it being one of those September days that didn't know whether it wanted to be hot or cold. Still in their tent, the St. Theresa's team was moments away from the last-minute rallying cry of Coach Jack, who first arched his bushy brows and threw his eyes around, followed by a silence meant to ready his varsity for a baptism of fire.

"It's like this, boys. We have a gigantic race today. At none other than Van Cortlandt, the damn mecca of meccas, where the ghosts of Prefontaine, Liquori, and shit, Bulldog Centrowitz, once stirred about the course. Today we get a chance to win a trip to D.C. to pay homage to our nation's capital, to shake hands with Gerry Ford, Tricky Dick Nixon having been sent into exile just last month. Nice? You better believe it. The chance of a lifetime. Yet it's even bigger than that. Do you know why?"

He tilted his neck as if peering over a cliff.

"Well, I'll tell you. It's for the bragging rights of all Catholic schools from here to Timbuktu. I bet you don't know just how many of the old boys are here, priests who once pounded these very same paths when they were young men. This is their race, and it means a hell of a lot to them. See, you just don't know what it'll do to your insides when your name is announced at Mass on Sunday, and all of Bellport knows you won the Cardinal Hayes Invite and are on your way to D.C. I get an apple in my throat just thinking about it! Yes, like my man Martin Luther King, gunned down in his prime just a few years back, I got a dream. A dream of being the best running program in the state of New York. So wadda you say, Fenny? Mumbles? And you, Carl Peterson, brought in from the bullpen? We need you boys to step up to the plate and fill the void."

He stole a look at Dennis and Peter, running without William for the first time.

"Remember, in order to conquer this course, you'll first stare down Ole Man Vanny on the starting line and tell the son of a bitch that you're gonna pick his pocket with a sleight of hand we call slow burn. Which means after bumrushing the opening straight for position, easy does it as you funnel into the narrow cow path in all its rutted glory. Then at mile mark one, after surging like hell, you start picking off the low-lying fruit in the Back Hills, one runner at a time." Now pausing to put out his hand, Coach Jack, with eyes that conveyed both anger and resolve, cried out the final salvo, "And never forget that you got to bumrush the goddam enemy over the final stretch! Or else! You just got to."

After slapping their coach's hand and shouting, "Sitting Bull," the team took off for the starting line. Soon the man in the zebra shirt blew a whistle and pointed his gun at the sky. The tense field toed the line during the long hush.

Then, the crack of the starting pistol.

The opening mile of a Van Cortlandt three-mile race is cutthroat. Not for the small group of leaders, but for the mass of runners whose initial charge passes over the Flats, aptly named so because of its flat-as-a-pool-table surface. The arrow gradually forming, the field after a few turns takes aim at the infamous cow path, a narrow trail, rocky and laden with tree roots and crevices, where runners are trapped until the race starts to thin out. More often than not, a few of the more bullish competitors grow impatient and burst through, a move that can cause others to stumble and fall over each other, arms and legs slashed by spiked racers.

Today, that honor befell the unlucky team from Boston's Albertus Magnus High, two of its runners going down after a Bishop Molloy runner busted through. As for St. Theresa's seven, they made it through the cow path without incident and now found themselves on a wider trail that in no time at all led to the short climb up and over Freshman Hill and then to the notoriously difficult Back Hills. There a meet official yelled out mile splits to the lead pack of three runners who came by in 4:54, among them the favorite from Delaware's Pope John XXIII. Soon, the St. Theresa's runners started to appear: Adam in the top ten at 5:03, Dennis and Peter some thirty positions later at 5:18, followed by Fenny and Mumbles in the fifties, at 5:35. Legs loafed by in 5:38, Carl Peterson in 5:46.

During the next half mile, after Dennis and Peter surged in slow burn and passed a good dozen runners, the captain started to feel the same burning fatigue he experienced the previous week at Staten Island. Struggling to stay up with Peter, he looked over his shoulder. Fenny and Mumbles were still together. Right behind them, Legs seemed to be running in slow motion.

Now finishing the backside of a rolling hill, Dennis welcomed a fairly short stretch that allowed him to compose himself. But not far along it, he blinked in disbelief. There stood Cassidy on the trail's shoulder.

Peter, also seeing the pastor, rasped at his friend, "Damn, Denny, head down...Don't look up."

But that's exactly what Dennis did at the last second. He lifted his eyes to confront the same stinging glare that he endured at the funeral Mass.

What the hell, he muttered as he passed Cassidy.

Several strides along he came to a full stop.

He looked back fully aware of the defiance on his own face.

Cassidy returned a look tinged with an ever so slight smirk, a smirk nonetheless.

"Denny!" yelled Peter who had slowed down and was now running in place. "Let's go."

Dennis resumed and caught up to Peter. And yet the effects of the Cassidy ambush remained, heightened as they were by the cool air that burned Dennis' lungs and a sodden path that grabbed his feet. So, too, did coaches and fans stationed along the way scream encouragement that exhausted runners received as unintelligible jumble. Still, Dennis managed to stay up with Peter through the Back Hills, and after passing the two-mile mark, they went down the long hill to the Flats to begin the final phase of the race. Coach Jack saw all of this, and as Legs now approached and flew by runners, he nearly pissed in his pants when he looked further down the trail and saw Fenny and Mumbles running what were perhaps the best races of their lives.

"Shit, yeah," the coach yelled as he shortcutted down through the trees and headed for the Flats. "Who needs Flanagan when you got the Fleabite and the Marvel!"

When Coach Jack reached the Flats, he saw that Adam had moved into the top seven, and that Dennis and Peter were also mowing down runners. They were somewhere in the twenties, and soon, with a half mile left in the race, when most runners are comatose, the two did not bat an eye when George Legstaff showed up out of nowhere.

"Gentlemen," said Legs, getting ready to impose his enormous ego on the field, "it's Miller time."

With that, Legs took off, his two teammates left behind but still passing runners. That led the frantic Jack Hogan in the middle of the field to count places on his clipboard.

"Yes!" he screamed looking up. His team was in the hunt.

He looked again. Adam had moved up to third place, Legs to tenth and powering along, Peter and Dennis, now in the high teens. Somewhere in the forties were Fenny and Mumbles, still running strong. The only goddam obstacle to victory was Boston's Bishop Holtz. Three of their runners were in the top fifteen, two others in the thirties.

Coach Jack again went to his clipboard and scratched numbers. After seeing that his team was now in first place, he yelled, "It's ours!"

He then watched Adam move into the lead, followed by Legs passing a few more into ninth place.

"Yes, ours!"

But little did Coach Jack know, as his third and fourth scorers had some six hundred yards left in the race, that his captain was in a world of hurt. In survival mode, Dennis was fighting to hold form, to hold level. But it was no good, and with aching shoulders, dead arms and throbbing calves, he soon was forced to tell Peter, "Got nothing left."

"No, Denny…we're just about there."

The captain was spent, and as they headed into the final stretch, he had to let go, the shame of which he immediately felt.

His coach, stunned by the development, dropped his clipboard and ran full bore across the field in a mad dash toward Dennis, now being passed by one runner after another.

Reaching him, Coach Jack with elbows out and snapping desperate council ran beside his captain. "Lift your arms, Dennis! Damn it, lift!" And the coach might have continued but for a field judge who converged on him and shouted that he was breaking the rules. Coach Jack initially resisted with fiery language and dogged his runner a while longer.

Dennis looked over his shoulder.

His coach had stopped, hands on knees.

In the final straight, Dennis was passed by a slew of runners, including Fenny. And as he crossed the finish line, a line judge handed him a card with the number 78 written on it. He stumbled through the chute, holding the rope for support. He knew what his collapse had meant. No critical acclaim for Coach Jack or his team, which would not be heading to D.C. St. Theresa's would finish 8th.

With hardly a word between them, Dennis and Peter broke down the tent and carried it back to the van. Their coach was already sitting behind the wheel, his face a dead gaze. When Legs didn't show up, Coach Jack shot a look at Peter, who ran to fetch him. The luminary finally arriving, Legs announced, "A staff writer from *Runner's World* clocked my last half-mile in a mind-boggling two minutes and six seconds. Didn't think I had it in me." Taking a seat, he asked, "Why aren't we waiting for the medal presentation?"

Coach Hogan started the engine and took off, number 78 burning Dennis' brain.

30

That night at the dinner table, Catherine Hurley turned to her son. "Dennis, Ida Feltman phoned a short while ago. To ask how you were doing. She said that Adam told Harry you had a subpar race. She wondered if you were hurt."

Dennis stood, scraping his chair out behind him, and tossed a half-filled plate of food into the trash. His mother looked to her husband, who wanted nothing to do with it.

"Mrs. Feltman," Dennis said, "is a nosy body. Worse than Mrs. Legstaff."

"Dennis!"

"She only called because she's afraid her darling Adam's season is going to end at sectionals later in the season. That we ain't going to state!"

"What's gotten into you? She's worried about you. So am I. You're moving with chains on your legs these days."

Dennis left for his room.

"Something's wrong, Dan. Terribly wrong. It's got to be William's expulsion."

Her husband grabbed the bottle and two glasses.

"Wonderful. The unflappable Dan Hurley."

LATER THAT NIGHT while Dennis stared down calculus homework, his mother entered his room with a basket of folded clothes. At first, nothing was said. But as she laid a stack on his dresser, she sighed and said, "I heard that Bill and Kay Flanagan are attending Sunday Mass at St. Pius. Did you know that?"

"No, I didn't."

"Yes, they're taking it badly. I can't imagine what it's been like for William, who's been roaming the halls of Bellport High a good week now. I mean, walking along Old Montauk on his way to school, he's twice turned down a ride from your father. I guess he'd rather face it alone. Anyway, how's the team reacting to his expulsion?"

"Okay, I guess."

"We all wish, we really do, that somehow, we could get William back in the fold. If they'd just let him paint a few walls? Scrub floors? A public flogging? Anything that would help get the poor boy back where he belongs!" She paused before adding, "You'll let your father and me know if it's all getting to you, won't you?"

"I'm fine, Mom."

She turned to leave before Dennis could register the doubt in her eyes. But then she stopped. "Oh, I was wondering. Since tomorrow's Sunday, a run-on-your-own day as Coach Jack likes to say, maybe after Mass you could find time to take your brother fishing at Mill Pond for a few hours. To try out the pole that he got for his birthday last month."

"Sure, I can do that."

No sooner was his mother gone than Dennis cursed the idea. The world's upside down, he muttered, and she thinks reeling in sunfish will make things right. But when morning came, he thought better of his mother's idea once he found himself and Tommy in a deep wood on the north edge of Bellport. They were fishing off the same ancient bridge that the early Quakers built and that Dennis once occupied with William and Peter.

Passing under the bridge were navies of guppies darting through the clear water and flitting in and out of shadows. Dennis told himself that it felt good to be away from all the noise.

"C'mon, Mr. Fish, come get me," said Tommy. He and Dennis had been fishing for a good while without any luck. "Dennis, are you sure this is a good spot?"

"Patience, Tommy, and pay attention to your float."

"Maybe we should go over by him."

His little brother pointed to the south bank. Dennis turned and saw a fiftyish looking stranger cast his lure that glistened like a spoon through the air. It fell near a duck that in response shivered its wings and flew off. The stranger had a weathered face and straggly grey hair falling out from under a ragged Yankees ball cap. He reeled steadily at first, then swiftly as his lure skipped along the surface of the water.

"He's got something, Dennis!" shouted Tommy, confusing the water's action for a fish.

The stranger peered into the water before casting again. Dennis recognized this breed of fisherman, the kind whose mind burrowed in deep imaginings.

Some ten minutes later, Tommy hollered out, "Got one!"

Dennis looked, and sure enough, his brother's float was being pulled along. It might have been dragged out farther but that it was snagged by a fallen tree that slanted off the bank into the water. Dennis felt an intense joy over the prospect of some cunning fish on the end of Tommy's line.

"We should be able to see," the stranger's voice boomed like a loudspeaker, "what kind of fish it is." He said that walking along the bank in their direction, his eyes on the float. "Son, I'd say you got yourself a big old largemouth bass. Two, maybe three pounds. You can try to reel him in on that mom-and-pop pole of yours, that is, if your line don't bust. Or I could mosey on out there and catch him with my hand. Won't be hard if it's a slow-poke bass. Done that before."

As Dennis studied the float, the stranger added, "I usually fish in the bay. Or the ocean when I get the bug. But I like to return every so often to the same spot I fished as a boy..." His words trailed off as the float again started to bob. The stranger kicked off his sneakers and tossed them, along with his cigarettes and lighter, up onto the bank. As if walking a high wire, he ever so carefully tread the fallen tree as far as he could before it disappeared into the water. He stepped in knee deep and took a few more steps, barely exciting the water.

Now standing over the float, "Yes, by daddy, there she is. Just like I said, a big fat bass. Well, I might as well reach down and get her."

"Or maybe," shouted Dennis, hackled by the stranger, "my brother can reel him in."

"Whatever," said the stranger with a shrug of the shoulders, trying to hide his disappointment. "I'm just a little old fisherman from Patchogue trying to lend a hand."

"My dad, he works in Patchogue," a proud Tommy volunteered.

"So you boys from Patchogue?"

"We're from Bellport. My brother goes to St. Theresa's and he runs-" The float again pulled below, this time the stranger's hand broke the water's surface and heaved the fish, still hitched to the line, high in the air and onto the bank. Tommy and Dennis bounded off the bridge, the stranger splashing back through the water. The three converged on the bass.

"Is it dead?" Tommy asked, to which the fish sprang and jumped, the stranger's bare foot nudging it back up the bank.

"That should answer your question," he said reaching down to pick up his cigarettes and lighter. He lit one and took a deep drag. "Just like I said. A bass. Good eating fish, I'd say."

The three of them studied the fish, now caught inside a bright shaft of sun, golden brown and blue with short wide fins and large multi-colored gills opening and closing. It lay on a patch of dirt, the hook lodged in the corner of its mouth trickling blood.

With nicotined hands the stranger rolled down his pant legs and knelt on one leg to inspect the fish. "Say," he addressed Dennis, his hand now pressing along the bass. "Being from Bellport, you must have heard of the number that custodian pulled. Some of us wonder how the old guy could butcher his kid, nail him shut in a box, and all by himself lug it into the cemetery like he's carrying a six-pack of beer."

Tommy added, "My aunt says he shot him in cold blood."

To that, the stranger looked up in the sunlight and let out a lurid laugh that traveled upwards in the trees. Dennis saw that his whiskers were heavy, the skin on his neck, blotched.

"And to top it off," the stranger looked at Tommy, "the old guy gave his .45 a goodnight kiss. So anyway," he again turned to Dennis, "did you ever have a run-in with him?"

"Mister," Dennis snapped, "you can have the fish if you want him."

"No," said the stranger standing up. "I'd have done it for any fellow fisherman. What's fair is fair. It's your fish to eat." The bass jumped as if reading the mind of the stranger. "Well, I best be going. I'm glad this little guy here got himself a keeper. Does my heart good to see a boy go home with a fish."

With that, he returned to the stump.

"Let's fill the pail with water, Tommy," said Dennis looking askance at the stranger, now back on his stump smoking and lightly kicking his feet at the water.

After a while, the stranger gathered his things and retreated on some self-styled path through the woods. His shoulders were bowed but not apologetically. That made Dennis think that his brother had every right to keep the fish, more so after the way the stranger took dead aim at Mr. Malagati.

THROUGHOUT THE SAME DAY, Cassidy had several times lifted the newspaper and angrily glanced at the back page headline, *The*

Meltdown of St. Theresa's Coach. The story, which covered the Cardinal Hayes Invite of the day before, included a photo of a meet official trying to prevent a crazed Jack Hogan from running alongside Dennis, the incident described in some detail. The race results were also printed. Way down the list was St. Theresa's seventh man, Dennis Hurley, whose 17:36 earned him the 78th spot. The reporter noted that it was his slowest time since his sophomore season.

"Christ," grunted the pastor. His appearance at Van Cortlandt apparently had backfired. He wanted only to unnerve the two boys a bit. Get them more wound up than they already were. Make Father Ken's job easier. Cassidy had no idea his appearance right there on the race trail would break the Hurley boy running-wise. Nor that it would result in a damned photo of Hogan. More bad publicity for the parish. It was time to send Coach Jack packing.

But the pastor also knew that he didn't want the parish to think Hogan's exile was the result of excessive passion by the coach for a beleaguered athlete. Some of the more generous diocesan donors over the years, jocks themselves, considered Jack Hogan a local hero. No, Cassidy needed a strategy. A strategy that would take time, that would work, and most importantly, would conceal his own hand in it. Once again, he would turn to his clueless assistant, for whom he now was waiting.

When the knock finally came, and Father Garland entered, Cassidy unlocked his desk drawer and retrieved the *Ledger*. "The book, Ken," he said handing it over, "that I promised you. To familiarize yourself with the parish finances as you take over brick and mortar. But how to begin is a mystery to me. Perhaps the fund-raising stuff?"

"Or the Christmas dance?" Father Ken asked.

"Or maybe," Cassidy ever so gently slapped the desk, "the annual parish picnic?"

"That's Jack Hogan's baby."

"Whatever you decide, Ken. I'll defer. You're the one who's running the parish now. And by the way, Mrs. Wooten told me that Bill Flanagan had been by again."

"Nothing to worry about. I put him in his place."

"I expected no less. But don't fret if the other two boys remain at large. I know you have far more important parish considerations on your mind. Like overseeing the completion of a capital construction project, the prayer garden."

"Yes, I'm in constant communication with Tobin Brothers. But Monsignor, don't think for a minute that those two are not on my radar."

Father Ken returned to his office and started scouring the ledger.

31

Over in the Bellport High parking lot the next afternoon, William opened the front passenger door and got in.

"Well?" Bill Flanagan asked his son.

"The coach said it's too late to join the team."

"Why?"

"State rules. September 2nd was the cut-off for all fall sports."

"That's a bunch of shit."

"But the coach at least said I could practice with the team. Get to know the distance guys. Be ready for winter track."

"You okay with that?"

"Got no choice, Dad."

On the drive home, Bill Flanagan cringed when he saw St. Theresa's team out on a distance run on the shoulder of Southern Boulevard. Adam and Dennis were in the lead. Fenny and Mumbles, not far behind. Legs and Carl Peterson trailing them. Peter was way in the rear.

William saw the team, too, Coach Jack having most likely sent them on an out and back to Cummings Lake. What stuck out like a sore thumb was Peter's dead-last position. William wondered if the demons had snuck up and put the hex on Peter, as they did to him in the days leading up to his meltdown in sixth-period religion.

William thought about calling his friend that night and warning him to be on the lookout. He never made the call.

That night Peter pushed his homework aside and climbed the stairs to his attic to hit baseballs off the tee into a large net. At one point he pulled up a floor plank and withdrew a bottle. He took a few small swigs and put it back. He had convinced himself that the increased imbibing of late was not a problem given that he was keeping his grades up. Just last week, he had aced a big Spanish test, after which on the way out the door he blew a kiss to his favorite lay teacher, the sultry Isabella Liberatos. And while the erratic running of these past few weeks, though novel, gave Peter pause, he lay in bed that night taking solace in the Munich wall poster of Pre, whose reckless abandon he salivated over. He told himself right there that he needed to do the same. Of course, he also knew that it would help if William was still around. He missed his friend. Things had gotten way too quiet. He couldn't depend on Denny and that worried-sick look of his to pick up the slack. Denny and that damn night. He can't leave well enough alone.

Before Peter fell asleep, he looked at the wall poster.

Like Pre, dammit, I'll start running from the front, beginning with Saturday's Yale Invite that we won the last two years in a row.

As practice got underway that week, Coach Jack knew that without William Flanagan it would be tough to repeat a team victory on the Yale course. By Friday, impossible, given that both Legs and Adam came down with a stomach virus and would miss the meet. Rather than call up anyone from JV, and without alerting the meet officials, Coach Jack sent five runners to the starting line that day. Dennis read his coach's decision as ominous, confirmed by a hollow, meandering pep talk that concluded with, "So, boys, all I can say is God must have his fucking reasons."

As if that wasn't bad enough, the captain could hardly believe it when the gun went off and Peter shot out with the leaders. For Dennis, that meant he would have to expend energy fighting through runners to reel Peter back in. Which over the first half mile he failed to do. As Dennis circled the windmill and approached the steep Patriot Hill, he saw that Peter, incredibly, had taken the lead.

The captain forgot all about his friend as he started his own climb, repeating Coach Jack's commands over and over. Short steps. Arms low to the ground. But Dennis could not ignore the fatigue already settling in. Reaching the hill's peak, he now saw that Peter, fading fast on the rolling stretch ahead, was paying a heavy price for his crazy stunt.

Going down the hill, Dennis found that the level terrain helped his shoulder pain simmer to a manageable ache. But as he soldiered on, positioned in the thirties, he realized that, like the previous week, he was not right.

"Surge, dammit!" he blurted out, hoping that it would help him pass the large pack in front of him. It didn't. He soon found himself snaking through a long agonizing incline of soft dirt, the end of which brought an extended series of ups and downs. Eventually reaching the two-mile mark, Dennis caught up to the spent Peter, both now positioned in the top fifteen.

"Let's go, Peter...Let's catch a bunch."

But Peter had fallen victim to his own crippling fatigue. "Can't, Denny...can't."

"You can!"

Peter intentionally slowed to a jog so that his teammate had no choice but to let him go.

As Dennis looped around the windmill, with less than eight hundred yards to go, he waited on George Legstaff to appear out of the blue and blow by him. He had forgotten that Legs was home nursing a virus. Still, he forged ahead, and on the final straight filled with the high-pitched screams of fans, he was passed by a runner who uncorked a wild sprint over the last fifty yards.

Crossing the line, Dennis was given a card with 21st place on it.

Fenny and Mumbles passed Peter, who fought off Carl Peterson at the finish line.

The team finished with 174 points, for 6th place.

The ride back to the Island was a quiet one.

On Monday the team ran five 440/880/440 repeats on the county cinder track. Adam ran but was still recuperating from the stomach virus. Legs was a no-show. Peter again went gangbuster on the first two intervals but faltered in the latter ones. After practice, Dennis approached his friend and asked, "What's going on, Peter?"

"What do you mean?"

"Taking the lead like you did on Saturday. Running out of gas. Just like at practice today."

"Hey, God hates a coward."

"Peter, you went out under five minutes on the Yale course of all places. That's nuts."

"You know what your problem is, Denny, you think too much. And for damn sure, you never take a risk."

The next day Legs returned to practice in time for an eight-mile fartlek along Ocean Parkway. But it was clear to Coach Jack that Legs, as well as Adam, were not in form. So he pulled the team out of the Hempstead Lake Invitational that weekend. Instead, that Saturday he would have his team do the second mile time trial, canceled a few weeks earlier on account of William's expulsion.

In anticipation of the time trial, Coach Jack ran the team hard through Thursday, light on Friday. After a good warm-up that Saturday, the team toed the Sitting Bull starting line.

"Set and go!"

His new-found audacity still intact, Peter took off like a bat out of Hell. Adam did not catch him until the U-turn at the plaque. Dennis, not at all. This time Peter held on for a PR on the Sitting Bull course. Coach Jack, impressed by the team's overall effort, hurried to get the results to the cross-country board for all to see after they showered.

Mile Time Trial
October 1974

Feltman: 4:20
Walker: 4:24
Hurley: 4:26
Fenny: 4:30
Mumbino: 4:31
Peterson: 4:44
Legstaff: 4:44

Late that night Dennis was awakened by taps at his side window. His alarm clock reported that it was past midnight. He got up and pulled the curtain aside to find Peter, who had climbed up on top of the garage.

"Damn!" said Dennis pushing the slider open.

"Couldn't sleep, Denny. Still all excited about today's time trial. And my Dad's out of town. So I'm off to the Apollo for some grub. Grab a bike and let's go."

"Shit, Peter," smelling the booze on his friend. "You're gonna find yourself over at Bellport High if you don't clean up your act."

"Clean up my act? Hell, I ran a 4:24 today. Not too shabby. C'mon, get your ass on a bike and join me at the Apollo. We can talk race strategy."

"You're deflecting."

"Pretty boy Steve Prefontaine ain't the only one who knows how to suck wind early in a race."

"What I'm talking about is you sharing homeroom with William if you're not careful."

"C'mon, Denny, we can get all philosophical over grub. Talk about life. You always wanna do that."

"Not after midnight."

"Why?"

"Because we got other things to worry about. Like that night!"

"Sure, that night. We can talk all about it in a corner booth. Let's go."

"How about tomorrow after practice?"

"Mark my words, Denny, Hogan's gonna choke on his tongue when we travel to Vanny and grab the big state championship. And we'll do it in honor of Wee Willy Flanagan."

"And how we gonna do that?"

"We run like hell, that's how. Now, you coming or not?"

"Not."

"Okay," said Peter, and after jumping down off the garage and mounting his bike, he yelled up, "I could kiss you, Denny Hurley, right on the cheek."

Dennis shook his head watching Peter pedal down Crocus and disappear into what for his friend was the sweet oblivion of night.

After the Apollo waitress delivered a vanilla milkshake along with the BLT and fries, Peter said, "I like it! Yes, I like it all."

While devouring his meal, he flirted with the waitress as best he could.

"Sonny boy," she said as he finished up. "How old do you think I am?"

"Same as me. Twenty-two. But with eyes of blue."

"Try thirty-four. And you, you look like you should be at home asleep in your jammies."

"Good God! Don't tell me you've been talking with my buddy, Captain Ahab."

"Not to mention that you smell like a brewery. I would stay out of your parents' liquor cabinet. Take it from one who knows, it'll catch up with you. It always does."

AFTER PRACTICE THAT NEXT DAY, Dennis on his way out of the locker room noticed a naked Peter lying on the bench, a towel draped over him. He had not yet showered.

Dennis asked, "Get home okay last night?"

"Always do."

"How about we talk now?"

"You shot me down last night."

"It was after midnight."

"That's when we do our best work."

"It's not gonna go away, Peter. The old man and his son stowed away in Brooklyn. William, across town at the public school. Cassidy, on cloud nine. And here we are. Still covered in bungalow blood."

Peter shot up, and heading to the shower, he shouted over his shoulder, "Wrong, Denny. A hot shower does the trick every time."

Shaking his head, Dennis left the locker room, and stepping out into a cool dusk air, he turned for home.

Not much later Peter, having showered and dressed, combed his hair in front of the bathroom mirror.

Denny, he muttered to himself, thinks he's got all the answers. Spouting off like he did about Brooklyn, and about William, and about some shit about Cassidy. And about bungalow blood. As if I give a shit about bungalow blood.

But what Peter couldn't deny were recent moments that left his own mind swirling in ways he had never felt before and couldn't fully grasp. Relief coming only after secret swigs of his father's booze. Refocusing the mirror, he recoiled at the dark rings about which his mother as of late had been nagging him. He leaned forward for a closer look at his eyes.

Suddenly, he felt a terrible pressure in his head, then the flare of anger. He grabbed a large garbage can and held it up to the mirror, as if posing for a photo. He waited just a few seconds before throwing it against the mirror, glass falling into the sink and onto the floor.

Father Ken had just left the sacristy, and was mounting the rectory steps, when through the murky dusk he recognized Walker across the way leaving the locker room and heading toward the convent. The young priest found it all so fantastic what happened next: Walker's lickety-split mounting of the convent garage roof, followed by his retrieving a bottle, from which he took swigs before collapsing on his back.

"You don't say," murmured the giddy priest.

Less than ten minutes later, Peter heard a familiar voice. "Walker, show yourself!" Crawling to the roof's edge, he looked down on Garland. Rosaleen stood beside him, a handful of nuns gawking from convent windows. "And bring the libation with you."

The next day, the news of Peter Walker's expulsion spread through the school like wildfire. By the time the final bell rang, Dennis had enough of all the gossip. On the way to the locker room for practice, he heard Eric Forgione telling others that Peter had used one of Mr. Malagati's ladders to gain entrance into the convent recreation room.

"Okay, boys," Coach Jack began, his team now stretching by the plaque. "Another kick to the gut. Which might bring most teams to their knees. But not us, not yet." Dennis saw that his coach uttered words he didn't believe. "So what's next? Next is that we are now into October, when Coach Jack's merry band transitions to bare-knuckles speed work. Such as today's six repeat half miles with a five-minute rest. The middle two repeats fast, fast, fast. Got it?"

"Got it, Coach," said Adam, the only one to reply, and the only one that afternoon to meet his coach's expectations. For everyone else, the workout was an abject failure. And with his exhausted team bent over afterwards, their coach looked through the woods and shouted a personal message to the occupants of the cemetery: "Hey, all of you out there in the long sleep, listen up. One day we're picked to win state. The next, we're a bag of broken bones, Flanagan and now Walker taking it right up the ass. You know what? I'm all out of ideas. In fact, I'm tired as hell. As tired as I ever can remember."

Dennis went straight to his room after practice, determined to get after calculus homework. A big test the next day. But unable to concentrate, he leaned over in his chair and took in the wall of trees.

"Dennis?" His mother nudged the door open. She was holding a large box, and apparently enroute to the attic storage closet.

"Yes, Mom?"

"I don't know what to say." Her face twitched as if the box had suddenly become too heavy for her. "Now, it's Peter. I'd die if it happened to you." She wanted to say more. But instead, she turned for the attic stairs.

Some hours later, Coach Jack in a sweatshirt sat in a beach chair at Field Six, just feet from the whitewash. He drank beer out of a cooler and took in the moon's swath of light on the ocean floor. At one point, he kicked off his shoes, tugged off socks, and rolled up pant legs. He cared not that the air was chilly. Nor that the water he trudged was cold. He stopped when it was knee high. His face fraught, he looked as if he was about to grip a thick rope and pull back to port a great ship lost at sea.

The next day, as bands of sunlight broke through trees and lit up the lush grass of the Malagati's rear yard, a Goodwill truck sat outside the gate. Father Ken came out the back door. He was supervising workers clearing the property of all items when he discovered the pastor leaning up against the pool and twirling his hand in the water.

"Oh, Monsignor, I didn't see you."

"You know, Ken, with you in charge now, I find myself in uncharted territory. Too much time on my hands. So I thought I'd take a stroll across the grounds. Hope I'm not interrupting."

"Not at all. It was about time to get all excess off to Goodwill."

"Speaking of excess," said Cassidy, pointing at Jack Hogan talking to his team under the Red Oak. "With the second hoodlum down for the count, which was brilliant on your part, only the Hurley boy is left."

"Not for the lack of trying, Monsignor. But I'm sure the third implosion's just around the corner."

A worker carried the restored St. Francis of Assisi statue past the two clergy and put it into the truck.

32

A cold October air settled into the region. The team in wool hats and thermals set out for an eight mile out-and-back to Percy Park. As they ran through downtown, Dennis glimpsed the showcase mannequin in the Horizon East clothing store, the same mannequin that the team sometimes saw Liz Pearce primping. Perhaps it was just coincidence. But his mind kept returning to the girlfriend. Indeed, the newspapers reported that she had twice passed a lie detector test. He still believed that she alone could put the night into context. Vinnie came out the door only moments after she had fled. Dennis felt if he could just learn what prompted her to take flight, he could march into the Bellport police station to set the record straight. But the word around town, as Legs had said, was that the "Eliza babe" had gone missing, that she was no longer living at her house on Fountain Lane.

On a hunch, he dropped to the back of the pack so that no one would see him turning onto Sawyer Street. The team left to itself, he maintained a good pace and stopped only when he reached the Gulf gas station. The phone book revealed that Liz Pearce lived at 24 Fountain Lane, which, Dennis learned upon arriving there, was a red ranch on a dead-end street. Its lawn was recently cut, its blinds drawn across the front windows. His knocks went unanswered.

"Can I help you?" asked an old woman crossing the lawn of the house next door. Her frail arms were doing all the work for her stiff legs. "You looking for Liz?"

"I am."

She stopped at a nearby Crape Myrtle, her hand grabbing a branch for support. "You know her?"

"I'm a friend."

"You look a bit young for her."

"I worked with her at the clothing store, Horizon East. I stock shelves."

"You were also probably a friend of the motorcycle man, the dead one?" When Dennis hesitated, the woman continued, "I am Peg Grant. Liz's neighbor. And you are?"

"Dennis...Dennis Smith."

"I see. Well, Dennis Smith," the woman said, her stern face softened by eyes that seemed gently amused, "how well would you say you knew him? The motorcycle freak, that is."

"I only read about him."

"Well, he was a real peach. Wish to God they had never met." Her eyes closed, as if to expel the thought.

"Mrs. Grant, Liz hasn't picked up her last paycheck. She helped me in a bad situation once. Now the newspapers say she's in a tight spot. I thought maybe she could use the money. I talked to our manager and he said, once I learn where she is, I can bring the check to her."

"Do you like fishing?" she said, readjusting her hand on the branch. "Liz's father did. Well, the drunk that raised her anyway. He managed to make more money on the water fishing than he did welding. Sold his catch to that fish market downtown. Yeah, Liz loved the ocean just like Pearce did."

"Ma'am, can you tell me where she is?"

"You know Oak Island, out east?"

"Never been on it. Passed it often enough, though."

"Her father left her the small cottage. Can't say she's there. All I know is that after the police interviewed her a few times, she dropped off money for me in an envelope. To have the lawn mowed a few more times before the weather breaks for good. Didn't get a chance to say good-bye."

Before turning back to her house, Mrs. Grant commented how Alexander Pearce meant well. She also noted how Liz was always left to pick up the pieces.

On the run back home, Dennis felt the juices flowing. Once he tracked Liz Pearce down at Oak Island, she would fill in the void, the exoneration of Mr. Malagati certain to follow. But what if her story doesn't absolve the old man? What if, like some about town suggested, the old man was the bad guy here? What if? What then?

He picked up the pace, nearly knocking over a girl emerging from the drug store. He slowed to a walk, mindful that he probably looked like a wounded soldier behind enemy lines. He adopted a lolling gait, his eyes fixed on the sidewalk. Farther along, after he dodged a bread delivery man, Dennis looked up at the sky and the dark shade of blue it gets at dusk. Against it, an arrowhead of geese beat wings.

That night Cassidy called Lambert. "Sorry, Nick, to bother you so late. But with Rome less than a month away, anything from the coroner?"

"I'm sorry about all the delays. First, confusion over the blood work. Judge Butler needed this document and that document. And, so I am told, it will be another few weeks before the coroner releases his report."

"I see. You'll stay in touch with any updates?"

"Indeed."

"Thanks very much, Nick. Yes, thanks."

The following day, Coach Jack sent his runners out for some

easy miles with a reminder. "Since you busted ass yesterday, and since tomorrow's a speed workout, today I want nothing but easy miles. Junkers, six of them, to Field One and back."

The team liked what they heard, and once they were up and over the inlet bridge, Dennis saw William and Peter on the boardwalk, also out running. He detoured over to them.

"Didn't know you two were still at it."

William picked up the pace.

"It was way too late," said Peter, "to join Bellport's cross-country team. So William and I decided we're gonna stay in shape... and run winter track."

"C'mon, Denny Boy!" William said, "last one to the boulder... is a lightweight pansy ass!"

It became an all-out dog fight that continued through downtown, over the parish grounds, and along the path, each boy finishing up with a tap of the plaque. Nothing was said for a while as the three boys paced about and caught their breath.

"Before you start, Denny," Peter was the first to speak, "we're done with that night."

"As in," William said, "leave it the fuck alone."

"Even though we'd get our lives back if we got some answers?"

William shot back, "From a couple of corpses in a Brooklyn graveyard? Are you retarded?"

"C'mon, Denny," Peter said. "What's over is over."

"Maybe for you two, but not for me. Even on blank bedroom walls I see the old man gurgling blood on the floor, the gun beside him, a hole in his head. I see his kid twitching in the box. And I'm the one who put the second bullet in him and whacked him to the ground."

"Now that you mention it," William said, "why the fuck did you not leave well enough alone? It's bad enough you shot him. But then you go ahead and bust up his face."

"Damn you," shouted Dennis as he took a step forward, "you were there. You heard him say he was going to kill my family."

"And just how was he gonna kill your family when he's on his knees with two bullets in him? Huh, tell me, how?"

Peter rushed to say, "C'mon, you two, let's call it a day."

"I'll call it a day, alright," William now shouted. "Though I'm not quite sure Denny here will ever let it go. And get us thrown in jail in the process."

Dennis shouted back, "Thing is, at the end of the day, we did nothing wrong. What if Liz Pearce can fill in the blanks?"

"Fuck, not her again!"

"And if she swears that the old man had no choice but to confront his son for what he did to Rosa?"

"We have no idea how that goddam dog died."

"Yeah, Denny," said Peter, "for all we know, Rosa choked on a chicken bone."

"Are you kidding? You heard Vinny throw out that *I mess with your shit* line. What do you think that meant? I don't know how he killed Rosa! I know only that he did!"

"And all we know," Peter countered, "is that Vinnie came out of his house looking for the Liz broad, like the old man had hurt her or something."

"The old man wouldn't do that."

"How the hell do you know that?" accused William.

"I just know. That's all. And once we know all the facts, our story would make more sense."

"Remind me again," said William, "what's our story?"

"Simple. Mr. Malagati shot Vinnie to stop him from killing us. I shot Vinnie to stop him from killing the old man. That's what we tell the police."

"Wonderful, Denny Boy! Felony count one: murder. Count two: accessory to murder. Count three: digging a grave the size of fucking Texas. And who knows what other shit the D.A. will heap on. Still, you want us to play the martyr?"

"You got to promise, Denny," said Peter, "you're gonna let this thing go."

"Say it, Denny. Fucking say it, once and for all!"

Dennis charged William, both rolling down the bank into the creek. They scrambled to stand in foot-high water.

Punches thrown and felt, both again rammed each other. It took Peter to untangle them. William was the first to walk away, then Peter.

Reaching his house not much later, Dennis found his aunt and uncle as well as his parents at the kitchen table, each with a drink.

"Dennis!" his mother said. "You're soaked! And what's that red welt on your face?"

"Just fooling around crossing the creek as we finished up a run. A few of us got carried away. Got elbowed."

"Say, Dennis," said Aunt Pearl, "everyone and their mother knows the coroner's report is coming out real soon. Rumor has it that Dizzy Lizzy will be cleared. I still think she and Charlie did the tango."

"For Christ's sake, Pearl girl," Uncle John said. "That mouth of yours!"

"Quiet, John. Just because you got nothing left in the tank doesn't mean that Ole Charlie didn't. So, Dennis, what's the buzz out there? About Dizzy Lizzy, I mean."

"The street's all quiet, Aunt Pearl."

"Street don't know squat. You wait and see. We'll learn she was in on it."

Closing his bedroom door, Dennis still couldn't escape the bluster. The baseless pronouncements below shot up through the floorboards. Aunt Pearl, the wrecking ball of gossip and innuendo.

Worse, he and William had exchanged punches.

33

Sophomore Alex Haskell, all legs, was brought up from JV in time for the Liberty Bell Invitational held in the rolling hills of Philadelphia's Fairmont Park. St. Theresa's had won the meet three of the previous four years. This year, however, after Adam and Legs took 1st and 4th, the other five ran races that their coach afterwards described as "dog crap." The team took seventh place. On the drive home, Coach Jack once again told himself that things looked downright bleak for the team without Flanagan and Walker. Just thinking about the next few races in the run-up to sectionals was more than he could bear. That night at Chief's, with two hands clutching his drink, he announced to a small crowd that he was all set to march over to the rectory and knock down the front door.

"Yeah, I'm gonna clobber those two idiot priests!"

"Hang in there, Jack," said Joe Mahoney.

The next race was the Jersey Shore Invitational on the brutal Holmdel Park course. After competitors struggle through a mostly uphill opening mile, they eventually find their way to the famous bowl-shaped path that ends with an impossibly short but steep hill, all of which drains the life out of most. Without any expectation for his once-prized team, Coach Jack's pep talk in the team tent was subdued, if not restrained. There was no hiding the fact that his team had fallen from grace. So did his captain approach the starting line with a sense of foreboding.

Even so, slow burn's muscle memory prompted Dennis to start passing runners as he entered the bowl. But halfway up the long incline, he heard from behind the sound of labored breathing, which turned out to be a gangly Colts Neck runner who beat Dennis by a nose the year before. The two ran today shoulder to shoulder, both nearly walking when they reached the crest. Once on level terrain again, they fought to stay up with each other. Soon, though, Dennis let the runner go. The captain could hardly believe he heard himself muttering the unthinkable, "Can't do this...anymore."

While a gusting wind did little to help the remainder of the second mile, Dennis tried invoking the spirit of Peter and William to get through it. But on the downside of a hill, his arms flung wildly, his feet in overly long strides smashed the ground. Several runners passed him on his way up another incline.

Coach Jack was positioned not far from the finish line. He wasn't too surprised that Adam was in the lead less than a few hundred yards left in the race. Or that Legs, in yet another stunning display, passed a slew of runners to take second place. But after that, the race was painful to watch as a pack from Christian Brothers Academy, hammering the final straight on the balls of their feet, flew by Dennis. Coach Jack felt a pit in his stomach watching the action slacken in his captain's arms and legs.

With each stride, Dennis also knew he no longer had lift. He barely finished ahead of Fenny and Mumbles.

Peterson and Haskell were way back.

The team, a routed outfit, took ninth place.

The following week at the Bear Mountain Invitational, the three varsity races were treated to a cold blustery rain that had started the night before. Once again, Dennis heard the sound of ruin in Coach Jack's pep talk.

As the first varsity race went off, Dennis from just outside the team tent watched the stampede of runners slipping and sliding as the arrow formed. The second race was no better. By the time Jack Hogan's team toed the line for the championship race, the trail had become a perilous mush. Over the opening stretch, St. Theresa's fought for position, a driving sleet of rain pelting their chests.

Positioned in the mid-twenties early in the race, Dennis followed the field that spilled onto a narrow, winding trail, runner after runner slipping in the mud. The rasping captain sucked in air when he could, the crowd with umbrellas all around sounding so far away. He didn't hear his time at the mile mark. In his ears was the metal of his cleats against the path's pebbles. Even so, Dennis refused to fall into a lull around Hessian Lake, and as he approached Beast Hill, and struggled his way up, he flew down the backside carpeted with wet leaves. At its bottom, his foot caught a tree root and he fell face first, his hands ploughing through muddy leaves. He jumped up and opened his mouth to catch air, the pelting rain still in free fall.

Dennis blindly surged, his legs pumping of their own accord. He had no idea his own stride was becoming dangerously vertical in the muddy trail. Then suddenly he felt his energy wane, like a spigot being turned off. One runner after another passed him. He glanced over his shoulder, waiting on George Legstaff. He didn't know at this point that the star half-miler had dropped out of the race. The culprit, or so Legs would say afterwards, was a bad fall.

Now approaching the deadly Upchuck Hill, Dennis knew he mustn't let any runners pass him. Which he was able to do.

As he continued on, he entered an up-and-down path that eventually led him to the final straight. There he saw Adam in the lead, Richie Calhoun from Elmont High just yards behind. It looked as if Adam would be able to hold him off. Legs was nowhere to be seen. In the final stretch, Dennis was squinting so hard from the rain that his vision was impaired.

Afterwards in the tent, with the team toweling mud off

themselves, Legs called over to Adam, who was not at all happy. "Hey, Moses, stop sulking. You won the race."

"Who you kidding, Legstaff? The team took seventh place today. And you dropped out."

"Hey, it got too dangerous out there. A second fall and my college career's down the tubes. My advice to my little friend is that you keep your eyes on the big prize, state."

"Shit, unless those two," Adam nodded at Fenny and Mumbles, "pull off a miracle next week at sectionals, we ain't ever gonna see state! If only Flanagan and Walker weren't such fuckups."

Dennis shot a look at Adam and left the tent.

THAT NIGHT COACH JACK drove over to East Patchogue, two towns over, where he sometimes took flight when his mind was fried and he wanted to drink in peace. Tonight, after parking in a fenced lot that stored old boats resting on wooden stilts, he crossed the street to Smitty's, a sleazy tavern whose clientele sometimes retired in pairs two doors down to Barney's B&B, long since dubbed Barney's Brothel.

Thank God, the coach thought as he found a near empty tavern. No irksome questions from Larry or Roger about his team's precipitous fall. Even so, over the course of an hour, as he nursed several beers, he pondered the plight of his bankrupt team. He pictured his captain that afternoon desperately trying to hold form on the final straight. Shit, Coach Jack muttered, Dennis Hurley has bumrushed hundreds of kids over the years.

It was a few days later, with the bell to end sixth-period religion just moments away from sounding, when Father Ken took off his glasses and said, "So, everyone, don't forget, we begin the Odyssey project tomorrow. I was thinking, groups of three." With that, he paused to spin the globe. "Any thoughts, Mr. Hurley, on possible partners?"

Dennis murmured inaudible words of disgust.

"You were saying?"

"I was saying, Father, that I will mull over the possibilities and get back to you."

"Not liking the tone. Not liking it at all!"

Dennis jumped up and took a step forward. But he stopped after noticing his wide-eyed classmates staring at him, as if they thought they had another blow-up on their hands. The bell sounded.

"Saved by the bell, Dennis Hurley. One doubts, however, that the same bell can save your team, depleted as it is, at sectionals this Saturday."

34

By the time Coach Jack's varsity stepped up to the Sunken Meadow starting line to join eighteen other squads, the temperature hit a cool sixty degrees. St. Theresa's captain took one last look at the course, which was moments away from rearing its ugly head and swallowing alive whole teams with its steep Snake Hill, its damnable tracts of soft sand, and its utterly diabolical Cardiac Hill. The season teetering on the brink, Dennis breathed in as hard as he could. Somehow, he thought to himself, if the team's ever to advance to state, I'll have to pull my old self up out of the muck. Same with Fenny and Mums. They've got to run the race of their lives.

Of course, it didn't help matters when a runner from a few team boxes over shouted, "Didn't think St. Theresa's would show up."

Dennis looked up. It was the same Longwood High runner who a few months back had harassed Adam at the Montauk Point Festival with an antisemitic remark, and who was then knocked to the ground by William. The kid now stood proudly with his teammates, among the squads favored to win.

"And why not?" Dennis shouted back.

"Two of your teammates have been relocated, in chains, to Bellport High. That's why."

"Shit, yeah," said another Longwood runner. "Your team's in a world of hurt."

A brick to the head, that's how the insult felt to Dennis. He was about to respond in kind, but the final whistle blew.

A gloomy Jack Hogan, having retreated into his van in the parking lot, saw none of this. Earlier in the tent, he didn't have the heart to tell his team that the night before, crunching the numbers, he figured they'd probably finish no higher than a piss-poor fifth place, with a spread of one through five approaching an ungodly ninety seconds.

No, with my crooner station on, I'll take in the race from behind the wheel, all so that I won't have to suffer up close the slings and arrows of outrageous fortune. Which, in fact, is where he was when the starter waited for silence and raised his arms skyward. The pistol shot, Coach Jack saw only the silver and maroon blur of General Custer's sorry seven charging into the valley of death in what would most certainly be a massacre of historic proportions.

Maybe it was best the coach was not front and center, and that he could see only parts of the race from a distance. For while Adam shot out into the lead, his captain did not get out near the arrow's front quadrant as he always did. Instead, Dennis was buried back in the field with Legs, Fenny, and Mumbles, Peterson and Haskell not far behind. Only Dennis and Legs knew that his lackluster start was intentional. The Longwood kid's taunting had so fired him up that right before the pistol cracked, he whispered to Legs, "Change of plans."

"Go on."

"No slow burn for me today. You and I run with Fenny and Mums the first two miles. We don't let them fade."

"Then what?"

"I turn on the jets at the two-mile mark."

"And me?"

"You keep Fenny and Mums at your side another half mile. Then shoot yourself out of a canon like you always do. Hopefully, Fenny and Mums will have something left."

"All in, but promise me something."

"Yeah?"

"A sub 5:00 last mile from you!"

"And a sub 4:50 from you?"

"In my sleep."

MORE THAN A FEW COACHES, who knew of the situation in Bellport, weren't too surprised that after Adam Feltman came by the mile in the lead in 4:58, the rest of St. Theresa's runners were nowhere to be found.

"Well, well," said the Commack North coach when four Longwood runners came by as a pack in the mid-teens, their fifth man not far behind. "With St. Theresa's down for the count, Longwood's the team to beat."

"Never count Hogan's boys out," shouted back the Longwood coach. "Bunch of wild animals is what they are."

Other coaches waiting on their runners, however, were ready to do just that when St. Theresa's next four scorers passed the mile in a middling 5:32, positioned way back in the fifties.

"They're toast," said the Patchogue coach, who added, "and where is Jack Hogan?"

Not much later, Coach Jack from inside his van caught a glimpse of his captain running alongside his three teammates. He shook his head in disgust. Dennis was too far back. But what the coach would not be able to see is that his four would stay together up and over Cardiac, passing runners in the process. Nor could Coach Jack know that, as the four were now nearing the two-mile mark, Dennis turned to Fenny and Mumbles and said, "You two got to hold on."

"Got it," panted Fenny.

The four passing the mark, Legs rasped, "Well, Denny...let her rip."

With that, the captain took off, leaving his three teammates behind.

"Sub five," Legs hollered ahead to Dennis who, waving a fist and feeling a savage intensity, flew by small packs from Sayville and Holbrook.

"Gentlemen," Legs said to Fenny and Mumbles, "take a look at Denny Boy."

"Fuck a duck," shouted Fenny.

"All day long!" from Bobby Mumbles.

"So," Legs cried out, "let's reel in fifteen...the next half mile... but steady does it."

With that, the three went to work, inspired as they were by their captain who up ahead was devouring runners. And as Dennis now headed past the picnic area, he could see Adam in the lead.

Coach Jack from his van also saw it, and jumping out of the van, he focused and refocused. It wasn't that Adam was in the lead and would win the race. It was that his captain, now with a half mile left, and approaching the bridge that would take him to the final stretch, had just passed Longwood's fifth runner with the same school's pack of four well within reach. And some twenty runners later, George Legstaff came into view. Coach Jack's head snapped back when he saw Fenny and Mumbles on Legs' heels. The coach did some quick calculating on his clipboard.

"Holy crap," he said, taking off for the finish line.

Approaching the thicket of fans lining the ropes, however, he could see only the flashes of school colors. But turning his gaze towards the top of the final straight, an unimpeded view revealed that Longwood's pack of four had broken up into packs of two.

"Damn!" he cried as moments later Dennis moved past the second pack. Coach Jack noticed Legs high-fiving both Fenny and Mumbles and taking off.

Barreling through fans, the coach reached the ropes in time to see Adam roar to victory, Harry Feltman's voice rising well above screaming fans.

Coach Jack turned back to watch his captain, now on the tail of the Longwood's lead pack, coming down the final straight. The fast-approaching George Legstaff blew by Dennis and Longwood's top two, catching all except Adam and a runner from Northport High. After several more runners crossed the line, Dennis, with one last surge and a face stretched in pain, lunged past the next two Longwood runners for a 9th place finish.

Haggard, pale, he stumbled just yards into the chute before collapsing to the ground. A cautious smile emerged on his face as he breathed in the smell of earth. He rolled over and sat up. A meet official lifted him and pushed him along in the chute.

Back at the ropes, Coach Jack cried, "Please, God, please," his eyes fixed on Fenny and Mumbles, both in horribly wincing pain and barely holding form as they took one exhausted lunge after another. Fenny's head bobbed up and down. Mumbles threw his arms widely across his front trying to muster up more speed. Unable to catch Longwood's third and fourth scorers, they at least held their own as St. Theresa's fourth and fifth scorers. And no sooner had they crossed the line than Coach Jack went to work on his clipboard.

He counted and recounted.

So far as he could tell, and he held his breath thinking this, his squad had just beaten Longwood High by four points. He counted one more time before shouting, "State, my Mary Janes! You've just qualified for state!"

It was Coach Jack who first reached Dennis just exiting the chute.

"How'd we do, Coach?"

"We won, dammit! That's how we did."

Arm in arm, they made their way to the team tent where families and friends shouted congratulations and hugged each other. Dennis looked at his teammates. It felt damn good watching

Legs lift Adam high in the air and twirl him around. And the proud exhausted look of Fenny and Mums, their faces drained, their lips white.

Less than thirty minutes after the race had finished, an official stapled the handwritten tally to the meet board. Coach Jack's seven had indeed won with 58 points. The St. Theresa team pumped their arms in wild jubilation as Adam accepted the championship trophy. This included Dennis, who hugged each teammate. Afterwards in the team tent, however, his mood fell off. In the van on the way home, he was silent. His two buddies. They should have been on board.

Coach Jack was also quiet, and when the van arrived back at the parish, he had just a few short words for his team. "Okay, boys, tomorrow's Sunday. I want you to take the day off. But Monday at three for practice. That's when we'll go over the week's schedule. As for Fenny and Mums, fucking outstanding, you two. Today's victory belongs to you. So outstanding that you are to bring your chessboards to Sal's tonight for a bowl of rigatoni drowning in marinara sauce. Six sharp!"

"Only if you promise, Coach," said Fenny, "you won't pout when I whip your ass."

From there, Coach Jack disappeared into his office to stare at walls, the harsh reality of the upcoming state race sinking in. He almost preferred a season-ending second-place finish to the Longwood team. That to avoid his own team getting embarrassed at state, which would surely be the case.

Out in the locker room, Legs laughed out loud as he began his post-race ritual, the cleaning of the skin between his toes. Pulling off his socks, he said to Dennis a few lockers down, "Lordy, lord, lord, to see athlete's foot up close and in person! It's like an overgrown vine snaking its way into every cubby hole. Which is why I keep an antifungal on hand at all times."

He reached into his bag and pulled out a plastic container.

"I mean, Denny, the enormity of my Mensa IQ aside, there's

also the thoroughbred factor, where a carefully nurtured toe to heel, a slight lean, and a floating style worthy of an Oscar over the first two-and-a-half miles gives way to a faster-than-light burst the final half mile. The Vegas bookies offer a 2-1 line that I break 2:05 at state."

Dennis shook his head as Legs dusted each foot with powder, the air coming alive with the white mite-sized dust.

"Yes, Denny, who would have thought, loins catching fire as they have around these parts? If I made a living as a contest judge, I'd have to say it's a three-way tie between William Flanagan's classroom romp on the cuddly Ken Garland, Peeping Peter Walker's private viewing from the convent garage, and Private First Class Vincent Malagati's taking two bullets for the team. It goes without saying that consolation prizes ought to go to Merlin for stepping out. And let's not forget, a few kudos to the Eliza babe for her disappearing act."

"Legs," said Dennis who tried to hide his annoyance, "let me ask you a question."

"Sure."

"Why do you think Mr. Malagati did what he did? I mean, how is it that a father can plug his own son with bullets?"

Legs gazed down at the floor, a cake board with flour spread over it. He stomped a stray sock as if squashing the life out of it.

Dennis tried again. "C'mon, Legs, you always got all the answers. Teach me a little something about life. How could something like that happen in the first place? A father shooting his son in cold blood?"

Dennis wanted Legs to take up the question, to burn his brain, even if it meant unraveling some tedious tale about Merlin's fiefdom.

Legs wanted nothing to do with it. "Denny, just got my license. I say I take you for a ride in my mother's Impala to Baskin Robbins. I'm in the mood for a butterscotch sundae. You know, to celebrate today's slaying of the infidels."

"I'll take a rain check, Legs. But thanks anyway."

Later that night a phone call came to the Hurley's from Coach Jack.

"Say, Dennis, just got back from Sal's where I skunked Fenny and Mums on the chess board. Also got talking to them about today's race. They said you ran with them most of the way. Which meant no slow burn, right?"

"Sorry, Coach."

"Was it to pull Fenny and Mums along?"

"Kind of."

"Brilliant. So brilliant that I think we'll try it all week long in practice. What do you think?"

"I like it, Coach."

"Yeah, I like it, too. It's all we got."

While Dennis agreed to the strategy, he couldn't help but think on the way up to his room that no matter what the team did in practice that week, they were toast at state.

35

It was late afternoon the next day when Catherine Hurley called up to her son, "Dennis?"

"Yes?" he shouted back down. He was doing homework.

"Listen, it being such a warm afternoon, Aunt Pearl just called to invite us over for a cookout on their deck. Still got a few hours of sunlight left. Uncle John's world-famous ribs. You in?"

"Thanks, but I think I'll pass. Got lots of homework."

"Sure?"

"I'm sure."

When the wagon took off not much later, Dennis leaned over his desk and looked out at the scattered headstones through the bare trees of late October. Cassidy needed only the coroner's report at this point to make official that Mr. Malagati was the Son of Satan. Dennis felt a familiar sinking feeling, and as was the case whenever that feeling arose over the past few months, his mind drifted to the whereabouts of Liz Pearce. Her neighbor, Peg Grant, had told him only that Oak Island was a strong possibility. That got him thinking about the cookout at Aunt Pearl's, and how it undoubtedly would move inside and linger into the evening as Uncle John offered brandy and dessert. Dennis threw on his training gear and soon found himself running down Crocus, through downtown, and over the inlet bridge. He didn't stop until he reached the eastbound shoulder of Ocean Parkway, which would lead him to Oak Island.

The hitchhiking underway, several times Dennis took note of the burning sun crashing the ocean's horizon. More time passed, and as an occasional car flew by him, and dusk settled in, he thought twice about the trip. Finally, a small pick-up, with fishing poles jutting out the back, pulled over.

Little was said during the ride. Yet as the driver steered onto the shoulder, he said, "Son, it's getting dark out there. I suppose you know your way around?"

"I do, thanks."

Once out of the truck, Dennis looked up at the night sky, then to the waves rolling in mounds toward the shore. Turning around, he saw the small bayside island and its handful of weathered cottages. With no cars coming in either direction, he cut across the road and headed down a footpath to a macadam lot with just two cars parked there. A wooden walking bridge led to the island itself, a few jon boats tossing lightly in their mooring.

Crossing the bridge, Dennis saw a sailboat with large wings gliding across the mainland lights, which upon closer inspection turned out to be a restaurant's torches on bamboo poles. There flashed a strange idea, that he was involved in the fragment of some story that would never be told.

Once across, Dennis found the name, *Agatha Humy*, carved on a porch board of the first cottage. Through a front window, he saw a gray-haired woman with a craggy profile putting glasses away in a cabinet. In the next cottage, a couple playing with a young child. From there, one cottage after another was dark throughout. He might have stopped but for the lights in the last cottage. A front window revealed sofas and chests. On one wall hung large, framed photos. One showed a man and a young girl on a fishing boat.

He knocked on the front door. When no one answered, he went around back where he saw the rollicking flame of a candle burning atop a wooden table a few yards from the bay. Beside the table, a bathrobed figure sat in a wicker chair looking out over the water. He stepped closer. Her fingertips circled the rim of a high stemmed glass, a bottle of wine on the ground beside her.

His approach startling her, she turned and looked up at him. "Who the hell?"

"Liz Pearce, my name is Dennis Hurley."

"God!" Her eyes, soft and round and drawn, recognized the face. "One of those parish brats, I see."

Wisps of hair blew about her face and down her neck as she swung her attention back to the water, a tiny cross just visible inside her robe's fold.

"I came to talk."

"Go away!"

"I need to know what happened that night."

"Little boy, let me tell you something." His abrupt demand had emptied her of the initial surprise and was now received with disgust. "I got drunk today, and I'll do the same tomorrow, and the day after that, all so I can crawl under a blanket while the rest of the world is at play." She paused to reach for the wine and filled her glass, drinking half of it in a gulp. "So, Hurley, an extra credit school project? Some nun sent you to follow my scent?"

"I just want the truth."

"The old man shot Vinnie. How's that for the truth."

"But what caused it?"

Liz finished off the glass and flung it into the bay, where it rocked atop the water before sinking.

"Tell me, Hurley, what's it to you?"

"A man's reputation, for one thing."

"That's a joke. The old man killed his only son. When one bullet wasn't enough, he put another one in him."

"The newspaper got it wrong."

"And you know that how?"

"As weird as it sounds, a few hours after the picnic ended, me and two friends were on the convent's garage roof that butts up to the bungalow. Star gazing, is all."

"Nice try."

"We heard the rear door. We saw you come out. You looked real scared. Once past the gate, you put on your shoes and took off in the direction of Main Street. But not before you stumbled and fell."

She shot him a look. He now had her attention.

"Not much time passed before Vinnie came outside looking for you. His father followed with a gun. That's when Mr. Malagati lifted the sheet off of the dog to show Vinnie what he had found. It got crazy after that."

She stood and glared at him. "How crazy?"

"Vinnie charged Mr. Malagati, who fell to the ground. Vinnie knocked the gun out of his father's hand and started kicking him real bad. The three of us jumped down and went after Vinnie, who got the better of my two friends with a shovel."

"And?"

"And he was about to do the same to me, but Mr. Malagati shot him. Vinnie buckled but didn't go down. He went after his father with the shovel, smacking his head, over and over. Then…"

"Then what?"

"I grabbed the gun. I shot him."

"You what?"

"So that he wouldn't kill his father."

Liz Pearce dropped to her knees and placed her hands over the candle's flame. Her face sagged, a mix of pain and grief.

Rather than tell her that he finished Vinnie off with a backhanded swipe, Dennis stepped over to the water's edge. She would need time.

The bay water lapping strong, he waited a good while before going back to her, and when he did, she said, "So, that's what happened. The newspapers kept spouting some shit about accomplices. And I suppose you all buried him. Had a big victory party."

"Vinnie was out of his mind. He would have killed his father. He would have killed my friends and me had he gotten his hand on the gun. As for afterwards, yes, we buried him. But it wasn't fun. I now wish we had gone to the police. If we had, Mr. Malagati would be still alive."

"You think so?"

"I do. Now it's your turn."

"For what?"

"What happened before? That's why I came."

Still on her knees, Liz Pearce went quiet for a while. Even after she had started to speak, she did so as if she was trying to make sense of it all. In the days and weeks following that night, any recall she had came in what seemed hallucinatory flashes, in bits and pieces. With Hurley looking on, she would now, as best she could, bring it all together in a way that made sense to her.

"WE WENT OUT EAST. To celebrate. We were happy, real happy. Vinnie had a job prospect up north that would get us out of Bellport. For good. But when we got back and Vinnie pulled under the carport, the old man, all stiff like, met us in the yard. He says all these things that got Vinnie really pissed off. It wasn't until he called me a whore that Vinnie took out his knife. The old man stood his ground, though. Turns out he had his own bomb to drop. Said he knew things. Said he'd go to the police. Vinnie exploded, telling the old man to take a hike. His father left for the cemetery. And that's when we went upstairs and found the safe in the closet pried open. Everything was gone. Everything."

"You mean Vinnie's little drug business?"

"Vinnie went ballistic. He turned the place upside down. But nothing. I talked him into waiting until the next morning to approach the old man. To pay us back for the drugs he cleared out. To get the gun back."

"Vinnie agreed?"

"We eventually heard his father come back. The house got quiet after that. We both fell asleep. Next thing you know, I'm awakened by Vinnie getting back into bed. Said he went for a swim. I thought nothing of it. That is until the old man, Vinnie's gun in hand, woke us up. The old man was soaking wet. Rosa, he said to Vinnie. He wanted to know why."

"Why what?"

"That's when I realized what Vinnie had done earlier. While his father was sleeping...he drowned Rosa. The old man must have awakened at some point and went looking for her. He found her in the pool, and knowing who did it, he came upstairs."

"Everyone in town thinks Rosa was old and just died."

"At this point," Liz continued, though she seemed lost in remembering. "I wasn't paying much attention to anything except the gun. He had it pointed at Vinnie, who started laughing, crazy like, daring his father to shoot him. I freaked. I threw on my clothes and beat it outside. One look at Rosa on the picnic table turned my stomach. Poor dog. Yeah, and you were right, I fell putting on my shoes. But I got out of there damn fast. I had to."

"Can you blame Mr. Malagati? The drug business. Getting the shit beaten out of him by his son. Then his Rosa. She was all that he had left. You tell me, how much more could the old man take?"

She looked away, and when she wouldn't answer, Dennis said, "Maybe, the time's come for Bellport to hear the truth."

"Hah! Lambert will twist you boys into pretzels. You won't know what hit you. Your family, Hurley, will feel it, too."

"But-"

"No. My advice to you is to lay low." And as she turned and walked back to the cottage, she yelled out, "This shit in our heads will never go away. None of us is ever getting our lives back. Ever."

Dennis watched her disappear into the house. He headed back to Ocean Parkway, where the blinding headlights of each passing car left him reeling in a blackness that soon gave way to a gloomy haze. He couldn't help but feel something like contempt for each driver. The low wailing of an unseen gull, which pierced the night, triggered an imagined scene: Vinnie waking up and creeping below to stand over his sleeping father, then luring Rosa outside and heaving her into the pool; jumping in and holding her under by the collar; his foot pressing firmly on her neck at the pool's bottom; his stomping down several times as if squashing the life out of a giant underwater rat.

The headlights of a sedan slowing to a stop pulled Dennis out of his morbid reverie.

After being dropped off in town, Dennis was relieved to find an empty driveway. Once up in his bedroom and looking out the window, he wished for a harvest moon, yellow and sleepy to soothe his frayed mind. Instead, he found a large pulsating disc, past three quarters and extraordinarily white. If Liz Pearce had convinced him of anything, it was that Vinnie Malagati put his father through hell. And yet, despite her supplying the pieces of the puzzle that he so desperately wanted, Liz also reminded him of something that William had been telling him all along—Lambert would crush them, and their families, if he went to the police.

36

"Okay, boys," Coach Jack said that Monday as the team stretched under the Red Oak. "Gonna be crazy around the parish this week. For one thing, we'll have to contend with all the bullshit hoopla surrounding Cassidy's departure for Rome on Friday, his coronation the next day. So what do we do? We ignore it! We get ready for state! Got it? Good. Now, here's the skinny for the week. One mile repeats today, three of them, a five-minute rest in between. The last two, blazing hot. Followed by a fartlek tomorrow to County Park. On Wednesday, we'll do our third and final time trial. Since Fenny and Mums beat the shit out of the sectional, I'd say they're ready for one hellava time trial. A PR for them. A PR for everyone. This will show all the naysayers that we're ready this Saturday to sneak up and steal the championship trophy. Understood?"

The team murmured, "Yes, Coach."

"Good, and come Thursday, to ensure that my merry band is well rested for Saturday, I want you all to take the day off. And I mean, no one runs. On Friday we'll meet at the plaque for a séance with the chief, our little pow wow to include stretching and a handful of bumrushes. Afterwards, high-carb spaghetti and meatballs at Sal's. Now, get nice and loose for the repeat miles."

While the team readied itself, Coach Jack pulled Dennis aside. "Again, let's use the sectional strategy. No slow burn. Just hang back with Fenny and Mums and hold steady for the first twelve hundred yards. Blast the last quarter. Hopefully, they'll stick with you."

"Will do, Coach."

By workout's end, Fenny and Mumbles had run their best mile interval workout to date, something that Coach Jack seized on as the exhausted team caught its breath. "Fenny and Mums, look at you two bad asses, picking up where Flanagan and Walker left off. A state championship in the offing. Right, Dennis?"

"Yeah, Coach. Fenny and Mums nailed it."

During the family dinner that night, Catherine turned to her husband. "Are we sure, Dan, the coroner's report is coming out this week?"

"Not to worry, Cat, if I know the Monsignor like I know the Monsignor, it will come out before he steps on the plane Friday night."

"You think so?"

"I know so. And speaking of Saturday, Dennis, the team ready for state?"

"We are."

Wednesday's time trial was a big success. Fenny and Mumbles once again stepped up to the plate, each posting a PR for the Sitting Bull course. Adam also killed it. The captain and Legs, not so good. Over the last few days, Dennis kept thinking about Liz Pearce, both her story and her words of caution.

After the time trial, the team was sent out for a cool down to the foot of the inlet bridge, and returning to the parish, they passed the marquee.

Join Bishop-Elect Cassidy
For Tonight's Bon Voyage Novena

Back in the locker room they huddled around the cross-country board where Coach Jack was stapling the day's results.

<u>*Mile Time Trial*</u>
<u>*October 30th, 1974*</u>

Feltman: 4:20
Hurley: 4:26
Fenny: 4:29
Mumbino: 4:30
Peterson: 4:35
Haskell: 4:36
Legstaff: 4:39

"You know, boys, I've been crunching the numbers. Today's five-man average of 4:28 is only three seconds behind the team's previous best average back on August 1st, when Flanagan and Walker were on board. I'd say when you boys toe the line at state this Saturday, you'll do so with a shitload of confidence. And remember, no running tomorrow. See you at the plaque on Friday. At three."

THAT SAME NIGHT Cassidy was about to retire up to his apartment when the phone line blinked red.

"Why hello, Nick."

"Monsignor, I can't tell you how sorry I am that we had to wait all these weeks for the coroner's report. I just received an advance copy. It will be released tomorrow morning at nine."

"Finally."

"But keep in mind that the report will make public at least a few new findings, sordid and otherwise."

"Such as?"

"Few know that there was serious trauma to Vincent's head

and face in addition to the two bullet wounds. And that he had THC and trace amounts of amphetamine in his system."

"Doesn't sound like closure to me."

"Which is why minutes after the report comes out, I'll throw water on it. I'll hold a press conference to announce my findings."

"And they are?"

"Essentially, that, yes, Charlie took his own life. This after he shot his son twice, apparently following an argument. And that all evidence points to his disposing of the body."

"The nephews?"

"Exonerated."

"And the girlfriend?"

"There I'll remind the public that we gave her not one, but two lie-detector tests. And that she passed all relevant questions. I like to think that most will conclude that Bellport has turned a page. And that the bishop-elect is all ready to cross the pond."

"Thank you, Nick. I cannot tell you how grateful I am."

"One more thing, Monsignor."

"Yes?"

"I got a call from Father Ken. He said he has information on Jack Hogan and financial irregularities in the parish ledger. My men checked it out. They think it amounts to low-level criminal activity. But criminal activity, nonetheless. I wanted to first talk with you."

"I have no idea what my assistant is up to. But it must be serious if your men think it is. Can we meet for dinner tonight at the club and see if there's not a way to entice Hogan to go quietly into the night?"

"Certainly."

37

Minutes after the coroner released his report that next day, Lambert, as promised, followed with a news conference on the steps of the courthouse, packed with cameras and reporters. News of both events reached St. Theresa's in no time. As if a powerful spell had been cast, a hush fell over the school building. Nuns and lay faculty alike gave their students busy work while out in hallways they discussed the findings in low, enthralled tones. When the final bell sounded, Dennis took off running along the path, and only when he reached the field did his stride fall off to an exhausted walk. Ahead he saw his mother in the kitchen window looking out at him.

"Dennis, you're home. Have you heard about the coroner's report?"

"Yeah, everyone was talking about it."

"I can imagine. Hey, why are you not at practice?"

"Coach Jack gave us the day off. To rest our legs for state."

"Yes, just two short days away..." Her voice trailed off as she saw the family wagon pull into the drive. "Huh, he's home early."

Dennis looked and saw his father in haste hop out of the wagon.

As an excited Dan Hurley entered the kitchen, he looked at his wife and said, "It's all over, Cat."

"So you heard?"

Dan undid his tie and folded it in half before slapping the counter with it. "How could I not! You should have seen it, my office practically shut down after the report hit. You'd think the Warren Commission had just released its findings. Well, maybe now we can get on with our lives. In fact, I think it's my turn to treat everyone to dinner. Chief's?"

"That suits me just fine, Dan Hurley." And to Dennis leaning against the wall, "And you?"

He shrugged his shoulders, the room's celebratory mood catching him by surprise.

"Your mother and I take that as a yes?"

"I think, Dan, that poor Dennis is ready for a night out. You should have seen him racing home across the field today, poor kid. Like a lunatic escaping from the asylum."

"A lunatic, you say?"

The jaunty voices made Dennis flinch, and as he turned to head upstairs, his father filled two glasses with ice cubes.

Dan and Catherine now sat with drinks and watched shadows move across the field. Neither would admit they were waiting for the paperboy to deliver the afternoon edition of the *Long Island Press* and the details of the day. They wouldn't have to wait long. Yet the details came not on the paperboy's bike, but via the green Nova.

"Hey, lookee here!" cried Aunt Pearl dropping the newspaper on the table. The article about the coroner's report included a dated photo of a handcuffed Malagati being led away. Aunt Pearl planted a fat finger on the old man's face. "You see contrition in that mug? I don't think so. If I remember, it was little ole me who told the whole world he was guilty!"

"Pearl," said Dan, "we all knew he was guilty. We just didn't like to say it all the time."

"If at all," said Uncle John.

Catherine looked at her sister. "Since you're here, won't you and John join us for dinner at Chief's? We are all going out. Right, Dan?"

Dan nearly swallowed an ice cube. "Yes, Pearl, by all means. You remember Chief's? Your old stomping grounds when you lived with us those few months?"

Pearl smiled at her brother-in-law. "Dan, you rascal! You meant to say, those long sixteen months. Anyway, the answer is, yes! John and I would love to join you."

Like a hard-hitting maître d', Aunt Pearl led the Hurley family through an overflowing dining room crowd to one of the few open tables in the bar area. Among the throng was Jack Hogan, who with a mug of beer, was looking down at the jukebox, Dean Martin in the middle of a breezy *The Way You Look Tonight*. As the Hurleys placed their order, the coach plugged the jukebox and tapped several more songs.

Somewhat later, as they were finishing their meal, an argument started up at the bar, at first sotto voce, then louder. "What the heck," Larry Mann yelled at Roger Greer, who sat with his wife, Mary. The room grew quiet. "I'm just saying Charlie ain't the devil people think he was."

"Okay, Larry," Roger snarled. "So what you're saying is that Charlie was an altar boy?"

"For Christ's sake, Larry," said Bill Munson at a nearby table. "Charlie shot his kid twice, once in the back of all places. But rather than pay the piper and stew in a jail cell, he takes the easy way out."

The music stopped. Coach Jack had jerked the jukebox plug out of the wall, and with his beer mug in hand, made his way up to the bar and said, "Yeah, Larry, do tell us why you think our venerable custodian should receive a Medal of Valor?"

Larry Mann was unwilling to take on the pugnacious coach, who now stood without an opponent. Jack Hogan was forced to turn to Cal Sims, the lone figure at the end of the bar.

"So, Cal, what about you? Tell us what you think. Does Ole Charlie Malagati, who we just today came to learn cracked his kid's skull in addition to shooting him twice, deserve our pity?"

Cal Sims lifted his bespectacled eyes from the newspaper and shook his head. "As far as I'm concerned, Jack, before that horrible incident occurred, Charlie never laid a hand on a person that I know of. As for his war-hero son, well, I have my doubts. And let's not forget that Lambert's press conference did not say exactly what caused the shooting."

"What caused it! As if there's ever a good reason to pump your kid full of lead!"

"Say, Jack," said Lou Fonzo, "you worked beside Charlie for what, ten, fifteen years. You know what he was like."

"Damn," said the coach as he slowly drew a complete circle with his upraised mug. "If I told you people the half of what happened over at the parish, you'd choke on your tongues. In fact, that young man right there," pointing at Dennis, "was present when Charlie went after me with big-ass electric hedge clippers."

Bill Munson asked, "Clippers alive, Jack?"

"Damn right. And two feet long, whistling Dixie. Being the hothead Charlie is, he could've taken off one of my fingers! Or a hand!"

"Is that right, Dennis?" asked Roger Greer. "Charlie went after Jack?"

Even the bar turrets turned for the captain's reply.

"Hey, leave the boy alone!" Uncle John yelled.

Aunt Pearl slapped her husband's arm. "Hey, yourself! Dennis is a big boy. He can answer if he wants to."

Coach Jack stepped over to the Hurley table, his hand gripping Dennis' shoulder. "I don't blame anyone for not wanting to cast aspersions on the legendary parish custodian. No one likes character assassination."

Juanita Munson said, "Well, Dennis, either Malagati did or he didn't."

All eyes on Dennis, the captain took a deep breath and said, "He got mad at Coach and ...and he...waved the clippers."

"And the clippers were on?" Bill Munson asked.

A barely audible "Yes."

"Hell!" Coach Jack called out as he headed back to the jukebox. "Who needs to go over that dirty business anymore. As for me, I got to get home and plan tomorrow's workout. Dennis Hurley here and his teammates have a big race ahead of them."

"Yeah, Jack," Lou Fonzo said, "the parish has one heck of a big weekend coming up. The Pope waving his wand over Cassidy in Rome. And your boys bringing home the gold at state."

"A forgone conclusion," said Jack Hogan plugging the jukebox with more coins. "That is, until Garland decided to gut the team." He chugged his beer and tapped selections.

As Benny Goodman's clarinet roused the room, Dan and Catherine knew it was time to shuffle their family out the door.

When the wagon rolled back into 32 Crocus, Dan's hands remained on the wheel.

"You okay, Dan?" his wife asked.

"What a night, Cat! A public trial of Charlie Malagati. And who else but Jack Hogan playing the prosecuting attorney, his closing argument even thumping Father Ken." Looking in the rear view, "And, Dennis, that must have been a doozy, Charlie with them clippers."

Dennis pushed open the door. "Coach got it all wrong! It's Cassidy who deserves the thumping."

Watching her son go inside, a flustered Catherine said, "What's gotten into him tonight? And what's Cassidy got to do with anything?"

"Dennis is no dummy. He must know that it was Monsignor, and not Garland, ultimately responsible for the decision to expel William and Peter."

Once sitting at his desk, Dennis tapped a pencil on its surface and thought, I must have looked like the village idiot at Chief's.

But it's funny what a gentle nudge from Coach Jack can do to a person.

IT WAS LESS than twenty-four hours after Dennis' affirmation of Malagati's killer instinct that Nick Lambert, the parish ledger in one hand, a pen in the other, stood over a distraught Jack Hogan, who sat staring down at a document in the district attorney's office. Father Ken hovered in the background.

"This is bullshit, Lambert!" said the coach. "Pure bullshit."

"Consider, Jack," the D.A. replied as he lay down the pen in front of him, "what kind of jail time you'd get if the parish allowed me to pass the ledger on to the grand jury. They'd see in a flash that you've been padding your pocket all along."

"Everyone knows I use the money for parish upkeep."

"Upkeep? You call fifty here, fifty there, upkeep?"

"Just the other day I goddam bought the girls' softball uniforms with the entry fees from the boardwalk race. Ask Cassidy. He knows how I operate."

"My men did just that after Father Ken discovered the transgressions. The pastor was appalled."

The fire going out of the coach, "So this is how it's going to be. With the state meet tomorrow."

"Just think of it, Coach Jack," Father Ken said, "as a friendly restraining order. The one condition, of course, is that you sever all ties with the parish. Which includes that team of yours. Or else, it's off to the state penitentiary!"

"Go fuck yourself, Garland!"

Jack Hogan took the pen, scribbled his name, and stomped off.

As Father Ken afterwards steered back into the parish, school having just been let out, he looked forward to the unfinished business. After parking his car, he retrieved a cloth sack from the rectory and headed over to the locker room where the team was dressing for practice.

"Boys," he said, "huddle around."

The priest explained in painstaking detail what had transpired at the courthouse. He made sure that the team had no doubt concerning Coach Jack's guilt.

"So," he said holding the sack open out in front of him, "it's time to surrender uniforms. I mean, how can a team compete at state when its coach is preoccupied elsewhere? When half its team is at a crosstown institution?"

Dennis fired a look.

But Garland at this point had no regard for what the Hurley boy was thinking. His priority was the uniform grab, after which he took a parting shot as he left, "Besides, this team never stood a chance at tomorrow's state meet."

Adam was the first to erupt after the priest was gone. "My whole career!"

A thundering racket filled the room as Fenny and Mumbles pulled over a locker.

Legs swung his gym bag at a wall light, busting it into pieces.

Peterson and Haskell exchanged bewildered looks.

Dennis knew only that he had to take flight. Once outside, he saw Garland tossing the uniforms into a school dumpster, this just as the claws of the municipal garbage truck lifted it up and dropped all contents into its bed. The priest making eye contact, yelled over, "Hey, Dennis Hurley, your time will come."

"Asshole," an angry Dennis said under his breath. He felt such rage that he actually thought about marching over to the Doughboy and beating him senseless. Then shaking his head, he realized that he needed to leave. So he set a trajectory for the beach.

A jog turning into a run, he soon pumped his arms madly as he ran up and over the inlet bridge. His heart pounded louder when, now atop a dune, the Atlantic came into focus, swaying back and forth. He trudged the sand, and reaching the waterline, he resumed running along the empty beach. Soon sweat streamed down his forehead and stung his eyes. He told himself when he returned home, he would go straight to his parents and tell them about what had happened to Coach Jack and how unfair it was. What he didn't know was that while he and the others were surrendering uniforms, Mrs. Wooten was calling around to alert parents of Jack Hogan's restraining order and what it meant—that Coach Jack was history, that there'd be no state meet the next day.

38

With the red-eye to Rome scheduled to leave out of JFK that night at ten, Cassidy had just enjoyed an early dinner at the country club. He was approaching his Cadillac when a member called out across the parking lot, "Have a safe trip, Monsignor."

"Thank you, Jerry."

"And do know that I'll be in the front pew when you return on Sunday to say your first Mass as bishop."

"God bless you and your family."

As the pastor steered back to the parish, he saw Hurley running all alone on the inlet bridge. By now, Cassidy was well aware of the day's developments, that both Hogan and his cross-country team were given the axe. That's why he was not too surprised when he saw the boy running alone. Even so, the sight of Hurley, still in good standing at St. Theresa's, continued to vex him, this despite his own best efforts. So, too, had his assistant been unable to break him. The implosion, he conceded, would have to wait.

As Cassidy entered the rectory lobby, up ahead he saw the Feltman boy on the hallway bench. So as not to have to greet him, he brushed invisible lint off his jacket as he approached. He was still brushing when an angry Harry Feltman emerged from Father Ken's office and nearly bumped the pastor.

"And damn you, too, Most Holy Cassidy," Harry shouted. "My son and the other boys deserve to run in the state meet tomorrow. We all know that!"

"I am truly sorry, Mr. Feltman," said Father Ken, stepping out into the hallway, "that you feel that way. But St. Theresa's can never afford to soft pedal serious ethical shortcomings by any member of our parish community. We owe it to our Christian God."

"Your Christian God will hear from my lawyer!"

It was a few hours later, dusk settling in, when Mrs. Wooten entered the office. A delivery man from Getz Nursery followed her with another bouquet to place along the credenza.

"Did you have a nice meal at the club, Monsignor?" she said as the delivery man left the office.

Without turning around in his swivel, Cassidy replied, "I did. Thank you."

"I hope all these lovely arrangements keep while you're in Rome. And I do wish you would stay a few days to relax and take in the sites."

"My dear woman, only so much olive oil one man can take…" His voice trailed off as he saw Hurley jogging across the grounds and heading toward the path.

That boy, he then muttered. That damn boy!

"Oh, Monsignor, isn't this nice?" She read from the card. "Congratulations. With warm regards, St. John's Monastery, Spokane."

"Mrs. Wooten, repeat for me what you said when you learned of the Hurley boy's recent defiance in Father Ken's class? When he assumed a belligerent stance?"

"A good old-fashioned flogging. That's what I said."

"Yes, I thought that's what you said."

"I mean, a kid like that, his two friends stewing over at the public high, has the gall to behave like that? A few students said that if the bell hadn't rung, there might have been another assault on Father Ken. You might want to have our third little pig in for a chat before you leave for the airport."

"Oh, I've turned that kind of thing over to Father Ken. And with my plane taking off later tonight, I barely have enough time to get my hair cut. That reminds me. Please call over and make sure the rear parking stall is open at Vito's."

Shortly before six, Cassidy in a VIP room rose from the barber's chair and looked in the mirror. By all indications, his hair had been nicely layered by Vito. The manicure by Vito's wife was quite fine, too. The pastor left a generous tip, then headed out into the night and to the rear parking stall. Once behind the wheel, he turned on the overhead light to look at his watch. Plenty of time for a hot shower and a light meal before the airport limo was to arrive and take him to JFK airport.

As he pulled out of his parking space and started down the dark alley, he slammed the brakes to avoid hitting someone carrying empty boxes to the dumpster. With the help of the headlights, he identified the Flanagan boy, who in his work frock flung the boxes off to the side and then pounded a fist against the car's hood, yelling, "Slow down, asshole!"

Cassidy jumped out of the car. "Have you lost your mind, Son?"

"Nearly running me over, and all you have to fucking say is, have I lost my mind!"

It dawned on Cassidy that he was in a dark alley. Still, he couldn't resist. "Apples, William Flanagan, never fall far from the tree."

William grabbed the cleric by the collar and shoved him against the car. He wouldn't let go. "My father's twice the man you are!"

Cassidy trying to writhe free, "How dare you!"

William pounded a free hand on the roof before releasing the priest. "Go on, you creep. Beat it back to that rectory of yours."

The pastor indeed got in and sped back to the safe confines of his office.

Disheveled and shaken, he twice poured a bourbon, downing each in a gulp. He was distracted to no end. He had never been treated in such a way. He poured a third glass and dropped into his swivel. He spun around to look out into the night. But how to get back at that pig of a boy who, no longer a parish student, wallows in the mud. As for fetching the police after him, that would result in more publicity. Hell, the boy will say, I tried to run him over. So how...

A smirk emerging, the remaining little pig, Hurley, came to mind. Cassidy told himself that despite the late hour, there was plenty of time for a point-blank attack on the boy before he left for the airport. Hurley wouldn't know what hit him.

The pastor swung back around and pressed a familiar button on his phone.

"Yes, Monsignor?" answered his secretary.

"Mrs. Wooten, please phone the Hurley residence and have the boy come right over."

"But the airport limo! And I thought that Father Garland-"

"Mrs. Wooten!"

"Right away, Monsignor."

"And do call it a day once he arrives."

"Yes, Monsignor."

WHEN DENNIS HAD REACHED 32 Crocus after his beach run that afternoon, he lost all nerve to tell his parents about Coach Jack's dismissal and the busted season. Instead, he bypassed them in the kitchen and went straight up to his room. Catherine made as if to follow him. Dan grabbed his wife's arm in a gesture that conveyed, for now, she let her son be.

But that was prior to the highly irregular summons by Mrs. Wooten, and now Dennis sat across from the pastor who, buoyed by several bourbons, started the meeting by moving his quill a few inches. The same with the ink well.

"Perhaps the best way to begin, Dennis Hurley, is to say it's a crying shame the parish will not be represented at state tomorrow." He held up one hand to the lamp to admire his manicure. "I had hoped to say a victory prayer in Rome even as the Holy See was extending his blessing. Anyway, I was out driving today when I saw a certain young man running all by himself. The loneliness of a long-distance runner, as they say. This time carrying around the memory of a late summer night."

Dennis shot a look at Cassidy, now inspecting the nails of his other hand.

"You see, I can't help but admire the way some have weathered our parish tragedy, quietly and without show. While others, such as the Walker boy, pole vaults atop roofs. Or-"

"Peter only went there to-"

"Or Flanagan. A slovenly boy raised in the mud. Speaking of pigs, what is the sound this farm animal makes? It's right there on the tip of my tongue." Dennis knew not what to say. "Please, I insist, do tell me the sound a pig makes." Cassidy pressed together the fingertips of each hand, as if to suggest the Church's very existence depended on an answer.

A confounded Dennis now shook his head and muttered, "Oink."

"Atta boy! Now far be it from me to pass judgment on what happened that terrible night, for the dealings lie well beyond my reach. I know only in the weeks that followed, your two friends reflected a festering quality, that is, until they chose to hot-rod it, the results for both," he paused to smack the desk, "to crash and burn."

"That's not at all how it was. Or is."

"What if, Dennis, an old farmer takes dead aim and shoots his favorite pig? Who'd help the farmer bury the animal?"

"You must be-"

"Local gravediggers, perhaps. And what if, while dirt's being tossed back in, there comes a sudden movement down in the hole, say, the jerking of a hind quarter?"

Dennis leaned forward and gripped the chair's arms.

With fake rapture Cassidy made the Sign of the Cross. "What if from the same hole there came a dull, mournful oink?"

Dennis sprang to his feet. "What if Vinnie Malagati deserved to die!"

"Oh, try to imagine, if you can, the poor animal's helpless moans slowly fading to nothing as the grave fills with dirt. As for the farmer, his own wife in the great beyond, he probably couldn't help but think that maybe his time had come, too."

Curling his palms at his side, Dennis spit out, "You sick, sick fuck! That's what you are!"

Doing his best to retain an inscrutable expression, Cassidy replied, "Lest Satan think he's won the day...."

But Dennis, already halfway to the door, never halted his stride. He slammed the door shut behind him and took off running down the empty hallway. Once outside, he bounded down the rectory steps, only to stumble and fall into an ornate sign, *The Parish Prayer Garden,* illuminated by a floodlight, which made visible the recently completed project. Now on all fours, he looked up and saw the pastor raising a side office window and yelling out, "Tell 'em, Son, that the devil made you do it!"

The window abruptly lowered, curtains drawn.

Dennis tore the sign pole out of the ground, and taking giant steps, he screamed out as he smashed one ceramic fauna after another. One swing catching a main, a geyser of water erupted as Father Ken and several nuns descended on the scene. They grabbed Dennis, who broke free and streaked away.

Now racing along the path, and about to cross the creek, he stopped to catch his breath. He noticed that the Sitting Bull plaque was gone, in its place a gaping hole. He looked all around until downstream he saw an object gleaming in the creek water. He slid down the bank and trudged the creek until he stood over the partially submerged plaque, still attached to the pole and cement crater at its base. He kicked the water and cursed. He climbed back up and sat on the bank.

"Cassidy," was all he could muster.

In a fit of anger, Dennis swore he'd go straight to his parents and tell them what just occurred at the rectory. But then he relented after realizing what telling his parents would lead to—a confession about the hideous details of that late August night. Besides, Cassidy would deny any and all accusations.

"He's a bloody coward," Dennis muttered. "But so am I."

As the limo driver put the suitcase and garment bag in the trunk, Father Ken held the door open for his boss. Before getting in, Cassidy surveyed the sorry scene, a torrent of water spraying about.

"I had hoped, Father Ken, to leave our little hamlet in one piece."

"Well, Monsignor, not exactly sure what happened here tonight, but at the very least, we've got a third implosion on our hands. And none too soon."

In no mood for Garland's bluster, Cassidy said, "In short order, do get this mess cleaned up. The parish can hardly afford more photos. And make sure the boy's parents are given notice."

After sitting on the creek's bank a long time, Dennis returned home and found his father in a hooded sweatshirt leaning forward on the porch rocker.

"Sorry, Dad."

At first Dan Hurley neither answered nor looked up. But raising a wizened face, he said, "Damn it, Dennis, how much more can we take! First, word spreads like wildfire about Jack Hogan getting canned over stolen money. Then we get a call that there will be no state meet. And if that's not bad enough, you go out and bust up the new prayer garden, that after cussing out the future Bishop of Rockville Centre. Then, you go missing! Your poor mother, worried sick, left to call all over town looking for you." His father rubbing his hands together, Dennis had never seen him like this. "Shit, your mom called all the parents. No one knew where you were! No one! Finally, she called the police."

"Dad…" Dennis felt himself breaking.

"And to think, while the state championship is being run in the morning, your mother and I will be over at the parish watching the legs cut out from under you. You, the newest addition to Bellport High."

His head dropping, he waved his son inside.

Dennis knew better than to stop in the kitchen where his mother sat in darkness.

Climbing the stairs, he heard the front door open, then his father's voice on the phone notifying the police that his son had made it home safely.

A STEWARDESS DIMMED the cabin lights as the private jet lifted off the tarmac. Nellenberger and Cassidy, both in sleeping masks, reclined in the rear section, their entourage up front.

"You know, Jim, with the Charlie Malagati business winding down, I'm hearing some very upbeat news. Two of the renegades have been exiled."

"Your source, John, needs to update the list to include the third boy."

"You don't say? A trifecta for St. Theresa. The old gal must be proud."

As the jet continued to climb, the masked Nellenberger could not see that a somber Cassidy, now pulling his own mask away, stared down at the white caps of the Atlantic. Word of the Hurley boy and his wreckage, the future bishop was thinking, had already spread about town. With any luck, the press would go easy on this latest incident. With any luck at all.

After his father's phone call to the police, Dennis paced about his room. He was at a loss. A mix of anger and shame. At one point, his right arm swept the framed photo of the Watkins Glen team off his desk. He dropped to his knees. He pounded the bed again and again. Only when he ran out of steam did he reach for the team photo on the floor. Through cracked glass, he peered at each face. He opened the bottom desk drawer, stuffed it in, and dropped into bed.

I fucked up. And there's not a damn thing I can do about it. Then looking over at his confidante, he said, "Right, Pre? I'm done?"

At first, the country's star distance runner, as was often the case, remained stone cold silent. But then, incredibly so, it seemed Pre's big eyes flashed an idea, a wild one that would require Dennis to wait until his parents were asleep before slipping out. Which he did, and once outside, his next hour was hectic, starting with his mounting the Flanagan's garage roof. There he woke up William, that followed by the two of them rounding up Peter.

As the three then huddled under a streetlamp, Dennis flailed about as he filled them in on what had occurred over the last week, everything from his visit to Oak Island to his busting up the prayer garden after Cassidy's ambush. He finished with the discovery of the Sitting Bull plaque in creek water. This time his two friends listened. Once Dennis was done explaining, deliberation among the three followed, which led to their scurrying over to the parish. There Peter jimmied the locker room's exterior door as his two friends stood guard. A few minutes later, after gaining access to the cross-country office, he returned outside with a box in hand. The three boys now had just a few more stops to make.

Finally back at 32 Crocus, the box atop his desk, Dennis pulled out paper and began writing. The text, taking a while to finish, was slipped into an envelope that he labeled, *The Memoir*. He scribbled on another piece of paper, set the alarm, and went to bed.

39

It was early afternoon in Rome. The newly minted bishops, Cassidy among them, streamed in pairs of two out of St. Peter's Basilica. Their heads were bowed, their hands pressed together in solemn prayer, their murmur all but lost on the crowds that cheered and lined the square. At the same moment, some four thousand miles away, with dawn emerging in Bellport, Jack Hogan was awakened by knocks. At the front door, he found his captain in race sweats.

"Dennis! You can't be here. I signed a..." Noticing something outside, he opened the door and stepped out.

Good God, he murmured, stunned by what he saw. Not only all seven members of his original team in meet sweats, but also the plaque and its cement-cratered pole hoisted on the shoulders of Peter and William.

"Gentlemen, on three," Legs declared, the plaque gently lowered to the ground.

William said, "Coach, Captain Denny discovered the chief wasting away in the creek. Like it was junk."

"The Doughboy," Peter added, "probably ran the operation."

"But," Dennis said, "Cassidy was ultimately behind it."

"I'd break both their legs," said Coach Jack. "If only I could."

From his bag Dennis pulled out an old uniform singlet with Chief Sitting Bull on it.

"Coach, we want to run. We deserve to run."

Less than an hour after the team awakened their coach, a groggy Catherine Hurley, still in her bathrobe, was filling the kettle when she saw a note on the table. Reading it, she bolted upstairs to find an empty bed. She then raced below and awakened Dan. A series of phone calls made, Dan carried a sleeping Tommy out to the wagon, his wife following. They headed to the K-Mart parking lot, where the Feltman's Dodge Monaco nearly rammed their wagon at the entrance. The Mumbinos, Walkers, Flanagans, and Legstaffs were already parked.

Bill Flanagan spread a map across the hood of his car, and as the fathers deliberated the best route to take into the Bronx, Walt Fennessy's Volkswagen bug showed up. The route established, the caravan took off, Flanagan's wagon the lead car.

"Bill!" Kay screamed as her husband took the winding entrance ramp to Southern State Parkway at a dangerously high speed. "You're gonna get us killed!"

"Damn it, Kay. We've got a fucking race to catch!"

The Monaco fell out of line when Harry failed to negotiate a lane transfer near the entrance ramp to the Throgs Neck Bridge. Knowing the area's back streets well, he made his way to the Whitestone and somehow caught up with the group on the Major Deegan Expressway. The contingent pulled into an abandoned parking lot of the Transit Authority. The wild-eyed cohort raced down Amsterdam Avenue to join hundreds of fans passing under the entrance banner.

Welcome to Van Cortlandt Park
Home of the 1974 New York State
Cross-Country Championship

As many fans headed to a bluff overlooking the cow path to

watch the early part of the race, some at first stopped to steal looks at the tent city where runners were engaged in pre-race rituals. Some sprinting, others stretching, still others adjusting spikes and pinning numbers to their singlets.

"Your attention, please," the P. A. voice boomed. "It is now 9:15. Forty-five minutes until race time."

At the registration table, the line of coaches dwindling, a meet official handed a packet to the Potsdam High coach.

"Next?"

"McQuaid Jesuit, Schenectady."

The official dug out the packet. "There we go, Coach. And take some extra safety pins if you need them. Next?"

"Buffalo Lancaster."

"Here you go. Next?"

"St. Theresa's of Bellport."

"Oh, Coach Jack. We didn't think we'd see you today. We got a call saying your team had pulled out."

"We had a big change of heart, we did."

The official reached for a packet in a box off to the side.

"Well, we're glad to hear that."

As Coach Jack scurried through the north woods to the team tent, raised in an isolated spot to prevent detection by the hostile cross-country forces, he found Dennis leading the team in stretching exercises.

The P. A. system came back to life: "Your attention, please. It is now 9:30, the race to begin in thirty minutes. All runners should be making their way to the starting line."

Coach Jack waved his runners inside the team tent.

He first looked into the eyes of each boy.

"So here we are again, at Van Cortlandt Park, the crème de la crème of high school cross country. Ready to take on a championship run that you and I have been waiting a lifetime for. There's no doubt that once the race is over, meet officials will come after our championship trophy, this after we have snatched victory from the jaws of defeat. So will District Attorney Nick Lambert come a-knocking at my door with offers of a solitary cell at Sing Sing. But as Sitting Bull would say, live like a coward or die a bloody hero. Well, boys, I'm here today to die on a hill for you. You ready to do the same for me?"

"Yeah, Coach!" the team shouted back.

"See, this group here hasn't trained as a unit for many weeks. Life kind of got in the way. But I've seen the likes of Flanagan and Walker out on the local trails running on their own. Kicking some mean ass, if you know what I mean. I also saw our team rise from the ashes last week at sectionals. Yes, I'd say we're back! And I'd say it's time to rain down on the upstate schools, who go by Syracuse Central and Albany Hamilton, not to mention newcomer Saratoga Springs. Are you ready to sling dirt back at them?"

"Yeah, Coach!" they again shouted.

"Damn, you seven, you're gonna make Coach Jack cry. But first, I want to send a little love back, starting with Fenny the Fleabite. Huh, Fenny, you ornery little bastard who brought that puke-green time of twenty minutes your freshman year down to a personal best last week at sectionals. Not to mention that you kicked the shit out of the mile time trial this week. Are you ready?"

"Fenny's ready, Coach. Ready to break balls."

"And you, Bobby Mumbles, who likes to chase tail, and who also ran the race of his life last week. You ready to die with Coach Jack?"

"Copy that, Coach. Mums is ready all day long!"

"And then there's Adam Feltman, the best goddam runner in the state, the yamaka of all fucking yamakas who I love more that life itself. Huh, Adam, ready to heave that barrel chest across the finish line in first place? Ready to take gold?"

"Damn ready, Coach Jack!" said Adam, steel in his eyes.

"As for King Arthur, the mouthiest piece of shit to ever roam the forest, you could be a top three in this race with your hands tied behind your back if you weren't so busy saving your energy for the big kick at the end, all so you can get that ugly mug of yours in the papers. Wadda you say, Legs, you up to the task?"

"Arthur's sword is ready to slice and dice."

"And last but not least, the hot molten core of this team! Do know that I am damn proud of you three boys. This team is yours. They go where you go. To the moon and back, if need be."

He stuck his hand out.

"Now I say to Jack Hogan's merry band of seven, as strong as the wind and tide, let's get 'em! And let's get 'em good!"

All seven, now locked in, placed their hands atop Coach Jack's and shouted, "Sitting Bull!"

As THE STARTER SILENCED the enormous crowd with the raising of his pistol, each runner snatched a last breath of air. The entire park going quiet, the long stretch of runners toed the line. The starter's muted call came, followed by a loud pistol crack that unleashed over two-hundred runners over the grounds. With a flash of arms and legs, the mad dash was underway.

The arrow gradually forming, the sleek Tom Parr of Chillicothe High, as expected, bolted to the front. He was the first to enter the cow path. Not far behind was a large cluster, that followed by an endless stream of runners squeezed in on the narrow trail of bulging roots and cheered on by fans up on a bluff, the St. Theresa contingent among them.

"Do you see the boys down there?" Catherine Hurley called over to the other parents.

"Not yet," Kay Flanagan shouted back.

"Where's my Adam?" Ida Feltman asked.

"No, no, no," shouted Harry, registering shock at seeing Syracuse's green and white singlets in a pack of four.

"Can't be," said Paul Mumbino.

"That damn team," cried Bill Flanagan.

"There's your boy, Ida!" yelled Rick Walker. Adam came into view surrounded by packs of three each from Albany and Saratoga.

"Good God," Harry said, "he's too far back."

Now the wait on the core three. And when they entered the cow path, their parents' immediate concern was that they were caught in a logjam.

"What do you think, Dan?" asked Bill Flanagan. "They look like they're in the fifties. But how to get out?"

Dan sighed, "Yeah, it's looking like they're not going anywhere soon."

A long line of runners passed before Fenny and Mumbles appeared, followed by Legs.

"Go, George, go!" yelled Carol Legstaff.

"Shit, no!" Walt Fennessy cried after a runner knocked into his son, who tumbled over. Fenny sprang up and continued.

The core three now leaving the cow path behind reached the bottom of the short but pesky Freshman Hill in time to see their team's top runner at its crest.

"Looks like..." yelled Dennis to his two friends, "Adam's broken away...from Albany....and Saratoga."

As St. Theresa's top runner went up and over Freshman Hill, an official in the Back Hills, ready to call out the mile split, was surrounded by a throng of coaches, all of whom waited on the field.

"Shame about the team from Bellport," joked the Albany coach to others.

"You mean Homicideville?" said the Baldwinsville coach.

Guffaws.

"Heard half their team got bounced from school."

"And word has it that Hogan's wearing an orange jumpsuit."

"Hey, look! Here comes Parr."

All by himself, Tom Parr breezed by in an effortless 4:47. Not far behind him, the same cluster of runners, then the pack of four from Syracuse, clearly the team to beat at this point. Soon, three from Saratoga came by, Adam on their heels. Right on point at the mile mark, Adam surged, passing runners and now running with the small packs from Saratoga and Albany.

"Holy crap!" yelled the Saratoga coach. "That's Feltman, Hogan's top kid."

"Thought they weren't here," another coach shouted back. Not much later, the same coaches looked a bit dazed as the core three passed by the mile mark in 5:18.

"You two ready to slow burn?" Peter called out moments later as he and his two teammates negotiated the Back Hills.

"Hell, yeah," William yelled.

Up on a bluff, Coach Jack looked down on his three runners who were surging and seemed to be in good shape.

"Burn, you three, burn!" he cried.

Hearing the muffled voice of their coach, the boys responded in kind, promptly passing a large pack in front of them. But that was little consolation to Coach Jack as he noticed the fifth man from Syracuse was right there with his three.

"Bastard!" the coach muttered. He wouldn't be surprised if that kid turned out to be the one to stand in their way of a championship trophy.

Fenny and Mumbles soon came by, Legs some ten positions behind them. Coach Jack took off through the woods and deeper into the Back Hills.

At one point he stopped for a bird's eye of his team in the distance. Adam had moved into the top ten, the Syracuse pack of four not far behind. His core three were now in the low thirties, the fifth man for Syracuse still with them. Fenny, Mumbles and Legs, all in the high forties.

Soon the core three found themselves on the same stretch of trail where Cassidy appeared some months back at the Cardinal Hayes Invite. Dennis recalled this and surged some, his two teammates right on his shoulder as they encountered a series of hard turns. Negotiating one turn, the three came to a grinding halt. They saw Adam down an embankment kicking leaves wildly about in an hysterical search for a racing shoe lost when he took the turn too fast and toppled down.

High up in the woods, Coach Jack winced at the scene: his core three side-stepping down to join his top runner in search of a racing shoe. Their coach's eyes went back and forth from the passing stream of runners to his four kicking leaves about. Though the scene lasted just a short while, it seemed an eternity before William held up the lost shoe and tossed it to Adam. And no sooner were the four back on the path than their coach, taking heavy steps in the direction of the walking bridge, cursed the high heavens that the last race he would ever coach had been lost to a bloody shoe.

"You okay?" Dennis asked Adam once they had resumed. Adam said nothing but picked up the pace, the core three going with him. The four passed a sign nailed to a tree:

1½ Miles
The Halfway Point

Grimacing, gasping, and in seeming slow motion, Adam and the core three together made their way up an incline of a few hundred feet. Their short steps and low digging arms helped them pass runners, including the fifth man from Syracuse. Once at the crest, Dennis looked back down and saw Legs fast approaching.

Dennis and his three teammates started the flight down the long descent, feet crunching ground all the way to the bottom. The four continued for a few hundred yards before they heard the familiar voice approaching from behind. "Boys," said Legs now reaching them and ready to impose his enormous ego on the race. "Time to slay the dragon."

"Let's go," William gasped.

"And," Legs said, "You ready, Adam...to dance a Yiddish jig?"

Adam's answer came in the form of a terrific surge, taking Legs and the core three with him.

SITTING BULL RUN

A SOMBER COACH JACK came through the woods where he joined a mob of coaches and fans, the St. Theresa parents among them. He did so in time to catch Tom Parr coming by with a healthy lead, followed by a small handful of runners.

"See the boys, Coach?" Dan Hurley shouted over to him.

Before he could respond, the faces of the St. Theresa parents went dull when they saw the approaching green and white of Syracuse in a pack of four. Coach Jack counted only twelve runners in front of them. The two giddy Syracuse coaches dodged trees heading down to the Flats. They saw their team in what seemed an insurmountable lead.

"In the bag, Coach," gloated the assistant.

"Let's hope."

Back at the mob of coaches, the small packs from Saratoga and Albany each passed by. Dan Hurley stole a sorry glance at his wife.

"My Adam, Coach," said Harry Feltman, "where is he?"

But as a gloomy Jack Hogan looked away, Catherine Hurley shouted, "There's your Adam! Look!" Sure enough, there he was. But no longer way ahead of his teammates, he was now just yards in front of them. Yet it was clear to the parents that the five boys, clustered together and flying by runners, had found a tremendous momentum of their own.

"In the low thirties, they are," yelled Dan who had been counting runners as they passed.

As the parents screamed at their immediate approach, Coach Jack fisted the sky as he slid down to the race trail to get in his team's face. "A title, boys! A goddam title!"

Adam was the first to make the turn down to the Flats, his four teammates now some ten yards behind. Coach Jack went weak. His eyes welled up. The same with the moms. For the first time today, they were all close enough to read the same phrase scribbled on the back of each uniform, *We Are Jack's Boys*.

"Hey, Coach Jack," Dan Hurley shouted, "get your ass down there. Still got coaching to do."

The coach wasted no time weaving through trees. He reached the Flats just in time to see Syracuse's four runners split into packs of two. They still remained the team to beat, a fact not lost on their euphoric fans, one of whom waved an enormous school flag. Soon, though, the same flag went limp as an impressive pack of silver and maroon singlets came into view, Adam and his four teammates powering by the small packs from Saratoga and Albany.

Coach Jack now reaching the Flats, and seeing what the Syracuse fans saw, hoped like hell that the real race was about to start. He tossed his clipboard in the air and made a mad dash to the race trail. He got there in time to catch Adam, who in a wild sprint was passing Syracuse's second pack of two.

"The leaders, Adam, get 'em! Get 'em now!"

Which Adam did in short order.

Coach Jack now waited on Legs, who having separated from the core three soon came flying by. "You son of a bitch, the whole world's watching. Think top ten."

Legs, all business, didn't respond, but blistered along.

A good dozen runners passed, including Syracuse's second pack, before the core three approached. "Syracuse, boys!" Coach Jack hollered at them.

The coach now charged full bore for the finish line. He barreled through frenzied fans who lined the ropes nine and ten deep. He did so in time to see Adam turn on to the top of the final straight, a few hundred yards out, and closing in on Syracuse's lead pack of two.

"Bring it home, Adam Feltman! Bring it now!"

Yet as Adam drew closer, the coach could see that his top runner was operating on borrowed energy. The slouching of his head, the clawing of arms. Still, Adam persevered even as his body seemed to disintegrate. Just yards from the finish line, incredibly, he passed Syracuse's first pack of two for fifth place.

Now it was Legs' turn, and in a hard-charging bumrush, and with proud anguish on his face, the one and only King Arthur moved inexorably past a good dozen runners to snag ninth place. The coach again looked to the top of the straight, onto which the core three now spilled, Syracuse's second pack of two right in front of them, their fifth man not far behind. Seeing this, Coach Jack erupted into giddy laughter. It had just dawned on him that he had a front row seat to a spectacle far greater than the Ali-Frazier Fight of the Century, and it hadn't cost him a damn penny.

As the core three drew closer, however, now some twenty yards out, the coach's jesting vanished. He saw that the three, fighting for every last spot, were in deep hurt. Jello legs, arms in a slow-motion fight, faces shrieking pain. Yet approaching the finish line, and with agony on their faces, the three surged into a tangle of runners that included Syracuse's third and fourth men. They did so as one of those Syracuse runners stumbled and fell just feet from the finish, causing a Saratoga runner to go down with him.

"Thank you, Jesus!" Coach Jack shouted out as his core three crossed the line unimpeded. Even so, as line judges scooped up fallen runners and pushed them into the chute, the coach kept a close eye on the process to make sure that his boys were placed in their correct positions. Once assured of that, he turned his attention to Fenny and Mums, who fought like hell to maintain their positions through the finish. Only then did the chaos of the moment hit Coach Jack. Except for Adam and Legs, he had no idea what position his core three landed in. Only that they had finished.

Dennis, William, and Peter found Legs and Adam at the end of the chute. Soon Fenny and Mumbles joined them. Barely coherent, the seven held onto each other for support. Family members surrounded them. Their utterly depleted sons exchanged looks at one another that seemed to ask, Was it enough? They did so while their coach took off in the direction of the officials' tent. There he'd lose his mind waiting on the results.

40

That next morning a row of local Bellport fishermen with five o'clock shadows cast their lines out over the breakers, the bright sun beyond dancing about the ocean floor. Back in town, the airport limo turned off Main Street and into the parish, today's marquee reading,

James Francis Cassidy
Bishop of Rockville Centre
To Preside Over Evening Mass

Suitcase in hand, and watching the limo drive away, Cassidy stood for a moment admiring the prayer garden repair. He was so impressed that he started whistling a sprightly melody, this despite the fatigue he felt from the night flight back across the Atlantic. The whistling, now playful, grew louder as he lifted the Sunday paper off the rectory porch and saw his formal portrait gracing the front page. A spring in his step, he went inside.

But as he entered his office, the whistle died off when he glimpsed the headline on the back sports page.

St. Theresa's Cross-Country Team
Disqualified After Winning State Title

The stunned cleric wondered why he hadn't been notified, unaware that Lambert and Father Ken had talked amongst themselves the night before and agreed that they'd let the new bishop enjoy what was left of his trip.

Cassidy pulled the newspaper up closer. He looked on in horror at the photo of Hogan, waving a colossal trophy and being carried on the shoulders of his runners, the backs of their singlets reading *We Are Jack's Boys*. The article's opening paragraph reported that meet officials, well after the awards ceremony ended, disqualified the team upon learning that two of its runners had been expelled and that the team's coach had been fired.

Before Cassidy could read any further, there came a voice, "Not a bad day's work, eh?"

The bishop turned. The words belonged to the Hurley boy who stood across the room, his two cronies flanking him.

"How did you…" stammered Cassidy, the newspaper lowered to his desk.

"Simple," said Peter pointing to a window. "A bit of jimmying."

"Some might call it breaking and entering," said Cassidy, his eyes scanning the boys' hands, searching for a weapon of some kind.

"Yeah! That's right, breaking and entering," echoed William. "Like we did over at Coach Jack's office the other night. A man's gotta do what a man's gotta do. After all, to win the granddaddy of them all, we needed uniforms, right?" And stepping closer to the now seething Cassidy, William added, "only problem is they disqualified us."

Cassidy's face flushed to crimson. "Do you three know to whom you are speaking?"

"Tell us, Oh Mighty One," said Dennis.

Cassidy lost all control. "I am the Bishop of Rockville Centre, and now I find myself accosted by three parish vermin who think they can barge in here and invoke a Third Vatican Council on American soil. You're nothing but petty felons. In fact," Cassidy lifted the phone's receiver, ready to turn the tables on them, "I think it's time to finally bring in the authorities and have you dragged away for good."

With sarcasm in his voice, Peter said, "Say, Denny, can he have us dragged off for good?"

"Believe it!" Cassidy rushed to say. "I'll have you three out of here faster than you can-"

"Well," Dennis interrupted, "it goes like this. The state race was stage one of our master plan." He pulled an envelope from his shirt pocket and waved it. "This is stage two. I call it, *The Memoir.*" Cassidy's hand around the phone receiver tightened visibly. "See, I tracked down Vinnie's girlfriend and learned the whole story." Sizing up Cassidy's stricken expression, Dennis savored the moment. "But don't worry. I wrote it all down. And you've got a starring role in it."

"How about you treat us to a summary, Denny Boy," said William.

"Well, after all hell broke loose one late August night, Bellport awoke to the arrest of the parish custodian. Mr. Malagati's guilt etched in stone, the natives nonetheless kept asking who else might have helped the old man bury his son. Some argued the nephews. Others that Mr. Malagati preferred to work alone. The bishop here conducted his own investigation."

The receiver ever so slowly went back down into its cradle.

"Perhaps because he's the Sherlock Holmes of our day, and perhaps knowing just how fond we are of the wee hours, he moved us to the top of his suspect list."

"You don't say," Peter said.

To which Dennis replied, "Ain't that right, Bishop Cassidy? But upon further reflection, you had a problem on your hands. Three parish athletes involved in such a grisly affair? What of your career? Bishops can't be all tangled up in such ugly business. So, you hatched a plot that began with scurrying to the bungalow to take control of the situation."

Unbidden, Cassidy's eyelids raised a fraction.

Dennis continued, answering the bishop's unspoken question, "Yes, I went back to the bungalow just hours before the old man killed himself. I wanted to talk him into telling the police the truth. But I never got the chance."

"Why, Denny?" William asked.

"Because the bishop here beat me to the punch. Indeed, I wasn't inside the bungalow. But when I crept up to a window, I could hear only muffled voices, the bishop's, dominating, of course."

Peter asked, "Wonder why this holy man was there in the first place?"

"For one thing, he needed to know our exact involvement in Vinnie's death, which he clearly squeezed out of the old man."

"Anything else, Denny?"

"Hell, yeah. With his flair for words, he surely magnified Mr. Malagati's guilt, convincing the old man that he disgraced his wife, his family, the parish, that he had nothing left. Gave the old man no choice."

"No choice but what?" asked Peter with a mocking smirk at Cassidy.

"What Denny's suggesting," William said, "is that the pastor reduced the old man to a bag of shit. All so that he had no choice but to shoot himself. Right, Denny, that's what you're saying?"

"Exactly! After the session with the old man, with my own eyes I saw the bishop, like a thief in the night, take the long way round to the rectory. Moments later, the old man left for the cemetery. For a final goodbye to his wife before, or so I thought at the time, he was hauled off to jail. I went home that night, suicide the last thing on my mind. Yet the bishop still had a small bit left on his plate after the old man blew his brains out, and that was us. Yes, it wouldn't be cool to have three parish students in handcuffs on the front page. He needed something far less public, but something that would get us off the parish grounds for good. So he sicced his lapdog Garland on us."

"And to think," William said, "we didn't believe Denny the first time he told us his theory. Or the second or third time. Told him to go pound sand."

"Garland," said Dennis, waving the envelope at Cassidy, "took out my friends in no time. But I didn't go so easy, did I? It took you yourself to pull that off right before you left for Rome."

Cassidy slammed the desk. "What do you boys want?"

Dennis replied, "This little piggy - oink, oink - goes to market."

"I repeat, what do you want?"

Dennis turned a visitor's chair around and straddled it, pocketing the letter and pulling out another piece of paper that he tossed on the desk. "There, take a gander."

As Cassidy looked it over, Dennis continued, "Oh, just a few changes to your announcements at today's evening Mass."

"Only after you've made them and we're satisfied," William added, "do we torch the memoir."

"And your part in the saga," said Peter, "will never be known."

"Capeesh?" said William.

Cassidy wasn't at all ready to dignify the outrageous blackmail with a response.

Dennis said, "Demand number one: Jack Hogan gets his coaching job back. For good."

"Never."

"Next. The three of us are reinstated. We finish the school year here."

"Never."

"Last, by week's end, your bags are packed, and you are gone. But not before you use your clout with Lambert to keep us out of real trouble."

Cassidy's head jerked some.

"And do make sure," Dennis added, "that once today's Mass is over, the parish knows full well that Mr. Malagati didn't have a mean bone in his body, that things simply got out of control."

As the three boys scampered back out the window, Dennis

stuck his head back in for a parting shot. "When someday, Preacher, you kick the bucket, and find yourself denied admission into the pearly gates, you might try telling St. Peter that the Devil Made You Do It."

The window slammed shut.

With the three boys scuttling away, Cassidy was left to convince himself that none of what just happened was real. But as the initial shock faded, his first instinct was to phone Lambert and have the boys rounded up. Then he recalled Hurley's threat, the envelope he carried in his top pocket. The boy's brash demeanor was evidence enough that he'd make good on his promise. There was no telling what Hurley was capable of doing next.

"CAN I HELP YOU BOYS?" asked the desk sergeant at the Bellport police station.

"Yes," Dennis said. "We have some information about the Malagati affair. And the D.A. will want to be in on it. Best fetch him."

The sergeant cocked his head at the kid's audacity. But hedging his bets, he said, "You three take a seat while I make a call."

Not much later in an interrogation room, the boys gave their version to a stunned Lambert and a lead detective named Watts. A few deputies stood guard. Dennis did most of the talking, which included Liz Pearce's account of the lead-up to the shooting as well as the blow-by-blow of the violent altercation and the burial that followed. He left out nothing except the role of Cassidy. The boys assumed that Cassidy's ties to Lambert would rescue them from serious legal trouble. They also agreed that no one, especially their parents, must ever know about Cassidy's involvement. Their dads, for one thing, would tear his eyes out if they were to learn of his role.

While Dennis was finishing up, the three sets of parents flew past the front desk and barged into the interrogation room. At the table's head, the district attorney motioned to a deputy that they be allowed to enter.

"What the hell's going on, Lambert?" Bill Flanagan shouted.

"Yeah," added Rick Walker. "Why didn't you call us before you started in on our boys?"

Detective Watts answered, "It was your boys who sought us out."

Dan Hurley looked at Dennis. "But why?"

"To confess," Watts said.

"To what?" asked a flabbergasted Kay Flanagan.

"You folks have surely heard about the tragic business over at the parish?"

Catherine clutched Dan's arm tightly as Watts read from his notepad, her fingers digging in deeper with each charge that was leveled: "We're looking at drinking in public. Trespassing. Cemetery malfeasance. Exceptional felony. Conspiracy to hide a felony. And, finally, manslaughter."

Each of the parents froze at the jaw-dropping charges.

"According to your boys," Lambert said, "they killed Vincent Malagati. After his father shot him the first time. This boy here," he pointed at Dennis, "admitted to getting his hand on the gun and shooting Vinnie a second time, after which he hit him with the gun and knocked him down for good."

William pounded the table. "That's not what we said! We said that Denny was stopping Vinnie from killing the old man. And us."

"Perhaps," Lambert said. "But since Charlie Malagati is no longer available for comment, and since you have no one else to corroborate, we might ask a grand jury to chime in."

Dennis leaned over to Lambert and whispered, "You might want to contact the bishop for a short chat. You'll be sorry if you don't."

Lambert had no idea what the Hurley boy was up to. But like the desk sergeant before him, he thought under the bizarre circumstance he better play it safe. So he stood and announced, "I need to make a call. Take these boys below. And folks," he said to the parents in as threatening a tone as he could muster, "it will be best for your boys if you wait here quietly."

"Are they being charged?" asked a desperate Kay Flanagan.

The detective's only reply, "We'll be back."

The parents were left helpless as they watched their sons led out of the room and down to a holding cell.

The phone line fell silent following the D.A.'s report to Cassidy that the three parish boys had just walked into the Bellport precinct of their own accord and conveyed in detail their involvement in Vinnie Malagati's death and burial.

"My God, Nick!"

"I agree. But while their story seems to make sense, we can't accept their assertions at face value. For all we know, their role was far more sinister. We'll need to interview each boy one at a time to really gauge their credibility."

"I see."

"But, here's where it gets strange. The Hurley boy said that I contact you. As if you had anything to add to the conversation in the first place. Trust me, I am going to get to the bottom of this. But I thought at the very least I should contact you before word of this gets out, if it hasn't already."

"Nick, would it be possible for us to meet right away. In the privacy of my office. It's urgent."

"Of course. Be right over."

"And, the boys, Nick?"

"For now, I'll send them home with their parents. Charges will come later. No avoiding that."

After hanging up, Cassidy bristled. That reprobate Hurley, using his little tell-all as leverage! Expecting me to negotiate for him and his two buddies! But...is it possible those three have me over a barrel? And how can I plead their case before Nick Lambert based on a confession from Charlie I claimed I never got?

Cassidy marched over to the decanter and poured a half glass.

He returned to his desk and sank into his swivel to take in the parish grounds. There his mind went to work, and by the time the district attorney was sitting in front of him, he was ready.

"Nick, I wish I had been honest with you, but like I told the archbishop, Charlie phoned and asked me to hear his confession. Which I did, though I had no earthly idea that suicide would follow the meeting. Yet I can't stand by anymore and allow the current false narrative to dictate the terms of Charlie's legacy. So the time has come to share with you what Charlie told me happened that night, which will include the three boys' role in it. Shall I proceed?"

Lambert's eyes narrowed, surprised by the omission. Yet his response was a polite, "Yes, please."

While Lambert shifted uncomfortably in his chair, Cassidy took just a handful of artful sighs to bang the matter into shape. The D.A. nodded back in earnest throughout, and once the fate of the old custodian and his son was explained in some detail, including the role of the boys, he said, "Well, this indeed puts the whole thing in a different light."

"Nick, I am now thinking that I should step down as Bishop of Rockville Centre."

"Step down?"

"Yes, the Vatican can hardly afford the publicity that will come once the public learns of my visit to the old man just hours before he took his life."

"Listen," Lambert replied, "The boys never mentioned your visit. Only that I contact you. As far as I'm concerned, your visit to Charlie has no relevance to any aspect of the violence that occurred at the bungalow."

"Are you sure?"

"Absolutely."

In a bit of theatre, a heavy sigh escaped Cassidy, before he gave Lambert a grateful smile and said, "Again, Nick, I apologize I didn't tell you this sooner. And while those three boys have been a thorn in my side for years, strangely enough, in this serious matter I find myself in their corner. But how to proceed from here?"

"Well, the boys' confession will surely leak out to the public in no time, so my office must charge them with something. I can arrange for a plea deal that avoids a trial and that includes a few misdemeanors, even as it takes all felonies off the table. Needless to say, I will make sure that your name is left out of it. We can't allow this unfortunate series of events to interfere with your tenure as bishop. Yes, just leave it to me. I'll handle it."

41

Making the Sign of the Cross to end Mass, Cassidy gestured to the congregation that they sit. His stepping down off the altar's marble steps onto the wooden floor might have struck most as unusual, if not unprecedented, except that Cassidy was no longer a mere parish priest. He was the new diocesan bishop of Rockville Centre in full regalia.

"Yes, please, sit," he said, his two hands patting his vestment down. "I have a very important announcement to make."

Waiting for obedient silence, he looked up at the rear balcony. He found the three boys in a shameless pose, arms lazily hung over the railing. "But before the big announcement, I'd like to congratulate our cross-country team for yesterday's state championship win. What a grand achievement! And," he paused to point up at the statue of St. Theresa high on the side wall, "the ole gal must be proud, despite the cruel technicality that stripped the title from them. But we'll show the cross-country universe that with Coach Jack Hogan at the helm for years to come, St. Theresa's will always be in the hunt for a title."

This was met with a surprised but resounding approval.

"Of course, regarding the boys at the heart of the disqualification, I was in the dark concerning any involvement they had surrounding the sad event this past August. Just yesterday, I learned that they met with the district attorney and explained their role in it."

Cassidy again paused, this time to gauge the congregation's body language. It was clear from the pursed lips that word of the boys' confession had already spread about town, which is what he had expected.

"Yet, suffice it to say, as long as I have an ounce of energy in my body, I will not allow these three to sit by in the town's public school and become the daily targets of lies, innuendo, and abuse. No, as members of the parish family, each boy will be brought back into the fold right away. They will graduate from St. Theresa's in May. In the meantime, we must not pass judgment on them until law enforcement, having done due diligence, issues its findings."

Approving murmurs.

"For the same reason, I would ask the parish community to suspend judgment on Charlie Malagati until we know further what exactly happened that night. Try to imagine, if you can, the painful grief our custodian of over four decades experienced after the death of his son. A grief ultimately based on a deep love for Vincent. So, yes, we must never forget that Charlie lived a Christian life, and that for many years, come rain or shine, he served our parish community as a faithful servant. Each of us ought to always remember what Jesus said, *As I have loved you, so you must love one another.*"

Cassidy looked up at the balcony. The boys, their impudence in full display, stared back at him.

"Now onto the big announcement. As most of you are aware, I had hoped to finish the school year right here at St. Theresa's, where I would temporarily run the diocese from Bellport. A long, fond farewell, that is what I had hoped for. But the archbishop on the plane trip home alerted me to several urgent needs that will require my immediate departure for my new home, the chancery in Rockville Centre. I leave Monday morning."

Disapproving murmurs.

"Now, now," Cassidy said, "my love for St. Theresa's notwithstanding, let me explain."

He again looked to the balcony. The boys gone, he carried on with some confidence, unaware that the three were now skirting the building and enjoying his humbug filtering through the glazed windows. A smiling Peter high-fived William, both patting their friend Dennis on the back.

The drone of the bishop's speech faded as they entered the path.

Meanwhile, the fathers of the three boys sat at the law office of J. Willard Forster, who agreed to represent their sons. As they sat in front of him, the lawyer wasted no time in dialing the district attorney to alert him of his new clients. Lambert responded by telling Forster that as long as the boys' story held up under scrutiny, a generous plea deal of just a few misdemeanors would follow. With a lawyerly smile, Forster relayed the news to the fathers, who, thrilled by the development, rushed home to tell their wives.

Hearing of the D.A.'s promise of leniency, Catherine grabbed Dennis, who had just arrived home from Mass, and hugged him. For his part, Dan looked at his son and said, "Dennis, we have a thousand questions. Your mother and I want you to start at the beginning and tell us everything that happened that night."

Dennis nodded.

"And I mean everything, dammit."

Dennis felt the flood gates about to burst open. He wanted to tell his parents the truth about Cassidy. Not only that the pastor ambushed him after having the Doughboy do the same to William and Peter, but also how it was all part of the Monsignor's grand scheme. He desperately wanted to unload about Cassidy's visit to the bungalow and all that followed. But he couldn't. He had made a pact. So, instead, he plowed through just the details surrounding Vinnie's death.

When Dennis reached his bedroom that night, he left the

lights off and fell into bed. He couldn't deny that part of him was relieved. The gambit he and his two friends decided on paid off. Not only would they escape harsh legal retribution, but also his own main goal would be accomplished, the public exoneration of Mr. Malagati. Yet even as he was thinking this, there flashed the image of Cassidy leaning back in his swivel and wearing that damn smirk as he gloated over the fact that his role in the whole affair would never be known.

MOST IN THE CONGREGATION, as they left the church that day, supported the bishop's resolve that the three boys return to school while the legal process played itself out. Many were also pleased that Jack Hogan would return to coach the cross-country team. While Coach Jack welcomed the development, the news of the core three's involvement in the bungalow mess left him shell-shocked even as it helped to put the pieces of the season's puzzle into place. He now understood their wildly erratic behavior, especially that of his captain. Still, as he drank heavily at Chief's that night, he kept asking just how he could have missed it! The fucking writing was right there on the wall. And yet any guilt the coach was feeling was softened somewhat by the words of encouragement from regulars who bought him drinks and congratulated him on being rehired as coach.

"Hey, Jack," Joe Mahoney at one point called over, "don't forget all of us consider yesterday's championship the first of many!"

"Damn right!" confirmed Larry Mann raising his glass.

So, too, did Dan and Catherine that same night receive words of encouragement from family and friends. Aunt Pearl called her sister to say she and John would be glad to help with legal fees. Hank Legstaff, Walt Fennessy, and Paul Mumbino phoned to tell Dan the same. Rick Walker dropped off a quart of Seagram's gin. Harry and Ida Feltman knocked on the Hurley door with a basket of fruit and a bottle of wine: "Your Dennis is a special kid," Harry told Dan and Catherine. "All these years, never a problem at our house. And always a kind word toward my Adam."

A few days later, however, a *Long Island Times* article offered a less sympathetic picture of the cross-country team captain. It included any number of new details. The most damning one was the article's vivid description of Dennis' assault on Vinnie. Not only his shooting of the war veteran, but also the whack of the gun barrel that followed. It read at one point, *The separate blow to the face by Hurley came while the victim was on his knees, the impact substantial.* The article went on to note: *The investigation also learned that the three boys had been drinking whiskey atop the convent garage when the violent interaction between father and son began, this after drinking beer on the parish path earlier.* More than a few parishioners whispered among themselves that at least the Hurley boy ought to face jail time. The same parishioners were left scratching their heads when the D.A. wasted no time offering the three boys a generous plea agreement.

Public sentiment had not much changed in late November when the three went to court. In return for a guilty plea to the misdemeanors of drinking in public and trespassing on private property, they received a suspended sentence and a probationary period of two years, after which their record would be expunged. Of course, the public never learned that Cassidy's hands were all over the deal. A clause in it forbade the boys from ever discussing any and all parish staff involvement related to the affair, a breach to result in several retroactive felony convictions which amounted to mandatory prison time. And while three sets of smiling parents afterwards huddled in the parking lot to reflect on what they considered a very good day, Dennis among the boys wore a somber look. His two friends couldn't help but note Dennis' demeanor.

"Why the sad face?" William asked. "The judge just slapped our wrists."

"Yeah, Denny," Peter said, "our plan to bring Cassidy on board worked like a charm."

Dennis replied, "It's just that...well, for me it's more than just escaping jail time. I wanted to clear the old man's name."

"And that's exactly what you did," William said. "The town knows, once and for all, that Malagati's no damn villain. That he's innocent!"

"But they don't understand that the old man should still be around. They'll never know what Cassidy did. Just as surely as if he pulled the trigger."

"Fuck, Denny," William grew red. "I thought we were past that."

"Yeah," Peter said. "We had an agreement."

William first looked over at the parents before he took a step forward to get in Dennis' face. "Tell us, Denny, that it's finally over. And say it like you mean it."

Dennis at first hesitated. "Okay, okay, I get it. It's over."

"So we're all good?"

"We're all good."

That night Dennis lie in bed unable to sleep. No, all is not good. Cassidy's left unscathed. And there's not a damn thing I can do about it.

42

It would take time to heal, Catherine kept telling Dennis over the next several weeks. And that it did, especially as he found his attention drifting off at school. He couldn't help but stare out classroom windows, at the gray that hung low in the sky and that didn't seem to want to loosen its grip on Bellport. Then there were his classmates who kept their distance from him. After all, he was the one who put the finishing touches on Vinnie Malagati. What most bothered Dennis, however, was that Cassidy continued to live the good life at the Rockville Centre chancery. Nor was it any consolation, as reported in the *Bellport Citizen,* that come January 1st, Cassidy in his final salvo, would banish Father Ken to St. Catherine of Sienna hospital in Smithtown, where he would take on a chaplaincy position. A Father Edward Eichen would take the helm as pastor of St. Theresa's.

It snowed the first week of December, which offered the nuns food for thought. Sister Grace Corde told Dennis' calculus class that "Souls fall into Hell like snowflakes." With big, looped letters on the chalkboard, Sister Miriam Gonzaga wrote that the perfectly formed crystals on classroom windows represent "unrepentant sinners on the loose."

During a brief thaw, Dennis in his bedroom heard the

drainpipes gurgle with water trying to break through the leaves clogging them.

One afternoon Dennis was in his bedroom filling out an application for the state college at New Paltz when out the window he saw a drab-looking Peter down on Crocus, his shoulders hunched as he gazed up and across the woods. He stood a bit longer before heading downtown. Dennis returned to the application. But unable to concentrate, he reached for his winter coat and left to find his friend. After looking in the windows of several businesses, he spotted Peter coming out of the shoe store.

"Denny, fancy meeting you here."

"Dancing shoes, Peter?"

"Nah. I was checking out the steel toes. Some staff sergeant will give me a new pair my first day of boot camp. But I thought I'd try on a few for the heck of it."

"Boot camp?"

"The Marines. I leave June 3rd, the week after graduation."

"You didn't!"

"And watch this. Gonna do fifty." Handing Dennis his jacket, Peter dropped into a push-up position, his hands flat on the cold pavement. "You keep count!"

Glancing around at the busy downtown when Peter hit the pavement, Dennis counted out loud. The first fifteen were swift. The next ten, mechanical. The boredom all but gone by thirty, at which point Peter took over the counting. Grunting the remainder, he then sprang up from the crouching position.

"Well?" he asked.

"God help Sitting Bull if you two meet in the field of battle."

Before breaking up, Dennis told his friend that he was looking forward to the first day of indoor track, less than a week away. "Yeah, then the Armory meet, the week before Christmas. Shit, Peter, time to collect hardware in the distance medley."

Back up in his room that night, Dennis was unable to keep Peter's new reality at bay. Even though the war in Southeast Asia was drawing to a close, he pictured his friend face-down in a rice field, submerged in a foot of water made cloudy by blood leaking from his head.

A few days later, Catherine Hurley came home with a bag of groceries and said to her son, "Did you know that Peter is working at the market with William?"

"No, I didn't," answered Dennis, trying to hide his confusion.

"Yes, I just saw the two of them stocking the produce section."

"But winter track starts next Monday!"

"Yes, that's what I thought, too. Peter said that he and William decided not to run indoor track. Or outdoors, for that matter. Said he wants to save money for the Marines."

Finding words inadequate, he retreated upstairs. There he paced some before throwing on his winter gear and slipping outside. The cold air tinged with pine resin, he took off running down Crocus. He found his two friends in the back storage area loading crates of fruit onto dollies. "When," he yelled over to them, "were you going to tell me that neither of you are running winter track? Why the hell not?"

"Got to save money," said Peter.

"That's a bunch of bullshit. It's the last time we get to run together."

William stole a look at Peter before saying, "You ever think, Denny, that it was running that got us into trouble in the first place?"

"What are you talking about?"

"If not for cross country, we never would have gallivanted all over the south shore. That includes the parish grounds."

"Plus, Denny," Peter added, "William and I agree that jail time might have been better than getting death stares everywhere we go. Like we're mass murderers."

"So, no," William confirmed, "I ain't about to run track and have every last car slow down and gawk at me while I train."

"Me, neither," said Peter.

"Ain't that just grand!" said Dennis. "Blaming it all on running. Not to mention that by walking away from indoor track, you put another notch in Cassidy's belt."

"Hey, you keep forgetting that Cassidy's the one who saved our asses from big trouble by talking with Lambert. You do remember that, don't you?"

Dennis worked his mind but came up with nothing to say to that.

Before storming off, he picked an apple out of the top crate and threw it against the cinderblock where it splattered. His agitation only increased on the walk home as he realized there was no denying what his two friends had just said. All the staring, all the whispering, the harsh effects of which he felt, too. Nor could he deny that the many cross-country trails over the years had inspired any number of wild adventures. And, finally, how at the end of the day it was Cassidy's winning over Lambert that saved them from the slammer.

But even as Dennis begrudgingly admitted those truths, he still could not swallow the fact that his friends had abandoned running. The pressure in his head grew until he cried out, "To hell with them!" And approaching 32 Crocus, he thought, I'll show them. I'll run killer times. A sub 4:20 mile and a sub 9:20 two mile. Both PRs. That's what I'll do. I'll run killer times.

Dennis might have achieved those goals had not Sister Jean pulled him aside the first day of practice to inform him that Sister Rosaleen forbade him to run either indoor or outdoor track, this based on what the principal described as "a conglomerate of past indiscriminate behavior." Hearing this, Dennis bolted home and demanded that his parents intercede. While sympathetic to their son's cause, they told him that it was best to leave well enough alone. As Dennis stormed off, Dan Hurley shouted after him, "And don't ever forget, you're skating on thin ice. The plea deal, remember?"

Catherine shuddered at the sound of her son's bedroom door slamming shut.

"Dan?"

"Yes?"

"Maybe you shouldn't be so hard on him. I mean, he shot someone. He buried a body. I'm sure he's been enduring the same looks from people that I, mother of convict Dennis Hurley, have been getting everywhere I go."

"I get it, Cat, though there's nothing we can do but carry on. And we sure don't want Dennis to know we are also in the line of fire."

A few days later, William phoned Dennis to tell him that he had heard about Rosaleen's decision. "Pure bullshit, Denny. That's what it is. But listen, me and Peter have off tomorrow. How about we nail a lighthouse run together? Slow burn the shit out of it. Just the core three. What do you say?"

Dennis was too startled by the invite to turn it down. "Sounds good."

"Good. We'll meet at your drive at five. Finish in the moonlight. Just like old times."

No sooner had Dennis lowered the receiver than he smelled a rat. William and Peter had huddled together for a Denny Hurley intervention. His hunch was right. During the round-tripper to the lighthouse the next day, his two friends carried on as if that night at the bungalow had never taken place. They instead recalled, with great fanfare, some of their killer races. So did his two friends' stagecraft continue over the next few weeks at the cafeteria table. There William and Peter reminisced about Coach Jack's more memorable outbursts. Dennis could not help but join his two friends in laughter. He even high-fived them at points. But he also knew their banter came with glances of guilt, like bank robbers seeing one another at Mass years after a big heist.

43

During the Christmas holidays, Dan and Catherine Hurley decided to hold their own version of a Healing Mass. But the altar was not located anywhere near Bellport. Instead, it was on the ice-skating rink at Rockefeller Center. Or in seats at an off-Broadway matinee. Or inside a horse-drawn buggy during a chilly ride through Central Park. Dennis knew the whole time what his parents were up to. They were seeking refuge from all the glaring with road trips to the city. He put on a front as best as he could.

Dennis did wish, however, that regrets had been offered to his father's first cousin, Tim Sheehy, who held an annual New Year's Day party at his Flushing Heights brownstone, serving up various fish and pasta dishes. For there, too, city cousins looked askance at Dennis. His parents saw this. Their only recourse was to offer up a strained joviality. Catherine at one point whispered to Dan "Thank God" for the large console television that preoccupied most watching Phil Jackson, the dirtiest Knick to ever play the game, take on the Lakers. It was Action Jackson himself who stole the ball from the Laker's Cazzie Russel to score a buzzer beater. Uncle Marty declared afterwards that the victory was a sign of good things to come. None could have predicted the Knicks' victory would usher in one of the harshest Januarys in history, the temperature often in single digits.

Back in school after Christmas break, Dennis groaned at Mr. Kealty's poetry project. The blathering, red-headed lay teacher asked each student in American Literature to recite a poem by a Long Island bard. His directions called for a brief introduction that explained how one came to be poetically inspired by the text. When it came time for the first student, Eleanor Fenwick, to introduce her poem of choice, Dennis was not surprised that her prefatory remarks, read from index cards, used the parish tragedy as illustration.

"When hamlets like Bellport are confronted with evil, such as domestic murder, its citizens must resist it like the rock in this poem and try as they may to live with beauty and grace. This is a theme close to my heart, and something that I picked up from Grace Buchanan Sherwood, a Long Island poetess from Southampton who lived from 1851 to 1927, and who wrote a masterpiece of a poem called, *The Rock*."

Eleanor said a few more things concerning rejuvenation before she lowered her index cards and began from memory,

> *How placidly this granite, by the sea,*
> *The rock receives the shock of billows...*

As she continued, Dennis thought she looked ridiculous, affecting as she did a noble calm. But he couldn't deny that, like the poem's rock, she glistened up there. He imagined, as did most of the other boys in the classroom, his hands all over the haughty Eleanor Fenwick.

Following her speech, Dennis at night would dream different versions of Arthur's knights thrashing about the stormy parish woods. He'd awaken knowing the dreams represented a crude power that could very well jostle about in perpetuity, even though the woods had been emptied of all visitors. Gone forever was the bluster and swagger of young men whose feet had moved about its floor with ease, and whose laughter excited the hidden creatures of its wood. He couldn't help but think that the forest would lie quiet for some time, maybe for long periods, until some happy band of warriors found the gumption to ride herd again.

A heavy snow fell the second week of February. School canceled, Dan Hurley called up and told his son that out front needed shoveling. So there he was in the cold afternoon sun, tossing snow off to the side when he saw Harry Feltman slowly steering the Monoco down an unplowed Crocus, Adam in the passenger seat. As the car passed, Dennis recalled an intercom announcement a few days earlier that congratulated Adam for his third-place finish in the Millrose Games high school mile. Dennis seethed then, and he seethed now, thinking that he would never again compete for St. Theresa's. Undoubtedly, Rosaleen's revenge on Bishop Cassidy for his forever having squashed any attempt on her part to fire Hogan.

After tossing another shovelful, Dennis looked up at the field covered deep in snow. An idea came. I'll show the Amazon, he murmured as he tossed the shovel aside and started running down Crocus. He was careful to keep his balance, the traction of his winter boots doing their job. He didn't stop running until he made it down Main Street and reached the parish entrance. Catching his breath, he liked what he saw, the grounds as yet unplowed. The thought of the tumult he was about to impose on the virgin snow got the adrenaline flowing. He walked over to the starting line, the convent mailbox.

"Set and go," he shouted as he took off running for the start of a ten-lap race around the high school, featuring the one and only Denny Hurley.

He charged forth as best he could, and after slipping a bit, he settled into a manageable pace. As he circled the school, he raised a fist as he passed by the empty bungalow. In honor of Mr. Malagati, he'd raise a fist each time he passed it.

It took only two laps before faces up in convent windows looked down on the Hurley boy. Sister Rosaleen not among them, Dennis knew she'd shortly present herself. But what's she gonna do, send me to the public school for frolicking in the snow? I'm a renegade angel protected by the imprimatur of His Excellency in Rockville Centre.

Dennis liked the thought so much that he surged a bit before settling back into a more sensible pace. And when he made it around for another lap, he mock-saluted the Amazon, now at a window. The appalled principal, who was not about to allow the brazen affront go unpunished, retreated back to her convent office to make a call.

As Dennis began his fourth lap, he knew that his little stunt came with a price. His calves started to throb, the cold air tickled his lungs. Over the next several laps, his shoulders tightened into a painful knot. The ninth lap began with the family wagon rolling into the parish. Out the driver's side window his father yelled, "Dammit, Dennis, get in the car. Now!"

Dennis, in response, lowered his head and forged ahead.

The wagon put in park, Dan Hurley glimpsed up at the eyes in various convent windows. He now understood what his son was up to. Payback. He felt a stitch of pride.

Dennis now coming around for the gun lap, he waved to the nuns and made his way to the backside. Fully aware that his breathing came in great uneven gasps, he brandished two fists at the bungalow, that followed by the mighty struggle of an all-out sprint. At the finish line he offered the nuns Frank Shorter raising his marathon arms at Munich.

Dan Hurley pulled the wagon alongside his utterly spent son, who leaned on the wagon's hood for support. His father got out and opened the passenger door. Before Dennis got in, Dan took his son's hand, and to let the nuns know whose side he was on, he raised it high, the signal to all that his son had won this championship ten-rounder.

Still sucking wind, Dennis managed, "Thanks, Dad," and got in.

The victory sealed, Dan steered the wagon back on to Main Street. "What do you say," he asked his son, "a pitstop for the champ at Sal's? Pepperoni calzones and root beer?"

"Sounds good, Dad. Real good."

When the two eventually made it home, Catherine was horrified by her husband's report. "I don't know what's worse, Dan, your son's exhibition or the celebration afterwards. So we wait. A suspension? Or worse, expulsion?"

Dan reaching for two glasses said, "Bring it on."

After Dennis showered and dressed, he heard his father below doing his Mae West. He went downstairs and found his mother doubled over in laughter. He loved seeing her like that. Returning upstairs, he nonetheless knew that Rosaleen would come after him. But like his father, he didn't care. After all, before God he had defended Mr. Malagati, the raised fist each lap testimony enough to that.

The convent phone never rang that night, even though the principal had marched over to the rectory for an emergency meeting with the new pastor. She declared for an expulsion. Father Eichen understood that she was right. But what he didn't tell the good nun was that the new bishop, in a closed-door meeting a month earlier, made clear to him the professional damage he'd experience if any of the three boys was sent packing. Cassidy cited Garland's chaplaincy transfer as an example. After Dennis received only two weeks of detention, an exacerbated Sister Rosaleen retreated to the gloom of the convent's chapel. She asked Jesus for the strength to forgive Cassidy for the outrage of his imperial conduct, for his hiring Eichen, another lackey, who was afraid of his own shadow.

Perhaps because Dennis had escaped severe punishment, over the next several days he felt something like renewal for the moral victory over the Amazon. It also got him thinking. He decided that once the weather broke for good, he'd buy a new pair of trainers and start running again. Who needs a team! And who cares if the locals stare at me. But a wet and soggy March on Long Island, which brought with it a cold rain that felt like small rocks, slowed down his plans to get back in running shape.

However, even after the winter stormers on 32 Crocus were taken down in early April, the house's stale air driven out by spring freshness, he didn't buy the new trainers. He hated to admit that, like William and Peter, he had not the courage to face the rubberneckers who'd slow down their cars for a look-see at the boy. The same boy who, after shooting and whacking the soldier to death, dug and deposited the body into a shallow grave, something that more than a few locals read as cold-hearted. So for the time being, Dennis postponed any resumption of running. The staring, however, still came while he was out and about, especially among the downtown merchants who whispered among themselves. But he had no idea they were telling one another how reedy he looked wrapped in a hooded sweatshirt, his hands dug so deeply into the front pouch that perhaps, like Charlie Malagati, he was contemplating the worst.

Walking along Main Street one afternoon, Dennis looked up at white clouds being pushed along by the wind. At ground level ahead was a cadre of female classmates, the skin under their skirt lines pink from the cool air. One reached and goosed another, which for whatever reason led him to stop at the Apollo for a black and white cookie. But as he waited in line, he noticed in a nearby booth the stranger from Mill Pond, still in the tattered Yankees ballcap. As his fork speared his hash browns and splashed it in a mound of ketchup on his plate, his green eyes, bold in their sockets, suddenly turned to Dennis. A smile started at the corner of the stranger's mouth, ketchup dripping out in a thin line. Dennis wheeled around and left without the black and white.

"What the hell," he muttered once outside. He fell into a slow jog all the way home where he found his mother sweeping the front porch.

"Dennis," she said as he climbed the steps out of breath. "You actually look like you've got some spunk. I wonder if the gremlins have all but disappeared."

Who's kidding whom, he thought. She knew he was still in the throes. And he knew that she was, too, as well as his father. But he also knew that it was best that everyone put on a happy front as best they could. Which is what he tried to do in the coming days. He even surprised himself one night at the dinner table laughing hard with his mother over his father's imitation of Alice Crimmins' evangelical-speak.

Of course, for Dennis, any sense of turning the corner was upended a week later at school. It was not so much that Eleanor Fenwick turned down his invitation to the prom. It was the way she said it. "See, Dennis," she peered around after everyone else had left the lunch table, "you were on my short list. But then that thing happened. I mean, you barely escaped a life behind bars."

In the days following the rejection, and with less than a week until the prom, he tried small talk with Eleanor at her locker. Her eyes might have shown interest and enthusiasm. But he could see that she was refusing to give way to any real emotion. On the morning of the prom, when it was just the two of them in the hallway, she said, "You know, Dennis, my butt is getting so big and fat that I want to cry." She looked up and down the empty hallway, and said while jutting out her ass, "But what jock in his right mind wouldn't want a piece of this on prom night?" Dennis refused to give her the pleasure of hearing from him that her butt, ample and round, was quite fine.

The final grading period was a bustle. The college applications, the crowds outside the counselor's offices, the visits to Stonybrook, Rutgers, and SUNY New Paltz. The closer it got to the end, the faster the shuffle became.

COMMENCEMENT TOOK PLACE on the Great Lawn in late May. The graduating seniors, on fold-ups in ordered rows, listened passively to Father Eichen, who up on a portable amphitheater stage with faculty and staff, started things off with a solemn invocation. Sister Rosaleen presided over an elaborately concocted ceremony. What stood out for Dennis was the bemused indifference of faculty up on the stage. At least a few of them must have felt the absence of the old custodian. In better times, he would have been standing off to the side, ready to tackle any issue that arose.

To conclude the ceremony, Father Eichen announced that this year's graduation would include a dedication. With that, he asked the crowd to turn their attention to the Prayer Garden where the new custodian, Buddy Burke, wheeled out a dolly. On it, a life-sized statue of Cassidy hidden under a silky purple drape. The statue was maneuvered onto a cement footer.

"To bring this commencement to a close, we will honor a very special man who gave his heart, his soul, his very being, to this parish. We will do so by presenting James Francis Cassidy, Bishop of the Rockville Centre Diocese."

Right on cue Buddy whipped off the drape. The likeness to Cassidy, even from across the way, was unmistakable, notwithstanding the kindly, retiring gaze the sculptor imposed on the subject's eyes. Afterwards Dennis watched in wonder as parishioners raced over for a family photo with the statue. The whole thing put Uncle John into such a foul mood that he hobbled over to the shade of a sycamore, where he lit a cigar and tapped his cane on a bulging root.

Some hours later, with a *Congratulations Graduate* streamer hanging proudly across the Hurley's front porch, Dennis and his parents stood at the drive's bottom saying goodbye to guests. The last to leave, Aunt Pearl, with Uncle John in the passenger seat, slowed the Nova to a crawl as she yelled out, "Don't cry for Auntie

Pearl." She waved her hand out the window as the car disappeared down Crocus.

"Well," Catherine Hurley said, "this has been a wonderful day."

"You can say that again, Cat."

"Hey," Dennis said, "would you two mind if I caught up with William and Peter? To chew the fat, is all."

"Go, enjoy yourself," his father said. "But make damn sure you stay away from area pools."

"Will do."

Not much later, Dennis bounded creek rocks to join his two friends at the boulder. "Any idea what he wants, Denny?" William asked.

"None. He just walked up to me after graduation and told me to make sure the three of us met here right at seven. Said he'd cut off our balls if we were late."

They heard a rumble.

"Wow," said Peter, pointing down the path to the cross-country van creeping along toward them.

The van stopped and out hopped Coach Jack. "You boys ready for a Sitting Bull workout?"

"Can't," William replied.

"Why not?"

"The chief's missing in action."

"Follow me."

As the van's back door opened, the boys marveled at the Sitting Bull plaque and its pole, the cement crater still at its bottom. They also found bags of cement, a wheelbarrow, a bucket, and a shovel.

"I figured it's high time to bring the chief back from the dead."

The boys took turns digging the hole in the same spot where it had stood. Coach Jack poured cement into the wheelbarrow and smacked his way out of the cloud of smoke, the boys doubling over in laughter. The plaque was set back into place with the cement churned with creek water.

All four stood by admiring it as they reminisced about several races, state taking the cake.

"Well, boys, you'll come visit Ole Coach from time to time?"

"Bet your ass, I will," said William.

"Me, too, Coach," said Peter.

"Every chance I get," Dennis said.

Jack Hogan gave each boy a hug and told them to get home and go straight to bed. He watched them tap the plaque one last time, each shouting "Sitting Bull" before bounding creek rocks.

As the three passed through the woods, Dennis turned around. Coach Jack offered a hearty wave, which the captain returned in spades before catching up to his two friends on the field.

"I love that fucker," William said.

44

The following morning, Dan Hurley called upstairs to ask Dennis if he could help move the couch outside to make room for a new one to be delivered that day.

"Listen, Dennis," he said once the couch was lowered curbside, where the Goodwill truck would pick it up. "I know another summer in Bellport will be tough on you. I talked to my boss who said he'd be glad to give you a job on county trucks that clean parks each day. At the very least, it will get you out of town."

"That sounds good, Dad."

"You can drive in with me each day."

"Okay."

"And for Pete's sake, don't go putting on a front if the going gets rough. Just track me down, and the two of us can sneak off for an ocean swim out east. Grab some grub afterwards. Got it?"

"Sure, Dad."

"And make damn certain that you don't lose touch with your two buddies. They are hurting, too."

"Now that you mention it, with Peter leaving Tuesday for the Marines, I was thinking about calling the two of them for a boardwalk run tomorrow, afterwards the last supper at Sal's."

"I think you should."

Dennis made the calls. Both liked the last supper idea. They agreed on a seven-thirty meeting time for an evening beach run. Early that next morning, however, the Walkers, to prevent their son from any last-minute shenanigans, surprised Peter by shaking him out of sleep and putting him on a train for Grand Central Station. They gave him just enough money to catch an Amtrak down to Charleston, South Carolina, where he'd hotel it before catching a bus to boot camp at nearby Parris Island the following day. Dennis heard about Peter's departure only after William called with the news and to cancel the run.

Bill Flanagan was thrilled when he heard of the premature departure of Peter Walker. One less thing to worry about. It got him thinking. Maybe it would be in the best interest of William, not due to leave for the University of West Virginia until mid-August, to also leave town sooner than later. He made a phone call. It resulted in sending William upstate to Lake George to work at a summer resort, which a family friend had managed for years. Dennis only learned of his friend's departure after the fact. He got quiet following the news. Like Peter, William had not called to say goodbye.

Less than a week after William left for Lake George, Dennis experienced another body blow. Overhearing his father tell his mother that the bungalow was being razed to the ground, he wasted no time racing over to the parish. There a small crowd had formed to watch a giant excavator rip the house apart, the debris dropped into one of several enormous dumpsters, the pool ladder jutting out of one.

"It's about time," one guy said.

"Yeah," from another, "Malagati was one bad egg."

Dennis wasn't surprised to learn that the rectory remained tight-lipped about the sudden demolition of the property. Eichen even refused an interview with the *Bellport Citizen*. By week's end, when Dennis again made his way over to the parish and found that Gise Nursery had already laid sod and planted a small handful of trees, he was sure the transaction, and the speed behind it, had Cassidy's hand all over it. Only the bishop would think to replace the property with a non-descript plot of land. All of which intensified Dennis' festering over Cassidy's escape from a retribution he so rightly deserved.

Dennis would forever remember that summer before he left for Rutgers as the longest of his life. The unrelenting staring whenever he found himself about town. Some locals even stopped him to inquire after that night. At the deli one day, Oscar from behind the counter asked, "How does it feel, Dennis?"

"How does what feel?"

"You know, *it*."

"Not so good."

Perhaps worst of all was the anxiety that he knew his parents continued to carry around. They had not mentioned the bungalow for some time. He could still read it on their faces.

A new life at Rutgers could not come soon enough.

PART 3

45

Dennis had been on campus only a few hours when there came a knock on his dormitory door. Ken Bradbury, once an All-American distance runner at Rutgers and now the school's head cross-country coach, invited him to join their D1 program as a walk-on. Jack Hogan, unbeknownst to his former captain, had put in a good word. For Dennis, however, his commitment to starting anew meant something other than cross country, which for him was still associated with that night. So after thanking Coach Bradbury for the interest, he told him that over the summer he had done some research and had made up his mind to join the school's hiking club. Over the last few weeks in Bellport, Dennis had indeed glimpsed the club offerings in the school catalogue. The description of camaraderie that the hiking club promised is what won him over. New friends seemed like a good idea.

But even as the hiking club president at the first meeting enthusiastically itemized each of the club's benefits, Dennis felt the old trainers in his footlocker tugging at his heart strings. That evening he set out for junk miles, and liking the novelty of running along the Raritan River, he abandoned the hiking club idea. In the days that followed, he discovered different trails along the river. Some spilled onto semi-rural corridors, still flush with late summer foliage. As the days turned into weeks, and brilliant fall colors came, he realized that without the daunting burden of team competition, running on his own each day helped to release the tension that arose from the full load of classes. And how good it felt waking up one day to notice the haunted look, which he had come to expect in the mirror most mornings, had taken a hiatus.

Maybe, just maybe, I've got myself a new lease on life. And maybe junk miles, if limited to my own private enterprise, can be part of that new lease.

But then came the trip back to Bellport for the month-long Christmas break, when he again faced the town's lookie-loos. Following that trip, Dennis decided he would stay in New Brunswick that summer and take classes. Of course, he would wait until the last minute to notify his parents of his intentions. To be expected, Catherine Hurley was none too happy when Dennis called with the news, which included mention of a part-time job at a coffee house that would support the furnished sublet on Orange Street with two other Rutgers students. She expressed her reservations to Dan, who replied, "The town, Cat, will never forget his role in it. No, a summer sublet at Rutgers is whip smart on his part. He has my blessing."

When the spring semester ended mid-May, and summer school started the following week, Dennis fell into an agreeable routine: a morning shift at the coffee shop, followed by classes and a library stint; an early evening run to finish the day off. Ignoring Coach Jack's slow burn, junk miles remained his go-to. In honor of Legs, he sometimes picked up the pace the last half mile, a bumrush on the final straight. As May turned into June, he was getting into such good shape that Coach Jack's mainstay running strategy crept back into the routine. One day, while slow-burning a six-miler, he was thrilled with the negative splits, his last three miles nearly a minute faster than the first three.

During the early days at Orange Street, he got to know his two new roommates whose names he found on an off-campus housing list. Pothead Donny Campbell from Paramus was a red-headed general studies major who was always talking about becoming rich someday. Dennis had no idea that Donny would become a wealthy Myrtle Beach chiropractor who drummed up business by delivering bags of bagels to transplants from New York. In the meantime, each weekend Donny drove his Audi to his boyhood home on the water in Sea Girt to do his laundry. His parents were loaded. Each visit his father would slip him a few fifty-dollar bills for spending money.

Terry Seagull, a gangly student with crimpy black hair and a dainty nose, was reared in suburban Montclair. A double major in philosophy and English, Terry stayed in New Brunswick for the summer because he had fallen in love with Pauline Myers, who moved into Orange Street rent-free. Terry called her the next Virginia Woolf. Dennis knew her to be a petulant brat whose bland personality best revealed itself during her shrill pillow talk with Terry in the next bedroom.

That first night on Orange Street, Terry announced that an annual ritual of his was to commence the next day.

"And that is?" Dennis asked.

"When I read one of my favorite books over the course of several days. *The Adventures of Augie March*. Been doing it for five years running."

"What the heck," said Donny, who broke out in laughter. "Why read the same book over and over?"

"I read Saul Bellow as proof that evil has no intention of hiding in the dark. And I should know. I've been the victim of every manner of evil since the day I was born. Starting with the day the sheriff showed up and handed my father, a Presbyterian minister, a summons to appear in court for swindling his congregation out of money. Which was practically a lie."

In the days that followed, as Terry lounged on the couch and smoked one cigarette after another, he described for Dennis the terrors he felt growing up in suburban New Jersey. Dennis could not help but marvel at how Terry, in excruciating and self-pitying detail, explained how this person or that person had committed some oppressive wrong against him. At times, Dennis wanted to interrupt Terry and tell him that he came across as a tender lightweight. But Dennis was too intrigued by this self-absorbed roommate who catalogued his hatred of others so completely and with such precision.

Dennis knew that it was Terry's weekend part-time job at a clothing store that was the source of any oppression he was currently feeling. Terry hated work, even if it was just a weekend job at a men's high-end clothing store. Which is why Terry's eyes went big when he learned that Donny came from money, and that his parents lived on the water. Terry started buttering him up by telling the stoned-out-of-his-mind Donny that since his surname, Campbell, was Scottish, and that since Scotland's capital, Edinburgh, was the Athens of the North, Donny undoubtedly possessed a keen intellect. The flattered Donny invited Terry and Pauline back to Sea Girt for a long weekend where they ate and drank for free. Dennis discovered that the buttering up extended to Donny's mother. Donny's description of her as a freethinker reminded Dennis of Alice Crimmins. Betty Campbell apparently was mesmerized by Terry's spectacular reading of the universe. The Campbells told Terry and Pauline that they were always welcome.

It wasn't long before Dennis tired of Terry. This was especially the case after Terry quit his job knowing that Donny would cover his rent if he fell short, lest they be kicked out. Dennis also tired of having to pick up the dog poop that Pauline's toy poodle, Spinoza, left all over the house. A few times Dennis wanted to clobber Terry. And he might have done so had he known at the time that Terry one day would become a famous cultural critic who would write a memoir that included a brutal section on the debilitating alcoholism of Donny's parents, both of whom treated Terry to countless bottles of wine during his bloodsucking leech days in

Sea Girt. Even so, it was good to get Terry out of the house on weekends.

ONE DAY, DENNIS HEADED out for some junk miles to Logan Park. On the way back, he stopped at *Wild Bill's Road Racing Outlet* to check out the new trainers, only to be greeted by outrageous sticker prices that depressed him. That led him to the book section to browse a few titles that Coach Jack had recommended and that he had read back in high school. Glanville's *The Olympian* and *The Four-Minute Mile* by Coach Jack's hero, Roger Bannister. Above the shelf was a poster of Steve Prefontaine. Dennis closed his eyes, the great Pre having recently been tragically killed in a recent car accident. Another shelf held a slew of Sillitoe's *The Loneliness of the Long-Distance Runner,* which Dennis read during the days he hid in St. Theresa's library waiting for county deputies to come drag him away.

"You looking for something good to read?" said a large man behind the register, who went on to laugh at Dennis' startled look. "I'm Wild Bill. A hundred pounds heavier than my harrier days at Scotch Plains High."

"I read some of these books in high school. I was a harrier also."

"Hey, I just got in a boxload of this running novel by a guy named Parker. Hold on."

Wild Bill retrieved a box that he opened with a utility knife. "Here," he grabbed a book out of it. "Called *Once a Runner*. Haven't read it, but it's all the rage. Here, on the house." He tossed it at Dennis, who marveled at the cover, a solitary runner pounding the shore's sand.

"You okay?" Wild Bill asked.

"I grew up out on Long Island. Ran along the water all the time."

"There you go!"

Returning home, Dennis started in on the novel about an elite college distance runner from Florida. Dennis couldn't put the book down. Nor could his pen stop scribbling marginalia. For one thing, the author got exactly right the myth of runner's euphoria, which is nowhere to be found *on dark, rainy mornings...when the click of stoplights seemed inordinately loud in the chilled air*. But the novel also confronted Dennis with a hard-to-swallow truth: while running for him had always been a romp among high school friends, Parker reminded him that more often than not, running is a deeply solitary venture that mostly resembles a lonely rite, something that Dennis had only recently learned while out on the Raritan trails. Still, Dennis looked forward to finishing the book, as the inside cover promised a climactic mile race.

He might have done so but that one night he returned to Orange Street and found Terry stuffing his face with a Pepperidge Farm chocolate cake, the novel wide open beside him. His roommate said, "I took a glimpse at your book here, Dennis. For starters, you should know that the dimwit author is the quintessential alpha male who claims that running teaches the basics of human nature." Terry waited for a reply, and when none came, he said, "Not sure what basics about human nature this Parker thinks a sport such as running grounds a person in? Basic knowledge about animal aggression? Or what is the proper running gait to use after robbing a convenience store? Or, maybe, the efficacy of the jock strap?"

Dennis was about to lay into his feckless roommate. Instead, he shouted out as he retreated up to his bedroom, leaving the novel behind with his roommate "All good questions, Terry. Let me finish the novel over this next week. Have an answer then."

"I'll be waiting."

As Dennis retreated into his own room, he told himself that he should go back downstairs and call Terry Seagull a freeloader, the kind that Dan Hurley liked to call a plucker of guitar strings who, when not trashing those who put food on the table, writes lyrics about heartache. Dennis never returned downstairs that night. But leaving for work that next morning, he first banged on his roommate's bedroom door.

"What the fuck," Terry screamed out.

"You want my answer?"

"Hey, asshole, you know what time it is?"

"The basics, dammit. I'll tell you what they are."

"Go straight to hell, Hurley."

"Trust me, I'll end up there someday. But in the meantime, jocks like me who run are grounded in such basics as cleaning Spinoza's dog shit off the floor before they go to work, all so that navel-gazers who wake up at the crack of noon can stroll over to my coffee house, and over a chapter of *Augie March* enjoy a latte and a croissant, all before an afternoon siesta. That's what loser jocks and the rest of the working public do while the enlightened Terry Seagulls of the world enjoy their beauty sleep."

Dennis banged the door and left for work.

When he returned home that day, Terry was gone. So was Parker's novel. A note from Donny said he was driving Terry and Pauline, both with packed suitcases, to his home in Sea Girt. "And not to worry about Spinoza. He came with us, too." Dennis had a hunch that the Parker novel now lay on the shoulder of the Jersey Turnpike. Sure enough, when Donny returned late Sunday night, he did so without his two passengers. Or the novel.

"My mom loves Terry to death," Donny reported. "My dad, well, the old lech that he is, likes to ogle Pauline's hot bod."

DENNIS KNEW his running routine would fall off once the two summer school classes picked up steam, which turned out to be the case. He was surprised, though, by how much he liked his World Civilization survey course even though Professor Albert Cooke liked to throw around the Bonaparte quote, *History is a set of lies agreed upon.* For illustration he used the ambiguity surrounding the tragic innocence of Joan of Arc. Dennis didn't have the nerve to tell Cooke that he himself knew of a larger-than-life tragic event from his own hometown that, in all its glory, could be reconstructed with precision and accuracy. Still, the survey course filled his mind with crises that made his own pale in comparison. Famines. Pestilence. The slaughter of millions in wartime. Perhaps there were other reasons why Dennis marched into his advisor's office and declared a history major. But the one that presently caught his fancy was that the study of history offered him, ironically enough, a sense of detachment from Bellport. Nine of the fifteen credits he signed up for the next semester were history courses.

As the fall of his sophomore year began, the daily regimen of junk miles resumed. He signed up for a 10K that took him back and forth over the Raritan. The race itself was a disaster, and afterwards he knew that a slow burn surge at 4K was a big mistake. The race was followed by a barrage of dreams about him and his two friends running marathons together all around the world.

Perhaps the thing's finally going out to sea.

During the second semester, Dennis trained for another 10K, this time in downtown Newark. Though the race timewise was another flat tire, he afterwards enjoyed time spent at The Old Queens Tavern with other runners whom he had just met. A good hour of Smithwick's pints gave him the courage to call Bellport and report that he had signed a year's lease for a campus studio on Ralph Street, this time as a solo renter. This meant that he'd remain in New Brunswick for another summer. Catherine Hurley again raised concern to her husband: "Dennis will be living all on his own, Dan. Without a roommate. Is that wise?"

"Hey, Cat, wake up and smell the coffee! He's getting on with his life. It's high time you and I celebrate that fact."

DURING HIS JUNIOR YEAR, Dennis took an upper-level seminar, entitled "The Industrial Revolution of Nineteenth Century England," offered by Professor Michael Corrigan, one of those corduroy academics whose thick salt-and-pepper brows would have made him look prematurely old but for his long, muscular face. Perhaps it was because Corrigan was always using scenes from Dickens' *Bleak House* to illustrate lecture points that Dennis got up the nerve to confide in him one cold, snowy afternoon at The Tomb, the campus bar that hosted the final class meeting. While a tipsy classmate's interpretation of the Corn Bill was boring the hell out of Corrigan, an equally tipsy Dennis leaned over and informed their professor that he had begun a fictional account of a dark boyhood event of his, and that its conclusion was all but inevitable.

At first, Corrigan's mouth went weak. For a few terrifying moments, Dennis thought it possible that his professor somehow knew that what his student had just told him was not true. But the professor, perhaps to lend encouragement, though more likely to conceal pity, confessed that he had several novels in him. "But unlike you, Dennis," Corrigan added, "I'm so plugged up with Victorian beat and measure that I'd be unable to capture the level of contemporary American idiom necessary for fiction." Lifting his beer mug, he concluded, "Good luck as you wrap up your story. It all sounds very promising."

The night gathering strength, Dennis slouched back over snow to his third-floor studio. A weary academic had to humor a student preoccupied with literary cant and pretense. Yet Dennis would make up for it by going straight to his desk as soon as he reached his studio and start fictionalizing the events surrounding the old custodian and that sorry night. The undertaking needing only pen to paper, chapter one, he told himself, would be given shape by midnight. The following morning, he'd start chapter two. He resolved to do a good bit each day thereafter. A draft, with the story's protagonist fully exonerated, would be completed by month's end. That Dennis was thinking in these terms suggested to him that the plan was not without merit. But when, in fact, he reached for a pen, he felt his mind shrinking, like a thin layer of Mill Pond ice, cracking and floating off in different directions. A good hour passed. He recorded only scraps of a scene, that of the core three taking flight after plowing dirt over the makeshift coffin.

The pen eased back down, the effort futile, he looked out the window at the snowy parking lot of the credit union bank, whose silver exterior blended into the icy ground around it. He imagined one of President Jimmy Carter's UFOs being sucked down out of the sky by the building's magnetic quality. The ship now clamped to the bank's side, the aliens with shit-eating grins waved at him. Perhaps Dennis' folly lay not in his attempt to record the affair, but in his not dropping the effort into the trash can. Instead, he slipped it into an old folder that had become a storehouse of cross-country memorabilia.

Someday, he thought, when the thing has been put to bed for good, I'll pull the false start out of the folder. Use it as a springboard to chronicle a martial tale that Merlin, Sitting Bull, and warriors of every make and persuasion will be proud of.

He turned off the desk lamp, and much like evenings back on Crocus, sleep didn't come right away. But then in floated an image of a giddy Coach Jack lifting Adam off the ground and swirling him around after his top runner as a junior won the Bear Mountain Invitational. Dennis smiled. Since my novel can't find its legs, I'll write me a letter when the sun comes up. A long one.

Good to his word, Dennis wrote to Coach Jack. By the time he finished, he had mingled the highlights of several big races, a few Peter Walker nuggets, and the time he caught a nude Ida and Harry Feltman in the hot tub. That led to him telling his old coach just how much he liked Adam's father, that it was the gruff Harry Feltman, an oil burner repairman of all things, who took the time to teach chess to Dennis as a young boy when he had his leg brace on, and who was forever reminding him that only hard work and discipline would right the ship. *See, Coach Jack,* Dennis wrote, *I had no idea how much Harry Feltman meant to me. In a strange kind of way, he gave me strength. He gave me hope. Just like you did.*

Little did Dennis think before signing off that he'd share so many private thoughts, filling up some four pages. He excluded any mention of the episode, about which Coach Jack back then never uttered a word.

After Dennis reread what he had written, he scribbled a postscript, *Miss the old days like hell.*

A week later he received a postcard with this on it: *You're killing me, Coach Jack.*

Dennis responded to the emotionally charged moment with long miles along the river.

46

The girl who pontificated about the Corn Bill at The Tomb that night, her name was Anne Graehler. She had been in past classes of his where they acknowledged each other with glances, but nothing more. Nor was anything much said beyond a passing hello when they ran into each other at the laundromat on most Sundays. One afternoon, she caught him staring at her whipping a mint green towel high in the air. Showing no mercy, she folded the towel in half, then in exacting quarters. She turned away, but not before their eyes, if just for a moment, made contact and held level.

Dennis had this hunch.

Over the next few days, he rehearsed the phone call, all so that he wouldn't botch the invitation to the fellow history major of striking features to attend Saturday's home football game against Boston College with him. The delight he experienced after she accepted the invite dropped off to dread when he realized that their previous encounters had been limited to classroom nods and dull smiles. That's why he was relieved when on the walk over to the stadium this Anne Graehler carried the conversation. It was all about her growing up in rural Oneonta, in upstate New York.

The more Dennis listened, the more he realized she was

simply venting the kinds of things you'd expect from someone who grew up on a country farm, and who wanted more from life than fighting the elements. That's why, Anne then explained, she was thrilled when during her high school graduation party, her mother announced she was moving to Buffalo to live with a sister of hers whose husband had recently passed. For the time being, Billy Trevor, the son of a nearby farmer, would rent the Oneonta house and the farmland.

"And with any luck, Dennis, Trevor will eventually buy the whole ball of wax from Mom. Be done with it, once and for all."

Anne might have had more to say except upon entering the stadium's lobby they were greeted by an echo chamber of fans thrashing about cement pillars. They paid each other polite smiles as they headed up the ramps to the middle tier. Once out in the open air, a bristling sea of red and white, they found themselves lurching toward their seats.

Dennis was not surprised that his date, given the keen curiosity she displayed in classroom discussions, was not at all interested in the game. Moments after Boston College grabbed a fumble recovery on the opening kickoff, she asked him what life was like growing up in Bellport. The question catching him off guard, he turned to his roots, starting with a bit about Granddad Paddy, how he was born 1891 in the small Irish village of Ballyduff. And how after he came to America, he married Grandma Nellie, from County Kerry, the two of them living in a Manhattan tenement before moving to Queens. Then, Dennis moved on to his mother and her antique fetish. How if someone was to drop a match at 32 Crocus, the house with all the old pieces lying about would go up in smoke.

"Poof, Anne, just like that!"

She fell to a jarring laughter, as if a hard tickling in a previous lifetime had taken effect. Dennis might have confessed that he had just employed a favorite tease that his father used on his mother, but Anne was having too much fun. And perhaps with the sun high in the sky, she might have forgotten all about the Oneonta farm, and its cows and chickens and raccoons and bores and field mice. In an unguarded moment in the fourth quarter, however, just after a disgruntled Rutgers player threw his helmet halfway down the field, Anne turned to Dennis and shouted over the crowd's roar, "So help me, God, I'll never again get caught in a downpour pitchforking bales of hay! Never!" She said that clutching a beer in her hand, her second of the afternoon, which is what probably roused the sentiment.

So, too, the words that came next: "So, Dennis Hurley, what took you so long?"

"So long for what?"

"To ask me out. I've been waiting, you know. Ever since I saw you running in the campus 10K last year."

"Oh, you ran that race?"

"Nah. On my way to the library I saw this lanky classmate, with not bad looks, come running by. Bet you were on a high school team?"

He scrambled for a deflection. "I had no speed. None at all. Running's a way to take my mind off the books."

"So, anyway, Dennis, what took you so long to pick up the phone?"

"Too nervous."

"Why?"

He chugged the remainder of his beer. "I always get nervous when I am within arm's length of natural beauty. Would you join me for a pasta dinner at my apartment next Friday?"

"Why not tonight?"

A few weeks passed, and one night in the darkness of his bedroom, Anne asked, "What's the worst thing you ever did?" The question rocked him, even though over the last several days he swore that this Anne Graehler was never to know. She was human, after all. She'd reject him if she found out. She'd have to.

"Mine, Dennis, was back in high school when I told my mother

I was sleeping over at my girlfriend's. Emma and me instead went to a Charlie Daniel's concert at the university. Afterwards, we danced the night away at a frat house. Got all crazy. But not to worry. We ended up sleeping on the student center couches. Your turn."

His wheels spinning like crazy, he finally said, "The worst thing I ever did, Anne, that's what you want to know?"

"If you're man enough, that is."

"I once was an altar boy."

"Go on."

"I'm ashamed to admit it. But one time I stole a look at a young nun, Sister Bernadette. She had rosy cheeks and blue eyes, oval shaped. Yes, Anne, with the sun barely over the horizon at early Mass, God caught me leering at a nun."

"If you can't be serious, Dennis Hurley, I'll punish you with more farm talk. Let's see, should I focus on the animals? Or the pre-dawn chores?"

He was about to tease her back, when he saw something shift in her eyes. Taking on a stony stare, she continued, "After Dad died when I was in ninth grade, I had to help my mother manage the workers, who could be-" She paused as she searched for the right word. "Gruff."

Dennis did not know how to reply.

Anne then spoke of a horrible tornado that ripped off the barn's sheathing, the farm crippled for weeks on end. "It was awful. I knew I needed to get away after high school. Cross state lines, if need be."

As she went into some detail about her Rutgers decision, Dennis realized that this person, with whom he had been sleeping night after night, had spent many hours learning the natural order of things the hard way. She had experienced real misfortune. And as she continued, he felt the flood within. He had fallen in love with this Anne Graehler. He was smitten by her. By her curious mind. Her unrelenting knowledge of the natural world. The wonderfully wild swerves in her conversation. And, yes, her lovely body in the dark of night.

But he didn't know how to tell her any of this.

He did make the mistake in a phone call with his mother to mention this girl he had met.

"Her name?" Catherine Hurley wanted to know right away.

"Anne."

"Is it serious?"

"We've become friends, Mom."

"Bring her home to Bellport, Dennis. And bring her home soon."

"I'd like to, but…"

"But what?"

"I'd die if Anne found out."

Dan Hurley called back that same night to assure him that the thing would not be brought up. Period.

"Aunt Pearl?"

"We'll duct tape her mouth shut if need be. You can bank on that."

While Dennis one day was studying at the library, Anne rented a tiller from a local dealer and tore up a 12 x 12 section of heavy weeds in the backyard of the Ralph Street apartment building. When he got home, he found her standing over a raked section of dirt, beside which was a table that held seeds in containers, each one marked with name and seed depth.

"Are you sure this is kosher, Anne?"

"I already told you that I called your landlord. He said it was perfectly fine."

"So, which seed you want me to plant first?"

"You choose."

"What are my choices again?"

"Tomatoes need a row of six inches in depth. Green beans and lettuce, four inches. Zucchini, eight inches. And baby red potatoes, twelve."

"Lettuce, Anne. I'll start with lettuce."

Over the next hour Anne helped Dennis with the process, which included a tutorial on fertilizing. The planting of all seeds concluded a good hour later with a dramatic sigh by Dennis, who settled into a lawn chair while Anne turned on the hose and gave the seeds a good soaking. Once she was done, and they were back inside, Dennis said, "Anne, I have a question for you?"

"Your question is?"

"Let's say after a few months of courtship, I fell in love with a farmhand and I-"

"What's she's like?"

"Striking! Eyes to die for."

"What I meant is, what's she really like? You know, her interior?"

"Oh, that."

"Yes, that."

"Sweet as can be. Super smart. Too smart, sometimes. But I like when she hovers over me."

"Like a warm blanket?"

"Now we're talking."

"Anything else about this farmhand?"

"She darns my darn socks. She makes me laugh. She folds the dough over thrice when making apple strudel. And I think I'm falling in love with her."

"Real love?"

"My gut's telling me, yes, which is why the weekend after next I take her to Bellport to meet up with the family. And I...."

He would have said more but that he needed to reach over and with a thumb wipe a tear off Anne's cheek.

AFTER A BUS INTO MANHATTAN and a train ride on the Long Island Railroad, Dennis and Anne arrived in Bellport for a long weekend. As promised, the Hurley clan was on their best behavior. During a tour of the house, Anne focused on a framed photo on the den wall. A horribly depleted Dennis coming across the line, flanked by William and Peter, at the Sag Harbor Invite their junior year.

"I thought," she said turning to Dennis, "that you weren't on a team?"

"No, Anne, I said I had no speed."

"And over here," Catherine Hurley stepped in, "is a picture of Dennis at the spelling bee contest in sixth grade."

From there, Anne pointed to a large group photo.

"That," said Dan Hurley, "is a family reunion on both sides. At Kissana Park in Queens. Just blocks where both Catherine and I grew up as kids."

Anne leaned closer to the photo. "That can't be you, Dennis! And what's that contraption on your leg?"

"Oh," Catherine Hurley said, "Dennis didn't tell you about the hip issue? The contraption is a leg brace that ran along the length of his left leg and that he wore for about five years when he was a young boy."

"It's hard sometimes, Mrs. Hurley, to get him to talk about himself. So, anyway, Dennis, did you hurt your leg or something?"

"Oh, no, Anne," his mother continued, "he had a condition called Perthes disease, which is a deterioration of the hip socket. The brace kept pressure off the leg to give the socket time to grow back. In fact-"

"Why, Mom," Dennis interrupted, "don't you take Anne into the den and show her the antique pieces from the Revolutionary Period."

"Better yet," said Dan, winking at his son, "how about you show her the country relics in the yard. Say, the jet-black cauldron. Or the wheelbarrow, potted with the most vibrant of colors."

"Mr. Hurley and my son, Anne, should have been stand-up comics."

"I'd like to see it, all of it," said Anne. Then to Dennis, "Hey, how about after lunch you give me a walking tour of your old stomping grounds?"

"Terrific idea," replied Dennis. A jaunt down Main Street and to the beach wouldn't hurt. That is, as long as they stayed out of downtown stores where locals who knew his rap sheet lurked about.

"Question," said Anne once they had reached the water that day. "Why did you not tell me about the brace years?"

"So, like my mother said, Perthes is a degenerative disease of the hip. Its origins-"

"No, no, no. I mean, why didn't you tell me what the experience was like? It must have been hard on you."

"Kids at school called me Corn Ball Harry as I hobbled around."

"No!"

"But the real killer was that my doctor prescribed that I lay the brace aside after dinner each night for bed rest."

"How'd you get around? Like, if you had to pee?"

"Became a world class hopper on my good leg, the right one. During the summers, I'd hop to my bedroom window and watch all the kids running all over the place on the field across from my house. Some even disappearing into the woods. I couldn't wait to run with them. I eventually did just that."

"Ever think that the brace is what turned you into a runner?"

"Maybe. Or maybe it was all the books and magazines that my dad brought home from the library that I read in bed. I couldn't wait for the newest edition of *National Geographic* each month. I told myself once the brace came off for good, I'd hightail it into the woods and discover all those places I'd been reading about. African villages. Indian riverbeds. Mount Everest. Shit, Anne, I'd fancied myself an explorer."

"Did Marco Polo discover anything big once the brace came off?"

"Nah. But I ran everywhere."

"So, what you're saying, Den, is that your passion for running was the result of a brace and a magazine?"

"And there were my two boyhood chums who…"

"Who were these chums, Dennis? Partners in crime?"

Right there and then he decided that it was best to go full monty with the actual boyhood adventures, minus the bungalow incident. Of course, tales that would pacify Anne. It might even impress her, the macho side to him. He'd change the names to protect the innocent.

"I knew Bob and Tom from school. I used to watch them from my bedroom window play and run about the field. But I really got to know them when the brace came off. At first, it was harmless fun. We loved cutting through the woods and running north along the creek, stopping when we saw something interesting. An old barn. An abandoned house. One night we stumbled onto the Henry Cavendish estate, which is on the historic registry. The plaque on the front gate read, *General George Washington Once Stayed Here*. So Bob jimmied the back door open. We raided the refrigerator in the volunteers' break room. Never stole anything. We knew better. Things started heating up, though, with skinny dipping in a few country club pools."

"Boring, Dennis Hurley. I want something juicy. Really juicy."

"Such as the times we'd climb a massive elm behind the Miller's house. Took a gander through the bedroom window of one Carol Miller, just home from a waitressing shift."

"A nice pair of grapefruits on her, Den, is that what you're telling me?"

"The gallivanting came to a grinding halt a few weeks after our graduation from the parish elementary school, when the three of us hid behind the theater curtains of the last showing of the *Planet of the Apes*. Once the manager locked up and left, we made our way to the concession stand grill and stuffed our faces with hot dogs. We were caught by the projectionist, who had fallen asleep on an office couch up top. Fortunately, the police were not called in. I got grounded for a month. Tom, two months, not to mention that his father threw him down into the basement for an entire weekend."

"And Bob?"

"His father cussed him out, is all."

"So no adventures for you three after that?"

"Not really. Besides, that was right around the time cross country kicked into gear."

On their final day in Bellport, Dan and Catherine insisted on a Southampton restaurant. Dennis recoiled at the sight of Mrs. Wooten, sitting across the dining room with a nun whose name he couldn't remember. Wooten stole one glance after another. On the way out of the restaurant, a kitchen worker looked at Dennis and said, "Hey, you that St. Theresa's kid in the newspaper?" Fortunately, Anne was walking ahead with his mother and didn't hear the remark.

The next morning, as Catherine was saying a final goodbye to Anne on the front porch, Dan approached his son packing the wagon. "That was pretty rough last night, Dennis. First, Ginny Wooten and her beady eyes. Then that ignoramus made that damn comment on the way out."

"Which is why, Dad, I was afraid to bring Anne home in the first place. Though it's been a blessing in disguise."

"How's that?"

"I mean, who knows what will happen with Anne and me. But one thing's for certain. If she's the one, I'll have to ask myself whether I want her bogged down with all the baggage that goes along with Bellport. Or move somewhere else, maybe out of state. I'm thinking the latter, a blank slate."

Dennis could see the sorrow on his father's face.

"Sorry, Dad, but that's how I feel."

"No need to be sorry. And how I wish I had been more supportive back then. I was so damn concerned with getting you over the initial hurdle, the legal one, keeping you out of jail. So now as you move on, I'll support whatever you do. I'll support you one hundred percent."

Dennis' need for a blank slate was confirmed on the train back to the city. Chip Jankowski, a classmate of his at St. Theresa's and now a train conductor, shot him a look while punching his ticket. He also glanced at Anne. Dennis told himself he'd never again live on Long Island.

47

The following May, hours after both Dennis and Anne crossed the stage to receive their Bachelor of Arts diplomas in history, he got down on a knee. Anne, with tears of joy, accepted his marriage proposal. She wasted no time pressing for a small ceremony in Buffalo, where her mother and extended family lived. A modest wedding, away from Bellport, was to his liking.

"And I have another favor to ask of you, Dennis."

"Anything."

"You know my mom's been renting our Oneonta farmhouse and land on Clydesdale Lane to a neighbor?"

"I do."

"Well, she and I have been talking. What would you say if my mother sold off just the acres of farmland and gave the house and the barn to us? Would leave us with half an acre to play with. Too small to farm but room enough to grow some crops each season. Taxes, yes. But mortgage, no."

"If you're asking me if I approve, the answer is, yes."

"And one more thing. The sooner the wedding ceremony, the better."

"Why's that?"

"Because over the next few months my belly's gonna start bulging. Just got the results. A shotgun wedding."

By all accounts, Buffalo was a big hit, and afterwards the honeymooners spent a glorious week in a Lake George cottage. Neither Dennis nor Anne wanted to return to New Brunswick. Once back in Jersey, Dennis couldn't wait for the move to Oneonta. Based on a few black and white polaroids of Anne's childhood home on Clydesdale Lane, he romanticized the lush waves of farmland and the magnificent vistas of the Catskill Mountains. But when a few weeks later he turned the U-Haul into their new home, their 1969 Rambler towed from behind, he was careful to hide from a pregnant Anne his disappointment at the row of drab farmhouses they passed, each one a good ways apart from each other. In front of one, tinker-like children in raggedy clothes played out front. Their young mother stared stonily at the passing truck. Dennis pictured junk miles during Oneonta's winter months on this bleak frontage road, the wind howling in all directions. And when he finally pulled into the macadam drive covered with weeds, he found the Graehler house in serious need of scraping and painting.

"Well, Den, there she blows. Home sweet home. What do you think?"

"I love it, Anne. I really do."

"And since you're at it, why not park in the barn. The garage is stock full of junk. And would you mind leaving everything in the truck till morning? Except the mattress and bedding, of course."

As directed, he steered the U-Haul into the barn without doors. In one corner was a rusted tractor and a stockade of rusty ploughshares on top of each other. Dusty weeds ranged about the barn's dirt floor, the result of the bands of sunlight coming through the roof's bare sections. A few old cars sat in the opposite corner alongside a clutter of furniture.

Anne was so exhausted that she fell asleep shortly after dusk. That left Dennis to roam about the empty old house, where it hit him that he now was rural. In this Irish literature course at Rutgers, rural meant the place where people existed in varying states of despair and desperation. Things improved, however, the next morning when Anne's first cousin, Nancy, arrived with a breakfast casserole, followed an hour later by her husband, Warren, a contractor with a wicked sense of humor. He showed up with a crew of workers, buckets of fried chicken, and a cooler of beer. Warren installed GFI outlets in the kitchen and bathrooms while his men unloaded all their furniture and belongings, after which they sheathed and shingled over the bad patches of the barn roof, the beer finished off in the process.

By the time Dennis fell asleep that night, he realized it had been light years since he had laughed that hard. He did wish that he hadn't agreed to join a bowling league with Warren. As it turned out, though, the league network secured him a social studies teaching position at The Filmore Academy, a private Oneonta high school just west of town.

A few weeks after moving in, Dennis returned home from a Sunday run, utterly depleted. Anne blindsided him by asking, "I take it that you like to torture your body." This was not the first instance that Anne had questioned what she called his "running fetish." She really didn't object to the running. Yet it galled her when Dennis would offer curt responses to her questions about his running. This time he'd have a little fun by throwing spaghetti at the wall and seeing what happened.

"Actually, Anne, I never torture my body. In fact, I always feel pretty good when I finish a long run. A sense of renewal. Of real accomplishment."

"Renewal from what, Den? And just for the record, you always look like hell in a handbasket when you finish up."

"See, Anne, there are all kinds of good reasons to run."

"Oh, yeah, my field hockey coach used running as a form of punishment. He'd make me and my teammates run laps when we did something wrong."

"Well, for many like me, running isn't all about winning. It's a way to find tranquility."

"Really?"

"And peace."

"So the horrible panting each time you return from a run is a manifestation of tranquility and peace?"

"Running is also a time, Anne, when one can brainstorm all the unrealized possibilities, all the untapped energy pushing to escape."

"Wow, Den, that's a mouthful. And deep."

Bullshit, that's what Dennis knew he was feeding Anne. Anyone who runs knows that it's all about sucking wind, and fatigue, and the chaos of unrelated thoughts, and wary eyes focusing laser-like on the ground so that you don't fall on your face and crack your skull wide open. If there's any compensation, it comes in those fleeting moments during a run when one realizes, as Coach Jack liked to say, that one is nailing the shit out of it.

"Perhaps most importantly, Anne, is that running can give new meaning to the natural world that surrounds us all. Can't tell you the high I get running along the shimmering Susquehanna River."

"So what you're basically saying is that running is a way to get out of the house and away from yours truly?"

"You, Anne, are the love of my life. Running's not even a close second."

"Okay, Den, go shower. And use lots of soap under the pits. And when you're next out running, you might want to harness that untapped energy of yours and paint the bedroom next to ours. For the twins who are going to be sleeping there."

"Twins?"

Sure enough, as the arrival of the babies neared, Dennis' running fell off. Under Anne's supervision, he scraped and scraped until all the nursery's wallpaper was torn away. Then came a fresh coat of paint to decorate the room for the two cribs. The floorboards on the front porch were treated to a glossy gray, the balustrades, a bright white. New screens replaced the ripped ones in the old back porch that was attached to the rear of the barn, a porch that some twenty yards from the house would become a favorite retreat for Dennis. On many an afternoon he would carry the newspaper out there and lay it down on the surface of an octagonal picnic table that Anne had bought at a garage sale. He came to love reading the paper out there, stopping occasionally to take in the distant Catskill range.

Not long after the boys were born the following February, Dennis again took to the roads, and as spring emerged, he discovered new trails. A special route of his became a six-miler along the Susquehanna that passed an old fire station and a dilapidated hotel, at which point he turned and ran up a long winding footpath. At its top was a rocky overlook of a mountain lake that had a primitive feel to it. He'd run around the lake on a beaten dirt path before his return trip. From time to time, he'd stick money in a sock, and on his way back to town, he'd stop off at McGillicuddy's and suck down a few cream ales with a bunch of regulars who liked off-color jokes. If Anne was lucky, he'd tell her one.

It was also during this early period of their marriage that Anne happily declared her intention to be a stay-at-home mom who would make money working a few crops. Dennis watched in awe as she tilled the slum side of the barn and planted vegetables, the barn's front soon becoming a profitable farmstand. One day stacking a bumper crop of red potatoes, he said to her, "We might want to drive over to the county courthouse, Anne, and change our name to Appleseed."

"And it goes without saying, Den, that one must put into perspective the difference between the soft brackish land of your boyhood home on Long Island and that of my birthplace here in upstate New York, known for its dark, iron-fisted soil of endless opportunity."

Dennis had been perfectly happy teaching at the Academy, and for several years he had no plans to move on. But with property taxes and other bills piling up, and Anne's farmstand cash not enough to cover it all, the salary scale in the public school system prompted him to apply for a job at Oneonta High. Just days after his hire, Dennis and Anne were at the kitchen table when the phone rang. Steve Capell, athletic director and future drinking buddy, phoned Dennis to offer him the head cross-country job. It was awkward with Anne sitting right there. Dennis begged off, and instead told Capell that since he played youth soccer and knew the sport, that he'd be glad to take freshman soccer, for which he knew an opening existed.

After the phone call, Anne asked, "Why not take the cross-country gig, Den? I mean, you ran on that state team! You still run all the time!"

"I love soccer, Anne, a global sport. And I was a pretty good striker, you know."

A sigh escaped her. "No, Dennis, I don't know. But I guess you have your reasons."

He was glad he turned down the job. Junk miles were one thing. Coaching, another. As sure as hell, cross country would bring back the onslaught of memories that only recently had started to take long holidays.

48

One Sunday afternoon, Anne put the boys, now rambunctious toddlers, in a playpen right outside the back door. She did that so she could keep an eye on them while Dennis, a shovel in hand, followed her out to a Japanese Elm tree. There she kissed him on the cheek and pointed down at the base of the elm.

"A new flower bed, Den, is to go around the tree."

She pulled out a crumpled glossy paper ripped from a magazine. A photo of Augusta's sixteenth hole, its perimeter spotted with beds whose peanut shape she wanted him to replicate. So as not to alienate the Japanese Elm, Anne had decided on a bed of Japanese Blood Grass, a shoot of hairy leaf blades tinged a red-onion color. Even as Dennis was still processing the fact that the page was ripped out of God-knows-what publication, there came a rueful smile on his part.

"Never to worry, Dennis. You're just the man for the job."

She watched him begin. A few times she wrenched the shovel from him and poked at the grass to reassert the grand shape of the bed. Finally satisfied that he was on track, she began her walk back to the playpen.

At the bird bath, however, she spun around and posed a

question that stunned him: "By the way, Den, who's this Mr. Macaroni, or Manicotti, or whatever he's called? I was putting the white socks away in your top drawer when I found this piece of writing in that ratty folder of yours. You know, where you keep all your old cross-country memorabilia. I had been through the folder before, but never saw this thing, stuck as it was to the back of an award."

Dennis could only manage a thin smile. Anne, to his disbelief, had stumbled onto the false start, that futile attempt of his back in college to turn that night into a novel.

He had forgotten all about it.

"Huh, Dennis, who is he?"

His face curling in pain, he stabbed the ground twice. "Not sure what you're talking about, Anne. Not sure at all."

"C'mon. It's your handwriting."

"Probably something I whipped up in that writing class of mine back in the day. I should have burned it. Just some pathetic attempt, I'm sure."

His response, trumped up as it was, didn't exactly fill him with confidence that she'd buy it. Fortunately, she turned and made her way back inside, the storm door clacking shut. Even so, his wife had stumbled onto his great secret.

LATER THAT AFTERNOON, the tilling finished, he was at the kitchen sink cleaning up when from behind Anne said, "Hey, Den!" He turned around and saw that she had showered, her hair in wet strings. She was in one of her pajama tops, an oversized long-sleeved shirt that went to the knees, and whose hem on occasion he lifted to his advantage. "Here's what I was talking about earlier." Pinched between her fingers was a yellow tattered paper. "That thing from your writing course. Thought maybe we could go over it together."

The water marks on her shirt included a conspicuous splotch

over her left nipple. Dennis focused hazily on it, desperate to snatch the paper away. Making his way around the table to her, he said, "Now tell me, Anne, what else of mine did you get into? The shoe boxes in the closet? The old briefcase under my bed?"

"Hey, buster, I was making room for your underwear in the world's largest junk drawer! Somebody's gotta do it. Anyway, there's that ratty old folder and who could resist? Not exactly Shakespeare. But listen to this." To heighten the dramatic effect, she held the text out in front of her as she read: "*Departing the cemetery in a feverish pace, we left Mr. Malagati behind.* Oh, so it's not Macaroni. *At a safe distance, Peter and William and I broke into a trot that erupted into a mad sprint.*"

Anne repeated *mad sprint* three times, her eyes at one moment businesslike, the next lighthearted, a transition that made Dennis shiver. "*Like wild dogs we tore out of the cemetery.* Ruf, ruf, ruf, Den. Ruf. *From there we splashed across a slow-moving creek, dodging all manner of trees, until the Forest, with a life of its own, was left behind.*"

Dennis was fighting all instinct to lunge and tear the page away.

"And, Den, who's this Peter and William? Guys on that team of yours?"

The sleuthing had reached grotesque proportions. Still, Anne again raised the text to continue. Dennis had no recourse but to grab her arm and lift the shirt's hem up to her neck and pull her close to him. She was startled at first, then curious, even as her mind flitted to the twins, wondering about their location. But when his hand went to snatch the paper, she stepped back, "Not so fast, Dennis Hurley."

"Okay, Anne," he said turning for the stairs, "have it your way. I'm off to the shower. Your farmhand's all mucked in down-home Oneonta soil."

Slumping in the shower, Dennis knew that his wife had just offered him a golden opportunity to finally tell all. But as happened before whenever that impulse came, his feet turned ice cold. He reminded himself that the truth would consume her, eventually finding its way to the twins. Their father's legacy amounting to little more than a heartless rogue who, so they someday would read on library microfiche, got good and drunk one night before shooting and whacking a defenseless Vietnam vet.

No, Anne must never know. She can't know.

He sucked in the shower's wet air, thinking he might hold it in forever.

The next morning, he went down to the kitchen and through the window spotted her out back. With the twins playing in the grass beside her, she was on her knees planting the blood grass. Turning back, he noticed the tattered paper that Anne had read from. It was now face up on the table. For Anne, it had become a game. But in no mood to play, he turned on the stove's burner and lit the paper. He watched the flames spread some before he turned on the water and dropped it in the sink.

He again turned to the window and saw a squirrel leap from one branch to another. Fucking stir-crazy is how William Flanagan once described the species. Once, over the course of a week, Peter, William, and Dennis watched one squirrel after another fall from the power wires that streamed over the alley behind Schmidt's liquor store. All of Bellport later discovered that Gary Schmidt's weird son, Davey, put lunch meat laced with poison on the store's roof, and though William was right about a good many things, Dennis doubted that the clever squirrel he saw from his kitchen sink on this particular day would fall headlong to its death. The water still running, he turned to the ash fragments being flushed down the drain. It reminded him of Cassidy, and how the pastor undoubtedly had convinced himself that the little tussle with the three little pigs back in the day had been flushed down the drain as well.

That following morning Dennis went downstairs and, pouring a cup of coffee, looked out and saw Anne weeding the flower bed by the bird bath. The twins playing in the grass beside her, she stood and stepped back to take in the progress. Tall, wide shoulders in a smudged T-shirt, cut-off jeans, and black socks pulled calf-high above work boots. Dennis shook his head. A damn force of nature is what she is. I can't stay up with her. No one can.

But that thought was tempered by another. Anne now had a new vocabulary. Cemetery. Peter. William. Malagati. All of which she would bring up again in due course. A white lie was needed to confront the new development head on. First, though, he needed to draw her attention. So he whistled a sprightly tune as he left for the porch with the *Oneonta Tribune*. It worked.

"Hey, Den," she shouted from across the yard, "what were you and your two friends doing in the cemetery anyway?"

He stopped. "Pure fiction, Anne, if you've got to know."

"Drinking with the boys, were you, and got caught by this custodian guy? Huh, Den, it wouldn't kill you to tell me what you were doing. Knocking over headstones? Plundering a grave?"

He lowered his head, and ready to unload a whopper of a tale, he walked over to her.

"Since you won't rest until you know, I signed up for this creative writing course, unaware that I was about to mimic classmates who spun yarns about abject loners possessing remarkable wit and acumen. My first story was about a homeless guy making friends with this bloodied mutt."

Anne seemed intrigued.

"My professor, however, the churlish Donald Costello, suggested I focus on a topic that wouldn't excite violent allegory. So like all good English majors who believe their destiny lay in a poetic universe, I kept at it."

"Huh?"

"I decided I'd write a tale about the time our family dog, Coco, was killed by a car on Crocus after being spooked by fireworks." That event did, in fact, take place. But Dan Hurley took the dog to the pound for cremation.

"Yeah, Den, I remember hearing your mom talk about a family dog being killed. But how does this Malagati, or William and Peter, for that matter, figure in?"

Dennis looked into the yard and blinked twice, his mouth chock full of jumbled words. He spotted a bee humming just above a potted geranium that rested on a decapitated birch. "It was tough, Anne, making the burial of a dog the story line. I knew from the moment I picked up the pen that I had a flat tire on my hands."

"If the tire was so damn flat, why didn't you throw it away? Why keep it all these years?"

Looking past her and the sun-drenched yard to the rolling farmland, he said, "I kept it because I wrote it right around the time I fell in love with a young beauty from upstate New York, Protestant country. A symbolic keeping, if you will."

"You're full of shit, Den. But God knows, I love you anyway."

As he watched Anne drop back to her knees, he was sure she wasn't done yet. But strangely enough, inexplicably so, in the weeks and months that followed, Anne dropped the whole thing. He waited for her to bring it up. But she didn't. That's not to say that there weren't times when Dennis, milling about the open spaces of the old farmhouse, felt the same old throes. Nor did junk miles always help, evoking as they sometimes did reminders of a lifetime that had been whisked away.

49

"Mind if I join you for some coffee?" asked Anne in her bathrobe to Dennis. He had gotten up early to look over faculty resumes. Now in his fourth year teaching at Oneonta High, and fully tenured, he was asked by the principal to represent the faculty on the School Board Review Committee. Anne leaned over and kissed him.

As she poured herself a cup, she inquired, "Den, if I was to love you, and that's a big if, should I count the ways?"

"What is it, Anne?"

"Did I tell you what I found in the dryer?" Sitting down opposite him, she dropped a shriveled wad of paper on the table as she took a seat. "A receipt, Den, I found inside a shirt pocket of yours in the wash, almost unrecognizable now. But as it turns out, it's the receipt for those fancy new pair of Brooks trainers you bought a few days back."

"And?"

"When are you ever gonna fess up that you're a running geek? I mean, the whole kit and caboodle?"

"C'mon. Anne, we've been down this road before."

"I take it you want to change the subject."

"If only I could."

"Okay. Let's mull over the presidential election. Less than two months away, you know." He perked up. He relished political banter with Anne. "And can you believe it, Den, that it's been years since we voted for Jimmy Carter back in 1976? Remind me again. Why exactly did we side with the peanut man from Georgia? He was an absolute disaster."

"We were young, that's why. Remember that seminar with that lunatic professor Carol Bates?"

"Oh, that's right."

"She convinced us that character, and not policy, is the only way to gauge a politician running for office. She was always talking about Gerry Ford being a crony capitalist who, of all things, played football in college."

"Now that you mention it."

"And how, Anne, can we forget the bus trip Bates took us on up to Rochester to hear Carter on the stump!"

"Yes, and we all got drunk on the ride home. You tried to take advantage of me in the back of the bus."

"That I did, Anne. I failed miserably. So, tell me, who you gonna vote for this time? Reagan or Mondale? It was Reagan in his first go-around, right?"

"You go first."

"I am obligated to pull the Democrat lever. My grandparents were saved by FDR during the Great Depression."

"You mean, the Adulterer in Chief?"

"I mean him, yes. So out of loyalty I must go with Mondale."

"Even though Mondale's a child, just like Carter? Not to mention the runaway inflation. And God bless Mario Cuomo, who in office less than a year has raised our taxes some twenty percent."

"You must know, Anne, that you've become a dyed-in-the-wool Republican."

"Not true. I voted a straight Dem ticket last year in the county election. It's just that Carter's policies failed. And I've grown up. Time for you to take off your diapers and follow the voice of history.

Speaking of history, Den, bet you didn't know I became a history major by accident?"

"No, I didn't."

"Yeah, my first semester I signed up for a biology course that got canceled. To fit the time slot, all that was left was a topics course on urban America that Dambroach was offering. A country girl, I was fascinated by what he had to say about the city streets. It was all so new to me. Anyway, what about you? Your love affair with history started how?"

Dennis's face went silly. Who was going to tell Anne that his decision was based on his studying crises in that world survey course that made his own personal crisis pale in comparison? Thus, he would have to tell her that history ironically supplied a much needed refuge from Bellport. He could never do that. So he searched his mind for a real-life incident other than the bungalow affair that Anne would perceive as having shocked his system in such a way that got him thinking more worldly.

"C'mon, Den, tell me."

"See, Anne, Father James Donovan was a pumpkin-faced Jesuit with a drinker's pulpy nose. He was both a first cousin and a good friend of my father who grew up one block over on 256th Street. Smart as can be, he worked his way up through the ranks in the Brooklyn diocese. To get away from the chaos of the city, he'd occasionally hop a train out to Bellport and enjoy Sunday dinners with us."

"And what, Den, does this have to do with the study of history?"

"Father James also came armed with elaborate commentary on what he called the cultural rot in America's society. My father liked to sit by with clasped hands resting on his stomach, utterly content with the pronouncements. My mother bit her tongue."

"Why?"

"What she wanted to say, but couldn't, was that like all priests of stunted growth, Father James was ultimately amused by the sorry lot of most people. Anyway, this one Sunday my mother prepared a meatloaf dinner. Pretty sure that the mashed potatoes and string beans were served in matching ceramic bowls."

"Funny, Den."

"Anyway, during dinner, Father James started choking. Real bad. My dad jumped up, and only after smacking his back a bunch of times did the wet glossy fragments of a once puffy dinner roll land on and around the plate. His face red in embarrassment, Father James took out his handkerchief, and as he began to clean the mess up, he stopped to look directly at me. 'This, Dennis,' he said, 'is almost as bad as that one night at Okinawa, when me and two buddies were trapped in a foxhole.'"

"Shit, Den," Anne replied, "that was the bloodiest battle of the Pacific campaign."

"He goes on to say that in the blink of an eye, his two friends got their heads blown off by enemy gunfire. 'All because,' I quote Father James here, 'of a misanthrope who goes by the name of Hitler.'"

"How awful."

"I was maybe fifteen. I knew who Hitler was. But I wasn't getting the connection between Hitler and misanthrope. That next day my father, who saw some bad shit in the war, told me that what Father James was getting at was that wars in this century were caused by thugs who grab power, and not by religious zealots. Or poor central planning, as some people think. My dad said once I got good at understanding that dynamic, I'd have a better grasp of human nature."

"And did you?"

"It took some time, and while taking the world survey at Rutgers, it started to make sense. More so, after subsequent history courses. Yes, I remember that day with Father James like it was yesterday."

"So what you're telling me is that you were drawn to history to better understand how thugs change the course of human history?"

Dennis raised his coffee mug and said, "Cheers."

"Pretty lame. But I guess I'll drink to that." The two clinked their coffee mugs. "So now that I have you opening up the deep recesses of your soul, let's get back to the subject at hand. Are you ever planning on owning up to your running geekiness?"

"I tell you what, Anne. Let me go up top and put my new trainers on. I'll give the notion of geekiness some thought during some early morning junk miles before work. I'll report back tonight."

"You do that. I'll finish my coffee in peace before Sean and Colin stir."

But Dennis didn't move. He suddenly seemed lost in thought. As sometimes happened, Anne watched her husband's mind vacate the present without warning. What she couldn't possibly see, however, were the random images appearing and colliding in his memory. This morning it was the frantic Eliza scrambling to put on her shoes. William and Peter slumping over. The blue tinge of Vinnie's skin stretched over his lifeless form. Cassidy, his face fraught with suspense, scampering past the St. Theresa statue.

Then, as if being transported back to the present in a flash, Dennis would come to. This morning, he realized Anne was looking on. So it behooved him to stand and, as promised, head up top to put on his gear.

Shortly later, he found himself running at a good clip on a country road that skirted the Susquehanna.

50

As head coach of soccer, Dennis ran up an impressive win-loss record, and as his twins grew, he tried as best as he could to instill a love of the game in them. Hoping to coach them someday, he often brought them to soccer practice and taught them the more important skills. Sean and Colin soon became a dynamic offensive duo in the youth soccer program. The two of them also excelled in little league baseball. So much so that as their high school years approached, it became apparent to Dennis that baseball would be their varsity sport.

Which is why one night in the summer of 1993, the twins a month away from becoming freshmen, Dennis was stunned when Colin asked him if he and his brother could run in the Oneonta 5K, a road race to be held the first Saturday in August. Sean added that some of their friends who were going out for the high school cross-country team would also run the race.

"Who?" Dennis asked.

"Dickie Benz and Carlos, Dad."

When Anne noticed that the topic made Dennis uneasy, she said, "Not quite sure why your father objects. After all, he's as big a running geek as there is."

"Didn't you once tell me, Anne, that your field hockey coach used running as a way to punish the team's slackers?"

"Not to mention, boys, that your father was a member of a star cross-country team back in high school. Right, Den?"

Boxed in by Anne, Dennis turned to his twins: "I thought you two were planning on fall baseball, you know, to get ready for spring ball?"

"Who said anything about canceling baseball, Den? The boys just want to enjoy what's left of the summer with their friends."

Anne had no idea that over the years, a wary Dennis had studied his twins and was not at all sure he liked what he saw. Whether in youth baseball, basketball, or soccer, they had this fluid stride, too fluid, in fact. And they never seemed to run out of steam. It rocked him, the thought of them someday running cross country. That's why he sighed relief on race day when he saw his twins, looking like death, turn onto Columbus Street for the final straight. Arms clawing, faces gasping for air, they crossed the finish line and dropped to their backs right there on the pavement. They stood only after meet officials helped them to their feet.

Dennis waited until they were at Waffle House before he thought he'd nail the running coffin shut. "So I guess you two would rather spray doubles and triples to the opposite field than suffer horribly unspeakable pain on a cross-county course like you did today."

"Actually, Dad," said Colin dousing his pancakes with syrup, "today wasn't bad at all. In fact, I really liked it."

"Yeah, Dad," Sean added, "I only wish we didn't go out so slow. Dickie wanted all of us to run together."

"Slow?"

"Sean's right, Dad. Dickie said to wait until we circled the World War II Memorial, not far from the finish line, before we started our kick. Sean and I couldn't take it anymore. The pace was too slow. So at the grade school, halfway into the race, we took off.

Was hard the last mile, real hard. But it was fun passing all those people. Right, Sean?"

"It was, Dad, real fun. Could ya pass the syrup?"

Dennis felt like he was falling backwards, hearing that the twins had somehow employed a version of Coach Jack's slow burn.

A few nights later, Anne waited until the twins had gone up to bed. "Hon, I'm rethinking this running business. Maybe it's not so bad after all. Your mom has a framed 8 X 10 of you in the den finishing a race. You looked like crap in the picture. But you survived, and the better for it, I might add."

"It's one thing to run junk miles like I do. Another to run competitively, which by any standard is death by a thousand cuts. Why would you want to put the boys through that when they could excel on the baseball field?"

"That's not how the two of them described Saturday's race. It was like love at first sight for the both of them."

"Give them time. With fall baseball right around the corner, they'll forget all about it."

"I have a confession."

"You're leaving me for Mel Gibson."

"While you were getting the oil changed this afternoon, the twins asked me to sign a permission form."

"For what?"

"A week-long cross-country camp at Cornell University in Ithaca."

"Anne!"

"And Carlos and Dickie are going. And it's relatively inexpensive. Starts a week from Monday. We drop them off at four on Sunday."

"Please, Anne! Tell me you're joking. I mean, we don't want them to blow their wad on a sport like cross country when baseball could bag them a college scholarship to a D3 school. High school teachers like me aren't exactly rolling in the kind of dough that can send two boys to a four-year institution at the same time."

"It's a done deal. I signed the form. By the way, they both told me they are committed to running for Oneonta's high school team."

Over the next several days, it was clear to Anne that her husband had neither warmed up to camp nor the idea of his twins running cross country. But by the time they left for Cornell, he knew better than to be anything but cheerful in front of her when it came time to drop the boys off. As it turned out, however, Dennis couldn't hide his astonishment at what the camp director and head cross-country coach at Cornell, Dr. Christopher Smythe, had to say at a parents' cookout, which turned into a painstakingly long description of all camp activities. These included yoga in the morning hours and diary writing at night. In addition, participants each afternoon would retreat to their dormitory rooms and study a chapter from a handbook on distance-training principles self-published by Smythe.

"By the time the week's over," he told the crowd of parents, "your sons will not only have logged seventy miles. They also will have a good handle on the biomechanical attributes of a well-trained distance runner."

Dennis pictured Coach Jack clocking the guy.

Dennis and Anne had only just gotten home from dropping the twins off when Anne, her eyes lit up like hot coals, announced an overhaul of the house while the twins were gone. "And, Den, don't say a word about money. The house is going to shine by the time the boys get home. And if you're good, I'll sleep in the buff upon the successful completion of the work." Happily, the list didn't include any major projects, such as taking on the spare bedrooms way up top that had never been used. Nor did Dennis mind that he was the errand boy, sent to town each time for semi-gloss or floor wax or utility blades or whatever else was needed. McGillicuddy's Tavern was a mere half block from the hardware store.

After several busy days, Anne announced Wednesday night that they should be able to finish up the next day. "I was thinking you could splurge for a ribeye dinner at The Lariat tomorrow night, followed by an inside-the-park homerun."

That Thursday afternoon, while Anne was painting the mud room, the final task on the list, Dennis went out to the barn porch to take in the *Oneonta Tribune*. It was one of those late summer days, warm and breezy and sweet smelling. While out there, Anne caught his attention crossing the yard in his direction, the portable phone clutched in one hand. He thought nothing of her approach. His wife was always fetching him for one thing or another. But then he noticed her eyes cast downward, her gait steady and tight, all of which was unusual for her work-a-day aspect. Yet it wasn't until she started rubbing her left arm with the phone, as if she was cold, that his hands went flat on the table's surface.

"Dennis," she said pushing open the screen door. Her eyes streamed confusion and fear. "It's your brother."

He looked up at her handing him the phone.

"Tommy?" he said.

"Dennis," a faint voice came, as if a continent away.

"What, Tommy? Tell me, dammit."

"Dennis…we lost Dad. A heart attack. A massive one. Just got home from Good Samaritan…"

The line went silent. Each brother heard little more than a fire smoldering deep within the line.

When Tommy resumed, he informed Dennis that their mother had heard a cry in the backyard where their father had been trimming bushes. Tommy explained that after the medics masked their father with oxygen, they got him into the ambulance and took off. But it stopped only a few blocks along to paddle his heart.

"Can you believe it, Dennis! Dad died right there on Crocus."

"I can't."

"Neither can I."

"Where's Mom right now?"

"At Christine's. She's a wreck. Pretty sure she'll spend the night there."

Tommy added that the three of them were to meet shortly and discuss funeral arrangements. "You okay with that?"

"Of course."

Tommy said he'd get back as soon as he knew something.

Placing the phone down, Dennis could think of little else except his father lurching up against the backyard fence. Anne looked away, her lips just touching.

A bird cry pierced the woods. Dennis' head fell sideways on the table as if he was listening for voices in the wood. Anne looped her arms around his neck, her wet face pressed on his head.

"Den," her breath was jumpy. "Imagine it's too late in the day to retrieve the twins from camp?"

"First thing in the morning."

"Off to Bellport right from there?"

"Yes."

She kissed his forehead and left for the house in short stiff strides that seemed to be measuring distance. Dennis noticed a black-billed magpie landing on the feeder, filled to the brim just the previous day. The clever bird poked at the seed as one might an old-fashioned typewriter. Dennis lingered out on the porch until a wind picked up that pasted white petals against the screen.

Tommy later called back to report that their father's wake was to be at Dalton's in two sessions on Friday. To that, Dennis asked, "And the Mass and burial?"

"This is where it gets strange."

"Strange, how?"

"Father Eichen told Mom that Dad could not be buried in the parish cemetery on Saturday because of a prior parish commitment. They could accommodate us early next week."

"What commitment?"

"A ceremony for a refurbished St. Theresa statue on the Great Lawn. I guess the statue was on its last leg, cracks all over. Some outfit hauled it away a few months back. Anyway, the ceremony will be at three on Saturday, followed by a Mass at five. Bishop Cassidy's to preside over both."

"Cassidy?"

"Yes, him. Father Eichen told Mom that dignitaries will be in attendance, and that the set-up will start early Saturday morning, the grounds closed to the public."

"Mom's response to Eichen?"

"Fucking out of her mind, Den, she hung up on him. She told Christine and me that Cassidy's using the ceremony to introduce some diocesan capital campaign. Several high parish rollers will slip him a check."

Dennis' thoughts were going everywhere and nowhere.

"So we made some calls. Mom decided on Mass at St. Margaret's, in Queens. Dad's church as a boy. Followed by the burial at Holy Cross in nearby Middle Village where his parents are. She asked Father James to say Mass. You're coming right down to the Island, Den, aren't you?"

"We are. But we first have to head west to Cornell. To fetch the twins from a summer camp."

"That will make for one hell of a day of driving."

The next few hours were rough, a miserably distracted Christine even calling with a series of grievances, starting with her concern that some zealous mortician type at Dalton's was getting it all wrong. "And Dennis, there's that loser, Cassidy. He probably still resents our involvement in you-know-what."

"You mean my hand in you-know-what?"

"Anyway, since I assume that you are staying at 32 Crocus when you get into town tomorrow, why don't you first stop at my place and say hi to Mom, who, I imagine, will be staying with us for the time being. You can also leave the twins here. They can stay up in the dormer with my Michael for some catch up. Give you and Anne some down time after a long day."

The bedroom was black that next morning, his wife standing over him.

"Den, honey, it's a little after five. Set to drive?"

"Think so."

"Good, I'm going to make the coffee and get things ready." After she left, Dennis lay there still drugged from sleep and trying to pull in the upcoming day. He must have pulled too hard, his mind snagged on the scene of his father crying for help. Dennis pushed himself up, the soles of his feet thumping the wooden floor.

Within the hour, a coffee travel mug in hand, he got behind the wheel, a catatonic Anne in the passenger seat, a blanket pulled over her. He tried to clear room in his mind for the trip to Ithaca. He knew as he followed the headlights' dim tunnel, he'd have to outwit long stretches of silence.

"Dennis," Anne's voice came not long into the trip, "I heard you talking with Tommy. What's the story with this Cassidy fellow?"

The steering wheel turned hot, accompanied by an impulse to swerve off into a corn field.

"Oh, you must mean James Francis Cassidy, Bishop of Rockville Centre and former pastor of St. Theresa's. Well, he's got this big statue ceremony planned on the parish grounds that caused the Mass and burial to be moved to Queens."

"You okay with that?"

"My grandparents on both sides are buried at Holy Cross. So now, my dad, and I guess my mom eventually, will join them. How about you get some rest. I'll need you to drive later."

As she lowered the seat and fell asleep, Dennis started to think about when it was just the pastor and him in the sacristy before Mass. Cassidy had this habit of yawning ceremoniously and stretching his shoulders to relax the muscles in his back. Remembering himself, he'd straighten up, and with arched brows depart for the lectern to arrange the gospel pages. Dennis recalled one all-school Mass. He was standing idly by in cassock and surplice watching the pastor break communion wafers into small pieces as the crowds of students were filing into the church. Cassidy did so with the usual look of annoyance, all those faces out there waiting for Mass to start. While snapping a wafer, his hand accidentally knocked the silver bread plate and all its wafers onto the floor. "Fuck," Cassidy muttered, causing his altar boy to scurry out onto the altar while the pastor cleaned up.

The memory brought a grin to Dennis, though it didn't last long. Bellport never learned the whole story, how the pastor had Lambert rush through a plea deal that omitted his role in the affair. Cassidy did so even as parishioners radiated a glowing righteousness over the incident, like sharks feasting on the threadbare corpse of Mr. Malagati. All the while, Dennis stood by like a sorry drunk, watching from the sidelines. That's what knotted up his stomach back then. That's what still did.

His hands regripping the wheel, his mind again went wandering, now to his poor father who awaited the crowd at Dalton's to pay him a last visit. During the period when Dennis' left leg was shuttered by metal, Dan Hurley would sometimes wait until dusk to take his son and Coco for a slow walk around the field's perimeter. Despite the brace, Dennis loved those walks. Not only the dying birdsong but also the haze of falling light that seemed to swell the field into something larger than it was, making it seem the expanse of a grand park. Then there were those nights when his father would drive him to Field Six. The brace taken off in the wagon, Dan Hurley would carry his son over the sand and into the water. The two of them would go out past the breakers and swim parallel to the shore. "It's God's gift to mankind," his father liked to say, "to be able to swim in the light of the moon."

Once a dilapidated triple-decker birdhouse followed his mother and Alice Crimmins home from an antique shop in Miller Place. The birdhouse laid on the kitchen table, his mother and Alice took turns describing for his father what he would need to do to refinish it. An incremental sanding process of three grit levels, followed by two coats of walnut stain. "And, Dan," Alice said, "apply the stain with a soaking wet cloth, and rub so as to get into the pores." Dennis remembered his father's tongue that day reeling back and his mouth closing to form some version of his justice-has-ground-to-a-virtual-halt look.

It was noon before the minivan reached Ithaca. Camp Director Smythe walked the family back to the van and shook the hand of each twin.

"Real nice to meet you, boys, and again, sorry to hear about your grandfather."

Then turning to Dennis, "Do know, Mr. Hurley, that your two boys are welcome back next year. Free of charge, given the circumstances. And while you may not be familiar with cross-country lingo, over the last mile of yesterday's five-miler, your boys running together on a very tough horse trail slung some mean dirt, staying up with some of the better kids at the camp."

"Oh?"

"Yes, the long and short of it is that both of your twins excel at the absorption and propulsion phases."

"See, Dad," said Colin, "absorption is the moment the foot contacts the ground and where the knee flexion point is."

"And," Sean added, "propulsion is the moment the foot leaves the ground, and the body is propelled forwards."

"That's right, Mr. Hurley, and elite runners reduce energy cost by optimizing these movements. Your boys do that better than most. In fact, some coaches here are plenty nervous thinking about how Oneonta High, with these two boys on the team, might clean their clocks in a year or two."

"Not to worry about that. They play baseball."

"Cross country is a fall sport."

"Oneonta has a fall baseball league. But thanks."

The drive to Bellport was indeed long, and at one point, Anne, who was now driving said, "Den, we won't race home from Bellport afterwards like we usually do, right? I mean, Tommy and Christine might need help regarding your mom and the house on Crocus."

He rooted his mind for a response to the bloody question. It would require immense discipline. Before the answer came, however, she said, "No big deal. Just relax and get some sleep."

    He leaned the seat back and hoped that indeed sleep would come. But Anne's questioning agitated. Of course, he'd be staying to help. After all, he resided in Bellport his first eighteen years. That ought to count for something, despite that Christine and Tommy, except for their college years, have lived in Bellport their entire lives, both now in houses just blocks from 32 Crocus. And it wasn't like the two of them didn't try to get him to move back. His sister once schemed to get him a teaching position at Bellport High. His mother, having vowed not to haggle with him, forgot herself during a phone call. "You're poured and encased up north, Dennis. And we all better get used to it." Little did she know that up north he often felt himself flapping like a windblown flag. He was at least grateful that whenever he and Anne made one of their rare trips to Bellport that the family was on their best behavior.

51

It was after eleven when Dennis pulled up to his sister's house. During a tearful hug, Christine told Dennis their mother was exhausted and had gone to bed. They talked a bit about the next day before leaving the twins behind. It was the oddest thing when Dennis and Anne arrived at 32 Crocus. It was as if he had never set eyes on the house.

"Say, Den, why don't you go in and turn the lights on. I'll get the van straightened up some."

The front door giving way to a firm push, Dennis passed through the foyer and hit a light switch. He wanted to reach for one of his mother's many trinkets lying about. But choking on emotion, he couldn't figure out if all that looked gloriously familiar was actually that or a horrible trick. He wheeled around, and as he returned outside to help Anne with the suitcases, there under a streetlamp walking in their direction was Roger Greer, a miracle of modern science who each day for his entire adult life had survived a slew of gin martinis. His wife Mary was a few steps behind, the two of them were undoubtedly on the way home from Chief's.

"Dammit, Dennis," said Roger coming up the drive and shaking hands. "I'm so sorry. We're all shocked."

"My condolences, too," said his wife, a stick figure now, her once black hair frizzled grey. "Your father was a great guy, a great neighbor."

"Say, Dennis, this is your pretty bride, if I remember correctly."

"Anne, you remember Mr. and Mrs. Greer?"

"Heck, Dennis, you should know by now. I go by Roger, she, Mary." But his wife had already taken a step backward, all part of the long humiliation of having her private life made public by a husband who approached life like a battering ram, which on this day revealed itself in his boasting of a retirement three years ago that included a long overdue vacation to Florida.

"C'mon, Roger," his wife cut him off. "It's time to go."

Roger felt the narrow range in her voice. "Well, I guess Mary's right."

Dennis nodded, thinking that was that.

It wasn't. With an eye tightly cocked past the field to the woods, Roger said, "Yeah, Dennis, it's been a number of years since Cassidy banished the ole jailbird, Charlie Malagati, and his son to an upstate cemetery. In fact-"

"Roger! Let's leave poor Dennis and Anne to rest up after a long day on the road. They don't need to hear about that thing again. No one does."

"Oh, my Mary's right again. You two must be awfully tired. We'll be seeing you over at Dalton's tomorrow to say farewell to your dad."

Dennis might have corrected Roger Greer and told him that father and son were buried in a Brooklyn cemetery but that Anne was standing right there. Instead, he nodded goodbye.

Dennis and Anne made their way inside, suitcases and garment bags in hand. Anne opened the armoire and hit a stereo button, a nocturne now floating about the main floor.

"Say, Den, you don't mind if we use your parent's room. Sure beats the pullout in the den."

"Good idea," he said following her in.

With Anne preoccupied in the master bathroom, Dennis

sat down on the bed, which clearly was a better prospect than the den's pullout. Still, Anne's forging ahead on a night like this was a bit too much for him. First, the stereo. Then taking over his parents' bedroom and unpacking toiletries in their bathroom. Now wheeling around to turn on the shower, she undressed. She might have at least closed the door. Of course, he knew that her brain was awash in the minutiae of the next few days. She stepped over into the tub and the squalling hiss, the curtain pulled closed.

Gradually his eyes moved away from the spindle of bathroom light to the room itself, dense in tone and meaning, beginning with the lone crucifix above the bed, a tired palm wedged behind it. The dresser held a framed photo of the bride and groom leaving St. Margaret's. On his father's nightstand was the laminated beer coaster with a Bill Dickey autograph on it. Dan Hurley used to tell Dennis that it wasn't just that Dickey's lifetime batting average dwarfed both Berra and Bench. His defensive stats were the best the game has ever seen. To make more credible his case for Dickey, his father would crouch into the squatting position and pull off a pretty good imitation of a catcher jumping up and whizzing the ball by his ear to throw the man out at second.

Dennis looked back to the bathroom where Anne, now dripping wet and shrouded in steam, had stepped out of the shower onto the bathmat and shivered as she always did. She dried herself with a towel and wrapped it around her waist. The mirror's mist wiped off, she readjusted the towel and shifted her position to a football coach's stance, hands placed on hips in the way of an aspiring pin-up, her breasts, however, drooping low.

"Dennis," Anne lifted a leg onto the toilet cover and ran her hand along it. "Can you answer me something?"

The question made him start. Just then, however, she discovered a nubby roughness on one leg, which she rubbed as if it ached. Her brow relaxed when she reached for a razor.

"So anyway, just what did the custodian do? That's who you wrote about, right? Your neighbor called him a jailbird. And where does the son fit in?" Anne couldn't resist, and Dennis had the chance meeting tonight with Roger Greer to thank for that. He might have changed the subject by telling her that her legs looked so smooth, so fine, that one couldn't tell where her razor had been and where it was headed.

"Oh, you must mean Mr. Macaroni."

"Get serious, Den. What did he do that was so bad? Molest some kid or something?"

"No, Anne, he didn't molest some kid or something. I really never found out the whole story because the smoke from it all hadn't settled until after I left for college."

"Tell me, Den." She resumed shaving. "Steal the collection basket?"

"Actually, I heard that money might have been involved."

"Dennis?" She held a tube of skin cream, about to pour some into an upturned hand. "You must know that your mother has such good taste in music. This melody is so lovely."

Dennis fell backwards on the bed, the air going out of him.

But as he lay there thinking that but for the grace of God he had dodged a bullet, the feeling was tempered by something Liz Pearce told him long ago, that the noise would never go away. And under the present circumstances, he had better prepare for the looks coming his way. Local well-wishers at the funeral home who'd remember him as the kid who sent the Vietnam vet to the great beyond. But surely those same locals, he could only hope, would not bring up the topic in front of Anne. Like Roger Greer did. Which got Dennis thinking about his neighbor's bizarre claim that Mr. Malagati and Vinnie were buried upstate.

"Den?" She was now rubbing white face cream in circles on her forehead. "Can you turn the music off? Make sure the doors are locked?"

"Sure." He did just that, but not before stepping out onto the front porch and the dark wall of summer trees. Tomorrow, family and friends would flock to Chapel C.

THE MORNING SESSION at Dalton's saw a small crowd. Christine was at her mother's side most of the time, the two positioned in the front row of chairs. Dennis and Tommy mainly stood next to the casket, shaking hands. At one point Bobby Mumbles approached. Except for a bit of the salt and pepper in his hair, he still looked like a Roman god.

"So sorry, Denny kid."

"Thanks, Mums. And it's damn good to see you after all these years."

"I still think the bastards robbed us of a state championship."

"Me, too, Mums. Me, too."

The evening session was packed, with Catherine Hurley and Christine commanding the reception line while Dennis and Tommy milled about. At one point, Jack Hogan on his way out of the chapel stopped to shake hands with Dennis and whisper to him, "It's gonna be fucking rough in the morning. Slow burn as best you can. And never forget that I love your sorry ass. Gotta go, but see you tomorrow."

Dennis had only just awakened when the brutal business came to mind. He had been to Holy Cross Cemetery just once, in grade school when his grandmother was buried. What he most remembered was the grubby-looking staff hovering by, anxious to dump dirt back over. His old coach was exactly right. The day would require a slow burn of sorts.

Less than an hour later, with Tommy joining Christine and his mother in the front row of Chapel C, Dennis stole glances at his father in the casket as he paced nearby like a caged tiger. He knew it was just a matter of time before one of Dalton's people would walk front and center and hasten the closing of the casket. That person turned out to be Mrs. Crowley, a bird-like creature who wore a red button-down sweater and carried a fresh tissue wherever she went. After a nun offered the final prayer service,

Mrs. Crowley coughed twice and asked everyone to pay their last respects.

A line forming with menacing speed, Dennis sat with his mother and two siblings. Their heads slightly tipped, they looked as if they were about to stretch their hands forward and touch Dan Hurley across the way.

A hulk of misery, the four of them left the chapel holding onto each other.

As the limo and the procession of vehicles followed the hearse out of town, they passed the parish marquee.

Welcome Back Bishop Cassidy
Ceremony at 3 p.m.
High Mass to Follow at 5 p.m.

Out the limo's window, Dennis glimpsed the Great Lawn, the staff busily setting up rows of chairs in preparation for the day's statue ceremony. He pictured Cassidy at the moment being served V8 juice and a poached egg on toast at the Rockville Centre chancery, his entourage fussing over this and that as they prepared to take him to Bellport for the big day. Surely, Dennis thought, Eichen had contacted the chancery with word of his father's death. But even if he had, such news wouldn't give Cassidy pause. He's not the kind to be affected by the death of mere mortals. For him, even an earthquake in some third-world country that opens up and sucks down bodies and then closes like a bloody zipper is little more than a pesky natural disaster.

The Mass at St. Margaret's began right at ten. Father James offered an impassioned but dignified Mass, his voice cracking a few times during the eulogy for his boyhood cousin. The short graveside service was no different. It was hard on Dennis listening to the priest intone somber words of farewell while his mother stood by, Christine leaning into her. Both shook when Father James asked God to receive Daniel Patrick Hurley into heaven.

Arriving back at 32 Crocus, Dennis found cars parked up and down the street. Once inside, he saw that the parish bereavement committee had neatly arranged finger sandwiches on the living room table and put a full cooler of beer and soda on the back patio. By the fireplace, his mother joined Alice Crimmins. Age had ravaged her face, lines and wrinkles all twisting about like an Algonquin squaw. A quiet Aunt Pearl, who the previous year had a slight stroke after her husband John died of colon cancer, sat by herself nibbling on cake. Tommy huddled with Larry Gordon, a first cousin who had retired as a city worker and always smelled of salty peanuts. At one point, Catherine Hurley stood and left for her bedroom, followed by Christine, who afterwards came out and told Dennis that their mother needed to rest. "She's a wreck, Den."

Hearing voices in the den, Dennis moved in that direction. He stopped near the room's entrance. Jack Hogan had the small crowd in there laughing over the time Cassidy tripped over a potted flower on the altar steps and uttered words unbecoming a priest.

"Speaking of Cassidy, Jack," said Roger Greer, "it's a damn shame he couldn't figure out a way to accommodate poor Dan on home turf. Instead, he shuffled him out of town. Just like he did back then with the Malagati boys, whisking the two of them away to an upstate graveyard."

"Wrong, Roger," said Jack Hogan, "the two of them are buried in Brooklyn."

"Mary, you tell them what you heard."

"It's never been verified, Jack, but I think my husband's right. After Ginny Wooten retired back in 1984, she told her sister about the last-minute decision to send the two hearses upstate. Yet by then the affair had lost traction. Few cared where they were buried."

Anne approached with two plates of food. She gestured to Dennis that they go into the den and grab a seat. At which point, he moved to block her way. Yet that did not prevent her from hearing the conversation in there.

"Hey," replied Jack Hogan, "whether it's Brooklyn or upstate, it doesn't matter to the church of Julius Caesar. What counts is that Hopalong Cassidy wasn't about to allow the Malagati boys to push up daisies in the parish cemetery. No choice but to send the two caskets off into the sunset."

Roger added, "Jack's hit the nail on the head. I mean, we're talking about carnage at a premium. The biggest story to hit Suffolk County since-"

"Roger!" cried Mary Greer nodding in the direction of Anne entering the room, a nervous Dennis a step behind. "We buried his poor father today, and all you can talk about is that!"

"Oh," said Roger. "Sorry, Dennis, didn't see you."

"Dennis Hurley!" Jack Hogan declared. "A member of the state championship team!" His former coach couldn't have looked more at home, legs limply crossed, dress slacks stretching as he lowered a can of Budweiser to the floor. "Why don't you and your lovely bride come sit by Ole Jack. We can regale this group with the blow-by-blow of the state race. See, folks, Dennis here was the nucleus of a team for the ages."

As Jack Hogan held his audience in check, Dennis' great aunt Dorothy, apparently disenchanted with the speaker, stood and started for the door. A wary Dennis didn't want to leave Anne alone with this crowd. But his great aunt looked unsteady. He stood to help her outside.

"Why, thank you, Dennis, if you could help me to a seat in the sun." And once outside in a lawn chair, she said, "You go inside, now. But first you must know that your father was a wonderful person, and he'll be in Heaven in no time, if he's not there already. Some say it's like stepping on home plate."

Dennis smiled back even as through the woods he heard the tinny sound of a parish speaker, the statue ceremony underway.

Returning inside, he joined a small crowd in the kitchen listening to Father James, who had stationed himself there to guarantee a convenient escape route. Dennis wasn't surprised at all that this priest with great ease was fielding questions on the decline of American norms. Dennis stood and listened, even as his mother, still groggy from sleep, walked into the kitchen and interrupted. "Oh, Father James. The eulogy, it was so, so beautiful." She hesitated. "Can I ask you something?"

"Of course, Catherine."

"Is it possible that Dan already could have contacted me? I mean, lying down just now I felt something."

The small crowd was struck dumb.

The priest first returned a smile. "Dear Catherine, at one time I would have told a grieving family member with similar sentiments that it's the shock of losing someone close. And that a ghostly presence is not without precedence in the folklore of old. But these days the experience is inevitably all part of a cottage industry that promotes mythologies of death, which, I'm afraid to say, is little more than the repression of it."

"Of course. It's silly of me."

"No, not at all. But do know that we must listen for the sounds of the true God. And believe that we can go on loving Him even as those we love are taken from us. Now, Catherine, would you mind if we all said the *Our Father* before I head back into the city?"

"That would be nice."

"Please, everyone, join us." He took her arm, and the ardent drone began.

Our Father,
Who art in Heaven,
Hallowed be Thy name,
Thy kingdom come,
Thy will be done on earth as it is in Heaven.
Give us this day our daily bread
And forgive us our trespasses,
As we forgive those who trespass against us,
And lead us not into temptation,
But deliver us from evil.
Amen.

"And may God grant His servant, Dan Hurley, eternal rest. Amen."

As everyone made the Sign of the Cross, Dennis felt wheezing on his neck. Turning around, he locked eyes with Coach Jack who whispered into his ear, "And to think Cassidy, the big weenie, is pontificating just across the way." Before Dennis could reply, his old coach was off to the beer cooler.

Father James sat with Catherine Hurley for a while before he stood to leave. His departure set off a mass exodus, including the gang in the den. Dennis soon sat with Tommy at the kitchen table, each with a bottle of beer. They said nothing at first but watched the thin sunlight giving way out on the field, where a teenage girl pulled another way back and forth on the swing set. The twins were also out on the field throwing the football with Christine's Michael. Dennis leaned back in his chair and looked into the living room. Shadows wrestled in the far corner where his mother lay resting on the couch.

Christine and Anne entered the kitchen, each with a glass of wine.

"How you two doing?" Tommy asked.

"Good," said Christine. "I take it that everyone's left to catch a glimpse of His Highness, as Mommy likes to call him, say Mass."

"Yes," Tommy said, "our parishioners are a curious bunch."

"Speaking of curious," Anne said. "Can someone please fill me in about this custodian guy everyone keeps buzzing about? The word *carnage* was used by the neighbors chatting away in the den. It must have been a big deal if my husband was doing his best to write about it in college."

"Oh," said Tommy springing to action, "the Malagati business. That, Anne, was a private family matter back in the day. The details are sketchy at best."

"I like sketchy."

"So do I," said Christine. "But unfortunately, officials kept the details to themselves. The town barely remembers it."

"Except," Anne remarked, "that gang in the other room."

"You know what," said Dennis standing, "let me run out and grab a couple of beers for Tommy and me."

Dennis didn't go to the cooler. He detoured over to his mother, still resting on the couch.

"Mom?"

"Yes, dear?"

"You doing okay?"

"I'm trying. But aren't we all? I just wish I hadn't made such an ass of myself earlier with Father James."

"You didn't, Mom."

"Even so."

"Can I ask you a question?"

"What is it, dear?"

"Earlier there was small talk. Roger Greer, Jack Hogan, mainly."

"My nerves, Dennis. I stayed clear of both."

"I thought I overheard them saying something about Mr. Malagati and his son not being buried in Brooklyn. But somewhere upstate. All on Cassidy's dime."

"Oh, Dennis, nothing's ever too terrible for the likes of Jack Hogan and Roger Greer. Years later and they still can't let go of it."

"So it's true? He's buried upstate?"

"Your father and I only learned about it a few years later."

"Do you know where upstate they were buried?"

"It seems that Brooklyn was too close for His Excellency." She paused. "In upstate Delaware County, Dennis. That's where they landed."

"Delaware's one county over from me!"

"Alice is the one who told us. She found out from a cousin. It's the St. Joe's on the Hill Cemetery, on the outskirts of Delhi."

"I know St. Joe's! Just twenty some miles from Oneonta. Anne goes to their flea market each year."

"Your father and I decided not to tell you. Back then, that was the last thing you needed. Yes, rumors swirled about town. But they soon died out. The incident was forgotten, like it should be."

"Of course, Mom. Of course. You rest now. I am heading out for a beer for Tommy and me."

"You boys won't overdo it tonight."

"Not tonight."

Once outside, Dennis passed right by the cooler and with a head of steam went down the drive and crossed the field. For good luck, he tapped Sitting Bull after straddling the creek rocks. Long ago he had schooled himself not to look in the direction of the makeshift burial spot as he entered the path on the way to the parish.

Reaching the grounds today, he paused to stare at the refurbished statue of St. Theresa. She now stood in gaudy enamel colors, no longer a sweet looking girl with an inquisitive countenance given to otherworldly things. Damn, Dennis thought, Cassidy fucked that up, too.

52

Dennis settled into an open seat in the balcony's front row just as the choir was finishing up the closing hymn, during which time the bishop placed his hands flat on the altar and leaned over and kissed it. Cassidy looked out at the congregation, and making the Sign of the Cross, he said, *"In nomine Patris, et Filii, et Spiritus Sancti."*

Dennis half expected Cassidy to shoot a look up at him. The bishop instead genuflected and disappeared into the sacristy, his entourage in tow. Dennis would give the congregation some time to empty out rather than endure their inevitable gawking. As he waited, he noticed that while Cassidy had slowed down some, his genuflection still had the same old majesty and rhythm, the momentary delay in it designed to catch the attention of all.

With only stragglers remaining, Dennis headed down the balcony steps. He felt a hurriedness as he made his way along a side aisle. He didn't bother knocking on the sacristy door before entering. Cassidy's back turned, his entourage had just taken off his vestments. It was only after the bishop's private secretary moved to block the intruder that Cassidy turned around. He paused for a second. Recognizing the face, he offered up a bright smile, which glinted above the small pectoral cross hanging over his vest. Dennis smiled back, taking in the long hollow face that had filled out some. Cassidy still wore a golden ring that dazzled those who shook his hand.

"Sir, you must leave," said the secretary, taking the intruder by the arm.

Dennis, not having it, yanked free. "I am an old friend of His Excellency, thank you. The two of us have been meaning to shoot the breeze for some time now. Isn't that right, Bishop Cassidy?"

"This," the bishop said to his entourage, "is Dennis Hurley. A former altar boy and member of the legendary St. Theresa's cross-country team. His peaceful existence has been sadly interrupted by the sudden loss of his father, lowered into the earth just this morning. Now this young man is left to sift through the ruins. In any event," turning directly to Dennis, "my condolences, Son. Not to mention that, yes, it has been a while since we last broke bread."

Dennis' head jerked some at the glib tone. Worse, Cassidy now looked at him in an open way, evaluating. It lasted just a few brief moments.

"Why, thank you, Bishop Cassidy. My dad was a simple man, which is to say a great man. And, yes, the last meeting between the two of us was a memorable one, the morning of your return from Rome."

Cassidy's smile widened. "Your memory is keen."

"In fact, we also spoke a few days prior, when you waxed poetic to me about the burial of a pig."

Cassidy's tongue rolled about in his mouth. He looked quietly around, and sensing that Hurley's words were lost on his entourage, he nodded to his dutiful secretary, who stepped forward with the bishop's clerical jacket.

"Yes," Dennis added, "had we more time that night, I might have asked why you whisked the Malagati boys off to some Potter's Field in upstate New York?"

Not to be rattled, Cassidy with an ever-so-slight wave of the hand sent the entourage outside to the waiting limo. Only his secretary remained behind to help him slip into his jacket.

"Still holding a grudge, Dennis Hurley? Not good. No, not good at all."

"Or better yet, what silky phrase did you use that night to get Mr. Malagati to jump off the cliff?"

The question died without an answer as Cassidy turned to his secretary. "Father Zeitler, would you be so kind as to escort this poor boy forthwith out of the church and steer him in the direction of Main Street. As mentioned, he just lost his father."

"But to think, the farmer at least joined his wife in Heaven, to which some of us will never gain access."

"You forget yourself," said Cassidy, now visibly angered as he opened the sacristy door and left, ready to hop in his limo and get out of town.

As the door slammed shut, the secretary put his hand on Dennis' shoulder, this to move him back out into the church and down an aisle to a side door.

Dennis pushed him aside and said, "I'll leave on my own, thank you."

Once on Main Street, Chief's came to mind. The thought of getting good and drunk. But he didn't want to bring shame to his father today. He instead turned for the inlet bridge, and once at its peak, he stopped to look east over the bay and along the shoreline. He wondered if Liz Pearce had ever left her Oak Island haunt. He peered down at the dark water, thinking if only the day would disappear quickly, like ocean fish darting back into the murky depth. He recalled one morning Alice Crimmins sitting at the kitchen table telling his parents about jumpers over the years, and how the bones of the inconsolable lingered on the bay's bottom.

Dennis soon trudged over dunes and weaved past scattered sunbathers on towels. Stopping short of the waterline, he sat down, eventually falling on his back to gaze up at gulls lazing about. The sand's initial warmth gave way to the cold underlayer, so he turned his face in the direction of the setting sun and shut his eyes. He thought of Anne, of his siblings, of his mother. They had to be wondering where he was.

Darkness had set in by the time he got back into town. So had the breeze fallen off, and except for a car teetering at a red light, downtown Bellport offered little signs of life. He passed one shop after another, the faint breath of night keeping time with his steps. Back in the day he might have taken off running, his thoughts bolstered by race pace. Tonight, he pressed on, his shoes scraping out of sync with the sidewalk. Up ahead, he saw Chief's. Just one drink, a little something to help him face Anne, who probably was still hell bent on solving the mystery of what she had heard in the den.

Though Billy Boyce had sold Chief's some years back, Dennis saw that the new owner left intact the Sitting Bull bust as well as all the nautical artifacts. He took a stool roughly halfway between two old men. A younger man in a tired suit stood over a juke box playing soft rock. Down at the sink, the bartender, a Groucho Marx look-alike, scrubbed the inside of a bucket like some petty sailor in the ship's hull, the cigarette in his mouth oozing smoke that seemed to burn his eyes. Noticing Dennis, he drew in a lungful and expelled it sideways as he made his way over.

"What can I get you?"

"Something strong."

"Something strong coming right up."

As the bartender poured a shooter and a beer, Dennis took in Sitting Bull, with whom Coach Jack had commiserated on many a night. Dennis nodded to the Chief before looking at the fishbowls half-filled with sand and peopled with plastic marine life. His mind growing larger, then smaller, he couldn't make out what he was hearing in his head. But then he recognized the cracking sounds a battered ship makes on the open sea. He dropped the shooter in the beer mug and chugged it. He laid money on the bar and left.

Once back at 32 Crocus, he saw that the minivan was gone. He walked in on an empty house, a note from Anne on the kitchen table.

We waited, Den. But you were a no-show. Christine invited all of us to her house for pizza. Come join us. If not, I sure hope you're okay.

Dennis on an impulse climbed the stairs up to his old bedroom, which his brother took over when he left for college. Tommy had torn Pre down and replaced him with a poster of Jerry Garcia during an outdoor concert at the beach theater, which still adorned the far wall. The wind lifting Jerry's frazzled mane, bay water sparkling in the background, the friend of the devil is a friend of mine. Dennis had never asked Tommy if he ever turned to Jerry for advice as he did to Pre. Dennis went to the window and looked across. He cursed the fact that, with his father barely in the ground, he got into a pissing match with Cassidy.

Dennis went back downstairs and phoned Christine. She said that their mother had gone to bed and that Anne and the boys were watching a movie over some pizza.

"You coming right over, Den?"

"Thanks. But tell Anne I'm exhausted and going to bed."

"Okay. But you should know she got all quiet when you disappeared without a trace. I told her that the day was tough on you. That you probably walked down to the beach."

"Which I did."

"She had questions about Peter Walker and William Flanagan."

"What'd you tell her?"

"That you three were rabble-rousers as boys. That you all climbed Bellport's biggest trees. I said little more than that."

"She didn't ask more questions?"

"No, she didn't. Will you ever tell her what happened?"

"For now, tell her I'm going to bed. Would you please?"

"I will."

Dennis awoke early that next morning, Anne asleep beside him. He looked to the window and pictured the creek water, cool and slow moving. He needed more sleep, the bulwark against the approaching day. But his mind's rhythms picked up, Cassidy's deflections in the sacristy floating in. Sure, Dennis thought as he threw the blankets aside and sat up, yesterday I won the rubber match over His Eminence. But it doesn't feel like I won.

"Den," Anne's voice startled him. "You okay?"

"Oh," he said turning to her, "you're awake. Yes, I'm fine. Just can't sleep."

"Your Dad, Dennis, he was such a wonderful person. We'll all miss him."

He leaned over and kissed her. "Yes, we will."

53

The drive back to Oneonta was a long, muddled affair. On the very day his father was buried, Dennis came to learn that Mr. Malagati and his son were dumped in the tundra of upstate New York. And that for the past fourteen years all that separated him from St. Joe's on the Hill was a breezy two laner of twenty some miles. If, Dennis muttered to himself, all those afternoons on the barn porch I had listened with half an ear, I probably could have heard the old man moaning in his casket.

The minivan didn't pull into the drive until well after midnight, and that next morning Dennis tried as best he could to put St. Joe's out of his mind. As he drove his twins to pre-season cross-country practice, his intention was to stay busy by taking equipment inventory for the upcoming soccer season. Perhaps work on lessons plans for the new school year. But once in the school building, he detoured to the athletic office and dialed the Rochester chancery. A Father Devlin McLeod was the name given as pastor of St. Joe's parish. Dennis looked up at the clock. A good hour and a half, that's how long he figured practice for the twins and their showers afterwards would take.

Back on the road, Dennis drove north along a winding Route 28. As he approached St. Joe's grounds, to the north he saw ancient headstones sagging in unkept woods, the cemetery entrance chained off with a *Keep Out* sign. A little further along, as he steered up the very steep parish drive, the first thing that came to mind was the avalanche of cars that a fire-and-brimstone sermon of this Devlin McLeod fellow would set off during the icy conditions of the winter months. Today, however, was midsummer, and after parking and walking along an old Gothic church in serious need of tuck-pointing, he smelled the decay of nearby apple trees. The rectory came into view. Next to it, a detached garage. In front of that, a man leaned under the hood of an old sedan.

"Hello," said Dennis approaching the man, who in jeans and a soiled thermal shirt turned around, the weary disposition softened by grime on his cheek. He placed the wrench on the car's grille and grabbed a cloth from a back pocket to rub his hands clean.

"Can I help you?"

"I am looking for a Father McLeod."

"Speaking."

"Oh."

"Yes," the priest laughed, "when not administering sacraments, I replace timing belts and the like. Anyway, what can I do for you?"

"My name is Dennis Hurley, Father. I drove here from Oneonta to pay my respects to a deceased parishioner."

"A parishioner of St. Joe's?"

"No, from St. Theresa's. Out on Long Island where I grew up."

Devlin McLeod resumed wiping his hands, this time rubbing between fingers. "I see. Which parishioner did you come to see? Father or son?"

Dennis was startled by just how matter-of-fact the question was. The priest seeing this said, "You see, Dennis, following the burial we were deluged with reporters."

"Is that why the cemetery is closed?"

"The cost of upkeep overwhelmed the diocese."

"The reporters, Father, did they want to know why St. Joe's? And not in Brooklyn? And how the whole thing came about?"

"Am I right that you are one of the three boys involved in the incident?"

"I'm the one who shot the son, yes."

"I take it the thing is still alive for you?"

"It is."

"Well, Dennis, I am not at liberty to get into the details. But suffice it to say that this area was an Italian immigrant stronghold back at the turn of the century. So, in that regard, it made some sense to bring father and son back to their people."

Dennis felt a rush of emotion. "Mr. Malagati was no killer. He should have been buried in Bellport, with his wife. The world back then should have been told how His Eminence-"

"Let me stop you right there. If it's closure you really want, I'd be glad to point you in the direction of the plot."

Dennis would not be deterred. "Was it Cassidy who called you? Or did he pass the dirty work on to his pal, Nellenberger?"

The priest raised an arm and pointed. "There, in the far southeast corner. The bottom row. The inscriptions on most headstones are somewhat obscured with moss. Not sure about theirs."

Dennis nodded, and realizing that his fight wasn't with this priest, he left to find the graves.

Passing through a side cemetery gate, he started along a walkway before stepping onto the grass and making his way toward the southeast corner. Reaching the two headstones, sleek and bare, he found them just as McLeod had said, moss starting to creep about, but the inscriptions in clear view.

Charles Malagati
1896-1974
Vincent Malagati
1943-1974

A respectful prayer, that was what he told himself he'd offer up on the drive over, perhaps something about the old man finding peace in heaven with his wife at his side. But once he dropped to a knee and turned to Mr. Malagati's headstone, he was unable to slow down other thoughts forming in his head, thoughts that without much effort seemed to spill out of him in a gushing cascade. Thoughts about his own guilt. About his own shame. Even about his cowardice when it mattered. It was only when his thoughts veered to Cassidy that Dennis stood. He knew it was time to go. As he stood, however, he turned to Vinnie's headstone and said, "As for you, a thousand years in purgatory."

As he walked back through the cemetery to his car, a voice came at him. Dennis turned and saw Devlin McLeod, a wrench still in hand. "Some lunch before you get back on the road?"

"Thanks," he shouted back, "but got to pick up my sons from practice."

"Okay, but be safe, and let me know if I can be of any help." The priest said that with a wave and a smile.

"Will do."

Dennis said nothing to Anne about the trip to the cemetery when he and the twins returned home an hour later. He'd get through the day as best he could. He stayed busy by shucking corn and putting steaks on the grill. During dinner he even forced on his family a hilarious story about the time as a young boy he got lost at Yankee Stadium. But as he got into bed some hours later, the trip to St. Joe's grabbed a hold of him. He eventually got up and went down to the kitchen hoping that the *Oneonta Tribune* would make him sleepy. It didn't, and he was about to move to the den and turn on the television when his wife appeared in her bathrobe. She sat across from him.

"You couldn't sleep either, Anne?"

"No, I couldn't."

"Everything okay?"

"That, Dennis, is what I was about to ask you."

Who knows why it happened just then, but he suddenly felt the thing stretching beyond the bearable limits. Even so, he'd rather crack his knuckles than offer up the grotesque secret to her.

Anne saw the trouble on his face. "Whatever it is, Den, it can't be that bad."

Only then did he feel a great knot in his body begin to loosen. He stood and filled a glass of water.

It's time, he told himself.

He drank some before sitting back down across from her, the story of the bungalow then told in full.

Some of it came out in torrents. Other parts as if he was repeating a solemn myth that had been told countless times before by others more willing and able.

He left nothing out, slowing down at one point to emphasize how Vinnie tumbled face first after he backhanded him with the gun's barrel. "It's that goddam image, Anne, my whacking him with the gun and his dropping with a thud, that has dominated my daydreams over the years. Not my shooting him, no. But my busting his face open. Like I was a crazed animal."

Anne never spoke during the telling, even during the long pauses. Nor did she have anything to say as he finished up with Cassidy's devious hand in the suicide and all that followed, everything from the plea deal to the visit to St. Joe's. Instead, she nodded her head up and down, as if she had been expecting such a story all along. When he was done, she stood and went over to him. She sat on his lap.

"Den…" She started to cry, first in low sobs, then like a siren, tears splashing his arms. He grabbed onto her, holding her tightly. He held her that way a long while.

"So," she broke away and stood, wiping her eyes with her hand. "Why now?"

"At first, I was afraid you'd leave me. For good."

"How, Dennis, how, could you ever think that?"

"I was afraid the story would reach the twins. And the Oneonta locals. They'd treat me like those back home after the newspaper stories got out. Like I was some kind of hardened criminal. I'm sorry, Anne. I'm sorry it took so long."

"You have nothing to be sorry about. Nothing at all."

"Would it be okay if we picked this up in the morning?"

But that next morning, the topic was not brought up. Nothing but small talk, which made Dennis think that the story had so overwhelmed Anne that it would forever reverberate in her, their marriage forever tainted. But he would soon learn that was not the case. He would discover that it was Anne acclimating herself to the reality of a monstrous story finally told. As they lay in bed that night, she said, "Den, not sure if I will ever fully understand what happened that night. But I do want to ask if the business of avoiding Bellport all these years was part of it?"

"It was."

"And the aversion to taking the cross-country job when Steve Capell originally offered it to you some years back? And several times since?"

"Yes, even though with the exception of that one night, those were the best years of my youth."

"What about the guys on that team of yours? Stay in touch with any of them?"

"Not really. Though my mom for a long time gave me updates. After Adam Feltman ran for Penn State, he moved to Atlanta with his parents. Opened a Sears garage door franchise. George Legstaff never left Gainsville after running up a storm at the university there. And James Fennessy, I think, works in Boston. Some kind of city job. Mumbino is the only one still in Bellport."

"The other two?"

"William's in Morgantown. Peter, a lifer in the Marines. San Diego."

"Ever think about contacting them?"

"It was clear that both wanted to move on. Even after the plea deal, I still wanted them to think like me, that the deal let Cassidy off the hook. I think I scared them off. I was good at that."

54

With the start of school just days away, Dennis was in the locker room storage finishing up soccer inventory when he was approached by Steve Capell. "Hey, Dennis."

"Steve, what's up?"

"Just got off the phone with Anne."

"Oh?"

"Yeah, I called over to your house. She told me you were here. Figured I'd drive over to tell you in person that Kevin Stone called me this morning."

Here we go again, Dennis thought, he's gonna pitch the job again.

"See, Kev wrenched his knee real bad over the weekend. The last straw. Submitted his resignation to the board last night. Can't blame him after all these years of teaching as well as coaching."

"Ain't happening. I coach freshman soccer."

"C'mon, Anne told me that it'd be good for you. After all, your twins are part of the team."

"What else did Anne tell you?"

"What I already knew. That you once ran on a damn good high school team that made it to state each year."

"What else?"

"Nothing except that she said you still got running in your bones. That you never lost your love for the sport."

"Anne's imagination run wild, is all."

"For crying out loud, Dennis, she even said that over the years you got a thing for what she calls junk miles."

Dennis kicked a box and asked, "What else did she say?"

"That lately you've been consumed with talking with those twins of yours about running. I believe her exact words were, 'Coaching cross country would be a catharsis for him.' Whatever the hell that means. Don't need to know, just need ya, Dennis. Give a guy a break!"

"How many times do I have to tell you that I'm happy coaching soccer."

"I don't believe you for a second. But I don't have time to pout. Got to find me a coach."

After pulling into the drive, his sons going inside, Dennis strutted to the barn. There he found his wife arranging vegetables on a table for the weekend sale.

"A catharsis, Anne, really?"

"And hello to you!"

"What the hell were you thinking?"

"Hey, I made sure not to bring up the thing."

"Sure, but you left Steve thinking that I got some kind of deep-seated psychological bug up my ass."

"All I told him is that you still are a running geek. That you still love running."

"Running, yes. Coaching cross country and all that goes with it, no! That jig's been up a long while now."

"Dammit, Dennis, you just recently told me that being on that team was the best part of your youth. Was that a lie? And what I didn't tell Steve, but should have, was that you often forget yourself after a run. You get all chipper. You sing in the shower. Sometimes you even slap me on the ass. To top it off, you get a boner just thinking about the boys on the cross-country team. No, the jig ain't up by a long shot. Yet, if you want the job to be offered to someone else, so be it!"

Anne now had his attention. He had not given any thought to which faculty Steve would approach to take the cross-country position. He recoiled at the only two available candidates. The nitwit Denise Braxton, who coaches girls' cross country. And Richie Urgo, a hurdler in high school, who's lazy as hell and does a half-assed job with the boys' field events during the track seasons. Dennis would have to wait until the next day when he drove the twins over to practice to learn who the new coach would be.

When that next morning he pulled into the school parking lot, the twins hopping out, his heart sank as he saw Urgo over at the track, a crowd of runners stretching on the ground around him. But chin up, Dennis told himself, and as he hurried inside, he had every intention of finishing up the soccer inventory. Once in the storage room, however, and unable to concentrate, he went out to a hallway window for a look-see.

Fuck, no, he muttered. We're only in damn August, and Urgo's got them doing repeat 220s on the track.

Dennis cringed a second and third time watching his twins strain horribly to stay up with the older runners. Like him, they lacked leg speed. Unable to bear it any longer, he headed for his second-floor classroom. There he'd work on lesson plans. Anything to keep busy. As he bound up the stairs, and heard how winded he was, Coach Jack's hill workouts at the Brookhaven Conservatory came to mind. And once on the second floor, and peering down the empty hallway, he recalled a late October snow his junior year, the day before the Bear Mountain meet, when the team was forced to run pre-race bumrushes in the school hallway. Just thinking about it, his heartbeat quickened when he saw his younger self, along with William and Peter, striding along, three ghosts, shoulder to shoulder.

"Damn," he yelled, the echo reverberating about. He wheeled

around and headed in the opposite direction toward the teacher's lounge. There he scoured his wallet for a phone number on a tattered index card that he had not dialed since his high school days.

Margie Mudhank was frying two hamburgers and sliced onions in a skillet when the phone rang.

"Hello?" she said.

"Oh, I must have the wrong number."

"Who you looking for?"

"Coach Hogan."

"Jack," she shouted into the den. "A call for you." Then back to the phone, "Who's this, by the way?"

"Dennis Hurley."

"Shit, not captain extraordinaire of the '74 team! And in case you're wondering, this is Marge Mudhank." Cupping the receiver, "Jack, it's Dennis, Dennis Hurley." Returning to the caller, "He'll be glad to hear from you. Damn glad. You doing okay? And sorry to hear about your father."

"I'm doing fine. And thanks."

"Oh, here he is."

Coach Jack took the receiver. "Denny Boy, that you?"

"It is."

"Great. And it was good to see you a few weeks back. Wish it had been under different circumstances. Your father was a damn good guy."

"Thanks, Coach."

"You know, we really didn't get to talk when you were in town. Did you know I retired a few years ago after a fourth-place finish at state?"

"I heard."

"Yeah, I wanted one more first-place trophy. A keeper this time. But God had other plans. So, I threw in the towel and caught a flight to Vegas and tied the knot. You remember Miss Mudhank, the broad with long legs that ran up to her once-upon-a-time pretty ass, that is, before that same ass decided it wanted to be a caboose?"

"Dennis," Margie leaned over and shouted into the receiver, "Don't let Jack fool you. I'm the one who will be putting a bib on him some day and spoon-feeding him applesauce."

To that, Jack Hogan howled. "The ole gal's right. I don't move like I used to. So, Marge, why don't you go outside and water the weeds while I take this call?"

She grabbed the receiver. "Dennis?"

"Yes, Miss Mudhank."

"When you're next on the Island, come visit Jack. He'd love to see you. That team still gives him goosebumps. And I now go by Mrs. Hogan."

"Will do, Mrs. Hogan."

Once she was gone, Coach Jack said, "So, Dennis, what's up?"

"Coach, I hated to call you out of the blue like this."

"Not a health issue, I hope?"

"No, nothing like that."

"So, tell me."

Dennis explained what had transpired with Steve Capell. How in the past he had turned down the cross-country coaching job, how he had just turned it down again, and how an asshole with no distance experience was hired. "And, oh yeah, my twin boys out of nowhere stumbled into running. And they're pretty good. Better than most. So now I don't know what to do. I mean, getting back into cross country for me is out of the question, and I…"

Coach Jack heard the emotion in his voice. "This is ballsy of me, Dennis. But the Malagati thing. You and I never talked about it…And that's on me. Must have been a hell of a thing to carry that around in your head. And I never even knew the half of it. I hope to Christ that the memories finally disappeared." The phone line went quiet. "Anyway, I'm thinking you called for advice? What to do with that Oneonta job?"

"I guess it wouldn't hurt."

SITTING BULL RUN

"My thoughts. Sure, Coach Jack's always got thoughts. But first, tell me, do you still get at it? Out on the road for junk miles, I mean?"

"I do. In decent shape as we speak."

"What could you run right now on Vanny?"

"On a very good day, eighteen and change."

"Hell, yeah, and if that's the case, it's time to rumble. But it will mean getting your hands dirty in all kinds of shit. Got it?"

"Got it."

"First, you get a hold of this Steve fellow. Drag his sorry ass down to a local tavern and treat him to a bar burger and a bubbly. Tell him you'll take the job if, and only if, he buys you a fancy new team tent."

"But I-"

"No buts. Life's too short. Besides, you're a natural. And just for the hell of it, have the guy throw in new uniforms. So far, so good?"

"I think so."

"Atta boy. Now, you've got a dirt path attached to the school grounds?"

"Several."

"Now we're talking. Any Injun history in that neck of the woods?"

"Mohawk. Lots of it."

"Perfect. I want you to clear one of those paths and turn it into a trail to train on, not to mention a course for area toddlers over the summer. We'll call it, The Mohawk Youth Running Series. All that's left is the big-ticket coaching item. Ready?"

"I am."

"You got to train your teams the same way each and every season, so it becomes second nature in your kids. You remember how that goes?"

"High volume in July. And more of the same in August with a sprinkling of soft intervals."

"September?"

"The volume shrinks some as fast intervals kick in. And come October, bare-knuckles speedwork of the gut-busting kind."

"And let's not forget, Denny Boy, tapering like hell before sectionals."

"To include garlic knots that sing in the pan."

"Like I said, you're a goddam natural!"

"And slow burn, Coach?"

"What about it?"

"I slow burn my runners, right?"

"Dennis?"

"Yes?"

"Can you keep a secret?"

"Sure."

"After you boys graduated, I continued to slow burn my teams. But in the early eighties, I started to notice all these young coaches springing up like mushrooms. Cross-country junkies, you know the type. Nostrils that flare. Steel in their eyes. The kind that gets intoxicated by the pain on their runners' faces."

"Kind of sounds like you, Coach."

"Except that I didn't run in college like them. Which means I wasn't exposed to the flood of new speed training hitting our shores. Sure, I read a shitload about the spartan approach of Olympian Herb Elliot, and felt I knew how to mix volume and intervals. But I couldn't imagine in a thousand years the kinds of crazy-ass speed workouts that these young coaches themselves did in college, and that was then passed down to their own teams. For example, this one nut who coaches at Seaford High on the Island, and who won back-to-back state championships, has his kids once a week during the entire cross-country season do twelve bare-knuckle 440s on the track, with a lap jog in between."

"No!"

"And by season's end in November, his varsity seven go from

a 72 average in August down to 65, his top kids popping high 50s on the last few."

"Wow! But how does all of that translate into cross-country racing?"

"Speed's so goddam ingrained in these teams that going out as a pack in five minutes is a walk in the park for them."

"You're kidding!"

"Sure, all of them fade a bit. But by the time they get to the two-mile mark, a few of them are still in the top ten, the others in the teens, each kid bumrushing the final straight. Anyway, these whack-job coaches also have their kids eating leafy greens and fish, washing it down with olive oil!"

Coach Jack couldn't help but laugh at what he had just said.

"Shit, Dennis, it's a goddam commie revolution out there in cross-country land. But a revolution that seems to be working. Packs of front runners with speed out the ying-yang hammering the first mile and losing the field in the process. At the Jersey Shore Invite a few years back, I counted over thirty kids from five different schools coming by the mile under five minutes."

"But what about volume? They run long miles?"

"Sure, they do. Lots of it. And some of these same coaches supplement the running side of things with this cross-training bullshit. Bike riding stints. Back-breaking hikes up and down hills in the heat. Lots of swimming. Hell, I could have had you guys swim from one jetty to the next."

"You had a good run, Coach. No one did what you did back then. No one."

"Yeah, that's what my bride keeps telling me. I thank God every day for Margie Mudhank. Heck, she's the one who after my retirement signed me up for this woodworking club. I'm now club treasurer. Can you believe it? The same guy whose hand got caught in the cookie jar by Lambert back in the day. Hey, I even raided Charlie's old parish office and treated myself to a table saw that was collecting dust." He paused, realizing what he had said. "Shit,

Dennis, sorry about that. Bringing his name up like that. So where were we?"

"The secret, Coach. You were going to tell me a secret of yours."

"So after all these new powerhouse programs emerged, I had to take a long hard look at myself in the mirror. Had to ask myself if maybe I should retire slow burn, replace it with the fast-charging race strategy. For a season or two I did just that. But I felt way out of sync. My runners, too. Even so, the experience made me realize that since I took the job at St. Theresa's back in the fifties, I had been living vicariously – big word, huh?—through my runners. See, I was training my teams to run the same way I ran in high school. I'm not so sure that I didn't hold a few of them back in the process. Damn, a kid like Adam Feltman, had he been trained by the Seaford guy, might have run twenty seconds faster. Same with the core three. The goddam secret, Dennis, is that I stepped away from the sport because slow burn was all I knew. Yup, it's all I knew, and the learning curve was way too steep for me to begin anew. You know what I'm saying?"

"I do, Coach. But can I ask you a question?"

"You can ask me anything you damn well please."

"If I was to start coaching, are you saying I should abandon slow burn for the new stuff?"

"Hell, Dennis, I'm scratching my head as we speak. But my gut's telling me that you start out with what you know. Maybe once you find your footing, move on to the fast stuff when and if the time is right. Now that I think of it, you can still call it slow burn. But a slow burn that begins at the crack of the starter's pistol." They both laughed.

The two talked for a good while longer about all things running, and before hanging up, Coach Jack said, "And don't forget, while you got to piss all over any kid who sandbags a workout, be sure to lift that same kid off the ground and kiss him on the cheek after he runs a PR. Put a hex on the fucker, Dennis. That's what you got to do."

"I will, and if it's okay, Coach, do you mind if I call you from time to time if the going gets rough?"

"You got to call. You must call. And by the way, have you stayed in touch with your two buddies?"

Dennis hesitated. "I need to call them."

"You do that. Or Coach Jack will come after you with Charlie's hedge clippers. Got it?"

"Got it."

When practice was over, the twins mounted the minivan and found their father staring into space.

"You okay, Dad?" Colin asked.

"Yes, yes. I'm fine."

Neither boy knew that their father was still processing the phone call he just had. Is it possible, he said to himself, that Coach Jack, the rock of Gibraltar, just told me that he retired on account of a new training philosophy that he couldn't adapt to?

Dennis then stole a look past the baseball field to a path whose entrance was wide enough to accommodate the stampede of runners in the first Mohawk Youth Running Series. And once on East Street with the minivan passing by Wilbur Park, he gawked at the training possibilities its hills offered.

"Boys," he said, "when we get home, could you tell your mom that I forgot to pick up the two-cycle oil for the mower?"

After dropping them off, he did a beeline to the Black Oak Tavern, just blocks from where Steve Capell lived. Once there, he called his friend, who rushed right over and was more than happy to foot the bill for a new tent. But not the uniforms. He thought the idea of a summer series for area youth was brilliant.

On the way home, Dennis made a stop at the strip mall.

Anne was at the sink when he got home and presented her with a dozen red roses. She, in turn, reading eyes that brimmed with nervous joy, said to him, "Congratulations, Dennis Hurley, head coach of the Oneonta cross-country team."

"Victor's on the River tonight?"

"Are you asking me on a dinner date?"

"I owe you, Anne. I owe you big time."

Throughout the meal, Dennis spoke endlessly about the upcoming season. At one point he said, "And I'm anxious about tomorrow. My first practice."

"Nonsense, you're back where you belong."

"You think so?"

"I know so."

She kept reaching for his hand, telling him that it would be fine.

After the waiter dropped off the key lime pie, Dennis filled her glass with the last drops of the Bordeaux, which suddenly left him feeling a distinct sense of victory. "What do you say, Anne, I stand on the table and announce to the dinner crowd here that the French were damned lucky America saved their sorry asses three times in one century?"

"Make my day, Dennis."

55

When Coach Hurley showed up that next morning for practice, he was not at all ready for the mob waiting for him out on the track. He counted twenty-one kids. Worse, only seniors Brian Foy and Mike Pitt from last year's varsity seven were among the number. Dennis told the group to start stretching while they waited on others who might show up. A handful did.

"Hey, Mr. Hurley, I have a question," said Dickie Benz.

"Yes, Dickie?"

"At summer camp, Coach Smythe told us that all coaches should check their runners' heart rate for aerobic capacity. You plan on doing that?"

"Yeah, Mr. Hurley," Carlos Torres added. "Maybe demonstrate proper foot-strike while you're at it?"

Sean and Colin gave each other a sideways glance, the questions having caught their father off guard. He was forced to deflect. "First, I go by Coach Hurley. And before we start throwing around fancy terms, how about today we just focus on a good old-fashioned run. On Monday, the first day of school, we'll meet in the cafeteria after school and get into training philosophy and other stuff. So, for now, let's all of us jog over to Wilbur Park, stretch, and circle the outer drive twice for a total of six miles, followed by a dozen hundred-yard bumrushes, which is what we call strides that accelerate into an all-out sprint."

Most had problems finishing the park's hilly first lap. Dennis was forced to pull up the rear with a large group who, looking traumatized, ended up walking most of the second lap.

After the bumrushes, he told the entire team that the next day being Sunday, there would be no formal practice. He encouraged them to stretch and to run some easy miles on their own.

Late that night, Dennis poked his head into the den where his wife was reading a biography of Amelia Earhart for her book club.

"Think I'm gonna call it a night, Anne."

"Sounds good. But, say, when you got home today, you didn't have much to say about your team. How'd it go?"

"The sanitized version?"

"That bad?"

"For starters, I was interrogated by Carlos and Dickie. That nut in Ithaca filled their heads with all this hypertechnical stuff."

"You're not telling me you don't know all this hypertechnical stuff, are you?"

"Oh, I know it alright. But in much simpler terms. Those of Coach Jack."

"As in the Coach Jack guy I met in the den after the burial?"

"The one and only. Now, Anne, I have less than a week to figure out who will run varsity at the Highland Falls meet next Saturday. Which is why on Monday they will run a three-mile time trial."

"So soon?"

"Sure, some kids will run for the hills after it. But for the kids who stick it out, I will make damn sure that when those same kids run a good minute faster by season's end—and trust me they will—I will pick each of them up and kiss them right on the cheek."

He blew her a kiss and headed above.

But as he climbed the stairs, he realized that come Monday's cross-country meeting he would need a rock-solid presentation if he was to appease the likes of Carlos and Dickie. Not to mention make a good impression in front of his two sons. He decided that behind the backs of Anne and the twins he'd sneak a look at Smythe's handbook to find what training methods overlapped those which Coach Jack used and with which he was comfortable. He also had decided that he would follow his old coach's advice and stick to the tried-and-true approach, slow burn. Perhaps down the road, if his teams were overpowered by squads nurtured on intense speed, he would try that method.

So, when the coast was clear the next day, he grabbed a pen and pad and absconded with the handbook out to the back porch. For a good hour he glimpsed its pages, whose countless physiological analyses intimidated him at times. Still, the reading paid off. By the time Anne called him in for Sunday dinner, he had created a few transparencies for the first team meeting. Dennis smiled at the work he had done. He told himself that he would try out some of the concepts on the twins at the dinner table.

And when he did, their hearty approval got their father thinking that the team meeting was his for the taking.

BEFORE THE HOMEROOM BELL rang the following morning, Dennis sought out the varsity soccer coach in the teachers' lounge.

"Say, Zim, was wondering if you could do me a favor?"

"And that is?"

Dennis asked him if he might consider asking two of his varsity soccer players, Ricky Mays and Joseph Newcombe, if they might consider jumping ship to cross country. Coach Jack had stolen Fenny and the Peterson twins from the parish soccer team. "See, Zim, I coached those two a few years back in freshman soccer, and I know they will see absolutely no playing time this year for you. Maybe you could tell them that?"

"Let me see what I can do."

"Thanks, Zim, and I wouldn't have asked except that I could

really use them. My team as it stands is shit. But those two kids can run forever. They would easily be in my top seven."

During the school day, Dennis had his students toward the end of each period start on their homework, all so that he could once again pour through this year's meet information that Kevin Stone left behind. He kept returning to the season's schedule, which included the sectionals in late October at the Oneonta Country Club.

Just my goddam luck, he muttered, we host the meet.

From there his thoughts again turned to which seven would represent his varsity squad that Saturday at Highland Falls.

As one by one the cross-country prospects entered the cafeteria, they found the overhead contents on the wall:

<u>*The Five Principles of Oneonta Cross Country*</u>

1. *Building a Culture of Running*
2. *Applying Slow Burn when Racing*
3. *Transitioning from Aerobic into Anaerobic during the Season*
4. *Building Core Strength and Speed via Stretching and Bumrushing*
5. *Staying Injury free via Junk Miles and Rest*

Coach Hurley wasted no time with a brief explanation of the principles, all except slow burn. He told his team that he'd save that for a later date. Reading the positive body language thus far in his audience, he thought the meeting was going well. More so, when he turned to the second transparency:

<u>*The Three Stages of Each Practice*</u>

1. *The Warm-up: a half-mile jog, intense stretching, and bumrushes*
2. *The Day's Workout: volume or intervals*
3. *The Cool Down: a half-mile jog followed by progressive bumrushes*

SITTING BULL RUN

Of course, while Coach Hurley smiled his way through the explanations, there nonetheless remained the dizzying roster number out there, which included six new faces. Now he understood why Coach Jack turned JV over to Sister Jean. It was some consolation, however, when the two soccer rejects, Mays and Newcombe, strolled in toward the end of the meeting. Maybe those two, he thought, along with Pitt, Foy, and the twins, can salvage the season.

As the meeting came to a close, he said, "Okay, now I want all of you to head to the Silver Maple, right beside the entrance to a path on the north field. That tree will be our hub. We'll always start and end practice there."

What he didn't tell his team was that earlier in the day he had grabbed the measuring wheel and walked off a mile loop on the perimeter of the school grounds. He dropped orange cones along the way to help his runners navigate the loop.

Once the team had gathered at the Silver Maple, he announced that they'd run a three-mile time trial. "Using the orange cones as guides, you'll loop the school three times." Given the dismal experience at Wilbur Park on Saturday, he also decided he'd hold off on incorporating the slow burn strategy. "And try to run a nice even pace the whole way."

The time trial was a nightmare. Most went out way too fast, no doubt the result of Pitt and Foy bounding to the lead in a 5:27 first mile. A half mile later, they died like dogs. The twins and Newcombe and Mays also paid for going out too fast. The workout turned into an ugly line of wobbly legs that included Dickie and Carlos. A death march, it seemed to Dennis, much like the crawl of those flies whose wings Fenny plucked off that day at the Montauk Point Festival before they were dropped into the pit of sand.

Still, a total of twelve kids all gapped the rest of the field by a good hundred yards. And all twelve broke nineteen minutes. Not great. But not bad. Equally important, the twelve fell into a large pack the last mile, which included his twins. At least he had the makings of a team that would not embarrass the school on Saturday. Yet which seven would toe the line?

"That was one heck of a practice," he said to the group once they finished their post-workout bumrushes. "So, tomorrow, we'll again meet at the Silver Maple. Thirty minutes of junk miles at Wilbur Park."

"Coach?"

"Yes, Carlos?"

"At camp, the director told us that junk miles are a waste of time."

Time for a Coach Jack intervention. "Well, that director of yours must drink the Kool-Aid of the low-mileage, high-intensity camp. I, on the other hand, subscribe to foundation building." Turning to the team at large, "I want all of you to think of a pyramid. The bottom represents a period of high volume, which leads to the top and to less volume and to more and more speed work. And never forget! Junk miles are all part of building endurance. It also gives the body time to recover, which increases the chances of an injury-free season. Got it? Good."

When Tuesday came rolling around, it was probably the three-mile time trial of the previous day that shrunk the numbers by a handful, including a few from the top twelve. To complicate matters, three boys who finished way back in the three-mile time trial on Monday decided to turn the day's junk miles into a race and finished up in the lead group led by Pitt and Foy. All of which turned the top seven deliberation into a mine field, especially when Foy asked his coach, "Do we know who's running varsity Saturday?"

"I'll be posting that on Friday. Not before."

Pitt followed that with, "What about tomorrow, Coach? What we doing for practice tomorrow?"

As Dennis looked over at the track, an idea flashed. Something down and dirty, a mile time trial on the track. Something to separate the men from the boys. A top seven for Saturday will emerge.

"Tomorrow's workout, you ask. Well, I want my merry band to begin with stretching, followed by an easy loop around the school for a good warm up, then a good half dozen bumrushes. Then, boom, a mile time trial on the track. And for the first time we'll use the slow burn strategy!"

Groans.

"And what exactly is slow burn?" asked Pitt.

Dennis explained how Coach Jack's brainchild works in some detail, both in races and in practice, emphasizing that slow burn depends on negative splits.

"So what you're saying, Coach," Foy said, "is that you jog the early part of race, and then slow burn the rest?"

"Not jog, just a controlled pace early on. In the three-mile cross-country race, for example, it means a steady first mile followed by a fast second and third mile. As far as the mile time trial goes, the same controlled pace the first lap. And not a sprint at the beginning of lap two, but a steady surge that you sustain as long as you can. And, after you have used this strategy in practices as well as races, over and over, slow burn becomes a state of mind."

56

Later that night, Dennis and Anne were at the kitchen table when the twins appeared, each with a copy of John L. Parker's *Once a Runner*. Eyeing the cover, Dennis' mouth opened big and round. But he dared not tell the boys that one summer in college he had gotten halfway through the novel--and would have finished it but for an aggrieved Terry Seagull, son of a felon, swiping it and tossing it out onto the Jersey Turnpike.

Dennis asked, "Where'd you boys get that?"

Colin replied, "It was on the reading list that Coach Smythe gave us at camp. Said it was a classic. Sean ordered two copies on interlibrary loan."

"Anyway," Sean added, "since tomorrow we run a mile on the clock, we were wondering if you could take a look at the author's advice for running the mile. See how it stacks up against your slow burn strategy. That's what you used in high school, right? What was your best time?"

When he hesitated, Anne said, "Den, your best time?"

"4:20."

"Wow," Sean said. "Remember your splits?"

Dennis knew them by heart. But he didn't like where this was going. "Boys, that was back in the dark ages."

"All we want to know, Dad," Colin said, "is which strategy, Parker's or your slow burn, makes the most sense?"

"See, Dad," Sean added, "the book's got Quenton, the protagonist, warming up for a big mile race. His chief opponent's this guy from New Zealand, John Walton."

Dennis chuckled. "Walton's based on the Olympian, John Walker, the first runner to ever break 3:50 in the mile."

"But we haven't gotten to the final pages where he describes the race itself. Only the section where Parker tells how you should run the mile, lap by lap. So, could you go through it? See what you think?"

"Yeah, Dad," said Colin now raising his book. "Here on page 353, the guy says that the first lap is *lost in a flash of adrenaline and pounding hooves.*"

Both looked for confirmation to their father. "That sounds about right."

"Yeah," Sean took over, "after the runners *crash into the first turn,* Parker says it's all about *the flashing of elbows and spiked feet all around.*"

Anne chimed in, "A bit dramatic, Den, don't you think?"

"Heck no. It's exactly right. The author was an elite runner who once owned the mile in the Southeastern Conference. So, he would know."

"Anyway, once the first lap's underway," Sean continued, "you got to be *calm in heavy traffic, control the panic, wait for opportunities.*"

"Go on. The second lap?"

"It's about not getting suckered into something too fast, but going *into a floating stride, the long ground eaters…just to cover territory.*"

"Lap three?"

Colin took over. "This, Dad, is when the *iciest resolve* is needed. And listen to this, the third lap *is cruel with no distinguishing features except that it had to be run, a microcosm not of life, but of*

Bad Times, the no-toys-at-Christmas times, the sittin'-at-the-bus-station-blues times, to be *endured and endured and endured."*

"This Parker guy," said Anne, "is painting a rather dark view of the sport. Too negative for my taste."

Sean asked, "Is Mom right, Dad? He's too negative?"

"In tone, maybe," Dennis replied. "Running-wise, he's describing the traditional approach to the mile, the steady grinding of the first three laps."

"And, Dad," Colin said, "here he says, the beginning of the bell lap is where it heats back up and you become a *competitive runner again, looking to size up the situation.* Wait...where's that one part? Here we go. So, the rest of the bell lap runners start asking themselves *Is this what death feels like?* Cool, huh?"

"I've heard enough," said Anne. "I'm heading upstairs to take a warm bath."

Dennis waited until Anne had left. "Go on, boys. Finish."

Sean replied, "Parker says despite the excruciating pain, the back straight is where the kick begins, *one by one, or all at once blasting away.* And entering the final turn, the runner must fight to *keep the integrity of the stride* over the last hundred yards."

"So," Colin said dropping his book on the table, "the bottom line is that Parker's all about a smart pace and a kick. Your slow burn, from what you told the team today, is all about an early kick."

"So, who's right? You or Parker?"

"I tell you what, boys. You go to bed and let me take a gander at Parker's final pages, where the race against Walton actually takes place. We'll talk tomorrow at practice."

Once the boys retired upstairs, Dennis wasted no time reading the novel's final section, the race itself. He was spellbound by Parker's description of it. From its opening moments, where Quenton *burned off the first rush and excitement and fear,* to the middle of the race where he felt *a slow, acid strain...organs closing down for the duration,* and to the race's final straight, when after reeling in the world's greatest miler, he let out a *scream, and with a violent wrenching motion he shook himself loose from this terrible force that gripped him, and forced himself into a semblance of a lean and it was over.*

Lowering the novel to the kitchen table, Dennis retreated out back to let his racing heartbeat settle down. He looked up at the dusting of stars against a black sky. In the stillness of the Oneonta night, he could hear the crowd's wild roars, Quenton lunging across the line ahead of Walton. But Quenton did so not via slow burn, but through grinding sausage for three laps, the hot sauce not coming until the bell lap.

Dennis looked north to the dark woods beyond the barn where there floated into view the memory of his 4:20 PR at the Loucks Games. It was nothing like what Parker described. After the gun went off that day, to avoid all jostling, Dennis went right to the back and stayed there throughout the first lap. And his second lap stride never relaxed into ground-eaters. Rather that's where Dennis poked the bear, the slow burn surge beginning with the help of Coach Jack, whose booming voice from the stands rang out, "63! Dennis, 63!" Which is why his second lap surge took him from dead last to the lead.

What Dennis couldn't tell his twins was that by their father's junior year, slow burn had been so drilled into his brain that the middle part of any race was not to be endured but conquered. So that by the time the third lap at Loucks came, he had built a good lead. As he would soon learn, however, his gapping the field would draw the wrath of Louie Oslo, known as the Mean Machine from Bishop Loughlin High, who already had run a 4:12 mile that year in anchoring the DMR to a victory at the Penn relays. Dennis' only hope, as he came by in the lead at the bell lap, was that Louie would not fly by him like Legs had done countless times on the cross-country course.

But Louie did just that, and over the back straight of the gun lap, Dennis fought like hell to fend off the pack of runners who were now breathing down his neck. The final straight resembled the comatose state he was in at state his senior year. There he and William and Peter, part of a tangle of runners, grimaced and bumrushed their way across the line, not at all aware where they had finished. Dennis would never forget that day at Vanny. Not so much at Loucks, when unlike Quenton, he was passed by three runners right before the tape.

Dennis turned and went back into the house, now remembering that the twins went to bed expecting an answer about strategy before tomorrow's mile time trial took place. What would William and Peter, if they were to appear out of thin air, tell his twins? Peter's advice would be that slow burn's early surging is hip. William would add a cautionary note, that slow burn is not for the weak of heart. All of which reminded Dennis that it was his two friends that day at Loucks who interrupted their own warm-ups for their two-mile run, all to lift him off the rubber track with hearty congrats. "4:20!" screamed Peter. And William, "What a run, Denny Boy!"

Once on his feet, he saw Coach Jack waving a congratulatory fist from the stands and mouthing, Way to go!

57

That next morning Dennis was not at all sure what advice he would give his twins. During a first-period lecture on the Battle at Shiloh, he looked out the window at the track and wondered if the mile time trial that afternoon was a smart idea after all. Perhaps wait a few weeks until a base was established.

But what would Coach Jack say if he knew I had caved.

Dennis wavered back and forth throughout the morning, though by lunch an executive decision was made: the team would do a fartlek instead of the time trial. Afterall, Foy, Pitt and the twins were a lock for varsity. If need be, he'd flip a coin for the remaining spots. As the bell rang to end the school day, however, Foy stuck his head in the classroom. "Gonna kick ass today, Coach. Slow burn a 66 for the middle two laps." Dennis saw the wild energy of Peter Walker in Foy. The mile time trial was back in play.

That afternoon the team met under the Silver Maple, and while stretching, their coach told them the time trial would consist of two groups. Group One to include anyone who broke 18:30 on Monday's three-miler. Group Two would follow.

"How fast do you want the second lap?" Pitt asked.

"What's your fastest mile to date?"

"Last May, Foy and I both ran a 4:29 in outdoor sectionals."

"And are you in the same kind of shape today as you were then?"

"Not really."

"I would suggest a conservative slow burn, one that establishes a baseline for later time trials. Perhaps today you can aim for a first lap of 72 that ignites back-to-back 67s. A 70ish mopping up on the bell lap. For a time of?"

"4:36, Coach."

"Good. As for everyone else, go out real easy, but remember a steady surge at lap two. Got it? Okay, a half dozen bumrushes for Group One, then on the line."

A brawny kid with curly black hair who Dennis had not seen before approached him.

"Coach, can I run in the first group?"

"Your name is?"

"Johnny Reid."

"And what year is Johnny Reid in?"

"Sophomore."

"Don't know that I've seen you at practice so far."

"My mom just took a job here. We moved down from Syracuse yesterday and got registered for school this morning. My sister and me."

"Did you run for your last school?"

"I had to help my uncle in his landscaping business."

"You like to run, Johnny?"

"Yes, I do."

"Get your ass on the line."

Dennis was not surprised that Foy and Pitt bolted out into the lead, and as Parker predicted, the first lap turned into a jostling affair as runners staked out positions. By the back turn, Pitt and Foy had gapped the fivesome of Newcombe, Mays, the twins, and the Johnny Reid kid, who had an impressive stride.

"70, 71," Dennis called out as Pitt and Foy came by the first quarter. "Now, dammit, back-to-back 67s!" Both surged. As did the twins when they came by after having gapped Newcombe, Mays, and the new kid.

But turning onto the back straight, Johnny Reid accelerated, passing the twins and catching Foy and Pitt by the back turn. The move wowed Dennis, the kid now drafting Pitt and Foy. Dennis also liked that packs of three, two, and two had emerged, packs that maintained a good clip through the third lap, where both Foy and Pitt twice attempted to lose the kid. Johnny Reid wouldn't have it, and at the bell lap he bowled Coach Hurley over with a burst of speed that, in an effortless toe-to-heel strike, brought to mind the mighty George Legstaff. Nor did the kid let up.

"4:30, 31," the coach yelled out as he finished up. That damn kid just ran a 63 final lap!

He then turned to watch the twins catch Foy and Pitt, the foursome coming by in 4:36. Mays and Newcombe finished in 4:39.

A few hours later, Dennis walked into the kitchen and kissed his wife who was cutting celery for a casserole.

"You're married to a bona fide genius, Anne."

"I take it the practice went well."

"Coach Jack would be proud. Slow burned the shit out of my team. The result, seven clear-cut Mary Janes for Saturday's race at Highland Falls. And one of them turns out to be a very special kid who goes by the name of Johnny Reid. He's built like William Flanagan but runs with the audacity of Peter Walker."

"That's all well and fine. But how many kids have your slave-driver workouts lost since Monday?"

Dennis laughed. "Damn! Slave driver is what my mom called Coach Jack back in the day."

"At last count, Den, we've been married a good hundred years. And that whole time, I've never heard so much as a peep about this Coach Jack guy. Now he takes center stage. Did he have that much of an influence on you?"

"So tomorrow, Anne, is recovery day when-"

"C'mon, Den."

"Anne, if I tell you that Coach Jack was God to me, and still is, can we leave it at that for the time being? I promise to tell you all about him. I'll even treat you to a few of the more delicious tales. I have a considerable expertise in time travel back to the past."

"Apparently so."

"So, anyway, the team. Tomorrow I'll have them run, say, some very easy junk miles, followed by them clearing out this path in the woods by the school. Got a custodian to give me all these rakes. Dante's Pizzeria will deliver sausage and pepperoni pizzas to help motivate my Mary Janes."

"You're gonna find yourself in hot water with some board members if you keep up the sexist language."

"Anyway, with pizza on the menu, the team will have no idea that they will be toiling over a path on which, come early October, they'll be doing repeat 880s."

The team loved Thursday's junk miles. The same with the pizzas they gobbled down after having raked the path clean. They all howled approval when Coach Hurley told them that in preparation for Saturday's race, the next day they'd again do some junk miles, after which team uniforms would be handed out. "And the bus leaves for Highland Falls seven sharp Saturday morning. Don't be late! Or to the moon, Alice!"

After dinner that night, Dennis went out to the barn porch. For the umpteenth time, he studied the meet information for Saturday's race, especially the map of the race trail on the Highland Falls golf course. As far as he could tell, the trail was little more than a fairly flat first and third mile, the second mile being a series of small rolling hills. No narrow trails with rocks and roots. No pebbles and sand to throb the calves. No monster hill with blind switchbacks. A smirk emerged thinking how Coach Jack would throw a fit if he was to learn that his former captain's coaching debut was to take place on an undulating carpet of green silk.

"Hey, Den," said Anne who appeared with two bottles of Rolling Rock beer and a wrapped gift, the items laid on the table right in front of him. She yanked off the bottle caps with an opener pulled from her shirt pocket and then sat opposite him.

"Don't mind if I do," said Dennis, grabbing a bottle. He took a swig, pretending not to see the gift. "The twins, Anne, how they doing?"

"Not to worry, Coach," she said taking a swig of her own. "I left the both of them doing those maniacal stretching exercises you taught them."

"Basic preparation, is all."

"Go on. I never remember you jumping the shark all the years coaching freshman soccer. And don't think I don't know this past Wednesday you smuggled a white board down to the basement where more brainwashing took place."

"The race trail at Highland Falls. Just showing the boys how to negotiate it."

"By the way, Den, if it helps any, I'm happy for you. I really am."

"I'll toast to that."

He leaned over and kissed her.

"Your team ready, then?"

"Not by a long shot. But this season's all about pouring a foundation. So," he paused to tap the wrapped gift with his beer bottle, "pray tell?"

"Oh, that. Found it on the side of the road."

Dennis knew the gift had to be a framed photo. Anne was notorious for that. He lifted it up and massaged it. "Has the feel of an extra-large putty knife." He held it up to his ear and shook it. "Nah, sounds like a five pack of disc sandpaper. May I open it?"

"You may."

"Here goes nothing."

Anne's eyes welled up as he tore the wrapping paper away and found a framed photo of the 1973 Watkins Glen team, from his junior year. He peered at the photo, going back and forth between William and Peter, the two flanking him, all three on a knee. Then to the back row, his four other teammates and Coach Jack, who proudly waved the third-place trophy for the crowd.

"How, Anne?"

"I promised myself after you finally told me about that night at the bungalow that I would let it go, that for your sake I would try not to bring it up. And I've actually done a pretty good job of that, don't you think?"

"Yes, you have, and for that I am grateful."

"But when you told me the story, blow by blow, there was something in your voice whenever you mentioned William and Peter. It was as if their names were stuck in your throat. The tone, Den, of unfinished business."

"Rarely a day, Anne, has gone by since that night that one or both doesn't pop into my head. I never got to say goodbye to either of them."

"So, I called your mother and told her about the cross-country job, and you being on cloud nine these days."

"No!"

"I also told her that you finally told me about that night. Two days later, UPS delivered a package. This photo was in it. I took the liberty to get a frame and wrap it up."

"Damn, if I had a nickel every time I reached for this back in the day and gawked at it, I'd be damn rich. Of course, what you don't know is that I shattered the original frame after the Cassidy ambush. I now remember stuffing it in the desk drawer. My mother must have found it when Tommy moved into my room and kept it all these years."

Anne stepped around the table and sat beside him, now pointing down at the photo. "Den, I bet those two kneeling with you are your two buddies. So, who's William and who's Peter?"

"That, Anne, is William Flanagan."

"Wow! Now that's one mean Irish mug! And that must be Peter Walker. What a smile!"

"And nerves of steel that still brings goose bumps." He lifted the photo for a closer look at his two friends. "Hard to believe I lost track of them."

With that, Anne reached into her shirt pocket and pulled out an envelope that was folded in half. She flattened it on the table. *For Dennis* written on it, in his mother's handwriting.

"She included this, too."

Dennis withdrew the familiar letterhead. He found two entries on it.

William Flanagan
12 Glenwood Drive
Charlotte NC 28105
756-465-7575

Peter Walker
Marine Base Quantico
PO BOX 212
Prince William, VA 22193
646-881-6666

"Damn, Anne, they moved!"

After the team's short run and uniform distribution that next day, Dennis returned to the cross-country office. Over the next hour he labored over the drafting of a letter. For moral support, he occasionally reached for the framed Watkins Glen team photo that now stood beside a family shot. He tore the paper in half after reading the first long-winded draft that dripped mush. Grabbing another piece of school letterhead, he decided to dash off just the bare essentials. That got the job done.

Sept 6, 1993

William and Peter,

In my very first year of coaching cross country at upstate Oneonta High, where I teach history, I sure could use some help. I would like to invite the both of you, and your better halves, to the New York Section IV Cross-Country Championship, held on Saturday, October 29th at the Oneonta Country Club Golf Course. My wife, Anne, and I will make available our spare bedrooms for a long weekend. With any luck you can watch me drink a bubbly at McGillicuddy's.

I would be glad to fetch you both at the nearby airport in Albany, home of one of our fiercest competitors back in the day.

Bumrush RSVP to 2011 Clydesdale Lane, Oneonta NY, 13820

Hope like hell you two can make it!

Your good buddy, Dennis

P.S. The fence of the county club pool is eight feet high and protected by security cameras. Bring your speedos.

The copying machine in the main office made two copies.

ANNE HAD ONLY just turned off the nightstand lamp that night when Dennis climbed into bed.
"Den, if it's okay, I think I'm going to pass on driving to Highland Falls tomorrow to watch the race."
"What do I tell the twins?"
"The truth."

"Which is?"

"That their mother's frail. Too nervous."

"Frail? Nervous? Impossible. Anne Graehler's DNA knows no such things."

"Where does the team run the following weekend?"

"Cobleskill."

"I'll plan on making that, okay?"

"Of course."

"Den?"

"Yes?"

"I'm hoping the coaching will help to chase off the demons. For good, I mean."

"Not a snowball's chance in Hell. But it will help to keep them at bay. And strangely enough, coaching also makes me want to reconnect."

"Oh?"

"Yeah, a weird craving of sorts, the kind that throws all caution to the wind. For one thing, a cleansing visit to Bellport. Spend a good week with my mom on 32 Crocus. Sit with her in the front pew and stare down Eichen. Maybe lace up and take the twins for a lighthouse round-tripper. Kick their boney asses up and down the dunes. Make up for lost time, Anne, is what I'm saying."

"I like it, Den, that you're reaching out."

"If you like me reaching out so much, how would you like it if I was to reach out to some old friends?"

"Meaning?"

"Meaning I invited both of them up to Oneonta for the sectional championship in late October."

She shot up in bed. "You did what?"

"Hey, you're the one who armed me with the two addresses. I dropped invites in the mail just today. They probably won't come."

"But if they do, where will they stay?"

"This old wreck of a house has spare bedrooms up top that have never been used."

"Yes, spare bedrooms that need a facelift...starting with a jewel-toned coat of dark paint to add serious drama to the dressers and armoires."

"Please, God, no!"

"And your dear mom will gladly UPS some spare doilies for the candle holders I've been meaning to buy at the antique store and that will go nicely on the walnut nightstands. You know, the ones that have been collecting dust out in the barn. Which indeed will need refinishing."

"You're killing me."

"Say, Den, we'll call the arrival of William and Peter, The Second Coming. Wadda you think?"

After a ragged night of sleep, Dennis was the first one out of bed. As he straggled down to the kitchen to make the coffee, there came the tug to go outside and see if the weather gods would be kind on race day. He stepped out and felt the warm haze of an early September sun. The morning humidity meant that his runners would experience a world of hurt later in the day.

Maybe it was a blessing Anne wasn't coming to Highland Falls. She'd have winced at the dangerous opening stampede unleashed by the starter's gun. She'd freak out when she couldn't locate the twins among the mass of faces out there. And God forbid, one or two kids go down and cause a pile-up. But nothing would unhinge her more than the otherworldly blisters of sweat on the grimacing faces of Colin and Sean as they fought their way down the final straight.

"Yes," he announced to a squirrel scampering up a nearby oak, "it's best my wife stays home today."

He went inside to wake up the twins.

58

By the time the bus returned that late afternoon from Highland Falls, Dennis half-jokingly told himself that it wouldn't have hurt had he, like Anne, stayed home that day. The meet turned into a fiasco, starting with the new tent set-up that took the intervention of several dads to raise. Then there was his having to extricate the team from the mob of families whose well-wishing was getting in the way. Two JV newbies forgot their uniforms. And then moments before the varsity race, after Newcombe announced he had puked in the woods, Coach Hurley had to bolt over to the team tent and yank a JV prospect, who ended up reaching the starting line just as the pistol went off. The mishap meant that Dennis couldn't reach the mile mark in time to rally his runners into unleashing slow burn.

At least, he reached the crest of a small hill off the twelfth fairway, the race's halfway point, in time to witness a shocker off in the distance: Johnny Reid leading a small group of front runners emerging from a thick wood. Dennis knew that the kid would eventually fade. And yet while Pitt did catch Johnny, he couldn't shake him, both of them coming by the two-mile mark shoulder to shoulder and positioned in the high teens. Another dozen runners went by before Foy and the twins passed in the high twenties, Mays, some ten places behind. The plucked JV runner wiping up the rear.

Much like Coach Jack did back in the day, Dennis hightailed it to the finish line, a flat, pristine lawn behind the club house where a roped-off crowd had already formed, and where Coach Hurley would commit a rookie mistake. Lost in the moment of screaming bumrush at his runners, he failed to look up at the clock and record the final time for each. His spirits were lifted, however, when the results were posted. His varsity took sixth place out of twelve. The JV team, eighth.

It all gave him hope, and at the smaller Cobleskill Invitational the next Saturday, he was treated to a third-place team finish. This time Johnny Reid was his top guy, placing ninth, followed by the pack of Pitt, Foy, and his twins in the low twenties. Mays and a rejuvenated Newcombe were a good ten spots back. Of course, Dennis also witnessed one of the up-and-coming teams in the state, Mayfield High, a team that illustrated the fast-charging race strategy that Coach Jack had mentioned over the phone a few weeks back. Seven of their runners were in the lead at the mile mark, five of them maintaining a lead position through the finish line for a perfect score. It gave Dennis pause. But he forgot all about the sweep when his own team mounted the podium to accept their third-place trophy and medals. It made him recall his first ever podium finish. Sectionals, his sophomore year at Sunken Meadow. But the flashback sparked a question that had crept up several times during the week. The two letters, had they reached his friends?

The following day being Sunday meant no practice. Dennis woke up thinking that he'd head out for a long run on his own along the Susquehanna. As he was about to leave the house, Colin from the couch yelled out, "Oh, Dad, yesterday I found a couple of letters made out to you in the mailbox when we got home from Cobleskill. They're in with other mail on the Lazy Susan. Weird, but one had *Attn: Denny Boy* on the envelope. The other a stick-figure smoking a cigar."

Dennis wheeled around, and after stuffing the two letters deep into his sweat bottom's pocket, he took off down Clydesdale Lane. There, based on his hot pace, neighbors might have thought that he was running away from home. Or that a rabid dog had sunk sharp teeth into a leg. He maintained the quick pace, even after he crossed the rickety old bridge. He had every intention of stopping there. But the chaos swirling about his head kept him running in the shadows along the Susquehanna. He finally stopped and cut down a foot path to the bank, where he started skimming rocks across the river's surface.

"Dammit," he shouted, the letters burning a hole in his pocket. This time he wound up and hauled a rock through the air, hoping that it would reach the opposite bank. Barely halfway, it fell for a splash.

"Okay, okay," he said, "it's time."

He lowered himself to the ground. The first seal torn open, William's reply read,

> *I typically smother my bratwurst with sauerkraut, grilled onions, and tangy stone-ground mustard. Moreover, Denny Boy, they'll be hell to pay if the accommodations are bush league!*
>
> *Yours, Wee Willie Flanagan.*

Even as Dennis ever so slowly nodded his head up and down, a broad smile forming, he murmured, "Now, on to Huck Finn." He pulled an index card out of the second envelope with the stick figure smoking a cigar on it. Peter wrote,

> *Bring it on, Denny! Bring it on.*
> *But never forget that speedos are for lightweights!*
>
> *Oorah!*
>
> *Peter*

When he returned home that day, he hid the two letters in the barn. With the sectional race still about two months away, he'd wait several weeks before he told Anne that the invites had been accepted. Anything to keep her out of the region's antique shops. Not to mention that he'd first have to get up the nerve to phone his two friends to make arrangements. It had been years since they talked. In the meantime, he also knew, with William and Peter coming to town, there was some coaching to do.

I have got to make sure, he thought, that the team, come sectionals, is ready to turn on the afterburners. A ton of volume throughout the remaining weeks of September. Followed by a month of bare knuckles on the Mohawk path. Serious tapering that final week of October. And wouldn't it be sweet to have my two buddies attend a team dinner at Dante's. A large bowl of spaghetti, extra marinara for the garlic knots. The next day, the three of us can hobble around the course together and curse my runners into a mighty slow burn.

But Dennis was rocked by another thought.

What if the two of them never stopped running? What if they themselves are in shape? I better get my ass in gear, starting with a pair of Reeboks that are all the rage, or so says Dickie Benz. Maybe even a phone call to my old coach for some training advice of the down and dirty kind. Damn, now that I think about it, I got to invite Coach Jack to sectionals. His paramour, too. Put them up in the recently rehabbed Holiday Inn. Yes, that's what I'll do, invite the two of them to upstate Oneonta for one hell of a weekend with William and Peter. Done.

As Dennis lay in bed that night, with the news of his friends' visit still whirling around in his head, he heard himself saying, bring it on. That meant he was ready for whatever onslaught of random images was about to come his way. True to form, the first one featured Coach Jack smashing his office chair to pieces after hearing that William had bumped Father Ken in religion class. Then there was that hot, muggy day, the team having just run a sub-par ballbuster workout that involved Cardiac Hill, when their coach, after a few choice words, hurled his stopwatch at the ground and stomped it. That wasn't the first time that a stopwatch had fallen victim to one of his tantrums. Dennis smiled at the recall. Yet he also knew it wasn't exactly peace and tranquility that the moment was offering him. But neither was it the dull resignation that had affected him for so long.

    A few other memories came that night, and before he faded off for good, there floated in his mother and father huddled by the sink, each with a drink in hand. She buckled over in laughter, he with bounce and verve finishing up a colossal tale from days gone by. The spirit willing, Dennis told himself, the good memories will continue to drift in and out of view, like gulls riding the wind on a sunny day. They must, and they will.

□□□

Acknowledgements

I want to thank copy editor, Suzanne Reamy, for her brilliant work, which among many other things, greatly helped to tame the text. I also want to thank my wife, Kathleen, for her tireless attention to the manuscript at its various stages, without which this novel would never have seen the light of day.

AUTHOR NOTES

SCORING

Of the seven runners who make up a cross-country team, only the first five count in scoring. Points are awarded to the position in which each runner crosses the finish line (first place gets 1 point, second place 2 points, and so on). The points for these five scorers are then tallied, and the team with the lowest score wins. Ties are usually broken by the position of each team's sixth runner. The lowest possible score in the five-to-score system is 15 (1+2+3+4+5), achieved by a team's runners finishing in each of the top five positions, considered a "sweep" or "perfect score" for the winning team. A sweep is quite rare in races with many teams, such as invitationals or championship races. More often, the winning team has its top scorers place near the front and its middle scorers in the top third of the race. A winning score might go like this: 3 + 8 + 12 + 21 + 25 for a score of 69 A team's sixth and seventh runners, while not part of the team score, are known as 'displacers,' as their place can count ahead of runners from other teams.

DISTANCE, TIMES, AND TERRAIN

For decades now, the American racing community has adopted the European metric system. High school cross-country runners thus race on 5 km (3.1 mi) courses. Back in the day, though, the common high school distance was 2.5 miles or 3.0 miles, the latter of which the author of *Sitting Bull Run* uses in races throughout the novel. It might help to know that while a five-minute per mile race pace is reserved for elite high school runners, the better teams who vie for championship status on a typical cross-country course will aim for a five-man average of 16:00, which for each runner breaks down to a 5:20 per mile average. Because running terrain varies dramatically from one course to another, final times vary according to the degree of difficulty. For example, the winner on a runner-friendly golf course, who one week turns in a 15:10, could win that next week with a time of 16:10, the minute slower based on a difficult course with steep hills and harsh trail conditions.

RACING STRATEGY

Most coaches have long held that a brisk but steady pace throughout the cross-country race maximizes physiological efficiency, acceleration (the "kick") taking place only towards the end. Readers of *Sitting Bull Run* will quickly realize that its fictional coach, Jack Hogan, embraced a strategy that asked his runners to surge at the mile marker and hold form as best they can.

THE RUNNING UNIVERSE

Competitive running maintains a hyper focus on the stopwatch, which never lies. For runners, splits and final times are the only arbiters. This is why the author of *Sitting Bull Run* sprinkled the novel with actual times and splits, even though this aspect of the story might present a steep learning curve to some readers.

CROSS-COUNTRY VENUES

For those well versed in cross-country lore of the northeast United States, they will realize that the author, a native New Yorker, while fictionalizing various cross-country venues throughout the novel, retained the names of some of the more iconic regional courses, namely, Van Cortlandt in the Bronx, Long Island's Sunken Meadow, and New Jersey's Holmdel Park. Regarding the Van Cortlandt course, the author took license in modifying the course's layout, this to suit the story's fictional needs. Former harriers who know "Vanny" well are asked to engage in the willing suspension of disbelief.

GLOSSARY OF CROSS-COUNTRY TERMS

Aerobic: literally meaning "with air," aerobic refers to the body producing energy with the use of oxygen. As a training term, aerobic means continuous running at a pace that keeps one's heart rate at roughly 70% of its maximum, a pace that prevents lactic acid build-up in the muscles.

Anaerobic: literally meaning "without air," anaerobic refers to the body producing energy without oxygen. Anaerobic training generally applies to intense interval running that does not rely on the body's ability to process oxygen and thus helps to develop stamina, endurance, and speed.

Aerobic vs. Anaerobic Training: whereas aerobic training builds endurance as it improves cardiovascular respiratory functions, which enables a runner to train harder and longer as fitness levels improve, the harder intensity in anaerobic exercise, often using 90% of a runner's maximum heart rate, allows a runner to significantly improve race times despite the lactic acid build-up.

Bib: a sheet with a unique number pinned to the runner's singlet that ensures accurate scorekeeping.

Bonk: also known as "hitting the wall," bonk generally occurs when major fatigue sets in.

Burnout: when a runner feels tired, weary, and unmotivated, typically after periods of long training seasons.

Carb Loading: loading up on carbs before a race or long run by consuming meals high in carbohydrates, which, in turn, stocks up on fuel for future racing.

Chute: the roped-off area after the finish line through which runners are herded after finishing. While the recent chip timing has made chutes a thing of the past, chutes were necessary back in the day.

Cool-down: easy running done after a workout or race to help with the recovery process.

Compression Time: also called "spread," compression means the difference between the finishing times of a team's first and fifth runners. A small spread, such as thirty seconds, usually represents team strength and cohesion.

Cross Country: an outdoor sport in which teams run races over natural terrain, such as parks, golf courses, and fields. Some courses, however, include running over paved roads.

Cross Training: refers to a kind of training where two or more types of sports are used in order to improve performance in one's main sport as well as reduce the risk of injury. Two popular sports that typically supplement running are swimming and biking.

Dead Period: refers to a short period of time, from a few weeks to a month, when high school athletes are prohibited from any formal contact with their coaches.

Fartlek: a Swedish term for "speed-play," fartlek is a distance workout that repeatedly alternates faster and slower speeds.

Foot Strike: refers to a runner's *strike* pattern on the toes and ball of the *foot*, heels rarely touching the ground between strides.

Footwear Nomenclature: while over the last few decades cross-country footwear terminology has expanded some to accommodate the new technologies, back in the early 1970s, roughly three kinds of footwear for runners existed: 1) "Spikes" are racing shoes that feature protruding metal spikes, which are used mainly on dirt/grass surface to help improve boost and traction; 2) "Racing flats" (or "Flats") are lightweight racing footwear used on hard surfaces where spikes can't be used; and 3) "Trainers," with far more cushion and stability, are footwear used exclusively for training purposes.

Harrier: another name for a cross-country runner.

Intervals/Repeats: a workout where a set distance(s) is run repeatedly with a recovery walk/jog in between. An example of a common cross-country interval workout for high school runners is 5 X 1000 meters with a set rest in between. Some coaches, like fictional coach, Jack Hogan, are fond of ladder workouts, such as three sets of 440/880/1200/880/440.

Invitational Meet: a large cross-country race comprised of many teams.

Junk Miles: a common tag for short distance runs at an easy pace that serve as recovery from harder workouts.

JV: acronym for the junior varsity team.

Kick: the sprint at the end of a race.

Lactic Acid: a substance that forms in the muscles as a result of the incomplete breakdown of glucose, which—once present—causes muscle fatigue and sore muscles.

Negative Split(s): refers to when the latter part of a workout or race is run faster than the earlier parts.

Out and Back: running in one direction for half of the total distance before turning around to finish the second half by running back to the start.

Overpronation: occurs when a runner lands on the outside of the foot and rolls inward toward the arch, often resulting in injury.

Pack Running: when a group of runners from the same team stay together during a race.

The Recovery Run: a short, easy run that allows the body to shed the metabolic waste of a previous hard workout.

Sectional: a qualifying meet in which the top team(s) advance to a culminating championship meet.

Singlet: a sleeveless cross-country uniform top.

Split: refers to the time associated with standard checkpoints in a race or workout. In a three-mile race, an official will typically supply the split times at the first and second mile markers.

Surge: a short burst of speed during a race intending to change rhythm or break the competition.

Switchback: a point on the cross-country course where the racing trail makes a tight turn and heads back in the direction from which it came.

Taper: refers to the reduction in both volume and intensity in the days leading to an important race to ensure peak performance on race day.

Team Box: a team's assigned portion on the starting line.

Tempo vs. Threshold Runs: though often used interchangeably, the two terms have their own technical meaning and thus purpose: whereas a tempo run engages a comfortable pace that is considerably slower than a runner's mile race, threshold runs involve a faster pace that is close to a 5K race pace and that is equivalent to what exercise physiologists call "lactate threshold," or the point at which muscles start fatiguing. Running at or near lactate threshold is believed to raise lactate threshold, which, in turn, should allow one to run faster in future races.

Toe the line: the term applied to runners literally toeing the starting line as the race is about to begin.

The Three Running Seasons: cross country in the fall, indoor track during the winter, and outdoor track during the spring.

VO2 Max: the maximum volume of oxygen a runner's body can use.

XC: the abbreviated form of cross country.

About the Author

A resident of Charleston, South Carolina, Pat J. Daly is a recently retired Professor of English at Indiana University Southeast. Prior to that, he taught high school English and Latin. Daly was reared on Long Island, New York, where he ran cross country and track for Holy Trinity High School. The author then went on to compete at the college level for Bradley University, in Peoria, Illinois. Following graduation, he coached cross country and track at Massapequa High School and Bradley.

Made in the USA
Columbia, SC
12 July 2024

38528806R00312